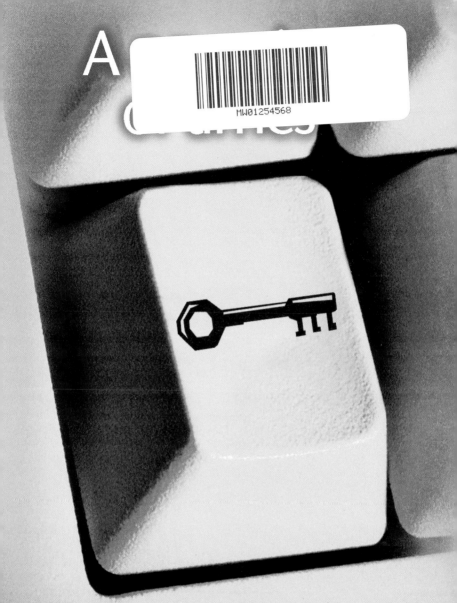

A

Make your vacation reservations through the Internet

You can now make your vacation reservations through the Internet or by phone with respect to security.

Look for this symbol. Several establishments already offer this premier service, a new sign of the times.

To obtain more information or make a reservation, the "online" bed and breakfasts in Quebec invite you to call:

1 877 Bonjour, extension 854
(1 877 266-5687)

Gift Certificates

for Inns and Bed & Breakfasts

The greatest gift is a sweet escape

GÎTES ET AUBERGES DU PASSA

Information:
1-877-869-9728

Inns and
Bed & Breakfasts
in Québec

AGRICOTOURS

Travel better, enjoy more

ULYSSES

Travel Guides

Project Coordinator	**Collaboration**	**Illustrations**
Odette Chaput	Odile Bélanger	Marie-Annick Viatour
(Féd. Agricotours)	Diane Drapeau	Lorette Pierson
Jacqueline Grekin	Isabelle Larocque	Myriam Gagné
(Ulysses Travel Guides)	Andrée Lyne Allaire	Sandrine Delbaen
	Evelyne Hébert	Sylvie Darèche
Publisher	Louis Hébert	Louca
Pascale Couture	Agathe Archambault	Stéphanie Thellen
		Richard Serrao
Translation	**Cartographers**	Émilie Desmarais
Danielle Gauthier	André Duchesne	Vincent Desruisseaux
	Bradley Fenton	
Copy Editing	Yanik Landreville	**Photography**
Eileen Connolly	Patrick Thivierge	**Cover Page**
		François Rivard
Page Layout	**Computer Graphics**	Auberge La Muse, Baie-St-Paul,
Julie Brodeur	Stéphanie Routhier	Charlevoix
	André Duchesne	

DISTRIBUTORS

CANADA: Ulysses Books & Maps, 4176 Saint-Denis, Montréal, Québec, H2W 2M5, ☎ (514) 843-9882, ext.2232, 800-748-9171, Fax: 514-843-9448, info@ulysses.ca, www.ulyssesguides.com

GREAT BRITAIN AND IRELAND: World Leisure Marketing, Unit 11, Newmarket Court, Newmartket Drive, Derby DE24 8NW, ☎ 1 332 57 37 37, Fax: 1 332 57 33 99, office@wlmsales.co.uk

SCANDINAVIA: Scanvik, Esplanaden 8B, 1263 Copenhagen K, DK, ☎ (45) 33.12.77.66, Fax: (45) 33.91.28.82

SPAIN: Altaïr, Balmes 69, E-08007 Barcelona, ☎ 454 29 66, Fax: 451 25 59, altair@globalcom.es

SWITZERLAND: OLF, P.O. Box 1061, CH-1701 Fribourg, ☎ (026) 467.51.11, Fax: (026) 467.54.66

U.S.A.: The Globe Pequot Press, 246 Goose Lane, Guilford, CT 06437 - 0480, ☎1-800-243-0495, Fax: 800-820-2329, sales@globe-pequot.com

Other countries, contact Ulysses Books & Maps, 4176 Saint-Denis, Montréal, Québec, H2W 2M5, ☎ (514) 843-9882, ext.2232, 800-748-9171, Fax: 514-843-9448, info@ulysses.ca, www.ulyssesguides.com

---

For information on the Fédération des Agricotours network:

Fédération des Agricotours du Québec
4545, av. Pierre-de-Coubertin, C.P. 1000, Succursale M.
Montréal (Québec) H1V 3R2
(514) 252-3138
Fax (514) 252-3173
Internet: http://www.agricotours.qc.ca
http://www.inns-bb.com
E-mail: agricotours-q@sympatico.ca

© May 2001, Ulysses Travel Guides.
All rights reserved
Printed in Canada
ISBN 2-89464-339-X

TABLE OF CONTENTS

INTRODUCTION 4

EXCELLENCE PRIZE WINNERS 5

SEVEN ACTIVITY AND HOLIDAY PACKAGES
    Bed& Breakfasts, Country Inns, Farm Stays, Country and City Homes, Country-Style Dining,
    Regional Dining, Farm Tours 7

TABLE OF SYMBOLS 9

PRACTICAL INFORMATION 10

HOW TO USE THIS GUIDE 13

COUNTRY-STYLE DINING 14

REGIONAL DINING 29

FARM TOURS 33

FARM STAYS 47

BED AND BREAKFASTS, COUNTRY INNS, COUNTRY AND CITY HOMES 57

LIST OF COUNTRY INNS, COUNTRY AND CITY HOMES 58

ABITIBI-TÉMISCAMINGUE 61

BAS-SAINT-LAURENT 63

CANTONS-DE-L'EST 77

CENTRE-DU-QUÉBEC 93

CHARLEVOIX 98

CHAUDIÈRE-APPALACHES 112

CÔTE-NORD, DUPLESSIS-MANICOUAGAN 123

GASPÉSIE 138

ÎLES-DE-LA-MADELEINE 159

LANAUDIÈRE 161

LAURENTIDES 169

LAVAL 193

MAURICIE 196

MONTÉRÉGIE 206

MONTRÉAL REGION 217

OUTAOUAIS 228

QUÉBEC CITY REGION 237

SAGUENAY - LAC-SAINT-JEAN 263

INDEX 279

EVALUATION FORMS 289

INTRODUCTION

Inns and Bed & Breakfasts in Québec 2001 features more than 659 properties categorized under seven "authentic" and "quality" vacation and leisure formulas.

428	**Bed & Breakfasts** Gites du Passant^{MD*}	
88	**Country Inns** Auberges du Passant^{MD*}	
75	**Country and City Homes**	
26	**Farm Stays**	
20	**Country-Style Dining** Tables Champêtres^{MD*}	
3	**Regional Dining**	
13	**Farm Tours**	

*Trademarks registered to the fédération des Agricotours du Québec. Only members may use this designation.

These establishments offer the warmth and hospitality of host-members, a family atmosphere and pleasant surroundings. *Inns and Bed & Breakfasts in Québec 2001* is perfect to discover the best of Québec. This guide is a judicious choice for its wealth of information, reservation advice, tourist maps, colour photos and descriptions of each property which includes: illustrations, price, itinerary, details about rooms, bathrooms and menus, etc. For explanations about each of the seven formulas, see **page 8**.

FARM ACTIVITIES

Take a "nature" break... At the end of each region in the "B&B and Country-style Inns" section of the guide, you will find a list of farm activities for accommodation, dining and entertainment possibilities.

TAXES

As per federal and provincial laws, customers may have to pay the federal Goods and Services tax (7%) and the provincial tax (7.5%). The taxes also apply to the deposit.

According to provincial law, some tourist regions (i.e. Montréal, Québec City, Laval) must charge an additional tax of $2 per night for each unit rented. This tax goes toward a partnership fund which is used to promote the region's tourist offerings.

ANNUAL REVISION OF THE GUIDE

Though the guide is revised each year, all information contained herein is subject to change without notice (i.e. application of taxes). However, the prices listed for each establishment are valid until the publication of the next edition, expected in Febuary 2002.

QUALITY CONTROL

All the establishments in this guide have submitted a request for accreditation review to the Fédération des Agricotours and must agree to respect a code of ethics as well as certain hospitality, room arrangement and food quality standards. To ensure that our norms are being respected, every two years, each establishment in the network is inspected by the federation (with the exception of the Country-Style Dining and Regional Dining establishments that are inspected every three years). On site, a sign indicating Agricotours membership is your assurance that the owner belongs to the Fédération des Agricotours du Québec.

EVALUATION FORMS

Do not hesitate to complete the "Evaluation Forms" sheets at the end of the book, as well as those available in all the establishments of our network, to let us know how you enjoyed your Agricotours experience. We need your feedback, suggestions and criticism to continue to improve the quality of the network and the services provided.

WIN A STAY

By filling out and sending your Evaluatin Form, you get the chance of winning a two-night stay for two persons in one of our member-establishments.

GIFT-CERTIFICATE

You wish to offer a stay in a B&B or a in Country Inn? For more information 1-877-869-9728.

EXCELLENCE PRIZE

Each year, the Fédération honours its members with two awards in two different categories:

- The "Peoples Special Favorite" category: awarded to the hosts who stood out for the remarkable welcome and service they have consistently offered their guests.

- The "Achivement" category: awarded to the hosts who stood out for the remarkable way they have developed, promoted and offered high-quality services.

You will find a list of the 2000 nominees in both categories on the next pages.

26 years of hospitality
1975 – 2001

For 26 years, the host members of the
Fédération des Agricotours du Québec have been
committed to offering you genuine, high-quality choices
for accommodation and agricultural tourism.

This has made Agricotours the largest
high-quality network in Quebec, and
your confidence has helped in its success.

For this reason, our network host members
hope that they may, with their traditional
warm welcome, continue to help you discover
the best of Quebec for many more years to come.

You'll always feel welcome in the Agricotours network.

The Fédération
des Agricotours
du Québec

www.inns-bb.com
www.agricotours.qc.ca

Prizes for...

« *People's Special Favorite* »
Category

« Congratulations to these hosts and hostesses for the remarkable welcome and service they have consistently offered their guests. »

Accommodation Sector
The Provincial Grand Prize-winner is

Le Gîte des Roses
Diane et Denis Lampron
Drummondville
CENTRE-DU-QUÉBEC

Country-Style Dining Sector
The Provincial Prize-winner is

La Conclusion
Chantal et Gilles Fournier
Sainte-Anne-des-Plaines
LAURENTIDES

Accommodation Sector
The Regional Prize-winners are

BAS-ST-LAURENT
Au Beau-Séjour
Louiselle Ouellet et Paul Gauvin
Saint-Louis-du-Ha! Ha!

CANTONS-DE-L'EST
La Maison Duclas
Ginette Canuel et Camil Duchesne
Granby

CHARLEVOIX
La Maison Frizzi
Raymonde Vermette et Marianne Frizzi
La Malbaie, Pointe-au-Pic

CHAUDIÈRE-APPALACHES
O' P'tits Oignons
Brigitte et Gérard Marti
Saint-Julien

CÔTE-NORD
Gîte La Nichée
Camille et Joachim Tremblay
Sainte-Anne-de-Portneuf

GASPÉSIE
Le Jardin de Givre
Ginette Couture et Gérald Tremblay
Matane, Saint-Léandre
Finalist for the Provincial Grand Prize
« People's Special Favorite »

LANAUDIÈRE
L'Andante
Lise Vézina et Claude Perrault
Saint-Gabriel-de-Brandon

LAURENTIDES
Aube Douce
Michèle Ménard et Gilles Meilleur
Saint-Adolphe-d'Howard

MAURICIE
Soleil Levant
Léonie Lavoie et Yves Pilon
Pointe-du-Lac

MONTÉRÉGIE
Le Relais des Îles Percées
Colette et Raymond LeBlanc
Boucherville
Finalist for the Provincial Grand Prize
« People's Special Favorite »

OUTAOUAIS
À Couette et Croissant
Anne Picard Allard
Hull

MONTRÉAL REGION
Gîte La Cinquième Saison
Jean-Yves Goupil
Montréal

QUÉBEC CITY REGION
La Maison D'Ulysse
Carole Trottier et Raymond Allard
Sainte-Anne-de-Beaupré

SAGUENAY-LAC-ST-JEAN
Aux Pignons Verts
Ghislaine Ouellet et Jean-Claude Villeneuve
Saint-Ambroise-de-Chicoutimi

...*Excellence* 2000

« *Achievement* »
Category

*« Congratulations to these hosts and hostesses
for the remarkable way they have developed,
promoted and offered high-quality services.»*

Agrotourism Sector
The Provincial
Prize-winner is

Accommodation Sector
The Provincial
Prize-winner is

Ferme Jean Duchesne
Diane Authier et Jean Duchesne
Saint-Pie
MONTÉRÉGIE
(Farm Tour)

Les Gîtes Makadan
Micheline Villeneuve et Daniel Bergeron
Normandin
SAGUENAY–LAC-SAINT-JEAN
(Bed & Breakfast and Farm Stay)

Special Mention by the Jury

Ferme La Colombe
Rita Grégoire et Jean-Yves Marleau
Saint-Léon-de-Standon
CHAUDIÈRE-APPALACHES
(Country-Style Dining and Farm Tour)

The Fédération des Agricotours du Québec
26 years of hospitality
1975 – 2001

www.inns-bb.com
www.agricotours.qc.ca

SEVEN ACTIVITY AND HOLIDAY PACKAGES

BED AND BREAKFASTS

Bed and breakfast offered in a private home, located either in the country, on a farm, in the suburbs or in the city. The house has up to five (5) rooms to let. For a short or a long stay, choose from one of our 428 bed & breakfasts. So many places to stay, so many ways to be welcomed while you discover Québec and its people!

COUNTRY INNS

Bed and breakfast offered in a small character inn with up to twelve (12) rooms to let. The majority of these inns offer additional meals in the dining-room. Although some of our 88 country inns are a bit larger than a bed & breakfast, you will always find attentive service and a personal welcome from the hosts.

COUNTRY AND CITY HOMES

House, chalet, apartment or studio apartment completely equipped for independent stays in the city, in the country or on the farm. Our 75 country and city homes welcome you with all the amenities necessary to make your stay a pleasant one. Some country homes offer farm-related activities. Linens and towels are provided. Rentals are by the month, week, week-end or day.

FARM STAYS

Bed and breakfast offered in the private home of a farmer. The home has up to 12 rooms to let. Farm-related activities are also offered. These vary depending on the type of farm and the kinds of animals. Choose from among our 26 farm stays to enjoy the unique experience of life in a farming community.

COUNTRY-STYLE DINING

Innovative menus, using mainly products grown on the farm. The meal is served in the intimacy of the dining room of the farmhouse or an outbuilding which has been tastefully and authentically furnished. The hosts of our 20 country-style dining establishments invite you to discover the fine flavours of their farm products. Share their passion by taking a guided tour of their farm. By reservation only. You may bring your own wine.

REGIONAL DINING (NEW)

Innovative menus, using products grown on the farm as well as those representative of the various regions of Québec. The meal is served in the intimacy of the dining room of the farmhouse or an outbuilding which has been tastefully and authentically furnished. It is best to reserve in advance. Some regional dining establishments sell foods made from produce from the farm or the region, and allow you to bring your own wine. Check with the establishment.

FARM TOUR

An educational and entertaining tour of a farm given by the farmer himself. Choose from among our 13 farm tours and treat your family or group to several hours of fun on the farm. Whether it's a picnic with friends, a country ramble or a school outing, a farm tour offers a choice of activities to please all ages.

In the case where a bed and breakfast or a country inn establishment doesn't offer a private bathroom, the establishment must confrom to the following norms:

- 1 shared bathroom for 6 people and less (including the residents)
- 1 shared bathroom and 1 shared wc for 7 to 9 people (including the residents)
- 2 shared bathrooms for 10 to 12 people (including the residents)
- etc...

TABLE OF SYMBOLS

SERVICES

⊟	Secure reservation through the Internet	♿	Wheelchair access
☀	Bed and Breakfast classification **(p 12)**	👋	Sign language
★	Country Inns classification **(p 12)**	**P**	Private parking
✎	Classification in progress	🚗	Pick-up from public transportation with or without additional charge
F	French spoken fluently	🐕	Pets on premises
f	Some French spoken	🏊	Swimming on premises
E	English spoken fluently (55% of establishments)	⊠	Restaurant on site
e	Some English spoken	**R3**	Distance (km) to nearest restaurant
🚭	Guest are requested to refrain from smoking	**M3**	Distance (km) to nearest grocery store
♿	Wheelchair access with the help of another person	**AV**	Establishment that accepts travel agency reservations

ACTIVITIES

🏛	Art gallery, museum	🚲	Cycling path
●	Summer theatre	🐎	Horseback riding
🚤	Boat cruise	🛷	Snowmobiling
🏊	Swimming	⛷	Downhill skiing
⛳	Golf	🏃	Cross-country skiing
🚶	Hiking	🐕	Dog-sledding

METHOD OF PAYMENT

VS	Visa	**ER**	En Route
MC	MasterCard	**IT**	Interac payment
AM	American Express		

PRACTICAL INFORMATION

COUNTRY-STYLE DINING AND REGIONAL DINING

- Menus:

The menus given in this guide are but examples of the type of meals served. In addition to the menu presented, the hosts may offer you a variety of other menus at various prices. You can bring your own wine in most of the establishments, this policy should be verified when making your reservations.

- Number of people:

The number of people welcomed during the week and on weekends is given for each establishment. Note that some hosts can accommodate more than one group at a time. In these cases, depending on the minimum number of people required by the owners, it is possible to reserve the whole establishment for your group (however, should any members of your group cancel some fees might apply, if the group becomes smaller than the minimum required by the host).

- Rates:

Rates vary according to the menus chosen. Service charges are not included in the prices.

- Reservations, deposit and cancellation:

You must reserve with the hosts directly. It is always advisable to get information about the deposit and cancellation policy. However, if the establishment has no deposit and cancellation policy, the Fédération des Agricotours policy will apply as follows: a 50% deposit to confirm the reservation. In the case of cancellation, 30 days or less before the reservation date, the entire deposit is retained. When cancelling, it is advisable to postpone the reservation to avoid losing the deposit.

FARM TOURS

- Reservations, deposit and cancellation:

Reservations should be made directly at the selected farm. It is always advisable to get information about the deposit and cancellation policy. However, if the establishment has no deposit and cancellation policy, the Fédération des Agricotours policy will apply as follows: maximum deposit of 40% (minimum $20) to confirm the reservation. In the case of cancellation, the money foreseen and received as a deposit will be kept by the host for damages according to the following rules:

- 8 to 15 days' notice, 50% of the deposit will be retained (minimum $20);

- 7 days or less before the reservation date, the entire deposit will be retained.

When cancelling, it is advisable to postpone the reservation to avoid losing your deposit.

BED AND BREAKFAST, COUNTRY INN AND COUNTRY AND CITY HOMES

- Reservations :

It's always advisable to reserve in advance, especially in high season (July and August). Since each place is different, it is usually a good idea to confirm details with your hosts: what time you plan on arriving, up until what time your room can be held in case of delay, and what methods of payment are accepted. Since bed and breakfasts are private residences, it is advisable to inform your hosts of a particularly late arrival. Also, if you have any special conditions or requirements (example if you are allergic to pets), you are strongly encouraged to advise your hosts before making reservations.

- Methods of payment:

Generally, expect to pay with traveller's cheques or cash. The establishments that accept credit cards, or interact payment have VS, MC, AM, ER, IT written under their rate charts.

- Deposit and cancellation:

For Bed and Breakfasts and Country Inns: it is very important to get precise details from the hosts about the deposit and cancellation policy. If an establishment doesn't have a specific deposit and cancellation policy, the policy of the Fédération des Agricotours might apply: a maximum deposit of 40% (minimum of $20) to confirm a reservation. In the case of a cancellation, the money foreseen and received as a deposit will be kept by the hosts for damages according to the following rules:

- **0 to 15 days' notice: 50% of deposit (minimum $20) is retained.**
- **7 days or less before the begining of the stay: entire deposit is retained.**

If your stay must be cut short before the end, 40% of the unused portion of the stay may be retained. When cancelling, it is advisable to postpone the reservation to avoid losing your deposit.

For Country and City Homes: check with owners of country houses for their individual deposit and cancellation policies.

FOR EUROPEAN CUSTOMERS

There are several ways to reserve your stay in advance: either contact the establishment directly, consult a travel agency that offers packages including stays in the bed and breakfasts or country Inns that are members of the Fédération des Agricotours, visit our web site: **www.inns-bb.com** or contact Hospitality Canada.

Hospitalité Canada
For a stay of **2 nights or more**, you can reserve through the Hospitality Canada network. There is no charge for these reservations from North America by calling 1-800-665-1528.

You can also make your reservations by telephone after you arrive or by visiting their offices located in the tourist offices in Montréal and Québec City:

Tel: (514) 287-9049
Fax: (514) 287-1220
Internet: www.hospitality-canada.com
E-mail: hosp.cam@iq.ca

In person:
Centre Infotouriste
1001 Square Dorchester
Montréal
(corner Ste-Catherine & Peel)

Maison du Tourisme
12, rue Sainte-Anne
Vieux-Québec
(opposite of Château Frontenac)

TOURISME CHEZ L'HABITANT

Reservations can be made by mail or by telephone with a credit card. All arrangements and payments are made in advance, so you head for Québec with the address in hand! An additional charge is added to the price for all reservation services. Information is sent free of charge.

Tourisme chez l'habitant
15 rue des Pas Perdus, B.P. 8338
95 804 - Cergy St-Christophe Cedex
Tel: 01 34.25.44.44,
Fax: 01 34.25.44.45
Internet: www.worldbandb.com
E-mail: wtch@casynet.fr

ACCREDITED BY AGRICOTOURS

Classified or not, all bed and breakfasts and country inns in this guide have been accredited by the Fédération des Agricotours du Québec. This accreditation greatly exceeds the evaluation criteria of a classification, as it ensures that each establishment conforms to higher standards of quality relating to hospitality, meals and facilities. Moreover, every owner undertakes to respect a code of ethics.

CLASSIFICATION «HÉBERGEMENT QUÉBEC»

In order to avoid confusion, we have included the following clarification with regard to certain establishments that do not post a rating result. Because adherence to the "Hébergement Québec" rating system is voluntary, there are three reasons for which no result may be posted:

– **the establishment is in the process of being classified**

– **the establishment decided not to publish its classification**

– **the establishment decided not to be evaluated by "Hébergement Québec"**

CATEGORIES LEGEND

BED AND BREAKFAST CLASSIFICATION	
☀	Basic comfort B&B
☀☀	Good comfort and quality B&B
☀☀☀	Very comfortable and good quality B&B
☀☀☀☀	Superior comfort and quality B&B
☀☀☀☀☀	Remarkable quality and comfort, refined and luxurious B&B

COUNTRY INNS CLASSIFICATION ALSO APPLIED TO COUNTRY HOMES	
★	Establishment with basic facilities and services that meets the quality standards
★★	Comfortable establishment with good quality facilities, providing some services and amenities
★★★	Very comfortable establishment, with excellent facilities, offering many services and amenities
★★★★	Establishment offering superior comfort, among the best, with superb facilities and a wide range of services and amenities
★★★★★	Exceptional establishment, in terms of comfort and facilities and the many amenities and impeccable services offered

Bed and Breakfasts and Country-style Inns are presented in the following format:

Country-style Homes and City Homes are presented in the following format:

3. DRUMMONDVILLE

Prize for Excellence "Special favorite" Provincial 2000. "Experience the house from long ago, where both roses and children grow. "Our small" family (11) welcomes you to its table set with home-made bread and jams, fresh eggs, juice and aromatic coffee. Make yourself at home! Halfway between Montréal and Québec City, between Sherbrooke and Trois-Rivières.

Hwy 20, Exit 175 twd Drummondville (Boul. Lemire Sud), 300 m from Hwy 20.

B&B
LE GÎTE DES ROSES

Diane and Denis Lampron
215, boul. Lemire, R.R. #6
Drummondville J2C 7X2
(819) 474-4587
fax (819) 474-1500
www.bonjourquebec.
com/info/gitedesroses
info@rose.ca

B&B	
single	$40-60
double	$55-75
triple	$65-85
quad.	$75-95
child	$10

Open year round

Number of rooms	3
shared bathrooms	3
room with private bath	1

Activities:

73. MONT-STE -ANNE, ST-FERRÉOL

Savour the tranquillity of our lovely country homes, ancestral or recent, 30 min from downtown Québec City, at the edge of Charlevoix. Dreamy, legendary spot, in a small typical Québécois town. Houses are well equipped and can comfortably accommodate 4 to 30 people, and even up to 50! We are nestled at the foot of Mt Ste-Anne, a year-round internationally renown resort. See colour photos.

1km after Mt Ste Anne, as you enter the small town of St-Ferréol-les-Neiges.

COUNTRY HOME
CHALETS-VILLAGE
MONT-SAINTE-ANNE

Marie Flynn and Gilles Éthier
C.P. 275
Ste-Anne-de-Beaupré G0A 3C0
tel/fax (418) 650-2030
toll free 1-800-461-2030
Visit us on the Internet:
www.chalets-village.qc.ca

No. house	8
No. rooms	2-8
No. people	4-30
WEEK-SUMMER	$525-2500
WEEK-WINTER	$500-6000
W/E-SUMMER	$150-1300
W/E-WINTER	$180-2000

Taxes extra VS MC

Reduced rates: spring and fall
Open year round

Activities:

Legend

A. Number corresponding to the one on the regional map
B. Localization of house
C. Type of service offered
D. Classification of Country Inns
E. Classification of Bed and Breakfasts
F. See table of symbols p. 9
G. Rate table (see the box on right)
H. Information about additional taxes and accepted methods of payment
I. Dates open and reduced rate period
J. Room and bathroom information
K. Nearby activities, see p 9
L. House information and table rates

G.
Shared room rates

B&B
Bed and Breakfast

MAP
Modified American Plan: breakfast and supper

*Child
12 years and younger staying in parents' room

When two prices are given, they refer to the comfort level of the room and not to high and low seasons.

Country-Style Dining

COUNTRY-STYLE DINING

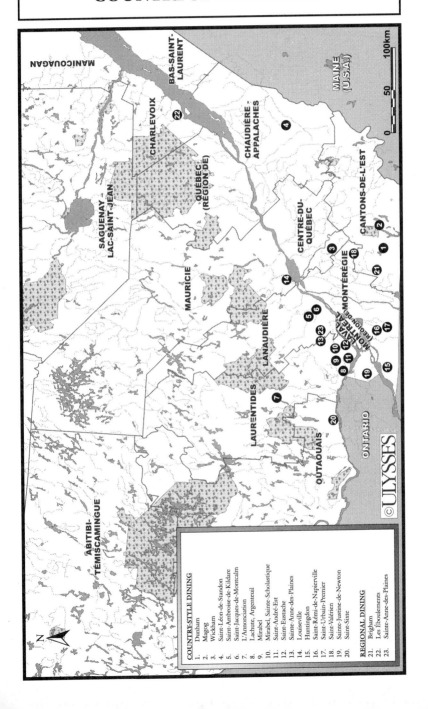

MANICOUAGAN

BAS-SAINT-LAURENT

CHARLEVOIX

MAINE (U.S.A.)

0   50   100km

CHAUDIÈRE-APPALACHES

SAGUENAY – LAC-SAINT-JEAN

QUÉBEC (RÉGION DE)

CENTRE-DU-QUÉBEC

CANTONS-DE-L'EST

MAURICIE

MONTÉRÉGIE

LANAUDIÈRE

MONTRÉAL (RÉGION DE)

LAURENTIDES

OUTAOUAIS

ONTARIO

ABITIBI-TÉMISCAMINGUE

© ULYSSES

N

COUNTRY-STYLE DINING
1. Durham
2. Magog
3. Wickham
4. Saint-Léon-de-Standon
5. Saint-Ambroise-de-Kildare
6. Saint-Jacques-de-Montcalm
7. L'Annonciation
8. Lachute, Argenteuil
9. Mirabel
10. Mirabel, Sainte-Scholastique
11. Saint-André-Est
12. Saint-Eustache
13. Sainte-Anne-des-Plaines
14. Louiseville
15. Huntingdon
16. Saint-Rémi-de-Napierville
17. Saint-Urbain-Premier
18. Saint-Valérien
19. Sainte-Justine-de-Newton
20. Saint-Sixte

REGIONAL DINING
21. Brigham
22. Les Éboulements
23. Sainte-Anne-des-Plaines

1. DUNHAM `F` `E`

LA CHÈVRERIE DES ACACIAS
Renée Ducharme and Gérard Landry
356, chemin Bruce (route 202)
Dunham J0E 1M0
(450) 295-2548

On the road to the vineyards, our homestead is a major goat-breeding, fodder-crop and poultry farm. The originality of the food served in the ambiance of a 19th-century house will charm you. Our menu constitutes a gastronomic adventure orchestrated around our farm products combined with those of our neighbours. Our home is just the place to end an unforgettable day in the region.

Located 1 hour from the Champlain bridge. From Montreal or Sherbrooke: Hwy 10, Exit 68 for Cowansville Rte 139. Then take Rte 202 to Dunham. In the village, Chemin Bruce (Rte 202) at the corner of "Boni-Soir". The goat farm is 1.2km from the village.

Open year round

Activities:

Jus de légumes et fruits frais
Fromage au pesto
et pâté de chevreau sur bruschetta
Mosaïque de légumes
au fromage frais de chèvre
Choux-fleur et pommes au cari
Gigot de chevreau sauce aux pommes
et/ou Cuisses de canard aux pruneaux
Granité aux trois melons
Salade de betteraves à l'aïoli
Meringue aux trois fruits
Other menus upon request

Meal : $35 taxes extra
week:12 to 30 people   w/e: 12 to 30 people
Able to accommodate more than one group / 2 dining rooms available
(exclusive use depends on season, nb. of people)

Includes: visit of the farm

2. MAGOG `F` `P` 🏊 🐕

AUX JARDINS CHAMPÊTRES
Monique Dubuc and Yvon Plourde
1575, chemin des Pères, R.R.4
Canton de Magog J1X 5R9
(819) 868-0665
toll free 1-877-868-0665
fax (819) 868-6744
www.auxjardinschampetres.com
auxjardinschampetres@qc.aira.com

Just steps from Magog and Orford in the magnificent Eastern Townships region, you'll give in to the charming countryside, the warmth of our hundred-year-old house as well as the "pure delights" that we will serve you. Our dishes are concocted from our various farm animals, organic vegetables and edible flowers. Do not resist, rather enjoy it with your friends and while staying at our B&B. One and two-day packages starting at $79 per person, double occupancy. Bring your own wine. **B&B p 87. See colour photos.**

From Montréal, Hwy 10 East, Exit 115 South-Magog/St-Benoît-du-Lac, drive 1.8 km. Turn right on Chemin des Pères twd St-Benoît-du-Lac/Austin. Drive 6.1 km, look for sign on your right. We are waiting for you!

Open year round

Activities:

Salade au confit de canard et vinaigrette tiède
balsamique ou
Rillettes de lapin au moût de pommes
Potage aux poires et cresson
Aumônière de poireaux sauce cheddar
et coulis de poivrons rouges ou
Croustade de lapin aux pistaches et au Pineau
des Charentes
Granité au calvados
Magret de canard au genièvre et Porto ou
Scalopini de volaille aux cerises de terre ou
Médaillon de cerf rouge à la crème de pleurotte
Crêpes glacées aux pommes et figues ou
Gâteau à la pâte d'amande ou
Péché mignon aux marrons et chocolats
sauce Sabayon au Grand Marnier
Other menus upon request

Meal : $42-47 taxes extra / VS MC IT
week: 1 to 50 people   w/e: 1 to 50 people
Can accommodate more than 1 group/3 dining rooms
(exclusive use depends on season, nb of people)

Includes: visit of the farm (in season)

3. WICKHAM

LA FERME DE LA BERCEUSE
Robin Fortin and Réjean Forget
548, Rang 10
Wickham J0C 1S0
(819) 398-6229
(819) 398-6411
fax (819) 398-6496

Small, old and comfortable, the Berceuse inn is a place where the fruits of our labour meet your desire to eat well. Farm-bred game birds, an herb garden and vast, organically certified vegetable gardens allow us to offer you original, healthy, balanced meals. La Ferme de la Berceuse, a shared passion... **B&B p 96, Farm Stay p 49.**

From Montreal, Hwy 20 East, Exit 157 toward Wickham. About 7km past the village of St-Nazaire, turn left twd Wickham Rte 139. At the church, turn left and continue for 1.8km.

Open: Mar. 31 to Dec. 23

Activities:

Terrine de petit gibier et confit d'oignons
Feuilleté de fromage de chèvre au pesto
Potage maraîcher
Petits fruits glacés à l'alcool
Perdrix ou colin de Virginie
ou pintade à la façon fermière
Salade saisonnière
Desserts cochons
Other menus upon request

Meal: $30-35 *taxes extra*/ IT	
week:8 to 28people	w/e:8 to 28people
Can accommodate more than 1 group/1 dining room (exclusive use depends on season, nb of people)	

Includes: visit of the farm (in season)

4. ST-LÉON-DE-STANDON

FERME LA COLOMBE
Rita Grégoire and Jean-Yves Marleau
104, rang Ste-Anne
St-Léon-de-Standon G0R 4L0
(418) 642-5152
fax (418) 642-2991
www.fermelacolombe.qc.ca
r.gregoire@globetrotter.net

Special Mention for Excellence "Agrotourism Success" 2000. Tourism Grand Prize 1997. One hour from Québec City in the heart of the Appalachians, come and experience the gourmet adventure of the Ferme La Colombe. You'll relish every moment in our cosy hewn-timber dining room, made all the more charming by the crackling fireplace and the beautiful panoramic view from the window. You will be won over by our regional cuisine, made of wild turkey, guinea fowl, rabbit and trout, while enjoying the lovely view. Edible flowers have a place of honour. Garden and dining packages available. **Farm Tour p 35.**

From Québec City, Hwy 20 E., Exit 325 twd Lac-Etchemin, Rtes 173 S. and 277 S. to Saint-Léon-de-Standon, Rue Principale. Go 0.9km beyond the church, cross the 277 at the stop sign, left on the Village road, 4 km. Turn right on rang Ste-Anne, 2 km.

Open year round

Activities:

Fromage frais aux fleurs d'onagre
Poitrine de dindon sauvage fumée en papillon
Velouté de citrouille et fromage de chèvre
Aumônière de pintade ou Râble de lapin au
cidre de pomme ou
Poitrine de poulet de grain à l'abbaye
Pomme de terre noisette
Tonnelle de courgette
Salade fleurie
Mousse aux pétales de rose
Fondant au chocolat et
coulis de gadelles noires
Thé, café, tisane
Other menus upon request

Meal: $30-34 *Taxes extra*	
week: 8 to 25 people	w/e: 8 to 25 people
Only one group at a time	

Includes: visit of the farm

5. ST-AMBROISE-DE-KILDARE

BERGERIE DES NEIGES
Desneiges Pepin and Pierre Juillet
1401, Rang 5
St-Ambroise-de-Kildare J0K 1C0
tel/fax (450) 756-8395
www.bergeriedesneiges.com
info@bergeriedesneiges.com

A life's dream... Goodbye law practice, so long teacher's summer holidays... Desneiges Pepin and Pierre Juillet (two "dyed in the wool" city dwellers...) took over this farm and settled with 11 ewes in 1985. What do they do for fun? They share their experience and show guests the daily renewed life of the farm. How? Over a good meal. More than 12 years and 400 ewes later, they have retained that "city kid" enthusiasm for the country. They offer you a gastronomic adventure at La Bergerie des Neiges. **B&B p 64.**

From Montréal, Hwy 40 E., Exit 122, Hwy 31 N. Rte 158 West, 1 km, left on Rte 343 N., drive for 15 km to St-Ambroise. At the flashing yellow light, go left on Rang 5 for 2 km. The farm is white and pink, on the left!

Merguez maison et mayonnaise harissa
Potage de carottes du rang 5
Rillettes d'agneau et compote d'oignons
Duo d'agneau, sauce ricaneuse
Légumes de Lanaudière
Salade de fromage feta de brebis
Tulipe et glace maison sur coulis de fruits
Thé, café, tisanes
New menu and decor, spring 2001

Meal: $39 *taxes extra* / VS MC
week:12 to 36 people   w/e: 12 to 36 people
Min. nb. of guests may
vary depending on the season
Only one group at a time

Includes: **visit of the farm**

Open year round
Activities:

6. ST-JACQUES-DE-MONTCALM

BERGERIE VOYNE
Lise Savard and Mario Gagnon
2795, rang St-Jacques, route 341
St-Jacques-de-Montcalm J0K 2R0
(450) 839-6583

In the beautiful Lanaudière region, we raise lambs and produce our own maple syrup. The ancestral home of the Venne family, also known as "Voyne", in green and white cedar, is ready for your visit. Lamb is featured in our cuisine, and the shepherd knows all the secrets of its preparation. You can see the herd on a tour of the farm.

From Montréal, Hwy 25 North to St-Esprit, 40 km. Rte 158 East to St-Jacques, left on Rte 341 North. It's 4.8km from the intersection with Rte 158.

Terrine de campagne
Tourte aux poireaux ou Feuilleté de canard, gelée de thym sauvage
Potage saisonnier
Gigot d'agneau sauce au porto blanc ou Rôti de veau forestière
Salade du jardin
Plateau de fromages fermiers de la région
Fondue à l'érable ou Gâteau aux noisettes et sucre d'érable ou Parfait aux bleuets et chocolat blanc
Thé, café, infusions
Other menus upon request

Meal: $35-36
week: 8 to 20 people   w/e: 10 to 20 people
Only one group at a time

Includes : **visit of the farm**

Open year round
Activities:

7. L'ANNONCIATION

F P

LA CLAIRIÈRE DE LA CÔTE
Monique Lanthier and Yves Bégin
16, chemin Laliberté
L'Annonciation J0T 1T0
(819) 275-2877

In the Hautes Laurentiennes, you are invited to our table to spend some peaceful hours in the clearing of a forest of varied species. We live in harmony with nature amongst a variety of small animals (lambs, rabbits, grain-fed chickens, calves and deer), which become succulent dishes accompanied by fresh vegetables from our organic gardens. **Farm Stay p 50 and B&B p 173.**

From Montréal, Hwy 15 North and Rte 117 to L'Annonciation. Drive 4.3 km beyond the hospital. Turn left on Chemin Laliberté. First house on right (almond Canadian-style house).

Open : Dec. 1 to Mar. 31, May 1 to Oct. 31
Activities:

Rougette crémière
Foie gras poulette
Pesto en pâte
Velouté de saison
Tournedos dindonneau au fouillis jardinier
Verdoyant potager, crémerie de fines herbes
Fromagerie raisinet
Fruiterie sauvagine en velours
Pouding paysan sirop d'érable
Thé, café, tisane
Other menus upon request

Meal : $30	
week: 6 to 20 people	w/e: 6 to 20 people
Only one group at a time	

Includes: visit of the farm

8. LACHUTE, ARGENTEUIL

F P

AU PIED DE LA CHUTE
Deschênes family
273, Route 329 Nord
Lachute J8H 3W9
tel/fax (450) 562-3147

In the calm of the country, our wood house offers charm, comfort and the delicacies of reputed country-style dining, where poultry and lamb are the specialties. Family-style welcome is both warm and personalized. Pastoral walks near our pond and at the foot of the falls will add to the magic of the countryside and the pleasures of dining. Welcome to our place!

From Montréal, Hwy 15 N., Exit 35. Hwy 50 to Côte St-Louis, go right to Rte 158 W., left to Rte 329 N. At the flashing yellow light, go right for exactly 1.5 km. It's on your left.

Open year round
Activities:

Amuse-bouche de bienvenue
Rillettes de cochonnet aux herbes du jardin
Feuilleté de champignons de nos sous-bois
Salade gourmande au confit de pintade
Croustillant d'agneau confit à l'estragon
Tartare de légumes et tomates marinées
Velouté de poireaux, crème à la ciboulette
Crème de carottes et rabioles
Civet de lapereau, sauce fumée aux pruneaux
Gigot d'agneau rôti, légumes au basilic
Pintade rôti aux champignons sauvages
Chapon braisé, crème à la moutarde
Navarin de daim aux pommes et canneberges
Raclette d'argenteuil à l'érable
Tarte aux fruits fous et amandes
Crousti-fondant poires-chocolat
Café-thé-infusion
Other menus upon request

Meal: $35-40 *Taxes extra*	
Reduced rates: Mar. 1 to Apr. 15	
week: 6 to 30 people	w/e: 14 to 30 people
Only one group at a time	

Includes: visit of the farm

9. MIRABEL

LES RONDINS
Lorraine Douesnard and François Bernard
10331, côte Saint-Louis
Mirabel, J7N 2W4
(514) 990-2708
(450) 258-2347
fax (450) 258-2467
www3.sympatico.ca/laptitecabane
laptitecabane@sympatico.ca

Located a few kilometres from Mirabel airport, Les Rondins henceforth welcomes you to their saphouse, situated on the edge of a vast maple grove, with trails laid out for walks. Farm-bred Barbary Coast ducks and grain-fed chickens are found here alongside Belgian horses. Antique furnishings and the piano create a warm and friendly ambiance in the two dining rooms, where guests savour our refined dishes, prepared in the adjoining kitchen. At Les Rondins, a peaceful, enchanting site is yours to enjoy.

From Montreal, Hwy 15 North, Exit 35, Hwy 50 West, Exit 272, Chemin Côte St-Louis. Left at the stop sign, 3km. Les Rondins and the "P'tite Cabane d'la Côte" are on the left.

Open year round
Activities:

Bouchées d'avant
Roulade de chapon farcie
Potage de saison et pain maison
Salade tiède au confit de canard
ou Tarte d'épinards-poireaux
Canard de barbarie à la framboise
ou Suprême de volaille aux mûres
ou Mijoton de veau au parfum de basilic
Fromage fermier «La Longeraie»
ou Verdure et chèvre chaud
Gâteau rhubarbe mousse au sirop d'érable
ou tartelette mousse au sirop d'érable
Crème glacée-sorbet maison
Other menus upon request

Meal: $35-37
week:10 to 50 people   w/e: 15 to 50 people
Min. nb. of guests may
vary depending on the season
Able to accommodate more than one group / 2 dining rooms available

Includes: visit of the farm (in season)

10. MIRABEL, STE-SCHOLASTIQUE

AUX DOUCEURS DE LA RUCHE
Danielle Rochon and Mario Morrissette
10351, St-Vincent
Mirabel, Ste-Scholastique J7N 2V7
tel/fax (514) 990-2450
(450) 258 3122
www.auxdouceurs.com
douceurs.ruche@sympatico.ca

Excellence Prize 1997-98. In the lovely Basses-Laurentides region, only 40 min from Montréal, come rediscover the calm of the countryside. A majestic drive lined by spruce trees leads to a home that has witnessed Québec's history. It is here that we await you. In the kitchen, our fowl is slowly being roasted and the sweet scent of warm honey house fills the room. A visit of the honey-house will reveal the secret world of bees you'll also taste "beehive sweets". A wood fire is already warming the dining room; the only thing missing is you.

From Montréal, Hwy 15 North, Exit 20 West, Hwy 640 West, Exit 11 Boul Arthur-Sauvé, towards Lachute. Drive 17.5 km. After Belle-Rivière Restaurant turn right on St-Vincent. 5km to 10351. We await your arrival at the end of the spruce drive.

Open year round
Activities:

Mousse de foies de volaille au cognac
Jus de légumes frais
Oeufs de caille dans leur nid et
terrine de volaille
Velouté de navet aux pommes
Perdrix rôtie, sauce moutarde au miel
Riz sauvage aux fines herbes ou
pommes de terre
Petits légumes de saison
Salade «Miramiel»
Fromages de chèvre frais
La ruche et ses ouvrières
Thé, tisanes, café
Pain maison, douceur «chocomiel»
Other menus upon request

Meal: $22-40 *Taxes extra*
week: 10 to 32people   w/e: 14 to 32people
Min. nb. of guests may vary depending on the season
Only one group at a time

Includes: visit of the farm

11. ST-ANDRÉ EST   F P

LA FERME DE CATHERINE
Marie Marchand and Robert Dorais
2045, Route 344
St-André Est J0V 1X0
(450) 537-3704
fax (450) 537-1362
fermecatherine@videotron.ca

Marie, Catherine and Robert invite you to come enjoy family ambience and country cooking close to the old wood stove whose warmth mixes with the warmth of the hosts. Robert will take you around the farm and you can admire a superb view of Lac des Deux-Montagnes and surroundings. If you love good food, have a seat and let the feast begin.

From Montréal, Hwy 13 or 15 to Hwy 640 twd Oka. From Oka, take Hwy 344 for 19 km. On the 344 it's 6 km after St-Placide. The road gets narrower and winding as you arrive at La Ferme de Catherine.

Open year round
Activities:

Crémant de pomme
Saucisse deux viandes sur
tombée de tomates au basilic ou
Terrine de bison au confit d'oignons
et vinaigre de framboises
Velouté du fermier
Médaillon de bison
Veau de grain braisé,
sauce aux cidre et gingembre
Suprême de volaille farci de canard
Plateau de fromages avec panaché de laitue
Délices de la saison au coulis fruités
Infusions
Other menus upon request

Meal: $36-42	
week: 12 to 36 people	w/e: 12 to 36 people
Only one group at a time	

Includes: visit of the farm

12. ST-EUSTACHE   F P ♿

LE RÉGALIN
Réjean Brouillard
991, boul. Arthur-Sauvé,
route 148 ouest
St-Eustache J7R 4K3
tel/fax (450) 623-9668
toll free 1-877-523-9668
www.regalin.com
regalin@total.net

Less than 30 minutes from Montréal, in the maple area of St-Eustache, a beautiful, typical old house with dormer windows overlooking a large orchard extending as far as the eye can see. Farm animals (rabbits, pheasants, guinea fowl, geese, ducks and ostriches) inspire the planning of our menus. We offer dinner-concerts where you don't have to be in group. 2 separate dining rooms, for your exclusive use, are available at each end of the house.

From Montréal, Hwy 15 North, Exit 20 West, Hwy 640 West, Exit 11. Boul. Arthur-Sauvé twd Lachute. 5 km from the exit, 8 houses after the Pépinière Eco-Verdure (tree nursery) on the right side.

Open year round
Activities:

Mousse de foies de lapereau et pain maison
Feuilleté de faisan au poivre vert ou
aumonières de pintade à l'érable ou
Potage de saison
Lapin aux abricots, au cidre ou à l'érable ou
médaillon d'autruche à l'hydromel ou
suprême de faisan au poivre rose
Salade verdurette
Plateau de fromages fins
Profiteroles au chocolat ou
gâteau mousse aux abricots
Café, thé, infusions
Other menus upon request
Breakfast menu on weekdays

Meal: $35-40	
week: 15 to 50 people	w/e: 15 to 50 people
Min. nb. of guests may vary depending on the season	
Can accommodate more than 1 group/2 dining rooms (exclusive use depends on season, nb. of people)	

Includes: visit of the farm

13. STE-ANNE-DES-PLAINES

LA CONCLUSION
Chantal and Gilles Fournier
172, rang La Plaine (rte 335)
Ste-Anne-des-Plaines J0N 1H0
(514) 990-7085 ou (450) 478-2598
fax (450) 478-0209
www.web-solut.com/laconclusion
laconclusion@web-solut.com

Prize for Excellence "Special Favorite" Provincial 2000.
By a stroke of good fortune, this elegant house caught our eye. We chose it in order to continue our adventure and receive you in a rural setting and relaxed atmosphere. In harmony with the seasons, you will enjoy refined cuisine made up of fresh products from our farm-bred animals. Our different cultures add flavour and colour to your dish. You are invited to share a moment in the country and let yourself be pampered by the Fournier family. In "conclusion," you will appreciate the warm welcome that has made our name, and you may hear the tale of our adventure...
See color photos.

From Montreal, Hwy 15, Exit 31. After the light, right at the stop sign onto Rue Victor, 10.7km. Left at the flashing light, 7.7km, Rte 335 North.

Open year round
Activities:

Potage ou crème du jardin
Pain maison aux cinq grains
Caille glacée au vinaigre de framboises ou
gâteau de lapin au vin blanc ou
aumônière de foies de lapin à la crème
Assortiment de pâtés
Lapin aux pommes et raisins ou
lapin farci aux abricots ou
lapin chasseur aux olives ou
cailles rôties, sauce porto et raisins verts
Salade de saison
Tarte aux framboises glacée au sirop d'érable
ou gâteau mousse aux fraises et à rhubarbe ou
crêpes de blé au Cointreau et bleuets ou
gâteau moka et mousse d'amandes
Crème glacée maison et gourmandises
Goat cheese available upon request
Other menus upon request

Meal: $30-40

week: 2 to 34 people   w/e: 2 to 34 people
Min. nb. of guests may vary depending on the season

Able to accommodate more than one group/2 dining
rooms available (exclusive use depends on seasons,
nb. of people)

Includes: visit of the farm

14. LOUISEVILLE

60 min from Montréal, La Seigneurie looks forward to spoiling you in its cosy home! You'll delight in our 9-course meal composed of produce from our small traditional farm. The vegetable garden, flower beds and herb garden make our food healthy, while the colours make for an attractive presentation. After a feast complemented by wine what could be better than joining Morpheus in one of our B&B's 5 cosy rooms! **Farm Tour p 40, Farm Stay p 51, B&B p 200 and country home (La Maison du Jardinier) p 56 and 205.**

From Montréal or Québec City, Hwy 40 Exit 166, Rte 138 E., 2.4 km to Rte 348 W. At the lights, left twd Ste-Ursule, 1.5 km, 1st road on the right, 1st house tucked away behind the trees.

Open year round

Activities: 🏛 🧍 🚶 🚲 🐎

LA TABLE DE LA SEIGNEURIE
Michel Gilbert
480, chemin du Golf
Louiseville J5V 2L4
(819) 228-8224
fax (819) 228-5576
www.bbcanada.com/3448.html
m.gilbert@infoteck.qc.ca

Bouchées cordiales à l'apéritif
Feuilleté de filet de perchaude
du Lac Saint-Pierre
Soupière de Bortsch ou du terroir (sarrasin)
Granité Bienfaisant
Le porc, le veau, le lapin ou
l'agneau de la Seigneurie sont à l'honneur
Légumes potagers
Laitue, vinaigrette «Fin Palais»
Éphémère triangle de fromages
Bagatelle «Seigneuriale» au sherry
Douceurs inoubliables
Other menus upon request
Exceptional menus inspired by cuisine from
Monet and Colette

Meal: $39 *Taxes extra*
week: 8 to 32 people   w/e: 10 to 32 people Min. nb. of guests may vary depending on the season
Able to accommodate more than one group/ 3 dining rooms available (exclusive use depends on season, nb. of people)

Includes: visit of the farm (in season)

15. HUNTINGDON

DOMAINE DE LA TEMPLERIE
Chantale Legault et Roland Guillon
312, chemin New Erin
Godmanchester (Huntingdon) J0S 1H0
tel/fax (450) 264-9405

Provincial 1999 Excellence Prize. Nestled in fields and woods, our ancestral home awaits you. Walking in the forest, visiting the sugar shack, outdoor activities. At your discretion: soccer field, volleyball court, bowling green and horseshoes space. Our farm-bred geese, guinea fowl, pheasants and ducks will treat you to an unforgettable concert. You will enjoy succulent dishes prepared by your host, who has some thirty years' cooking experience, in a relaxed ambiance.

From Montréal, Rte 138 West twd Huntingdon. 9km after the stop in Ormstown, turn right at the Montée Seigneuriale, drive 4.7km, turn left and you're at New Erin. Drive 1.3km.

Open year round

Activities:

*Petits fours apéritifs, Velouté en cachette
Plateau de trois charcuteries fines, au choix :
Truite farcie en croûte, Foie de veau au raisin,
Ris de veau aux poires, Mousse de saumon.
Selon votre goût : Filet d'oie sauce Bordelaise,
Suprême de faisan au cognac, Confit de canard
sauce béarnaise, Sauté d'agneau paysanne,
Tournedos de canard au roquefort, Médaillon
d'autruche à l'hydromel et bleuets
Également nous vous offrons :
Chapon, lapin, pintadeau, porc et caille
Pommes château, Jardinière de légumes
Salade de cœurs et de gésiers confits
Plateau de fromages, Crêpe soufflée au Grand-
Marnier, Clafoutis aux fruits de saison,
Coupe de la Templerie,
Café, thé, infusion
Other menus upon request*

Meal: $35-45
week:10 to 38 people   w/e: 12 to 38 people Min. nb. of guests may vary depending on the season
Only one group at a time

Includes: visit of the farm (in season)

16. ST-RÉMI-DE-NAPIERVILLE

FERME KOSA
Ada and Lajos Kosa
1845, rang St-Antoine
St-Rémi-de-Napierville J0L 2L0
tel/fax (450) 454-4490

On the wide expanses of the Rive-Sud, only 15 minutes from Montréal, come experience true gastronomy. A charming entrance, lined with apple trees and forest, a dining room redolent with the wonderful smell of well-browned chicken at the edge of a property near a pond provide a warm and soothing ambiance. While we prepare a feast for you, what could be better than an early evening drink on the terrace whose charm is only enhanced by your presence.

From the Champlain bridge, Hwy 15 twd the U.S.A., Exit 42, Rte 132. Rte 209 South, to St-Rémi. From the church, drive 2.2 km, 1st road on the right is Rang St-Antoine. Or from the Mercier bridge, Rte 207 South and 221 South until Rte 209 South, to St-Rémi.

Open year round

Activities:

*Cocktail de bienvenue
Amuse-gueule
Crème de légumes de saison
Tomate à l'antiboise
Tagliatelle aux asperges ou aux poivrons
Magrets de canard au vinaigre balsamique
et aux navets confits
Légumes du potager
Salade de saison
Quelques fromages fermiers (chèvre)
Couronne de pommes
caramélisée au jus de cidre
Café, thé, infusion
Other menus upon request*

Meal: $35 *Taxes extra*
week:10 to 40 people   w/e: 14 to 40 people Min. nb. of guests may vary depending on the season
Only one group at a time

Includes: visit of the farm (in season)

17. ST-URBAIN-PREMIER

F P ♿

LA BERGERIE DU SUROÎT
Nathalie Laberge and Stéphane Couture
440, rang Double
St-Urbain-Premier J0S 1Y0
(450) 427-1235

Pâté de foie et son confit d'oignons
Terrine de cerf, sauce à l'orange
Potage de cresson et champignons
Papillotes d'agneau, sauce au yogourt
Feuilles de vignes farcies sur coulis d'abricot
Gigot d'agneau aux trois parfums
Carré d'agneau aux herbes de Provence
Noisettes d'agneau sur lit de crème aux herbes
Filet de cerf rouge, sauce à l'érable
Verdure aux herbes fraîches
Chèvre chaud en salade
Aumônière de brie aux pommes
Douceurs glacées aux fruits de la saison
Surprises chocolatées
Méchoui d'agneau

A country house set back from the road, nestled in the midst of a perennial-flower garden and hilly fields. In season, outdoor games let you appreciate the setting. Inside, the fire crackles in the woodstove, the table sports its Sunday tablecloth with place settings from the pine cupboard. We'll share with you little details on lamb breeding, growing mixed herbs and edible flowers. Welcoming you to our home is both a pleasure and a passion.

From the Champlain bridge: Hwy 15 S., Exit 42, Rte 132. At 5th light, take Rte 209 S. twd St-Rémi. Drive 26.6km. Then take Rte 205 for 2.4km. From the Mercier bridge: toward Rte 138 W., 1st exit right on Rte 221 to St-Rémi for 7 km. Rte 207 S. Drive twd St-Isidore for 16km. Rte 205 S. for 3,4km.

Open year round
Activities:

Meal: $30-40	
week:12 to 30 people	w/e: 12 to 30 people
Only one group at a time	

Includes: **visit of the farm**

18. ST-VALÉRIEN

F P ♿

LA RABOUILLÈRE
Pierre Pilon, Denise Bellemare and Jérémie Pilon
1073, rang de l'Égypte
St-Valérien J0H 2B0
(450) 793-4998
fax (450) 793-2529
www.rabouillere.com
info@rabouillere.com

Cocktail de fruits
et assiette de canapés
Terrine de pintadeau aux avelines ou
Foies de lapin au porto
Potage provençal (tomates, ail,
pesto, chèvre frais)
Cuisseau de lapin farci à l'estragon ou
Pigeonneau à la niçoise ou Suprême de pintade
aux pommes et au cidre ou Magret
de canard au vinaigre de framboises
ou Gigot d'agneau au miel et au romarin
Salade mille fleurs (en saison)
Fromages de chèvre
Gâteau au fromage, amande et
fruits sur crème anglaise
Aussi menus brunch, méchoui
Other menus upon request

Depending on the season, you will be welcomed either by our gardens or a fire in the hearth. Rabbit is on the menu, as well as lamb and farm birds including delicious pigeon, our new dish. Edible flowers cheer up and flavour our dishes. Arrive early, as there is a lot to see. Visit our website for meal and lodging packages. **Farm Tour p 43. Farm Stay p 52. B&B 215.**

From Montréal, Hwy 20 East, Exit 141 twd St-Valérien, about 20km. In the village, 1st flashing light, staight ahead for 3km. Turn right at the 2nd flashing light, 1.3km. From Québec City, Hwy 20 West, Exit 143, twd St-Valérien... or Hwy 10 Exit 68, Rte 139 twd Granby, Rtes 112 and 137 North twd St-Hyacinthe. After Ste-Cécile right on ch. St-Valérien, left on 1st flashing light.

Open year round

Meal: $35-42 *Taxes extra*	
wk:12 to 100 people	w/e: 15 to 100 people
Min. nb. of guests may vary depending on the season	
Can accommodate more than 1 group/3 dining rooms (exclusive use depends on seasons, nb. of people)	

Includes: **visit of the farm**

19. STE-JUSTINE-DE-NEWTON

LA SEIGNEURIE DE NEWTON
Lucille Fournier Lavallée
750, 3ᵉ Rang
Ste-Justine-de-Newton J0P 1T0
tel/fax (450) 764-3420

At the heart of a farming region, share the intimacy of our hundred-year-old house with Victorian decor. Enjoy meals with fresh bread baked daily in our authentic bread oven. The piano is always at your disposal. Full range of products from our maple grove. Visit the pheasants, horses, chickens and other animals at our farm. Percheron horses can take you for a carriage or sleigh ride (reservation). Our windmill pumps water for the garden. Welcome!

From Montréal, Hwy 40 W., twd Ottawa, Exit 17, Montée Lavigne. Left on Rte 201 S. for 9.6km to Rang Ste-Marie-de-Ste-Marthe. Take this for 4.6km, at the first stop, go left for 5.1km

Open year round

Activities:

Spécialité faisan :
Terrine de foies de faisan et rillettes au poivre vert
Potage saisonnier
Feuilleté aux épinards
Faisan au cognac
Carottes persillées ou légumes saisonniers
Riz aux fines herbes
Salade de la maison centennaire
Fins fromages régionaux
Crêpes divines to l'érable ou tartelettes paysannes au sirop d'érable
Café, thé, infusions
2nd menu: Festin d'agneau
Other menus upon request

Meal: $35-40	
week:10 to 24 people	w/e: 10 to 24 people
Only one group at a time	

Includes: visit of the farm

20. ST-SIXTE

FERME CAVALIER
Gertie and Marc Cavalier
39, montée St-André
St-Sixte J0X 3B0
(819) 985-2490
fax (819) 985-1411
marc.cavalier@sympatico.ca

In our beautiful valley, beside the Rivière St-Sixte, lamb and poultry from our farm are served in the two traditions: the richness of French gastronomy and the exotism of Moroccan cuisine. Give in to temptation with our changing menu, depending on the seasons and available products and the vision of your hosts. And don't forget our package including accommodation in a cosy and comfortable B&B.

One hour from Hull, 2 from Montréal. From Hull, Hwy 50 to Masson, then Rte 148 to Thurso. Route 317 North for 18 km to Montée Paquette. Turn and continue to Montée St-André. Turn left, the farm is 800 m away.

Open year round

Activities:

Velouté de saison
Filet de truite et sa crème de persil
Noisettes d'agneau marinées aux herbes
Raviole aux champignons des bois
Flan de courgettes et tomates
Bouquet de fraîcheur du jardin
Fromages de la Petite Nation avec pain
aux noix et au miel
Mille-feuille à la mousse d'érable
Café, thé, tisanes, pain maison
Ask about our Moroccan
spreads and other specialties.
We can assist you in
planning your special occasions.

Meal : $23-35 *Taxes extra*
week:10 to 35people   w/e: 15 to 35 people
Min. nb. of guests may vary depending on the season
Able to accommodate more than one group/ 2 dining rooms available (exclusive use depends selon saison, nbre de people)

Includes: visit of the farm (in season)

Regional Dining

21. BRIGHAM

LES DÉPENDANCES DU MANOIR
Lucie Paulhus and Jean-philippe Gosselin
1199, boul. Pierre Laporte, Brigham J2K 4R2
(450) 266-0395
toll free 1-888-266-4491
fax (450) 266-0823
www.dependancesdumanoir.com
agrotourisme@dependancesdumanoir.com

"Les Dépendances du Manoir" offers you a dining experience that honours the product of their lands (fruit, vegetable, fish, chicken, eggs, beef, lamb etc...). The table d'hôte is complete by locally-bred deer, duck, wapitis. A whole specialized team is at your service to make your visit an unforgettable experience: entertainer, chef, *Maître d'hotel*, waitress, cheese maker, pastrycook. Our goal is "from the field to your plate". On our 235ha property, you will find a peaceful place, with a charming rustic decor where you will be warmly welcomed by your hosts. Reservartions suggested. **Farm Tour p 34.**

From Montréal, Hwy 10, Exit 74 twd Cowansville, boul. Pierre-Laporte, exactly 12km.

Open: Feb. 8 to Jan. 8
Activities: 🦐 🎿 🚶 🚴 🐎

*Crème d'oignons caramélisés au porto,
gratiné au vieux cheddar Perron
Verrine de truite aux herbes
Salade d'automne
(laitue, légumes de saison et ventrèche)
Terrine des Dépendances
Foie gras selon Philippe**
*Magret de Canard sauce foie gras accompagné
de son tian confit, gratiné au chèvre
Flétan poèlé au jus d'escargot accompagné de
pommes de terre purée au Gouda
Agneau du moment
Pintade roti, sauce au cidre de pommes Jodoin
Pavé de Cerf et poèlé de champignons
de nos sous-bois
Feuilleté de légumes au fromage et
pesto de notre jardin
Fondue des Dépendances (for 2 people)
Raclette (for 2 people)*
* additional cost

Meals: lunch $15-18 diner $25-35
Taxes extra VS MC AM ER IT
week: 1 to 110 ppl.　　W/e: 1 to 110 ppl.
Able to accommodate more than one group / 3 dining rooms available
(exclusive use depends on season, nb. of people)

Includes: visit of the farm (in season)

22. LES ÉBOULEMENTS

FERME ÉBOULMONTAISE
Lucie Cadieux and Vital Gagnon
350, rang St-Godefroy, rte 362
Les Éboulements G0A 2M0
(418) 635-9888
(418) 635-2682
fax (418) 439-0616
fermebou@cite.net

La Ferme Éboulemontaise, located in the heart of the Réserve Mondiale de la Biosphère at the foot of Mont des Éboulements and facing the majestic St. Lawrence River, offers you the opportunity to discover the sheep breeding in Charlevoix. After visiting the sheepfold and organic gardens or hiking in a bucolic decor, you will be cordially invited to our table. "Les Saveurs Oubliées," a designation of regional gastronomy, will let you discover the many aspects of our regional cuisine at its best. A taste to discover offered by Régis Hervé and Guy Thibodeau.

From Québec City, Rte 138 twd Ste-Anne- de-Beaupré and Baie-St-Paul. In Baie-St-Paul, panoramique Rte, 362, 1km after Les Éboulements village.

Apéritif et amuse-bouche
Rillette de canard au confit d'oignon,
Gâteau de presse d'agneau
et Salade folle au goût du jour
ou carpaccio d'agneau à l'huile de tomates
séchées et râpe de parmesan
Soupière du moment ou verdurette des jardins
et croûtons de fromage Le Ciel de Charlevoix
Tartiflette à la truite fumée des Éboulements
ou Foie d'agneau poêlé aux pommes
et tombée de choux rouge
Assiette d'agneau de la maison sur le grill
ou Navarin d'agneau Éboulemontaise
ou Souris d'agneau et sa pipérade au cari
ou Carré d'agneau à ma façon
et salsa rhubarbe maïs
Lapereau aux petits lardons,
vin rouge et pomme cloutée
Jambonneau de canard confit, caramel d'érable
Mes coups de cœur sucrés
Café Mignardises
Other menus upon request

Open year round
Activities:

Meals: $36-45 *Taxes extra*/ VS MC AM IT
week: 2 to 50 ppl.   W/e: 2 to 50 ppl.
Able to accommodate more than one group /1 dining rooms available
(exclusive use depends on season, nb. of people)
Includes: visit of the farm

23. STE-ANNE-DES-PLAINES

BASILIC ET ROMARIN
Jocelyne Parent
12, boul. Normandie
Ste-Anne-des-Plaines J0N 1H0
(450) 838-9752
basilicetromarin@sympatico.ca

Barely 45min from downtown! And there you are in the heart of a maple grove, the sweet cocoon of Basilic et Romarin. The dining experience awaits you in the solarium that opens out on the kitchen garden and a magnificent forest. The farmyard, maple grove, vegetable garden and regional products provide the raw materials for our creativity, inspired by a five-year journey through both the American and European continents. Are your taste buds curious, insatiable and ready to be surprised? Then come sample our original flavours in small groups of two to six people. The menu varies according to our whims throughout the year as well as the evening. Two different menus are served to each two guests.

Hwy 15, Exit 31. Head East for 14km along Victor, then Lepage. Turn right, heading south for 500m to Blvd. Normandie.

Open year round
Activities:

Gravad lax à la coriande et lime
Rillettes de lapin aux noisettes
Mousse de légumes
sur coulis de poivron rouge
Potage au zucchini et basilic
Feuilleté de mousse de foie à l'oseille
Tourte de cailles et d'amandes
Pâté de lapin sur coulis de champignons
Granité de vin blanc et de lime
Lapin farci à la courgette et pacanes
avec sauce à l'estragon
Pintades avec sauce à l'orange
et aux canneberges
Caille au riz sauvage et oignons caramélisés
Faisan aux petits fruits
Gâteau à la mousse d'érable
Marquise au chocolat sur crème anglaise
Gaufrette farcie de crème glacée au basilic
Tuile de mascarpone et framboises
Other menus upon request

Meals: $45	
Week: 2 to 6 people	w/e: 2 to 6 people
Able to accommodate more than one group of 6 people/1 dining room available	
(exclusive use depends on season, nb. of people)	

Includes: visit of the farm (in season)

Farm Tour

1. BRIGHAM

LES DÉPENDANCES
DU MANOIR
Lucie Paulhus and
Jean-Philippe Gosselin
1199, boul. Pierre Laporte
Brigham J2K 4R2
(450) 226-0395
toll free 1-888-266-4491
fax (450) 266-0388
www.dependances
dumanoir.com
agrotourisme@
dependancesdumanoir.com

70km from Montréal
10km from Bromont
15km from Granby

Les Dépendances du Manoir is a unique agro-tourism venture which combines a passion for cheese and a love of apples. With us, you'll discover animals in an enchanting environment, an orchard and garden, and friendly hosts ready to answer all your questions. You'll savour delicious meals at Les Dépendance; a cheese shop and pastry shop are also located on the premises. **Regional Dining p 30.**

From Montréal, Hwy 10 Exit 74 twd Cowansville, Boul. Pierre Laporte exactly 12 km.

For families and small groups (5 to 20 people): mid-May to mid-Oct., reservation needed

---

Visit:

- Flower and herb garden
- Vegetable garden
- Lakes: trout farm
- Apple and plum orchards
- Basse-cour: Hens, turkeys, chickens
- Sheep farm: Mohair goats and sheep
- Family friends: horse, donkey, dog and cat

- Tractor rides
- Farm visit
- Home-made cheese presentation and tasting

Duration 1hr.

Rates:
   $5 adult
   $2 children (under 8 years old)
   Taxes included

2. ST-LÉON-DE-STANDON

JARDINS DES TOURTEREAUX
DE LA FERME LA COLOMBE
Jean-Yves Marleau
104, rang Ste-Anne
St-Léon-de-Standon G0R 4L0
(418) 883-5833
(418) 642-5152
fax (418) 642-2991
www.fermelacolombe.qc.ca
r.gregoire@globetrotter.net

90km from St-Georges-de-Beauce
100km from Québec
70km from Lévis

Special mention for Excellence "Success" Regional 2000. Nestled in the heart of the mountains, this unique concept will introduce you to 500 varieties of plants laid out in 11 thematic gardens. Trails are graced with swings, a pergola, little bridges, ponds, aviaries and animal parks. Come enjoy your relaxing picnic by the gently babbling brook. This excursion will rouse all your senses and fill your daily life with romanticism and reverie. Country-style dining here will allow you to further enjoy our gardens. Packages available. Rare ornamental plants for sale. **Country-style Dining p 18.**

From Québec, Hwy 20 East, Exit 325 twd Lac-Etchemin, Rtes 173 and 277 South twd St-Léon-de-Standon. At the stop sign, 0.9km from the church, cross Rte 277, left on Rue du Village, 4km. Right on Rg Ste-Anne, 2km.

FOR FAMILIES AND SMALL GROUPS : mid-June to beginning of September
For groups of 20 to 80 people : mid-June to beginning of September (with reservation)

- horticultural farm: tending and reproducing plants
- Visiting the various theme gardens:
- edible flowers (75 varieties)
- fragrant flowers (rose gardens, lilacs, etc.)
- gardens of colours or garden of Eden
- garden of birds and hummingbirds
- secret garden
- garden of indigenous plants
- berry garden
- lovers' garden
- water garden (6 ponds and a lake)
- sampling garden
- nature-interpretation relay, with 15 points, and a mystery to discover

- Dinner on the farm and feeding the animals*
- For school groups: "Tour of Noah's ark"*
- guided visit of the animals (20 species)
- treasure hunt
- edible flower sampling garden
- plant arrangements
- tour of gardens

Rates:
$4.50 per person
$3.50 Senior citizens
$2.50 students
$1.50 children from 2 to 6
$2.50 to $3.95/pers. for group (20 to 80 people)

*additional charge

3. RAWDON

ARCHE DE NOÉ
Bernard Boucher
4117, ch. Greene
Rawdon
J0K 1S0
(450) 834-7874
(450) 834-3934
fax (450) 834-5090

55 km from Montréal
80 km from Longueuil
30 km from Joliette

You can begin your stroll immediately upon your arrival by visiting the different animals. This guided tour through the property introduce you to more than 15 animal species, some of which run free. The flower gardens and the different landscapes are sure to make your visit most enchanting. You may make reservations to take part in the daily tasks of farm life. Moreover, pleasant footpaths lead you through our valleys to peaceful picnic and rest stops. We can organize a party*, a spit-roasted-lamb barbecue* or other event* for you: just contact us!

From Montréal, Hwy 25 North to Rawdon. Rte 337 North, left on Rue Queen, at the IGA. Cross the village to 16e Avenue, then turn left at the Chemin Morgan intersection. We are 6km farther.

FOR FAMILIES, SMALL GROUPS AND FOR GROUPS
of 15 people and more: May 1 to October 31

- The Arche de Noé is 1 hour from Montréal!
- Ostriches, boars, Vietnamese pot-bellied pigs, miniature goats, horses, (Limousin) cattle, birds, cats and dog.
- Footpaths and picnic areas able to accommodate up to 200 people..

- Landscaped volleyball court and horseshoes space.
- Unforgettable scenery and family ambiance that will brighten up your day!

Rates :
$6 per person
$20 for groups of 4 people or more
groups on reservation

4. LA MINERVE

FERME ÉCO-FORESTIÈRE DE LA MINERVE
Carole Alarie
86, chemin des Grandes Côtes
La Minerve J0T 1H0
(819) 274-1366
fax (819) 274-1296
www.chez.com/
fermeecoforestiere
foresterie@intlaurentides.qc.ca

60 km from St-Jovite
60 km from Mont-Tremblant
190 km from Montréal

A century-old farmhouse with a magnificent panoramic view overlooking three lakes and surrounded by 276 acres of managed land and forest. Discover all the beauty and diversity of the Upper Laurentians forest...(Terre de Chez Nous, Oct 2000). Close, safe and easy contact with the farm animals. Our little family, the fourth and fifth generations to live here, offers you a warm welcome.

From Montreal, Hwy 15 North, Rte 117. 4.2km past the Labelle traffic light, left on Chemin de La Minerve, 16.3km, right on Chemin des Fondateurs. At the miniature-golf course, left on Chemin des Grandes Côtes, 1.2km.

For families and small group: June 1 to Oct. 30, Wenesday to Sunday 9am to 4pm
For groups of 15 to 60 people: Apr. 1 to Oct. 30

Come and brush Grognon and Bouchon the pigs, feed Biquette the goat, stroke the rabbits, gather eggs, say hello to Frisotin the sheep and his large family, pet Ciboulette the cow, quack at Saturnin the duck and cuddle my Vietnamese pig. Gus the dog and cats Ti-Mine and Blanchette keep you company.
- Kite
- Interpretive trails on the forest and the fauna and forest rally
- Cottage in the enchanted forest with play area

- Picnic area, with swings and a sandbox
- Group activities: farm animals, the forest and its inhabitants, ornithology, information about aquatic environments, foot rally, sugaring-off, hay ride.
- Mini rural boutique, farm products (maple, lamb and eggs), interpretive centre, baby-carriers available, picnic basket and ornithology equipment.

Rates:
$4.50 adult
$2.50 child
$5 for group of 15 to 60 people, with animation
$10 for family (parents and children)

5. MIRABEL, ST-BENOIT

INTERMIEL
Viviane and Christian Macle
10291, rang de la Fresnière
Mirabel, St-Benoît JON 1K0
(450) 258-2713
fax (450) 258-2708
www.intermiel.com
intermiel@sympatico.ca

15 km from St-Eustache
45 km from Montréal
25 km from Mirabel airport

In St-Benoît, come to the largest beekeeping area in Québec. The guided tour includes a visit to the mead cellar, a video, demonstrations of our various products and a "Bee Safari" in season. Free entrance to the educational games room and our "honey boutique".

From Montréal, Hwy 15 North, Exit 20, Hwy 640 West, Exit 8. Follow the blue tourist information signs, 18 km.

Open year round/ 7 days a week
Groups: with reservations
adults **$3**, children **$1** taxes included
Guided Tours (1h30 long) including sampling.
School package: 2-hour educational visit in 4 workshops.
Price: $6 (includes snack and a pot of honey)
other packages available (mini-farm)

- Movie on the beekeeping activities of the farm
- Learn about the bee
- Observation of living hives
- Handling of an active hive by the beekeeper (in summer)
- Demonstration of prodution techniques
- Visit the mead cellar

- Mead tasting (honey wine)
- Honey products sampling (honey ganache, caramel...)
- Educational games room
- Marionette theatre (schools)
- Exhibition shop (candles, crafts, gifts, cosmetics, etc.)
- Picnic area with interior space in case of rain
- Mini-farm

6. ST-FAUSTIN

FERME DE LA BUTTE MAGIQUE
Diane Gonthier
1724, ch. de la Sauvagine
St-Faustin-Lac-Carré J0T 1J2
tel/fax (819) 425-5688
www.citeweb.net/bmagique
fermedelabuttemagique
@hotmail.com

25 km from Mont-Tremblant
115 km from Montréal
180 km from Ottawa

Take a typical Laurentians piece of land, and add a herd of "multicoloured" sheep that liven up the scenery as well as a farm and a small, utterly picturesque B&B. Meet genuine artisan-shepherdesses who enjoy updating ancestral traditions, with boundless creativity. Our farm excursions are actually an open window onto the many aspects of the shepherd lifestyle. It is a great pleasure to introduce you to this way of life through various options... **Farm Stay p 51, B&B p 179.**

From Montreal, Hwy 15 North. In St-Faustin, 2km past Mont-Blanc, turn left on Chemin la Sauvagine and continue for 7km. From St-Jovite, Rte 327 Sud toward Arundel, drive 2km. Turn left on Chemin Paquette, 6km.

Guided tour of the farm
FOR FAMILIES AND SMALL GROUPS, every Saturday afternoon, from early July to mid-Oct.
Departure at 1:30pm (2hr tour).
Adults **$6**, children (2 to 12 years old) **$4**
* or at any other time by reservation for a group of at least 10 people
** vacationers staying at our B&B are invited to participate in our guided tour free of charge

---

- Guided tour of the farm: an eventful day, animals (various breeds of sheep, pigs, chicks, laying hens, roosters, llama, dog, cat and kittens), gardens and a demonstration of a spinning wheel at work in the "Grenier des Souvenirs."
- Courses (year-round): spinning, wool felting by hand
- Stay: one-week farm stay for young "artist" women 10 to 12 years of age ("accompanying" mothers are also welcome!

- The sheep's bounty from every angle: an amazing "picnic" day with choice of workshops. For all types of groups of 10 to 40 people (with reservation from April to October).
  - Presentation on the history of spinning.
  - Making of a wool-based souvenir.
  - Characteristics of ewe's milk.
  - Guided tour of the farm.
  - Visit to the wool-washing pavilion, the carding workshop and a collection of spinning wheels...

Rates: $15/adult
$8/children (2 to 12 years old)

7. LOUISEVILLE

LES JARDINS
DE LA SEIGNEURIE
Michel Gilbert
480, chemin du Golf
Louiseville J5V 2L4
(819) 228-8224
fax (819) 228-5576
www.bbcanada.com/3448.html
m.gilbert@infoteck.qc.ca

26 km from Trois-Rivières
160 km from Québec
120 km from Montréal

All around a traditional little farm, these gardens have been restored and enlarged, taking inspiration from 19th-century bourgeois farm life. You'll get an inside look at Québec's natural farming heritage, raising animals and ecological farming, and the art of country living. Your five senses will be charmed. "One of 20 gardens to visit in Quebec" (l'Essentiel, July 98; La Semaine Verte, August 98). The **Gîte de La Seigneurie p 200** at the **Maison du Jardinier p 56**, at the **Farm Stay p 51** and the **Table Champêtre p 24**, are the best places to stay to take advantage of these romantic gardens. **Advertisement end of Mauricie-Bois-Francs region, accommodation section.**

From Montréal or Québec City, Hwy 40 Exit 166, Rte 138 E., 2.4km to Rte 348 W. At the lights, left twd Ste-Ursule, 1.5km, 1st road on the right, 1st house tucked away behind the trees.

FOR FAMILIES AND SMALL GROUPS : June 15 to September15 (with reservations)
For groups of 10 to 40 personnes : June 15 to September 15 (with reservations)

- Identification of old flower varieties, fruits and vegetables in flower beds, a rose garden, groves and vegetable gardens
- Enclosed herb garden and an exhibition on their medicinal properties
- Buckwheat fields
- Composting and complementary gardening
- The advantages of a greenhouse
- Visit sheep, goat and horse pastures
- Demonstration on how to use some old gardening tools
- Identification of 60 tree varieties
- Visit the farmyard (turkeys, geese, chickens, ducks, guinea-fowl)

- Iroquois vegetable garden
- Cut-flower garden (900 gladiola)
- Visit heritage buildings and their "residents": pigs, calves, rabbits and cats

Price: $6 per person including tasting of farm products in the garden.

Schedule: guided tour (90 min) every day at 3 pm or otherwise with reservations.

Supper on the farm (5 courses, $20) is available after the tour, with reservations.

The tour is free for those staying at the Seigneurie.

8. ST-ISIDORE-DE-LAPRAIRIE

LES ÉLEVAGES RUBAN BLEU
Denise Poirier Rivard
449, rang St-Simon
St-Isidore-de-Laprairie J0L 2A0
tel/fax (450) 454-4405
www.rubanbleu.net
chevre@rubanbleu.net

Recipient of the Montérégie Grand Prize of Tourism 2000, category tourist attraction for less than 100,000 visitors. 10min from the Mercier bridge, come pet the adorable goats who are the first to greet you on site! Also, discover some 21 kinds of handmade cheeses offered year-round in our on-site shop. And if the goat world intrigues you, take part in the narrated tour in our interpretive centre, the Ruban Bleu pavilion, where you will learn everything about goats, from breeding to cheese.

15km from Châteauguay
15km from Montréal
25km from Longueuil

Rte 132, Hwy 30 West, Exit 86, turn left at the stop sign, take Rte 221 toward St-Rémi. 1km past the first stop sign, turn right on rang St-Simon and continue for 3km.

Narrated tours for families and small groups: May 1 to Oct 31
(May, June, Sep, Oct.: Sat and Sun 2pm; July and Aug.: Tue to Sun 1pm, 2pm, 3pm)
For groups of 10 to 55 people: year-round (by reservation)

- Independent walk through the site.
- Feeding and petting the goats
- Close contact with the animals
- "From breeding... to cheese" narrated tour
- Video
- Commentary
- Sampling of goat's milk and cheeses, July and Aug: Tue to Sun 1pm, 2pm, 3pm, May, June, Sep, Oct: Sat and Sun 2pm
- Educational school program

- Farm shop:
- 21 kinds of goat's-milk cheese
- goat's-milk bubble bath, bath milk and soaps
- mohair socks
- Shop hours:
Tue to Fri 10am to 6pm
Sat and Sun 10am to 5pm
closed Mon
- Wine-and-cheese tasting by reservation*
- Theatre package during the summer season (wine-and-cheese tasting and stage play), in collaboration with the Châteauguay Quatre/Corps theatre*

Rates:
$5 adult
$2.50 children
free for children under 6, with an adult
bus : 2 free entrance

Taxes included
* rates on request

9. ST-PIE

FERME JEAN DUCHESNE
Diane Authier and
Jean Duchesne
1981-84, Haut-de-la-Rivière Sud
St-Pie J0H 1W0
(450) 772-6512
fax (450) 772-2491
www.geocities.com/
fermejeanduchesne
fermejeanduchesne@
hotmail.com

60 km from Montréal
20 km from St-Hyacinthe
15 km from Granby

Prize for Excellence "Success" 2000. Our farm turns your children into little farmers, with everything fully designed with them in mind. The adventure is crowned with a "farmer for a day" certificate of merit, officially presented by the "big farmer." **See colour photos.**

Hwy 20, Exit 123. At the stop sign, left on Rte 235 South. At the flashing light after two bridges, left on Rang Emille Ville, left at the end, left at the stop sign. Hwy 10, Exit 55, Rte 235 North. Past Rte 112, right at the flashing light, left at the stop sign, left at the next stop sign.

FOR FAMILIES AND SMALL GROUPS : 1 to 30 people April to October (with reservations)
For groups of 2 to 150 personnes : April 11 to October 31 (with reservations)

- Guided tours: educational, recreational or participatory program, depending on the age group (see the 6 programs)
- Introduction to several farm-bred animals, including rabbits and their hutch, the cow and its dairy, goat milking. Over 200 animals and 100 poultry.
- Feeding the animals, goat milking, hay ride to the sheepfold, the maple grove and the sand quarry. Whew! What an adventure in the woods!
- Hike to the maple museum and the sugar shack.
- Children's ranch, horse ride*
- Farm games (tractor, hay...) and several big surprises!
- Facilities in case of rain. Indoor and outdoor game and picnic areas.
- Farm, local and maple products.

- 6 programs for group or family
- Day (10am to 3pm): guided access to the whole farm, diplomas for all our little farmers (times can be changed)
- Day (noon to 4pm): semi-guided, unguided access to the farm and cart ride to the maple grove.
- Night (5pm to 9pm): private reception for 25 people or more. Semi-guided tour and campfire. Perfect for corn-husking party* or birthday. Spit-roasted lamb with caterer* available.
- The farmer's trick*: apple and pumpkin in season, guided or semi-guided tour.
- Halloween: 3 last weekends of Oct, walk in the haunted forest resplendent with fall colours, and access to the farm.
- Children's birthday: guided tour with special attention for the birthday girl or boy.

Rates :
   $6 per person
   $5 For groups of 25 to 150 people
* additional charge

10. ST-VALÉRIEN

LA RABOUILLÈRE
Pierre Pilon, Denise Bellemare
et Jérémie Pilon
1073, rang de l'Égypte
St-Valérien JOH 2B0
(450) 793-4998
fax (450) 793-2529
www.rabouillere.com
info@rabouillere.com

80 km from Montréal
20 km from St-Hyacinthe
20 from de Granby

La Rabouillère, a unique farm. Your host, a veterinarian, has an infectious enthusiasm for animals and flowers... A unique collection of many animal species and breeds in magnificent countryside. (Ideal site for family parties, anniversaries, weddings, etc.). **Country-Style Dining p 26. Farm Stay p 52. B&B p 215.**

From Montreal, Hwy 20 East, Exit 141 toward St-Valérien, about 20km. In the village, at the first flashing light, continue straight ahead for 3km. Turn right at the 2nd flashing light, continue for 1.3km. From Quebec City, Hwy 20 West, Exit 143 toward St-Valérien... or Hwy 10 Exit 68 Rte 139 twd Granby, Rtes 112 and 137 North twd Ste-Hyacinthe. After Ste-Cécile right on chemin St-Valérien, left at 1st light.

Our farm is now open from May to October, weather permitting,
for families and small or large groups.
RESERVATIONS ALWAYS REQUIRED
Snacks available upon request*

- The garden: large variety of perennials and herbs (flowers in the kitchen, composting, water garden, the flora and fauna)
- The rabbit hutch: rabbits of different breeds (giant, dwarf, Angora...)
- Goats: care of the different breeds (dwarf)
- Horse breeding: dwarf-horses
- The farmyard: more than 50 types of birds
- The sheepfold (rare breeds): four-horned Jacob Sheep, Barbarian sheep and katadin (wool-less)

- Curiosities: llamas, donkeys, deer...
- Other activities: pony rides, pool, volleyball, musical shows (folksinger or classical)*, campfire*, spit-roasted lamb (méchoui)*, corn-husking party*, brunch*, sampling of terrines, potted meat and other farm products*

Price: $5 per person
* additional charge

11, PIERREFONDS

FERME ÉCOLOGIQUE DU
PARC-NATURE DU
CAP-SAINT-JACQUES
D-TROIS-PIERRES
183, ch. du Cap-Saint-Jacques
Pierrefonds H9K 1C6
(514) 280-6743
fax (514) 624-0725
www.d3pierres.qc.ca
info@d3pierres.qc.ca

30 km de Montréal
100 km de Joliette
180 km de Hull

On the western part of the island of Montreal, immerse yourself in a universe of organic agriculture. We are the only farm in Canada associated with an international organization of educational farms. More than 15 species, greenhouse displaying cultivation, organic garden, cultivation fields. Everything to introduce the young and old alike to the agicultural world. We also offer a whole range of complementary services. The country ambiance will charm you!

Hwy 40, Exit 49. Follow the blue signposts. The park entry is at 20099 Boul. Gouin West. Inside the park, follow "La Ferme Écologique" indications.

Free visit for families, year round, animation services: Feb. 15 to Oct. 31, weekends.
Guided visit for group of 10 to 120 ppl.: Feb. 15 to Oct. 31, with reservations. Rates $5/ppl.
Sugar shack*: Feb. 15 to Apr. 15, visit and traditional meal, with reservations.

- Free animated visit on weekends (mid-Feb./late Oct.).
- Guided visits: educational/recreational program
- "Farm visit": May/late Oct.
- Special programs*: sugar shack, farm/beach, Halloween
- More than 15 species in their indoor and outdoor habitats.
- Organic greenhouse cultivation.
- Organic garden: identifying crops, composting...
- Sleigh ride*
- Interpretation centre (Feb./late Oct.)

- General store, local farm and craft products.
- Dining
- Hiking trails and picnic site
- Cross-country ski trails
- Playground, thematic festivals, harvest festival* (2nd Sunday in August)
- Complementary services*: Country-style dinners, children's birthday parties, conference and reception rooms, outdoor reception areas

*Additional charge
Rates:
    Parking $4

12. CHÂTEAU-RICHER

MUSÉE DE L'ABEILLE-
ÉCONOMUSÉE DU MIEL
Redmond Hayes
8862, boul. Ste-Anne
Château-Richer G0A 1N0
(418) 824-4411
toll free 1-877-449-4411
fax (418) 824-4422
www.musee-abeille.com
info@musee-abeille.com

30km from Québec
5km from Ste-Anne-de-Beaupré
5km from Château-Richer

An unforgettable experience awaits young and old alike at the honey economuseum. At the Bee Safari, observe a beekeeper at work in a real apiary. Giant glassed-in beehives. "Bees and Humans" exhibit, interactive quiz, bee rally. Savour dry or sweet, light or frothy, mead, "the nectar of the gods," produced on site. Shop abounding in beehive products, gift wrapping. Honey-chocolate and pastry shop, healthy meals on the terrace in season. Multipurpose room for presentations, workshops, happy hour or functions.

From Québec City, Hwy 40 toward Ste-Anne-de-Beaupré. Follow the blue Tourisme Québec roadsigns.

For families and groups of 15 to 60 people: open year round

For individuals and families:
- Free admission to the exhibit and shop year-round.
- Sampling of our seven kinds of mead (honey wine)
- Bee Safari from St-Jean-Baptiste (June 24) to Thanksgiving for individuals and families.

For groups:
- Educational activities for school groups year-round.
- Candle workshop.

- Honey-chocolate workshop.
- Humorous presentation for groups of adults.
- Coffee break, top-of-the-range pastries and dessert plates.
- Package with individual gift (wine, chocolate, etc.).
- Wine-and-cheese tasting.
- Bistro and gourmet meal.
- Cocktail and snack.
- Lunch-box service.

Rates:
-**12 years old and over $1.75**
-**free for children under 12 years old with parents**
-**various rates for groups of 15 to 60 ppl.**
Taxes extra

13. NEUVILLE

LA FERME L'ÉMEULIENNE
Émilienne and Jacques
Chouinard, Houle
307, rue Petit-Capsa
Neuville G0A 2R0
(418) 876-2788
fax (418) 876-3280
www.quebecweb.com/emeu/
emeu@globetrotter.net

30km from Québec
100km from Trois-Rivières
60km from Lévis

Just 30min from Quebec City, discover a lifestyle that will delight all your senses. Meet the animals and the ratites (ostriches, emus, rheas) in our mini-farm. Let your family or group take part in an exceptional 90min outing, with a tasting session.* We are an educational farm specializing in agro-tourism. Nature is an open book for those with a sense of wonder and desire for knowledge. Come experience all this at L'Émeulienne! **B&B p 245, Farm Stay p 53.**

Hwy 40 East or West, Exit 285 Neuville. Right and then left, twd Pont-Rouge on Rte Gravel, around 5km, right at Petit-Capsa.

Guided visit and sampling for groups and families of 2 to 100 ppl.
Open year round, reservation required

- Emu breeding farm.
- Visit of the breddings (ostriches, emus, rheas)
- Visit incubation room
- Observation of embryo development
- Lively visit to mini farm, with ponies, Vietnamese pigs, ducks, rabbits, chickens...
- Tasting of emu meat
- Boutique (decorated eggs, jewelry, emu oil, soaps)

- Volleyball and horseshoes
- Picnic area
- Free visit for the poeple staying at the B&B
- Old-fashioned supper, upon reservation*
- Creative activities: decorating eggs, making featherdusters...

Rates: $4/people (includes emu meat sampling)
$2.50 children (includes emu meat sampling)
Free for children under 2 years old
*Additional charges

Farm Stay and Country Home on a Farm

BAS-ST-LAURENT

		RATES			ANIMALS	ACTIVITIES
		1 meal	2 meals	3 meals		
St-Jean-de-Dieu Ferme Paysagée ☎ (418) 963-3315 (page 73)	single double child child alone	30 40 10 --	40 80 15-16 --	-- -- -- --	Deer, lamas, ponies, lambs, sheeps, goats, rabbits, ducks, cows, peacocks, golden pheasant.	Milking a cow, bringing the cows in from pasture, gathering eggs from chickens and quails. Feeding the small animals. Trout fishing. Walking along our trails and through our fields.
Rimouski Ferme Flots Bleus Inc. ☎ (418) 723-1578 (page 70)	single double child child alone	45 60 10 --	-- -- -- --	-- -- -- --	The Ferme Flots Bleus is a dairy farm, with a herd of 60 cattle, including 30 purebred dairy cows, plus bulls and calves.	The small farm behind the bed & breakfast is made up of hens and ducks as well as Cannelle the goat and Mylène the ewe. Two horses, Tristan and Bel-Ami, are waiting for you to come pet them. During the summer season, I invite you to help out with farm chores, such as milking the cows, tending the animals, gathering eggs, haymaking, harvesting and gardening. If this work proves too hard, I propose you take a stroll in the fields or along the river.

CANTONS-DE-L'EST

		RATES			ANIMALS	ACTIVITIES
		1 meal	2 meals	3 meals		
Courcelles Ferme Auberge d'Andromède ☎ (418) 483-5442 (page 79)	single double child child alone	40-60 50-70 25 --	70 140 30 --	-- -- -- --	Pinto pony, Appaloosa horses, Canadian quarter-horses, Indian paint-horse pony, angora goats and rabbits, hens, vietnamese pigs. Dalmatian and Labrador dogs, ducks, partridges, geese, stripped kitten.	Rejuvenate yourself at our magnificent farm with its dazzling panorama. Feed the animals in our stable, gather eggs, ride my horses and brush them – bring along some apples. Equestrian package available for adults with horseback-riding experience including: room, country-style breakfast, table-d'hote with regional specialties, 2hrs horseback riding. $125 per person. Relaxation guaranteed.
Danville Le Clos des Pins ☎ (819) 839-3521 (page 80)	single double child child alone	50-65 65-80 10 --	65-80 95-110 -- 20-25	-- -- -- --	Cows, calves, horses, pigs, cats, sheep, rabbits, ducks, chickens, quail, guinea-fowl, partridges, Bernese bouvier dogs and cats.	Walks (135 acres), horse-drawn carriage rides, animal care, swimming, campfires, outdoor games, fruit picking, maintaining the organic vegetable garden, swing, children's playground. Daycare available for a small fee.

CENTRE-DU-QUÉBEC

		RATES			ANIMALS	ACTIVITIES
		1 meal	2 meals	3 meals		
Wickham La Ferme de la Berceuse ☎ (819) 398-6229 (page 96)	single double child child alone	55 60 9 ---	70 90 15 ---	--- --- --- ---	Laying hens, goats, northern bobwhites, partridges, guinea fowl, wild turkeys, dog and cat.	We invite you to share a moment of sheer delight in a bountiful space. A small organically certified farm, we grow 80 different varieties of more than 25 vegetables, herbs and raspberries. Take part in an educational tour, stroll through the woods or simply laze around on the farm. Renew your connection to the earth and sample the joys of the countryside. La Ferme de la Berceuse, a shared passion. **Country-Style Dining p 17.**

CHARLEVOIX

		1 meal	2 meals	3 meals	ANIMALS	ACTIVITIES
St-Urbain Centre de l'émeu de Charlevoix ☎ (418) 639-2205 or 1-866-639-2205 (page 110)	single double child child alone	43-45 55-70 17 ---	--- --- --- ---	--- --- --- ---	Emus and rheas (in same family as the ostrich). Price includes the guided tour.	Located on the site of the Chez Gertrude B&B (see colour photos). The guided tour (1hr) allows you to observe emus of all ages, to differentiate them from their cousins (ostriches and rheas), to get acquainted with their habitat and habits, to see the hatching of a chick and to become familiar with all emu-based products and their benefits. On-site shop. Tour schedule: Jun 22 to Aug 25 and Sep 1 to 3. Check out our Web site.

CHAUDIÈRES-APPALACHES

		1 meal	2 meals	3 meals	ANIMALS	ACTIVITIES
St-Cyprien, Barré Le Jardin des Mésanges ☎ (418) 383-5777 (page 117)	single double child child alone	40 55 5-15 ---	50 75 15-25 ---	--- --- --- ---	Poney, ox, cows, calves, pigs, laying hens, grain-fed chickens, wild turkey, quails, rabbits, dog and cats.	As the seasons drift by, discover different activities. In spring, participates in maple-syrup making in our sugar shack. In summer, discover the organic garden and it's original produce, as well as the flowers and the birds. Help take care of the animals. Visit the region on the bike paths. Enjoy the beautiful colours of automn while hiking, wood cutting or picking mushrooms. In winter, skate on the lake or do some snowshoeing. B&B accessible by skidoo. In summer, baby-sitting for a small additional charge.

		RATES			ANIMALS	ACTIVITIES
		1 meal	2 meals	3 meals		
CÔTE-NORD						
Sacré-Cœur Ferme -5- Étoiles ☎ toll free 1-877-236-4551 ☎ (418) 236-4833 (page 127)	single double child child alone	40 45-50 10 ---	64 88 29 ---	--- --- --- ---	Buffalo, stags, deers, boars, wolves, cows, horses, more than 32 species of farm birds...	Guided tour of the farm and its animals, the daily care of the animals, tractor and horse rides, excursions: hiking, all-terrain vehicles, kayaking, sailing or boat trips on the Saguenay Fjord, whale-watching cruises, backcountry camping. **Country home p 132. For activities: see advertisement in Côte-Nord and Saguenay-Lac-St-Jean regions.**
GASPÉSIE						
St-René-de-Matane Gîte des Sommets ☎ (418) 224-3497 (page 145)	single double child child alone	30 50 15 20	40 70 20 30	50 90 25 40	Cattle breeding, goat farm, chickens, rabbits and Ti-Lou, our friendly dog.	Guided tours of the farm, hikes on the well-marked and maintained trails. Fishing in the brook, mountain biking, picnics, campfires, mushroom picking, wild-berry picking, photo safari. Mountain climbing, visit to beaver pond. In winter season: snowshoeing, cross-country skiing, sliding, skidooing (equipment not provided).
LANAUDIÈRE						
St-Alphonse-Rodriguez Ranch 4 saisons ☎ (450) 883-0933 toll free 1-877-883-0933 (page 164)	single double child child alone	--- --- --- ---	115 230 60-85 ---	150 300 60-85 ---	Horses, pony, dogs, donkeys, hens, pheasants, wild turkeys, speckled and rainbow trout, etc. Free for children of 0-3 years old.	Horseback riding, sledding, skating rink, trapper's trail, ranch tour, western jail. Equipment supplied: fishing, pedal-boating, mountain biking, snowshoeing, cross-country skiing, water slide, tubes or "crazy carpets," food to feed the small animals.
LAURENTIDES						
L'Annonciation La Clairière de la Côte ☎ (819) 275-2877 (page 173)	single double child child alone	35-50 50-65 15 ---	65 90 20-25 ---	70 100 30 ---	Cows, calves, goats, sheeps, rabbits, grain-fed chickens, turkeys, geese, dogs and cats.	Visit of the farm. Forest walks (300 acres). Organic gardens, fine herbs, flowers, greenhouse. See chicks hatch. Transformation of farm products. Smoking of meat and fish. Rest areas. Campfires. Games. Life on the farm is busy. **Country-Style Dining p 20.**

LAURENTIDES

		RATES			ANIMALS	ACTIVITIES
		1 meal	2 meals	3 meals		
St-Faustin Ferme de la Butte Magique ☎ (819) 425-5688 (page 179)	single	47-57	67-77	---	Friesian (dairy), merino, Jacob and Icelandic (wool) lambs and ewes, turkeys, laying hens, roosters and chicks, pigs in the forest, llama, collie dogs and cats.	Passionate farmers guide you through everything from daily animal care to seasonal farming. What is truly magical is holding a chick in your hands, seeing a spinning wheel in operation, lifting a big carrot, finding a warm egg or witnessing the birth of a lamb... All this, and exploring the lake, trails and fields, too. Inquire about our one-week stays for young "artist" women of 10 to 12 years of age. **Farm Tour p 39.**
	double	67	107	---		
	child	20	28	---		
	child alone	---	---	---		

MAURICIE-BOIS-FRANCS

		RATES			ANIMALS	ACTIVITIES
		1 meal	2 meals	3 meals		
Hérouxville Accueil les Semailles ☎ (418) 365-5190 (page 199)	single	40	50	60	Cattle, horses, goats, sheep, pig, rabbits, kittens, ducks, pheasants, turkeys, hens, grain-fed chickens.	Feeding the animals, gathering eggs, horseback riding, petting kittens and having fun in the hay barn will put a smile on any child's face. A herd of 200 cattle allows you to immerse yourself in the farmer's daily life, in keeping with the passing seasons. Finally, take advantage of our outdoor facilities: swimming pool, volleyball court, sandbox, horseshoes, campfire vegetable garden and swings.
	double	50	70	90		
	child	12	17	22		
	child alone	---	---	---		
Louiseville Ferme de la Seigneurie ☎ (819) 228-8224 (page 200)	single	45-70	65-90	---	Goats, calves, sheep, horses, rabbits, ducks, turkeys, chickens, geese, guinea-fowl, dogs, cats.	Get close to nature at this small traditional farm: observe and feed fowl and other animals, identify birds. 40 varieties of trees, 86 varieties of flowers and medicinal herbs. Learn about the organic farming of the large vegetable garden and go all the way to the river through the fields. The guided tour of the farm and its gardens, at 3pm, is free. Winter: dogsledding, excursions. **Country Home on a farm p 56 and 205, Country-Style Dining p 24, Farm Tour p 40.**
	double	60-90	100-130	---		
	child	20	30	---		
	child alone	---	---	---		

MONTÉRÉGIE

		RATES			ANIMALS	ACTIVITIES
		1 meal	2 meals	3 meals		
Howick Hazelbrae Farm ☎ (450) 825-2390 (page 210)	single double child child alone	30 50 5-9 ---	40 80 15 ---	45 90 12-30 ---	Cows and variety of small animals. Dairy farm.	Campfire, carriage ride, inground pool, bikes, fruit picking, farm activities. Observe the milking of the cows, haymaking, collect the eggs, gardening, country walks, dairy farm.
St-Valérien La Rabouillère ☎ (450) 793-4998 (page 215)	single double child child alone	50-70 60-80 15 ---	70-85 110-130 25 ---	--- --- --- ---	Exotic animals (llama, donkeys, miniature horses, bearded sheep, katahdin, Jacob and pygmy goats, pot-bellied pigs, rabbit hutch (100 females, 10 varieties), 50 varieties of birds, peacocks, pheasant, geese, ducks, hens, pigeons and more.	Observation and care of animals, identification, feeding, gathering eggs, incubator, births. Tour of gardens and organic kitchen gardens (perennials, herbs, edible flowers). Forest walk (marked trails, plantings, mushroom and berry picking, peat bog, ornthology). Fishing, swimming in the pond. Pool, playground, summer theatre, zoo, downhill skiing, bike paths. **Country-style Dining p 26. Farm Tour p 43. B&B p 215.**
Ste-Agnès-de-Dundee Chez Mimi ☎ (450) 264-4115 1-877-264-4115 (page 215)	single double child child alone	45 55 10 ---	55 90 25 ---	70 120 35 ---	Bullock, cows, dogs, cats, hens, rabbits.	Taking care of the garden and flowers. Feed the rabbits, collect eggs, make hay, pick vegetables. Bird-watching, river fishing, golf courses, snowmobile stopovers, horseback riding, country walks, bike paths, archeology.

		RATES			ANIMALS	ACTIVITIES
		1 meal	2 meals	3 meals		
OUTAOUAIS						
Gatineau Ferme de Bellechasse ☎ (819) 568-3375 (page 229)	single double child child alone	60-90 75-110 15-20 ---	--- --- --- ---	--- --- --- ---	Breeding of Colombian Paso Fino horses renowned for their ease and refinement. Rearing of goldfish in the farm's artificial pond.	Charming site where you can feed, admire and tend to the horses, stroll through the flowery gardens, relax by the goldfish pond, savour the peacefulness of the countryside right near the city, pick edible flowers, or lounge with a good book in front of the fireplace.
Vinoy, **Chénéville** Les Jardins de Vinoy ☎ (819) 428-3774 (page 235)	single double child child alone	50-65 65-80 10 ---	69-84 103-118 19 ---	78-93 120-150 29 ---	Goats, pigs, sheep, wild boar, rabbits, guinea-fowl, ducks, geese, chickens, hens, dog, cats.	Yesteryear's charm, modern comforts. Animal husbandry, old-time sugaring off, sleigh rides (dogs, horses), soap-making, preserves, bread making, spinning, medicinal plants, forest trekking, cross-country skiing, snowshoeing, playground, campfire, organic garden, regional table d'hôte. **See colour photos.**
QUÉBEC CITY REGION						
Neuville La ferme l'Emeulienne ☎ (418) 876-2788 (page 245)	single double child child alone	50 60 12 ---	68 96 20 ---	--- --- --- ---	Three ratites: ostriches, emus, Rheas and their young. Pony, 10 varieties of hens, ducks, geese, rabbits, dogs, cats, sheep, goats, Vietnamese pigs...	Guided tour of the farm. Visit the incubation room, observe the development of an embryo, feed the animals, tame an animal, gather eggs, pick berries. Smoke and savour emu meat. Take part in a rally. Campfire, play area: volleyball, bowls, badminton. Have a picnic. Enjoy an old-fashioned dinner with emu meat*. Play with Ti N'homme the dog. Babysitting available for children*. Explore the region by bicycle. Experience a therapeutic "Swedish" massage*. Family special: 2 adults + 2 children $80/B&B $100/PAM. **Farm Tour p 46.** *extra charge

		RATES			ANIMALS	ACTIVITIES
		1 meal	2 meals	3 meals		
QUÉBEC CITY REGION						
Stoneham Ferme St-Adolphe ☎ (418) 848-2879 (page 260)	single double child child alone	45 55 15 ---	--- --- --- ---	--- --- --- ---	Sheep, rabbits, ducks, hens, egg incubation, speckled trout. Wildlife observation in the forest of animals such as moose, deer, hares, partridges eagles and herons.	Guided tours of the farm, wildlife observation, river fishing, rest area in a pergola, heated swimming pool. In the spring, take part in the making of maple products. In winter: snowshoeing. The delicious farm products (eggs, maple syrup, maple jams) will win you over at breakfast. Packages on request: guided visit to the sugar shack with sampling of maple toffee, speckled-trout fishing and cooking area.
SAGUENAY - LAC-SAINT-JEAN						
La Baie Chez Grand-Maman ☎ (418) 544-7396 (page 268)	single double child child alone	40-45 50-55 10-15 ---	60 100 15-20 ---	--- --- --- ---	Cows, calves, chickens, hens, turkeys, cats, dogs.	Try milking a cow. Feed the animals and see to their care. Walk along the shores of the Baie des HA! HA!. Outdoor fireplace, pool, and ice-fishing during winter.
Hébertville Ferme Jacques et Carole Martel ☎ (418) 344-1323 (page 266)	single double child child alone	35 45 10 ---	--- --- --- ---	--- --- --- ---	Cows, heifers, calves, dogs, cats, fowl.	Tour of the farm and observation of farm activities (milking, maintenance, etc.) Grain farming square and round hay baling. Capacity: 5 people.

SAGUENAY - LAC-SAINT-JEAN

		RATES			ANIMALS	ACTIVITIES
		1 meal	2 meals	3 meals		
Lac-à-la-Croix Céline et Georges Martin ☎ (418) 349-2583 (page 270)	single double child child alone	28 42 12 ---	40 72 16 ---	--- --- --- ---	Cows, heifers, calves, dog.	Visit of the farm.
Normandin Ferme Nordan ☎ (418) 274-2867 (page 273)	single double child child alone	40 55-75 15 ---	60 95 25-35 ---	--- --- --- ---	Dairy cows, goat, sheep, rabbits, hens, pheasants, partridges, ducks, cats, etc.	Charming little farm where everyone can feed and take care of the small animals, gather eggs and cuddle these engaging little creatures. At the dairy farm, tour and observation of farm chores (milking, maintenance, etc.). Dinner available for families of six or more.
St-Félix-d'Otis Gîte de la Basse- Cour ☎ (418) 544-8766 (page 275)	single double child child alone	40 50 5-15	60 100 15-20		Sheep, chickens, ducks, rabbits, partridges, pigeons, quails, dog, cats, trout pond.	Observing and feeding the animals, collecting eggs, feeding trout, bird watching and identification, tending of organic vegetable garden, vegetable and berry picking, preparing and baking bread in the outdoor bread oven, hiking, campfires, regional table d'hôte. Winter: cross-country skiing, snowshoeing, walking, skidooing (local trail 383 only 3 kilometres away). Available with reservation: kayaking on the fjord, dogsledding, ice fishing and skidoo rental.

COUNTRY HOME ON A FARM

	RATES	ANIMALS	ACTIVITIES
ABITIBI TÉMISCAMINGUE			
Île Nepawa Ferme Vacances ☎ (819) 333-6103 (page 62)	Activities included in the rental rate of the country home	Cattle, goats, horses.	Feed the animals. Help with the farm work. Harvest the hay. Aquatic activities, hunting and fishing, hiking trails.
CENTRE-DU-QUÉBEC			
Princeville Au Paradis d'Émy ☎ (819) 364-2840 (page 97)	Activities included in the rental rate of the country home	Jersey cows and calves, cats, rabbits and Plume, our miniature-schnauzer dog.	At the "Ferme Norjo," you can watch the cows being milked in the cowshed or have fun with the children climbing haystacks in the barn whenever you feel like it. In the summer, set off to gather hay on our vast prairies where we can take you by tractor. Take advantage of our large expanses to relax and observe the wildlife. Enjoy the seasons, in the comfort of "your" home!
MAURICIE			
Louiseville La Maison du Jardinier ☎ (819) 288-8224 (page 205)	Activities included in the rental rate of the country home	Goats, calves, sheep, horses, rabbits, ducks, turkeys, hens, geese, guinea-fowl, dogs and cats	Small, traditional farm where you will have easy access to nature: observing and feeding the farm birds and other animals, bird identification, 60 species of trees, 86 species of flowers and medecinal herbs. Information about organic gardening and the fields that lead to the river. Free guided tour of the farm and the gardens at 3pm. Picnic at the farm package available. Winter, dogsledding, excursions. Ask for information. **Country-Style Dinning p 24, Farm Tour p 40, B&B p 200, Country Home p 205, Farm Stay p 51.**
SAGUENAY - LAC-SAINT-JEAN			
La Baie La Maison des Ancêtres ☎ (819) 544-2925 (page 277)	Activities included in the rental rate of the country home	Dairy farm	Snowmobile trails run through the farm, snowshoeing, cross-country skiing on the farm, ice fishing…

Bed & Breakfasts

Country Inns

Country Homes

City Homes

58.

WHERE TO FIND THE...

COUNTRY INNS

Bas-St-Laurent	Bic	Auberge Chez Marie-Roses 64
	Cabano	Auberge du Chemin Faisant 65
	Kamouraska	Auberge des Îles 66
	Pointe-au-Père	Auberge La Marée Douce 69
	St-André-de-Kamouraska	Auberge La Solaillerie 73
	St-Éloi	Au Vieux Presbytère 73
	Ste-Luce-sur-Mer	Auberge de l'Eider 74
Cantons-de-l'Est	Austin	Auberge Les Pignons Verts 78
	Lac-Brome, Foster	Auberge du Joli Vent 83
	Lac-Mégantic	Manoir d'Orsennens 84
	Magog	Aux Jardins Champêtres 87
	Pike-River	Auberge La Suisse 90
Centre-du-Québec	Bécancour	Manoir Bécancourt 94
Charlevoix	Baie-St-Paul	Auberge La Muse 99
	Baie-St-Paul	Aux Petits Oiseaux 100
	Cap-à-l'Aigle	Auberge Petite Plaisance 102
	La Malbaie	Auberge la Romance 104
	La Malbaie	L'Eau Berge 105
	Les Éboulements	Auberge La Bouclée 105
	Les Éboulements	Aberge la Pente Douce 106
	Les Éboulements	Auberge Le Surouêt 106
	Petite-Rivière-St-François	Auberge La Courtepointe 107
	St-Irénée	La Luciole 108
	St-Irénée	Le Rustique 109
Chaudière-Appalaches	L'Islet-sur-Mer	Auberge La Marguerite 114
	Montmagny	Auberge La Belle Époque 115
	St-Eugène-de-l'Islet	Auberge Des Glacis 118
Côte-Nord	Baie-Trinité	Le Gîte du Phare de Pointe-des-Monts . . . 124
	Bergeronnes	La Bergeronnette 125
	Bergeronnes	La Rosepierre 125
	Les Escoumins	Auberge de la baie 126
	Les Escoumins	Auberge Manoir Bellevue 126
	Natashquan	Le Port d'attache 127
	Tadoussac	Auberge «Maison Gagné» 128
	Tadoussac	Maison Gauthier et les suites de l'Anse . . 131
Gaspésie	Cap-Chat, Capucins	Auberge de la Baie-des-Capucins 138
	Carleton	Auberge la Visite Surprise 139
	Escuminac	Auberge Wanta-Qo-Tí 140
	Gaspé	L'Ancêtre de Gaspé 142
	Les Boules	Auberge du Grand Fleuve 143
	Les Boules	L'Auberge «Une Ferme en Gaspésie» 144
	Matane	Auberge La Seigneurie 144
	Percé	Auberge au Pirate 1775 149
	Petite-Vallée	La Maison Lebreux 151

Lanaudière	St-Alphonse-Rodriguez	Ranch 4 Saisons	164
	Ste-Émélie-de-l'Émergie	Auberge du Vieux Moulin	167
Laurentides	Ferme-Neuve	Auberge au Bois d'mon Coeur	171
	Lac-Nominingue	Auberge-Restaurant «Chez Ignace»	172
	Lac-Nominingue	Auberge Villa Bellerive	172
	Mont-Tremblant	Auberge La Petite Cachée	174
	Mont-Tremblant	Auberge Le Lupin	175
	Mont-Tremblant	L'Auberge à La Croisée des Chemins	175
	St-Faustin, Lac-Carré	La Bonne Adresse	179
	St-Hippolyte	Auberge Lac du Pin Rouge	180
	St-Joseph-du-Lac	Auberge Roche des Brises	181
	St-Sauveur-des-Monts	Auberge sous l'Édredon	182
	Ste-Adèle	Auberge au Nid Douillet	183
	Ste-Adèle	Auberge le Clos Rolland	184
	Ste-Adèle	Auberge-Restaurant La Bruyère	185
	Ste-Adèle	Aux Pins Dorés	185
	Ste-Agathe-des-Monts	Auberge Aux Nuits de Rêve	186
	Ste-Agathe-des-Monts	Auberge de la Tour du Lac	186
	Ste-Agathe-des-Monts	Auberge «le Saint-Venant»	186
	Ste-Agathe-Nord	Manoir d'Ivry B&B	187
	Val-David	Auberge Charme des Alpes	188
	Val-David	Le Relais de la Piste	189
	Val-Morin	Les Jardins de La Gare	189
Mauricie	Batiscan	Le St-Élias	197
	Grandes-Piles	Auberge-le-Bôme	198
	Ste-Anne-de-la-Pérade	À l'arrêt du Temps	201
	Ste-Anne-de-la-Pérade	Auberge du Manoir Dauth	201
	Trois-Rivières	Auberge du Bourg	202
	Trois-Rivières, Pte-du-Lac	Auberge Baie-Jolie	204
Montérégie	Chambly, Richelieu	Auberge la Jarnigoine	209
Outaouais	Messines	Maison La Crémaillère	232
	Vinoy, Chénéville	Les Jardins de Vinoy	235
Québec City Region	Château-Richer	Auberge du Petit Pré	239
	Château-Richer	Baker	239
	Château-Richer	Le Petit Séjour	240
	Deschambault	Auberge Chemin du Roy	240
	L'Île d'Orléans, St-Pierre	Auberge Le Vieux Presbytère	243
	L'Île d'Orléans, St-Pierre	L'Auberge sur Les Pendants	244
	Québec	B&B Chez Pierre	250
	Saint-Raymond	La Voisine	259
Saguenay-Lac-St-Jean	Hébertville	Auberge presbytère Mont Lac Vert	265
	L'Anse-St-Jean	Auberge des Cévennes	270
	Métabetchouan	Auberge La Maison Lamy	272
	Petit-Saguenay	Auberge Les 2 Pignons	273

COUNTRY HOMES

Abitibi-Témiscamingue	Île-Nepawa	Ferme Vacances	62
Cantons-de-l'Est	Wotton	La Maison des Lacs	92
Centre-du-Québec	Princeville	Au Paradis d'Emy	97
	St-Pierre-Baptiste	Domaine des Pins	97
Chaudière-Appalaches	La Durantaye	Le Coudrier	122
	St-Henri	Tempérament Sauvage	122
Côte-Nord	Baie-Comeau, Pointe-Lebel	Villa Petit Bonheur	132
	Baie Trinité	Le Gîte du Phare de Pointe-des-Monts	132
	Sacré-Cœur	Ferme 5 étoiles	132
Gaspésie	Percé	La Maison Laberge	157
	Petite-Vallée	La Maison Lebreux	157
Lanaudière	Rawdon	Chalets des Pins	168
Laurentides	Mont-Tremblant	Le Vent du Nord	191
	Rosemère	La Maison de l'Enclos	191
Mauricie	Louiseville	La Maison du Jardinier	205
Montérégie	Massueville, St-Aimé	Maison Bois-Menu	216
Outaouais	Lac-Simon, Chénéville	Domaine aux Crocollines	236
Québec City Region	Cap Tourmente	L'Oie des Neiges	262
	Mont-Ste-Anne	Chalets-Village Mont-Ste-Anne	262
Saguenay-Lac-St-Jean	La Baie	La Maison des Ancêtres	277
	St-David-de-Falardeau	Les Chiens et Gîte du Grand Nord	277

CITY HOMES (APPARTEMENTS-STUDIOS)

Montréal Region	Montréal	Condotelogan	226
	Montréal	Appartements meublés Mtl centre-ville	226
	Montréal	Loft l'Escale	226
	Montréal	Maison Grégoire	227
	Saint-Laurent	Studio Marhaba	227

ABITIBI-TÉMISCAMINGUE

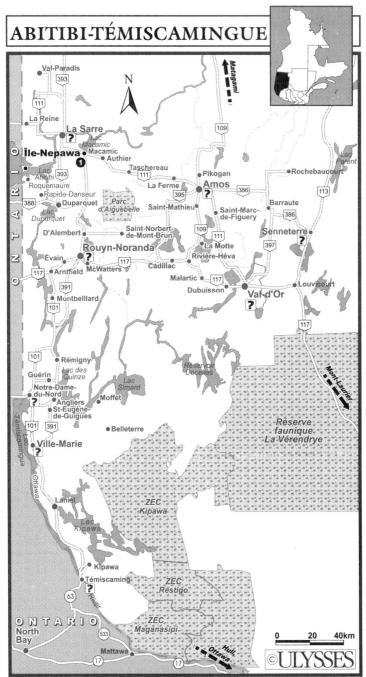

*The numbers on the map refer to the numbering of the establishments in this region.

1. ÎLE-NEPAWA

★ F E 🐕 🚗 P 🏊 R30 M1(

Three comfortable chalets in the wilderness on the shores of Lac Abitibi, including a Swiss-style with fireplace, as well as two bungalows. We raise cattle, goats and horses. Water sports, hunting and fishing. Near the Aiguebelle conservation park. Come and enjoy a visit with Quebecers of German descent. **Country home on a farm p 56.**

From Rouyn, Rte 101 to La Sarre. 3 km past La Sarre, follow the signs for Ste-Hélène and Île Nepawa, half-paved gravel road. 1st house on the right after the bridge to the island.

COUNTRY HOME
FERME VACANCES

Hélène and Hermann Wille
695 Île-Nepawa, R.R. # 1
Ste-Hélène-de-Mancebourg
J0Z 2T0
(819) 333-6103

No. houses	3
No. rooms	2-3
No. people	6-8
WEEK-SUMMER	$250
W/E-SUMMER	$125
DAY-SUMMER	$50

Open: May 1 to Oct. 31

Activities: 🐟 🚶 🐎

FARM ACTIVITIES

Country home on a farm :

1 FERME VACANCES, Île Nepawa 5

BAS-SAINT-LAURENT

© ULYSSES

0 15 30km

N

GASPÉSIE

NEW BRUNSWICK

MAINE (U.S.A.)

CHARLEVOIX

MANICOUAGAN

CHAUDIÈRE-APPALACHES

ZEC Bas-Saint-Laurent

Réserve faunique de Rimouski

Réserve Duchénier

ZEC Owen

ZEC Chapais

Réserve de Parke

Baie-Comeau

St. Lawrence River

Rivière Saguenay

Les Escoumins
Grandes-Bergeronnes
Tadoussac
Baie-Sainte-Catherine
Île aux Basques
Île Verte
Phare
Île aux Lièvres

Saint-Siméon
La Malbaie

Saint-Donat
Mont-Joli
Luceville
Sainte-Luce-sur-Mer 32 33
Pointe-au-Père 16 17
Rimouski 18 19
Sainte-Odile
Sainte-Blandine
234
Sainte-Marcellin
Saint-Narcisse-de-Rimouski 20
Trinité-des-Monts
Pointe-aux-Anglais 2
20
Parc du Bic
Le Bic 1 3
Saint-Eugène-de-Ladrière
132
Saint-Fabien 4
Îles du Bic
Saint-Mathieu
Esprit-Saint
Lac-des-Aigles
Biencourt
232
Bienpourt
Squatec
Saint-Simon 35 36
Saint-Éloi 29
Trois-Pistoles
2
Sainte-Françoise
296
Saint-Jean-de-Dieu 30
Sainte-Rita
293
Saint-Paul-de-la-Croix
Saint-Cyprien
Lejeune
Lots-Renversés
Dégelis 7 8
Saint-Jean-de-la-Lande
185
295
Rivière Madawaska
Cabano 2 5
Saint-Eusèbe
Packington
Notre-Dame-du-Lac
Témiscouata
232
Saint-Pierre-de-Lamy
Saint-Hubert
291
Saint-Honoré
185
Saint-Louis-du-Ha! Ha! 31
Saint-Elzéar
Saint-Éleuthère
Estcourt
Sully
289
Rivière-Bleue
232
2
L'Isle-Verte 13 à 15
Saint-Épiphane
20
Cacouna 6
Saint-Antonin
Saint-Moceste
145
Withworth
Rivière-du-Loup 21 à 24
Saint-Alexandre 25
26 27
Saint-Patrice
132
Saint-Hélène
230
Saint-André 28
Sainte-Hélène
Saint-Pascal
2
Saint-Bruno
289
Pohénégamook
Lac de l'Est
Kamouraska 9 à 11
132
20
La Pocatière 12
132
Saint-Gabriel
Saint-Onésime
Saint-Denis
St-Philippe-de-Néri
Lévis
Québec
138
172
170
St-Clément
St-Hélène

*The numbers on the map refer to the numbering of the establishments in this region.

1. BIC, LE

★★★ F e ⊗ ✕ 🚗 P R.2 TA

Bas-St-Laurent Excellence Prize 1999. Hundred-year-old house deep in the country. Great sunsets on Rivière-Hâtée cove. Ambiance where flowers meet the magic of Christmas. King-sized beds, private bathrooms. Old-fashioned or healthy breakfast, tea time, outdoor barbecues. Hiking in the mountain, or on the sea shore. Patio, balcony, family garden. Enjoy seaside solitude.

From Québec City, Hwy 20 E., Rte 132 E, East Bic exit, left at flashing light on Rte 132, 2km. From Ste-Flavie or Mont-Joli, Rte 132 W. twd Bic.

INN
AUBERGE CHEZ MARIE-ROSES

Jacqueline Caron
2322, Route 132 Est
Bic G0L 1B0
(418) 736-5311
(418) 736-4954
fax (418) 736-5955
www.marie-roses.qc.ca
marieroses@globetrotter.net

B&B	
single	$60-65
double	$65-75
triple	$80-90
child	$10

Taxes extra VS MC IT

Open: Mar. 1 to Jan. 1

Number of rooms	7
rooms with private bath	5
rooms in basement	1
shared wc	1
shared bathrooms	1

Activities: 🏛 ☕ 🚶 🚴

2. BIC, LE

☀☀☀ F E ⊗ P 🚗 🐕 R2 TA

On the shore of the St. Lawrence, in Bic Harbour, our century-old house awaits you in its calm setting with its old-fashioned decor and ambiance. Idyllically situated hugging the seashore. From the porch, a spectacle of sea birds follows the eternal movement of the tides.

From Québec City, Hwy 20 East, Rte 132 to Bic. Take the Aux Cormorans and Club de Golf exit. 2km on the point, «Aux Cormorans» is the last house on the left, on the seashore.

B&B
AUX CORMORANS

Judy Parceaud
213, chemin du Golf
Pointe-aux-Anglais
Bic G0L 1B0
(418) 736-8113
fax (418) 736-4216
www.bbcanada.
com/2982.html
cormoran@globetrotter.qc.ca

B&B	
single	$40-75
double	$50-75
triple	$60-65
child	$10

VS MC

Open year round

Number of rooms	5
rooms with private bath	1
shared bathrooms	2

Activities: 🏛 ☕ 🚤 🚶

3. BIC, LE

☀☀☀ F e 🐕 ✕ 🚗 P R3 TA

Quintessential Québec house dating from 1830. "Aux 5 Lucarnes" offers you 4 large rooms with sink, a «table d'hôte» prepared with local products, sea-kayak packages and access to the sea... Lunchbox service for your hikes, and so much more...

From Québec City, Hwy 20 East and Rte 132 East. At Bic exit, left at flashing light, about 3km along Rte 132.

B&B
AUX 5 LUCARNES

Johanne Desjardins
2175, Rivière-Hâtée,
Route 132
Bic G0L 1B0
tel/fax (418) 736-5435
www.cam.org/~bsl/lucarnes/
polyfilm@globetrotter.net

	B&B	MAP
single	$45	$70
double	$55	$105
triple	$70	$145
quad.	$85	$185
child	$10	$20

Taxes extra VS MC ER

Reduced rates: Oct. 16 to May 15
Open year round

Number of rooms	4
rooms with sink	4
shared bathrooms	2

Activities: ☕ 🚶 🚴

4. BIC, ST-FABIEN

☀☀☀ F E 🚫 🚗 P R3 TA

At the gates of Parc du Bic, come experience the charm of yesteryear, modern comfort, tranquillity (away from Rte 132) and a lavish breakfast of homemade bread and jam. Warm welcome. We love company!

From Gaspé, Rte 132 East. In St-Simon, 11km from Petro Canada. Left on Rang 1 West. From Montreal, Rte 132 West. 3km from St-Fabien tourist office. Turn right on Rang 1.

B&B
CLAIREVALLÉE

Marguerite Voyer
178, Route 132 ouest
St-Fabien G0L 2Z0
tel/fax (418) 869-3582
(450) 922-9054
www.cam.org/
~bsl/clairevallee/
marguerite_voyer@
hotmail.com

	B&B	MAP
single	$40-50	55-65$
double	$55-65	85-95$
triple	$70-80	115-125$
quad.	$85-95	145-155$

VS

Open year round

Number of rooms	5
rooms with private bath	1
shared bathrooms	3

Activities: 🦪 🛶 🚶 🎿 🚴

---

5. CABANO

★★ F E 🔪 🚗 P R.3 TA

Located near Lac Témiscouata and the bike path, guests at the Auberge du Chemin Faisant enjoy our fine Magdalen Island-style cuisine, as well as our delectable breakfasts. Your host will entertain you on the piano, and the fireplace completes the cosy atmosphere. A great place for rest and relaxation.

From Québec City, Hwy 20 E., at Rivière-du-Loup, Rte 185 S. At Cabano, first exit, Rue Commercial for 1km, then turn right in Rue du Vieux Chemin.

INN
AUBERGE DU CHEMIN FAISANT

Liette Fortin and Hugues Massey
12, rue du Vieux Chemin
Cabano G0L 1E0
(418) 854-9342
toll free 1-877-954-9342
www.cheminfaisant.qc.ca
info@cheminfaisant.qc.ca

	B&B	MAP
single	$45-85	$65-105
double	$50-90	$90-130
triple	$60-100	$120-160
quad.	$70-110	$150-190
child	$10	$10

Taxes extra VS MC

Reduced rates: 3 nights or more, 5$/night

Open year round

Number of rooms	6
rooms with private bath	2
rooms with sink	3
shared bathrooms	1
shared wc	1

Activities: 🚣 🎿 🚴 🛶 🏊

---

6. CACOUNA

☀☀☀ F E 🚫 🐴 P 🏊 R.02

La Berceuse is the pendulum swinging back, a bit of equilibrium in our busy lives. A warm, century-old house with many comforts and the joy of living, ideal for getting back to one's roots. Cozy queen-size beds, gourmets breakfasts, swimming pool, outdoor fireplace and rocking chairs! Now that's a real vacation!

Hwy 20, twd Cacouna Exit 514. Turn left at the stop sign. Rte 132 to the heart of the village. 12min from the Rivière-du-Loup ferry.

B&B
GÎTE LA BERCEUSE

Julie Gendron and
Jean-Luc Potvin
45, rue Principale Ouest
Cacouna G0L 1G0
(418) 868-1752
www.laberceuse.qc.ca
info@laberceuse.qc.ca

	B&B
single	$40-50
double	$50-60
triple	$70-75
quad.	$90
child	$10-15

VS

Open year round

Number of rooms	4
rooms with shower and sink	3
rooms with bath and sink	1
shared bathrooms	2

Activities: 🛶 🎿 🚶 🚴 🐴

7. DÉGELIS
☀☀☀ F E 🔲 🐾 🚗 P 🏊 R1.5

Located in a forest by Lac Témiscouata. Great comfort, clear panoramic view of the lake, famous à-la-carte breakfast. Come nightfall, around a fire on the beach, the song of the loon and golden sparks meeting the stars make up nature's sound and light show. Reserve from Oct. 15 to May 15.

Hwy 20, Exit 499, Rte 185 South. In Dégelis, Rte 295 North twd Auclair, for 6km. By bike, cross the Dégelis dam and follow the 295 North, turn left and ride 2.5km.

B&B
GÎTE AU TOIT ROUGE

Dominique Lagarde and
André Demers
441, Route 295
Dégelis G5T 1R2
(418) 853-3036
(418) 853-2294
www.bbcanada.com/
giteautoitrouge
andr.demers3@sympatico.ca

B&B	
single	$45
double	$60-70
triple	$85
quad.	$100
child	$5-12

Reduced rates: Oct. 15 to Apr. 15
Open: Jan. 6 to Dec. 20

Number of rooms	4
rooms with private bath	1
rooms with sink	3
shared bathrooms	1

Activities: 🚣 🎿 🚲 🏇 🚶

8. DÉGELIS
☀☀☀ F e P 🚗 R.13

Welcome to our welcoming B&B: water garden and falls, fragrant with flowers. Private entrance, big parking lot. Direct access to "Le Petit Témis" bike path; bike storage. Balcony, lounge, TV, fridge. Lavish breakfast in sunroom. Family picnics in gazebo. Restaurant nearby. Children welcome. See you soon!

From Québec City, Hwy 20 E. to Riv.-du-Loup, Rte 185 S. In Dégelis, 1st exit on left on Ave Principale. From New Brunswick Rte 185 N. In Dégelis, 1st exit on right, Ave Principale.

B&B
LA BELLE MAISON BLANCHE

Monique and André Lavoie
513, av. Principale
Dégelis G5T 1L8
(418) 853-3324
fax (418) 853-5507
www.maisonblanche.
asdweb.com
monand@icrdl.net

B&B	
single	$40
double	$55-60
triple	$70-80
quad.	$80-90
child	$15

Reduced rates: Nov. 1 to April 30
Open year round

Number of rooms	5
shared wc	1
shared showers	1
shared bathrooms	1

Activities: 🚶 🎿 🚲 🏇 🛷

9. KAMOURASKA
☀☀☀ F e ❌ 🚗 P TA

Situated on a hilltop, the Auberge Des Îles has a magnificent view of the Kamouraskan Islands and the sunsets. In the evening, whether you're in the dining room, solarium or in your room, the twinkling lights on the north coast will captivate you. A cordial welcome with a touch of class, as well as some little extras, will make your stay a memorable one.

Hwy 20, Exit 465. Drive to Kamouraska. Once in the village, turn left on Av. Morel (Rte 132), 1.5km.

INN
AUBERGE DES ÎLES

Liette and Rita Lévesque
198, avenue Morel
Kamouraska G0L 1M0
(418) 492-7561
fax (418) 492-7695
www.iquebec.com/aubergedesiles
aubergedesiles@iquebec.com

B&B	
single	$45-50
double	$50-60
child	$10

Taxes extra VS MC IT

Reduced rates: Nov 1 to Dec. 31
Open: May 1 to Oct. 31,
Nov 1 to Dec. 31, on reservation

Number of rooms	5
rooms with private bath	2
rooms with sink	1
shared bathrooms	1
shared wc	1

Activities: 🏛 🛶 🎿 🚶 🏇

10. KAMOURASKA ☀☀☀ F e 🚫 P 🚗 R.5 TA

This beautiful century-old house will leave you with unforgettable memories, marked by the rhythm of the wind and the tide. Comfort, cleanliness, and *joie de vivre* await. Close to the sea, with a 2km-long promenade: what memories are made of. The sea air will whet your appetite for the gourmet breakfast to come. Prize for Excellence "Special Favorite" Regional 1995-96. Access to the St. Lawrence River.

From Québec City, Hwy 20 East, Exit 465. Drive 5km to Kamouraska. Once in the village, left Ave. Morel (Rte 132).

B&B
CHEZ JEAN ET NICOLE

Nicole and Jean Bossé
81, av. Morel, route 132
Kamouraska G0L 1M0
(418) 492-2921
www3.sympatico.ca/
titesouris/gite.html

B&B	
single	$45
double	$55-65
triple	$85
child	$15

VS

Open year round

Number of rooms	4
rooms with private bath	1
shared wc	1
shared bathrooms	1

Activities: 🚤 ⛷ 🚶 🚴 🐎

11. KAMOURASKA ☀☀ F e 🚫 🚗 P R.6 TA

A bed and breakfast in the heart of the village of Kamouraska, one of the most beautiful villages in Quebec, "Au Petit Bonheur" welcomes you year-round. Comfortable rooms, living room with TV and kitchen. Period decor and warm ambiance. Magnificent view of the river. All-you-can-eat breakfast in a relaxing, convivial atmosphere. Various services 0.6km away: bank, bakery, museum, restaurant. "Come to 116, by the St. Lawrence River."

Hwy 20, Exit 465, twd Kamouraska. In the village, turn left on Ave. Morel (Rte 132).

B&B
GÎTE AU PETIT BONHEUR

Céline and Jean-Guy Charest
116, avenue Morel
Kamouraska G0L 1M0
tél/fax (418) 492-3247

B&B	
single	$45
double	$55
triple	$70
child	$15

Reduced rates: 1er oct au 31 mai
Open year round

Number of rooms	3
shared bathroom	1
shared wc	1

Activities: 🏛 ⛷ 🚶 🚴 🏃

12. LA POCATIÈRE ☀☀☀☀ F e ♿ 🚗 P 〰 TA

More than an inn, this is a place where we get to know our guests. A place whose charm and landscape inspires peace and love, where the aromas of regional dishes mingle with the fragrances of the ancient woods. Discounts for longer stays. Children welcome; 3 kilometres from various attractions...

One hour from Québec City, Hwy 20 East, Exit 436, turn right (west) at the stop, continue for 500 metres and you're here. From Gaspé, Exit 436...

B&B
AUBERGE AU DIABLO-VERT

Manon Brochu and Luc Gagnon
72, route 132 Ouest B.P.9
La Pocatière G0R 1Z0
(418) 856-4117
fax (418) 856-5161
www.quebecweb.
com/diablovert
diablove@globetrotter.net

B&B	
single	$55
double	$65
triple	$75

Reduced rates: Sept 1 to May 31
or 20% more than 3 nights
Open year round

Number of rooms	5
shared bathrooms	3

Activities: 🏛 🍁 🚤 ⛷ 🚣

13. L'ISLE-VERTE

☀☀☀ F E 🚗 🚤 P R1 T

La Grande Ourse is a 19th century Anglo-Norman house. The babbling Rivière Verte is just a stone's throw away from our flower garden, where birds congregate. In winter, warm up by the hearth before going off to your cosy bed. In the morning, a hearty breakfast awaits. Welcome to La Grande Ourse!

From Québec City, Hwy 20 East, Rte 132 East. After the Rivière Verte bridge, turn right and then right again. From Rimouski, Rte 132 West, L'Isle Verte exit, straight until end of the village, then left.

B&B
LA GRANDE OURSE

Martine Girard and
Paul-André Laberge
6, rue du Verger
L'Isle-Vert G0L 1K0
(418) 898-2763
fax (418) 898-3717

B&B	
single	$45-80
double	$55-80
triple	$70-80
quad.	$80
child	$0-10

Open year round

Number of rooms	5
shared wc	1
shared bathrooms	2

Activities: 🏛 🛶 🚤 🚶 🚲

---

14. L'ISLE-VERTE

☀☀ F e 🐕 P R.5

A Victorian-style house with centenary charm that extends a warm and genuine welcome. Large tree-lined property. In the early morning wake up to the crowing of the cock and birdsong mingled with the aroma of a hearty breakfast. View of the river and access to nearby leisure activities. Make yourselves at home.

From Québec City, Hwy 20 East, Rte 132 East. In the village, turn right at the caisse populaire. House on the left, on the hill. From Rimouski: Rte 132 West, turn left at the caisse populaire...

B&B
LA MAISON ANCESTRALE

Diane Lévesque and
Joseph-Marie Fraser
5, rue Béland C.P. 245
L'Isle-Verte G0L 1K0
(418) 898-2633
(418) 898-2053
http://lamaisonancestrale.
iquebec.com
maisonancestrale@caramail.com

B&B	
single	$40
double	$50
triple	$65
child	$10

Open: June to Sep. 15

Number of rooms	4
shared wc	1
shared bathrooms	2

Activities: 🏛 🛶 🚤 🎿 🚶

---

15. L'ISLE-VERTE

☀☀ F 🚤 P R.5 T

On the road to Gaspésie, enjoy this quiet place, in a warm home surrounded by flowers, with a relaxing solarium. Friendly reception, living room, wood stove, washer and dryer and bike shed. Hearty breakfast including homemade jams and muffins. We have been welcoming guests for 13 years. Ladies are treated to a small souvenir.

From Quebec City, Hwy 20 East. After the flashing light, at L'Isle Verte, drive 0.5km along Rte. 132. Left on Rue Louis-Bertrand. From Gaspé, Rte 132 to L'Isle Verte, second street on the right. 1km from the ferry.

B&B
LES CAPUCINES

Marie-Anna and Yvon Lafrance
31, ch. Louis-Bertrand,
C.P. 105
L'Isle-Verte G0L 1K0
(418) 898-3276

B&B	
single	$40
double	$55
triple	$70
quad.	$80
child	$10

Reduced rates: 5% 3 nights or more from Nov. 1to Apr. 30
Open year round

Number of rooms	3
rooms in basement	1
shared bathrooms	2

Activities: 🐎 🛷 🚤 🎿

16. POINTE-AU-PÈRE

★★★ F e ☒ P TA

Come to our Victorian home, built around 1860, and dream of traveling. Former property of Sieur Louis-Marie Lavoie, known as "Louis XVI", who was master-pilot on the St. Lawrence and upriver for the city of Québec. This charming home has since become an inn where you'll be spoiled by serenity and a warm welcome. **See colour photos.**

From Québec City, Hwy 20 East, Rte 132 to Rimouski, Rte 132 to Pointe-au-Père, drive 1km past the church.

INN
AUBERGE LA MARÉE DOUCE

Marguerite Lévesque
1329, boul. Ste-Anne
Pointe-au-Père, Rimouski
G5M 1W2
(418) 722-0822
fax (418) 723-4512

	B&B	MAP
single	$80-100	$105-125
double	$85-105	$130-155
triple	$115	$185
quad.	$125	$225
child	$15	

Taxes extra VS MC IT

Open: May 1 to Oct. 31

Number of rooms	9
rooms with private bath	9

Activities: 🏛 🏃 🚶 🚲

17. POINTE-AU-PÈRE

☀☀ F E 🚭 P 🚗 R.5 TA

Magnificent location, panoramic view, warm welcome, comfortable bed, affable host, nearby restaurant, quiet walks, sunsets, beach campfires, starry nights, northern lights, lapping waves, deep sleep. Quiet mornings, fragrant coffee, talks... Activities: kayaking, museum, cycling, hiking... Enjoy your stay!
André, sculptor

Drop anchor at the end of the 20! Past Rimouski, Rte 132 East, between Bic and Métis, below the Pointe-au-Père lighthouse (Rue du Phare).

B&B
GÎTE DE LA POINTE

André Gamache
1046, rue du Phare
Pointe-au-Père G5M 1L8
(418) 724-6614
(418) 750-3332

B&B	
single	$50-70
double	$60-75
triple	$70-85

Taxes extra VS

Reduced rates: Sep. 15 to June 15
Open: Jan. 15 to Dec. 15

Number of rooms	5
rooms in semi-basement	3
shared wc	4
rooms with private bath	1

Activities: 🏛 🛶 🏃 🚲 🎿

18. RIMOUSKI

☀☀☀ F e 🚭 🚗 P R2

At Chez Charles et Marguerite, visitors are greeted with a sincere and friendly welcome and the hosts respect your privacy. Breakfast is served in the dining room and solarium, with soft music playing in the background. Located close to the centre of town, this large, beautifully landscaped property has bike and walking paths that lead through the woods near the seashore. A wonderful opportunity to discover the lively, artistic character of the region!

From Québec City, hwy 20 East, Rte 132 East. At the eastern Bic exit, turn left at the flashing light, Rte 132. 1.3km past the church.

B&B
CHEZ CHARLES ET MARGUERITE

Carmen Parent
686, boul. St-Germain
Rimouski G5L 3S4
(418) 723-3938
charlesetmarguerite
@moncourrier.com

B&B	
single	$45
double	$60
triple	$70
quad.	$85
child	$15

VS

Open: June 1 to Sept 3

Number of rooms	3
shared wc	1
shared batrooms	1

Activities: 🏛 🍷 🏃 🚶 🚲

19. RIMOUSKI, BIC   ☀☀☀ F e 🐾 🚗 P R6 TA

An ancestral home
A family farm
A friendly ambiance
Amazing breakfasts
Enticing eggs, crepes
That young and old alike will enjoy
The house, the rooms, the stay
Are lovingly decorated
So that you will always remember
That at La Maison Bérubé
You are like family
Who visit us yearly
Farm Stay p 48

3 hours from Québec City, Hwy 20 East, Rte 132 East. At the Eastern Bic exit, at the flashing light turn left Rte 132, 6.4km to the left. 11.5km from Rimouski.

B&B
LA MAISON BÉRUBÉ

Louise Brunet and
Marcel Bérubé
1216, boul. St-Germain Ouest,
route 132
Rimouski G5L 8Y9
tel/fax (418) 723-1578

B&B	
single	$45
double	$60
triple	$80
quad.	$100
child	$10

Open year round

Number of rooms	5
rooms with sink	1
shared wc	1
shared bathrooms	2

Activities: 🏛 🍷 🛶 🎿 🐎

20. RIMOUSKI, ST-NARCISSE   ☀☀ F e 🦌 P 🏊 R4 TA

For dreamers, romantics or nature-lovers. Rural, rustic-style home with log interior; warm, comfortable and quiet. Small private lake, picnic table, swimming and canoeing included. Waterfall and canyon nearby. A real vacation, only 15min from Rimouski.

From Quebec City, Hwy 20 East, Exit 610, Rte 232 West for 16km, left on Chemin de l'Écluse, 1km.

B&B
DOMAINE DU BON
VIEUX TEMPS

Hélène Rioux
89-1, chemin de l'Écluse
Rimouski-St-Narcisse G0K 1S0
(418) 735-5646
www.chez.com/
bonvieuxtemps

B&B	
single	$45
double	$50-65
child	$10-15

VS

Open year round

Number of rooms	3
rooms with private wc	2
shared bathrooms	1

Activities: 🛶 🛷 🎿 🏃 🧍

21. RIVIÈRE-DU-LOUP   ☀☀☀ F E 🚫 P R1

A superb 1895 Victorian house. Come and admire the sunsets from the solarium while breathing the fresh, salty air. Rest in the shade of hundred-year-old trees. Two living room perfect for relaxation. Prime Ministers John A. MacDonald and Louis St-Laurent once stayed in the neighbourhood. Magnificent surroundings!

Via Hwy 20, Exit 503, turn left at the stop sign, 11th house on the left. Located on Rte 132 between Notre-Dame-du-Portage and Rivière-du-Loup.

B&B
AUBERGE LA SABLINE

Monique Gaudet and
Jean Cousineau
343, rue Fraser ouest
Rivière-du-Loup G5R 5S9
(418) 867-4890
www.bbcanada.
com/4386.html

B&B	
single	$60-75
double	$65-80
triple	$80-95
child	$10

Taxes extra VS MC

Reduced rates: Sep. 4 to June 21
Open year round

Number of rooms	3
rooms with private bath	1
shared wc	1
shared bathrooms	1

Activities: 🛥 🚤 🧍 🚲

22. RIVIÈRE-DU-LOUP

☀☀☀ F E P 🚗 ❌ TA

"Who sleeps, eats" at Au Bonheur du Jour, a rural B&B by the sea in L'Anse-au-Persil. As night falls the dining room offers 5-course meals to guests with reservations. The next morning there will be fresh bread toasted on the wood stove. Bring your own wine and binoculars. Io parlo più che meno l'italiano.

L'Anse-au-Persil is between Rivière-du-Loup and Cacouna. From Riv.-du-Loup, Rte 132 East to #284. A short, private marked road leads to the B&B hidden from the road.

B&B
AU BONHEUR DU JOUR

Marie Anne Rainville
284, Anse-au-Persil, rte 132
Rivière-du-Loup G5R 5Z6
tel/fax (418) 862-3670
www.bbcanada.
com/3922.html

	B&B	MAP
single	$45	$65
double	$55	$100
triple	$70	$140
child	$10	$35

Open: June 23 to Aug. 31

Number of rooms	3
shared bathrooms	1

Activities: 🦆 🚤 ⛷ 🚶 🚴

23. RIVIÈRE-DU-LOUP

✎ F 🚭 🚗 P R.03

Prize for Excellence "Special Favorite" Regional 1997-98 and the "small tourist business" Grand Prix du Tourisme Bas-St-Laurent. Home sweet home! Charming, antique-furnished house with rustic decor, terrace and garden, river view and lavish breakfast with homemade bread and jams. Near the ferry, whale-watching cruises, museum, summer theatre and good restaurants. Come share in our happiness—the only thing missing is you.

Hwy 20, Exit 503, turn right at the stop sign, drive 1.4km to Rue Fraser.

B&B
AU TERROIR
DES BASQUES

Marguerite Filion and
Pierre-Paul Belzile
197, rue Fraser
Rivière-du-Loup G5R 1E2
tel/fax (418) 860-2001
sans frais 1-877-647-8078
marpierre@sympatico.ca

B&B	
single	$45
double	$55
child	$10

Open: June 15 to sept. 15

Number of rooms	3
rooms in basement	1
shared bathrooms	2

Activities: 🏛 🦆 🚤 🚤 🚴

24. RIVIÈRE-DU-LOUP

☀☀☀☀ F E 🚭 🏊 P R3

Summer residence of Canada's first Prime Minister, Sir John A. Macdonald from 1872 to 1890. Magnificient heritage house which gives visitors a splendid view across the St. Lawrence River to the mountainous north shore. Enjoy your stay in a quiet and peaceful environment, as well as our delicious home-made breakfast. Many activities and day trips nearby. **Country Home in Percé, Gaspésie region, p 157, no°60.**

Hwy 20 to Rivière-du-Loup then west on Hwy 132 twd St-Patrice.

B&B
LES ROCHERS

L'Héritage Canadien du Québec
336, rue Fraser
St-Patrice, Rivière-du-Loup
G5R 5S8
(514) 393-1417
(418) 868-1435
fax (514) 393-9444
www.total.net/~chq
chq@total.net

B&B	
single	$60-80
double	$75-90
triple	$85-100
child	$10

VS MC

Open: June 15 to Sep. 10

Number of rooms	5
rooms with private bath	2
rooms with sink	3
shared bathrooms	3

Activities: 🦆 🚤 🚤 ⛷ 🚶

25. RIVIÈRE-DU-LOUP, ST-ANTONIN

☀☀ F e P R.5 TA

Located less than 5km from Rivière-du-Loup, on the road to Edmunston, "La Maison de Mon Enfance" awaits you. A perfect stopping place on the way to the Maritimes or Gaspésie. Whale-watching cruises, museums, theatre, golf. Only 1km from the Petit Témis bike path; motorcycle/bicycle garage, free parking. See you soon, *Roseline*.

Rte 185: In St-Antonin, at the flashing light, turn twd the Trans Canadien restaurant; it's at the stop sign. From Rivière-du-Loup, twd Edmunston, Jct. 185, straight ahead for 4km.

B&B
LA MAISON DE MON ENFANCE

Roseline Desrosiers
718, ch. Rivière-Verte
St-Antonin G0L 2J0
(418) 862-3624
fax (418) 862-8969
roselinedesrosiers
@sympatico.ca

B&B	
single	$40-50
double	$50-60
triple	$60-70
quad.	$80

VS

Open: June 15 to Sep. 15

Number of rooms	5
shared wc	1
shared bathrooms	2

Activities: 🚣 ⛴ 🎣 🚶 🚴

26. ST-ALEXANDRE, KAMOURASKA

☀☀☀ F 🚭 P R.08 TA

Enjoy a warm welcome in a spacious house in the heart of the village. It's a quiet place on a large property with fruit trees, vegetable gardens and flowers, and a large solarium for your relaxation. Sizeable, well-equipped rooms with queen-size beds, lavish breakfast with homemade jams, healthy meals. Welcome!

From Quebec City, Hwy 20 East, Exit 488 twd St-Alexandre, Rte 289. After the church, turn right on Ave. Marguerite D'Youville.

B&B
GÎTE DES FLEURS

Alice and Julien Ouellet
526, av. Marguerite D'Youville
St-Alexandre, Kamouraska
G0L 2G0
(418) 495-5500

B&B	
single	$45
double	$60
triple	$80
quad.	$100

Open year round

Number of rooms	4
shared bathrooms	2
shared wc	1
room in basement	1

Activities: 🏛 ⛴ 🚤 🎣 🍎

27. ST-ALEXANDRE, KAMOURASKA

☀☀☀ F e P 🚗 R.3 TA

Spend your holidays in the beautiful ancestral home of Marie-Alice Dumont, first professional photographer in Eastern Québec. Mouthwatering breakfasts served by the stained-glass window of the former photography studio. The warmest of welcomes awaits. Prize for Excellence "Special Favorite" Regional 1994-95.

From Québec City, Hwy 20 East, Exit 488 twd St-Alexandre. 1ˢᵗ house left, at the junction of Rte 230.

B&B
LA MAISON AU TOIT BLEU

Madame Daria Dumont
490, avenue St-Clovis
St-Alexandre G0L 2G0
(418) 495-2701
tel/fax (418) 495-2368

B&B	
single	$45
double	$60
child	$10

Open year round

Number of rooms	3
shared wc	1
shared bathrooms	1

Activities: 🏛 🚣 ⛴ 🚤 🎣

28. ST-ANDRÉ, KAMOURASKA

F e P ☒ TA

A charming inn, La Solaillerie welcomes you with open arms. Rustic rooms with period decor, in the ancestral house that invites you to dream of the past or luxury room with romantic decor in which to lounge with your loved one under the goosedown duvet. We also offer the best food in the region: creative, refined, lavish regional cuisine. Tourism 1999 Grand Prize: "Hospitality and Customer Service". **See colour photos.**

Hwy 20, Exit 480 twd St-André. In the village, turn right on Rue Principale. Or direct acces with "Route des Navigateurs" (rte 132).

INN
AUBERGE LA SOLAILLERIE

Isabelle Poyau and Yvon Robert
112, rue Principale
St-André-de-Kamouraska
G0L 2H0
(418) 493-2914
fax (418) 493-2243
www.focus-com.qc.ca/
solaillerie/sol.html
lasolaillerie@globetrotter.net

	B&B	MAP
single	$50-90	$90-130
double	$59-99	$139-179
triple	$125	$245
child	$16-26	

Taxes extra VS MC IT

Open : May 1 to Oct. 31

Number of rooms	11
rooms with private bath	6
rooms with bath and sink	3
rooms with sink	2
shared wc	2
shared bathrooms	1

Activities: 🛶 ⛷ 𝆑 🚶 🚴

29. ST-ÉLOI

☀☀☀ F P 🚗 ☒ TA

Come share the comfort and tranquillity of this venerable house (1863), located in the heart of a peaceful village. Smell the fluwers and admire the splendid view of the St-Lawrence River. Paintings relate the history of your painter host. Hearty homemade breakfast and meals. Spend a night with us and you'll be in heaven. Children welcome.

From Quebec City, Hwy 20 East to the end, then 19km along Rte 132. Turn right on Rte St-Éloi, continue for 5km. Turn left on Rue Principale.

INN
AU VIEUX PRESBYTÈRE

Raymonde and Yvon Pettigrew
350, rue Principale Est
St-Éloi G0L 2V0
(418) 898-6147
toll free 1-888-833-6147
aubergepresbytere.
citeglobe.com
aubergeauvieux@qc.aira.com

	B&B	MAP
single	$40	$55
double	$55	$85
triple	$70	$115
quad.	$85	$145
child	$10	$20

Taxes extra VS MC IT

Reduced rates: Nov. 1 to May 1
Open year round

Number of rooms	4
rooms with sink	4
shared bathrooms	2

Activities: 🏛 🛶 ⛵ 𝆑 🚴

30. ST-JEAN-DE-DIEU

☀☀☀ F P 🚗 R4

Family with children, all happy to have you as guests. Dairy farm. Fishing and small animals: peacocks, ducks, rabbits, sheep, goats, deer, llamas... Crepes with maple syrup for breakfast. A warm atmosphere and healthy food. 20 min from the river. Families welcome. **Farm Stay p 48.**

From Québec City, Hwy 20 East, Rte 132 East to Trois-Pistoles. Rte 293 South to St-Jean-de-Dieu. Drive 4km past the church.

B&B
LA FERME PAYSAGÉE

Gabrielle and Régis Rouleau
121, Route 293 Sud
St-Jean-de-Dieu G0L 3M0
(418) 963-3315
www.lafermepaysagee.
freeservers.com
rouls@globetrotter.net

	B&B	MAP
single	$30	$40
double	$40	$80
child	$10	$15-16

Open year round

Number of rooms	3
shared bathrooms	2

Activities: 🛶 🎿 𝆑 🚶 🐎

31. ST-LOUIS-DU-HA! HA!

☀☀☀ F e 🚗 P R6 TA

Prize for Excellence "Special Favorite" Regional 2000, this typical 1920s house located in the heart of the mountains offers a magnificent view. Situated on the road to the Maritimes and in the middle of the "Le Petit Témis" bike path. Shuttle service, bike shed, luggage carrying services. Our priorities: welcome, warm ambiance, comfort, cleanliness and a delicious breakfast. You'll want to come back.

From Quebec City, Hwy 20 to Riv.-du-Loup. 60km along Rte. 185 South. At flashing light, turn right, drive 1.6km. Left on Rang Beauséjour, continue for 5km.

B&B
AU BEAU-SÉJOUR

Louiselle Ouellet and
Paul Gauvin
145, rang Beauséjour
St-Louis-du-Ha! Ha! G0L 3S0
tel/fax (418) 854-0559
www.multimania.
com/gitebeausejour/
lgauvin@sympatico.ca

B&B	
single	$40
double	$55-60
triple	$70
quad.	$80
child	$5

Open year round

Number of rooms	4
shared bathrooms	2

Activities: 🏊 🎿 🚴 🛥 🏃

32. STE-LUCE-SUR-MER

F E ♿ ✗ P 🏊 TA

Right on the beach and just a few kilometres from the Jardins de Métis, we offer an oasis of peace in harmony with the rhythm of the seas. In concert with the setting sun and our fine regional cuisine (included in the menu), you will experience a magical sound and light show. **See colour photos.**

From Québec City, Hwy 20 East, Rte 132 twd Ste-Flavie. After Pte-au-Père, watch for "Camping La Luciole", drive 500 ft. and turn left, then right on Route du Fleuve.

INN
AUBERGE DE L'EIDER

Johanne Cloutier
and Maurice Gendron
90, route du Fleuve Est
Ste-Luce-sur-Mer G0K 1P0
tel/fax (450) 448-5110
(418) 739-3535
auberge-eider@sympatico.ca

B&B	
single	$55-65
double	$60-85
triple	$75-95
quad.	$105
child	$10

Taxes extra VS MC ER

Open: June 15 to Sept. 30

Number of rooms	14
rooms with private bath	14

Activities: 🦆 🛥 🏊 🎿 🚴

33. STE-LUCE-SUR-MER

☀☀☀☀ F E P 🚗 🐕 🏊 R.1 TA

On the banks of the St. Lawrence, charming 1920 house with country colours, landscaped grounds and private beach. Creative "eye-catching" breakfast will whet your appetite. Relaxing gazebo. Unforgettable evening show as the fiery sun kisses the sea. Cocktail hour. 15 minutes from Jardins de Métis, Parc du Bic, Côte-Nord ferry.

Mid-way between Rimouski and Mont-Joli via Rte 132. Enter the picturesque village of Ste-Luce along the river; we are 0.2km west of the church, near the river.

B&B
MAISON DES GALLANT

Nicole Dumont and
Jean Gallant
40, rue du Fleuve Ouest,
C.P. 52
Ste-Luce-sur-Mer G0K 1P0
(418) 739-3512
toll free 1-888-739-3512
www.bbcanada.com/1951.html
jean.gallant@cgocable.ca

B&B	
single	$45
double	$60
triple	$80
child	$10

Open year round

Number of rooms	3
shared wc	1
shared bathrooms	1

Activities: 🏛 🏊 🎿 🚴 🎿

34. TROIS-PISTOLES

☀☀☀ | F | E | P | R1

You will be captivated by our convivial home, and the nearby bird- and whale-watching opportunities. A feast for the senses, your stay here will be one of your fondest memories. Let us enchant you with our stories and legends about this stretch of the river. You can take the ferry, just 2.7km away, at your leisure. Packages available.

Halfway between Montreal and Percé, 0.5km from the west entrance to the town of Trois-Pistoles. From the dock, continue to Notre-Dame and turn right.

B&B
AU GRÉ DES MARÉES

Jeanne Riverin and
Marcel Hardy
525, Notre-Dame Ouest
Trois-Pistoles G0L 4K0
(418) 851-3819
fax (418) 851-4232
jeanne.riverin@sympatico.ca

B&B	
single	$45
double	$55
triple	$75
child	$15

VS

Reduced rates : Dec. 15 to June 15
Open year round

Number of rooms	3
shared bathrooms	2

Activities: 🏛 🦆 🚤 🚲 🧍

---

35. TROIS-PISTOLES, ST-SIMON

☀☀☀ | F | E | 🛏 | P | 🐕 | R4 | TA

Ancestral (1820) house. Bucolic setting. Farmhouse. Rooms with old baths. Private beach. Packages: excursions (Île aux Basques, whale-watching), theatre. Footpaths: Trois-Pistoles river, Parc du Bic... 2km from the Littorale cycling path. Hearty breakfasts, homemade bread. Cooking opportunities. Reduced rates off-season, group packages. **Ad end of this region.**

Direct access via eastbound Rte 132, 7km east of Trois-Pistoles. Heading west, 4km west of St-Simon. 10min from the ferry.

B&B
CHEZ CHOINIÈRE

Alain Choinière
71, rue Principale Ouest
St-Simon G0L 4C0
(418) 738-2245
www.bbcanada.
com/chezchoiniere
chezchoiniere@hotmail.com

B&B	
single	$40
double	$60
triple	$75
quad.	$90
child	$10

Reduced rates: 15% Sept. 15 to Oct. 15 and April 15 to June 15
Open : April 15 to Oct. 15

Number of rooms	5
rooms with sink and bath	2
rooms with private bath	3
shared bathrooms	1

Activities: 🏛 🦆 🚤 🧍 🧍

---

36. TROIS-PISTOLES, ST-SIMON

☀☀☀ | F | E | 🚭 | 🛏 | P | R.5 | TA

Located 15km west of Parc du Bic, our large century-old house has preserved its original character and charm. Guests enjoy our peaceful setting and cordial welcome. Breakfast includes home-made *reine-claude* (greengage) plum jams, as well as pancakes, maple syrup, muffins and excellent coffee. See you soon! **Ad end of this region.**

From Québec City, Hwy 20 East, Rte 132 East twd Saint-Simon, 15km east of Trois-Pistoles. Right on Rue de l'Église.

B&B
GÎTE DE LA REINE-CLAUDE

Jane O'Brien and Claude Daoust
39, rue de l'Église
Saint-Simon-de-Rimouski
G0L 4C0
tel/fax (418) 738-2609
www.bbcanada.com/3325.html
jcdaoust@quebectel.com

B&B	
single	$42
double	$55
triple	$75
quad.	$90
child	$10

Open year round

Number of rooms	4
shared wc	2
shared bathrooms	1

Activities: 🦆 🚤 🚗 🧍 🚲

FARM ACTIVITIES

Farm Stay:

29 LES FLOTS BLEUS, Rimouski   48

29 FERME PAYSAGÉE, St-Jean-de-Dieu   48

26 years of hospitality
1975 – 2001

For 26 years, the host members of the
Fédération des Agricotours du Québec have been
committed to offering you genuine, high-quality choices
for accommodation and agricultural tourism.

This has made Agricotours the largest high-quality
network in Quebec, and your confidence has helped in its success.

For this reason, our network host members hope
that they may, with their traditional warm welcome, continue
to help you discover the best of Quebec for many more years to come.

You'll always feel welcome in the Agricotours network.

www.inns-bb.com
www.agricotours.qc.ca

CANTONS-DE-L'EST

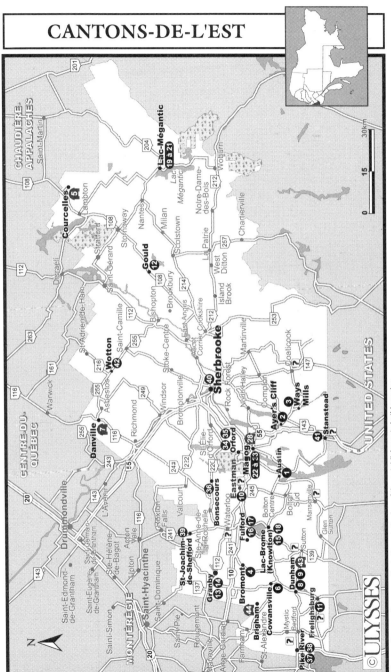

*The numbers on the map refer to the numbering of the establishments in this region.

© ULYSSES

1. AUSTIN

☀☀☀☀☀ F e ✕ 🚗 P TA

This Georgian manor is located in an impressive setting with a breathtaking view of Abbaye Saint-Benoît-du-Lac, Lac Memphrémagog and Mont Owl's Head. Depending on the season: ski, golf or summer theatre packages can be booked. Lovely scenery. Enjoy the fine local cuisine, which offers a choice of four different *table d'hôte* with five or six-course dinners. Bring your own wine. **See colour photos.**

From Montréal, Hwy 10, Exit 115, drive to Austin and St-Benoît-du-Lac, about 12km.

INN
AUBERGE LES PIGNONS VERTS

Raymonde and
Florian Landry
2158, chemin Nicolas-Austin
Austin J0B 1B0
tel/fax (819) 847-1272
www.aubergepignonsverts.qc.ca
pignons-verts@sympatico.ca

	B&B	MAP
single	$75	$105
double	$90	$150
triple	$120	$210
child	$30	$60

Taxes extra VS MC IT

Open year round

Number of rooms	5
rooms with private bath	5

Activities: 🛶 🏊 ⛷ 🚴 🎿

2. AYER'S CLIFF

F P R5

Hundred-year-old house in the country, panoramic view, quiet place. Home cooking. Swimming in Lake Massawippi 3km away, summer theatre, Coaticook Gorge, cross-country skiing, downhill skiing 15 min. away, 8 min. from golf, 200 ft. from skidooing. Near North Hatley, Mont Orford and Magog. Horseback riding 15 min. away. Ideal for hiking and cycling.

From Montréal, Hwy 10 East, Exit 121. Hwy 55 South, Exit 21, Rte 141 South. About 2.5km. after intersection of Rte 143, left on Chemin Audet. Big white house on the hill.

B&B
CÉCILE LAUZIER

Cécile Lauzier
3119 ch. Audet, Kingscroft
Ayer's Cliff J0B 1C0
(819) 838-4433

B&B	
single	$45-50
double	$55-65
triple	$75

Open year round

Number of rooms	5
shared bathrooms	2

Activities: 🛶 🏊 ⛷ 🚴 🛶

3. AYER'S CLIFF

☀☀☀☀ F E 🚭 🐕 🚗 P 🏊 R10

Unique Norwegain-style log house surrounded by 7 acres of private woods and field. 2 large bedrooms with fireplace and TV or grand piano. Whirlpool and sauna in house. Landscaped pond, brook and water-lily garden. Kitchen access for long stays. Picniking anytime.

From Montreal, Hwy 10 East, Exit 121, Hwy 55 South, Exit 21, rte 141 South twd Coaticook. 2km after crossing rte 143, turn right on Way's Mills road. Drive to village, then staight ahead for 3km on Ballbrook road.

B&B
LA CHAUMIÈRE
EN PAIN D'ÉPICES

Claudine Trudel
1488, ch. Ballbrook
Way's Mills
Ayer's Cliff J0B 1C0
tel/fax (819) 876-2686
www.bbcanada.
com/3853.html
chaumiere@sympatico.ca

B&B	
single	$65
double	$85
child	$20

Open year round

Number of rooms	2
rooms with sink	2
shared bathroom	1
shared wc	2

Activities: 🏊 🚶 🚴 🐎 🏃

4. BROMONT

☀☀☀☀ F E 🐕 P 🏊 R4 TA

closed

This completely renovated B&B in Bromont combines quality, tranquillity and hospitality. Located in an idyllic setting in the middle of a vast, wooded 19-acre area dotted with lakes and rivers, La Clairière has large, tastefully decorated rooms with an added personal touch. Our breakfasts are a gourmet delight. Less than 10min from all the region's attractions.

From Montréal, Hwy 10, Exit 78. At the light, right on Rue Shefford. At the stop sign, left on Rue Gaspé, 6km. Left on Rue Frontenac, 2km. Right on Rue des Perdrix, then 1st street on your left.

B&B
LA CLAIRIÈRE

Lyne and François Girardin
3, des Mésanges
Bromont J2L 1Y8
(450) 260-1954
fax (450) 260-1955
pages.infinit.net/girardin
la.clairiere@videotron.ca

B&B	
single	$75-90
double	$85-100
triple	$100-115
child	$15

Reduced rates: Nov. and Apr., 10% 2 nights and more
Open year round

Number of rooms	3
rooms with private bath	1
rooms with sink	3
shared wc	1
shared bathrooms	1

Activities: 🥾 🚶 🚴 🐎 🎿

5. COURCELLES

F E 🚗 P 🏊 🐕 🍽 TA

You will be won over by French traditions and rural life. Local cuisine, homemade foie gras. We open our hearts and our cottage to introduce you to the pleasures of agrotourism in a first-rate place. Packages: long holidays, equestrian, deer/pheasant-hunting, calm and relaxation. Pool, large lake. Located 2.5hrs from Montreal, 1.5hrs from Quebec City. Greetings, *Gina and Gilles*. **Farm stay p 48.**

Hwy 10, East Angus Exit twd Lac-Mégantic. Rte 108 twd Beauceville and Courcelles.

B&B
L'AUBERGE D'ANDROMÈDE

Gina Hallé and Gilles Leclerc
495, Rang 6
Courcelles G0M 1C0
tel/fax (418) 483-5442
www3.sympatico.ca
/andromedetour
andromedetour@sympatico.ca

	B&B	MAP
single	$40-60	$70
double	$50-70	$140
child	$25	$30

Taxes extra VS

Reduced rates: 10% Nov. 1 to May 1
Open year round

Number of rooms	3
rooms with private bath	3

Activities: 🚴 🐎 🏛 🚶 🚣

6. COWANSVILLE

☀☀☀☀ F E 🚗 P 🏊 R.5 TA

Prize for Excellence "Special Favorite" Regional 1999. Enchanting site near Bromont and Lac Brome. Discover our paradise on a 10-acre hill, overlooking Lac d'Avignon with view over the mountains. Flowery expanses, pond, footpaths, in-ground pool, VIP suites, hearty and varied breakfasts. Near cultural and sports activities. Gift certificates and "golf, bike, relaxation, ski" packages available. "Sheer bliss."

From Montréal or Sherbrooke, Hwy 10, Exit 74, Boul Pierre Laporte twd Cowansville. At BMP hospital, left on Rue Principale drive 0.5km.

B&B
DOMAINE SUR LA COLLINE
B&B

Nicole and Gilles Deslauriers
1221, rue Principale
Cowansville J2K 1K7
(450) 266-1910
toll free 1-888-222-1692
fax (450) 266-4320
www.surlacolline.qc.ca
info@surlacolline.qc.ca

B&B	
single	$70-100
double	$75-115
triple	$135
quad.	$150
child	$10-20

VS MC

Reduced rates: Oct. 14 to Dec. 8 and Jan. 15 to May 11
Open year round

Number of rooms	4
rooms with private bath	2
shared wc	1
shared bathrooms	1

Activities: 🥾 🚶 🚴 🚣 🐎

7. DANVILLE

☀☀☀ F e 🚭 🚗 P 🛶 ✕ R3

Nature lovers: spacious estate with forest, trails and animals, where only the beauty of the landscapes rivals the peace and quiet. Table d'hôte served by the fire or on the terrace in summer. Hiking, cycling (path), swimming, X-country skiing. Packages: theatre, golf, cycling, riding. **Farm Stay p 48.**

From Montréal, Hwy 20, Exit 147, Rte 116 East. In Richmond, at lights, 13.9km, left on Demers 2.5km. From Québec City, Hwy 20, Exit 253, Rte 116 W. In Danville at lights 3km, Demers to the right 2.5km.

B&B
LE CLOS DES PINS

Josée Brouillette and
Daniel Godbout
60, chemin Boisvert
Danville J0A 1A0
tel/fax (819) 839-3521
www.closdespins.qc.ca
closdespins@sympatico.ca

	B&B	MAP
single	$50-65	$65-80
double	$65-80	$95-110
triple	$95	$140
quad.	$110	$170
child	$10	$20-25

Taxes extra VS

Open year round

Number of rooms	4
shared bathrooms	2

Activities: 🚣 🎿 🚶 🚴 🎣

8. DUNHAM

☀☀☀☀ F E 🚭 🚗 P 🛶 R4

A great find, "with a lovely name... A superb house run by a young couple. The stately trees along the road here form a leafy tunnel... It's just like being in Vermont... lavish breakfast..." (Pierre Foglia, La Presse). Heated pool, hiking trails, maple grove. If you stay 3 nights, get maple product for free. Free tour of the L'Orpailleur vineyard (May-Oct).

Hwy 10, Exit 68, Rte 139 South for 20km. In Cowansville, turn right at 2nd light onto Rte 202 South twd Dunham and continue for 2km. Turn left on Chemin Fitchett for 2km, then left on Chemin Vail for 2km.

B&B
AU TEMPS DES MÛRES

Marie-Josée Potvin and
Pierre Cormier
2024, chemin Vail
Dunham J0E 1M0
(450) 266-1319
fax (450) 266-1303
toll free 1-888-708-8050
www.tempsdesmures.qc.ca

B&B	
single	$50-70
double	$65-80
child	$10-20

Taxes en sus VS MC

Reduced rates: Nov. 1 to May 1
Open year round

Number of rooms	5
rooms with private bath	3
shared bathrooms	2

Activities: 🚶 🚴 🏃 🐎

9. DUNHAM

☀☀☀☀ F e 🚭 P R.25

After touring the vineyards, unwind at our magnificent Victorian manor. Terrace, living room with fireplace, air-conditioned suites and private bathrooms. House with a dream-like environnement and many possibilities. We look forward to seeing you soon.

Hwy 10, Exit 68, Rte 139 to Cowansville, 18km. At traffic light, Rte 202 to Dunham (8km). 200 metres past the corner store, Rue du Collège (left).

B&B
AUX DOUCES HEURES

Lyette Leroux Dumoulin and
André Dumoulin
110, rue du Collège C.P. 40
Dunham J0E 1M0
(450) 295-2476
toll free 1-877-295-2476
fax (450) 295-1307

B&B	
single	$65-95
double	$85-95
child	$40

Taxes extra

Reduced rates: 10% Mar. 1 to Nov. 30, 2 nights and more from sunday to thursday
Open: Mar. 1to Nov. 30

Number of rooms	5
rooms with private bath	5
shared wc	1

Activities: 🚣 🎿 🚴 🎿 🏃

10. EASTMAN

Small details that make up a great whole: a divine setting, a lake in which to swim, with Mont Orford as a backdrop. Gourmet breakfasts served in the solarium, by the fire or on the terrace. Packages: show, ski, business meeting, gift certificate. Home sweet home; stay at the bed and breakfast, and have dinner too! Bring your own wine. A great place to sin without fear of repentance.

Hwy 10, Exit 106, Eastman, Rte 112 East, 3km past the village.

B&B
GÎTE LES PECCADILLES

Christine and
Jean-Marie Foucault
1029, route Principale
Eastman J0E 1P0
(450) 297-3551
(514) 482-5347
www.bbcanada.
com/3828.html
jmfoucault@videotron.ca

	B&B	MAP
singlr	$50-90	$75-115
double	$70-90	$120-140
child	$20	$45

VS

Reduced rates: 1 complementary night after 7 in a row
Open year round

Number of rooms	3
rooms with private bath	1
shared bathrooms	2

Activities:

---

11. FRELIGHSBURG

Come gather wild fruits or mush-rooms, surprise the deer in the or-chard or on wooded trails, feed the small animals or simply relax in one of Québec's loveliest villages, at the foot of Mont Pinacle. French spe-cialties. Packages available.

Hwy 10, Exit 22, to the end of Hwy 35 S. Left, twd St-Alexandre, to Bedford. Rte 202 for about 7 km. Right at Frelighsburg sign. We are 1 km past village, on right.

B&B
À LA GIRONDINE

Françoise and François Bardo
104, Route 237 sud
Frelighsburg J0J 1C0
(450) 298-5206
fax (450) 298-5216
www.netc.net/lagirondine
lagirondine@netc.net

B&B	
single	$60
double	$70

Taxes extra VS MC

Open year round

Number of rooms	3
shared batroom	1
shared wc	1

Activities:

---

12. GOULD

Welcome to our bed and breakfast, located in the heart of a Scottish village settled around 1837. Period furniture, traditional cooking, *tables d'hôte* and scotchs, plus our unique breakfasts will mark your stay. Meals served in the area's first gen-eral store. A unique experience in Quebec, a trip to Scotland!

From Montreal, Hwy 10, Exit 143, Rte 112 East. In East Angus, Rtes 214 and 108 East. From the U.S., Rtes 3 and 257 North. From Quebec City, Hwy 73 twd Ste-Marie, Rte 173 twd Vallée-Jct. Rte 112 twd Thetford and Weedon, Rte 257 South.

B&B
LA MAISON MC AULEY

Daniel Audet and
Jacques Cloutier
19, Route 108
Gould, Lingwick J0B 2Z0
tel/fax (819) 877-3446
toll free 1-888-305-3526
www.rueegouldrush.com
info@rueegouldrush.com

	B&B	MAP
1 pers.	$45	$70
2 pers.	$60	$115

Taxes extra VS MC IT

Open : Feb. 1 to Jan. 10

Number of rooms	4
rooms with sink	2
shared bathrooms	2

Activities:

13. GRANBY

✸✸✸✸✸ | F | E | 🚗 | P | 🚭 | R1 | TA

Prize for Excellence "Special Favorite" Regional 2000. From the terrace of our bed and breakfast, on Lac Boivin and a short bike ride away from l'Estriade, you can admire stunning sunsets in an enchanting setting. Private living room with fireplace, barbecue in season, skiing, skating, hiking: everything for your comfort and relaxation.

Hwy 10, Exit 74 twd Granby. At the traffic light, turn left on Rte 112, right on Rue de L'Iris, left on Rue de la Potentille and left on Rue du Nénuphar. By bike: at Km 1 on L'Estriade.

B&B
LA MAISON DUCLAS

Ginette Canuel and
Camil Duchesne
213, rue du Nénuphar
Granby J2H 2J9
(450) 360-0641
www.maisonduclas.com
info@maisonduclas.com

B&B	
single	$55
double	$70
triple	$90

Reduced rates: Nov. 1 to May 1
Open year round

Number of rooms	2
rooms with private bath	2
rooms in semi-basement	2

Activities: 🍴 🎿 🚲 ⛷ 🏃

14. GRANBY

✸✸✸ | F | E | 🏊 | 🚭 | P | R.2 | TA

Carole and Michel welcome you to their charming raspberry-coloured house. Let us mapper you in this relaxing setting on Lac Boivin located near a park. Enjoy coffee on the waterfront among flowers and facing the Estriade cycling path. Close to the downtown shops and restaurants. Rooms with air conditionning, heated pool.

From Montréal, Hwy 10 East, Exit 74 to Granby, at the traffic lights make a left on Rte 112 West. Right at the 1ˢᵗ traffic lights on Rue de la Gare, right on Drummond.

B&B
A FLOWER ON THE
RIVER FRONT

Carole Bélanger and
Michel Iannantuono
90, rue Drummond
Granby J2G 2S6
(450) 776-1141
toll free 1-888-375-1747
fax (450) 375-0141
www.clubtrs.ca/fleurvtg
fleurvtg@login.net

B&B	
single	$55-70
double	$60-75
child	$10

Taxes extra VS MC AM

Reduced rates: Jan. 8 to Apr. 15,
Oct. 31 to Dec. 15
Open year round

Number of rooms	4
rooms with private bath	2
shared bathrooms	1

Activities: 🍴 🚣 🎿 🚲 ⛷

15. KNOWLTON, LAC BROME

✸✸✸✸✸ | F | E | 🚭 | 🐕 | 🚗 | P | R4 | TA

Our B&B offers a breathtaking panoramic view. All three rooms have a balcony, a homey décor and a window with a beautiful view of the stars. Comfort, tranquillity and relaxation guaranteed, not to mention a hearty breakfast!

Hwy 10, Exit 90, Rte 243 South to Knowlton. After 2 stops, exit Rte 243 in the centre of town. Straight down Chemin Mt. Écho for 4km, 2ⁿᵈ street on your left is Rue Benjamin.

B&B
RÊVERIE AUX QUATRE-VENTS

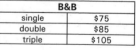

Jacqueline and Guy LeRoyer
46, rue Benjamin, C.P. 82
Knowlton Lac Brome
J0E 1V0
tel/fax (450) 243-0867
reveriequatrevents@citenet.net

B&B	
single	$75
double	$85
triple	$105

Open year round

Number of rooms	3
shared bathrooms	1

Activities: 🚣 🎿 🚶 🚲 ⛷

16. LAC-BROME, FOSTER

F E ✕ ▬

Joli Vent is a century-old house, a place to forget all your troubles. Our rooms are quiet and comfortable. Library, large living room, fireplace and bar. Hans offers a European menu with Asian accents. A large property with fields and a forest, a pond, trails, a swimming pool and private access to the lake. Steps away from golf courses, ski hills and Knowlton. **See color photos.**

Hwy 10, Exit 90, Rte 243 twd Lac-Brome for 3.6km, Rte 215 for 1km.

INN
AUBERGE DU JOLI VENT

Patricia Provencher
667, ch. Bondville
Lac-Brome J0E 1R0
(450) 243-4272
fax (450) 242-1943
www.aubergedujolivent.com
jolivent@sympatico.ca

B&B	
single	
double	$8. 95
triple	$95-105
child	$10

Taxes extra VS MC IT

Reduced rates: 20% 3 nights and more
Open year round

Number of rooms	10
rooms with private bath	10

Activities: 🛶 🎿 🏃 🚲 ⛷

17. LAC-BROME, FULFORD

✹✹✹✹ F E P 🐕 🏊 R5 TA

A warm welcome to our English "Tudor" house, located between Bromont and Knowlton. Come and stroke our pure-bred norwegian horses (Fjord). Enjoy a walk on our property of 26 acres. You'll find a brook, a wooded countryside, a pool and patios. Golf club 5 min. away. Snowshoeing on the site and snowmobile trail access 35-45.

Hwy 10, Exit 78 twd Bromont. Straight ahead for 7km, turn right at red flashing light (Brome road). We are 1km further on your left.

B&B
LE TU-DOR

Ghislaine Lemay and
Jean-Guy Laforce
394, chemin Brome
Ville de Lac-Brome J0E 1S0
(450) 534-3947
fax (450) 534-5543
www.bbcanada.
com/1431.html
lemay.laforce@citenet.net

B&B	
single	$65
double	$75-80
triple	$95-100
quad.	$115-120
child	$15

VS MC

Reduced rates: on long stay
Open year round

Number of rooms	4
rooms with private bath	4

Activities: 🎿 🚲 🐎 ⛷ 🏃

18. LAC-BROME, KNOWLTON

✹✹✹ F E 🚫 🐕 🚗 P R.5 TA

Take a break and enjoy of our peaceful ancestral home, the only B&B located within walking distance of the village. We offer you a warm welcome - just like a member of the family! Our specialty: fruit-filled crepes, a recipe passed down by our great-grandmother.

From Montréal, Hwy 10, Exit 90, Rte 243, to Knowlton, turn right at 2nd stop sign, Rte 104, 0.8km. From Québec City, Hwy 20, Hwy 55 South, Hwy 10, Exit 90, Rte 243...

B&B
LA DORMANCE

Jocelyne Rollin and
Normand Faubert
402, ch. Knowlton, C.P. 795
Lac-Brome, Knowlton J0E 1V0
(450) 242-1217
www.ladormance.com
ladormance@sympatico.ca

B&B	
single	$65-75
double	$80-90
triple	$95-105
quad.	$110-120
child	$10

VS MC IT

Reduced rates: Nov 1 to May 1, 20% 3 nights or more
Open year round

Number of rooms	5
rooms with private bath	5

Activities: 🚣 🛶 🎿 🚲 ⛷

19. LAC-MÉGANTIC

☀☀☀☀☀ | F | E | P | 🚭 | R1

B&B
AU SOLEIL COUCHANT

Visit our B&B perched on a hill over-looking the lake, located 1km. from the golf course. Near the Observatoire & Astrolab. Peaceful setting. 34 hectares of woodlands. Ponds and trails leading to the beaver dam. Panoramic view, ideal for fall colours. Private beach nearby. 2 large rooms with queen-size beds. Breakfast on solarium overlooking the lake.

From Montréal or Sherbrooke, Hwy 10, Rtes 143 S., 108 E., 161 S. From Mégantic, 8km twd golf club. From N.D. des Bois, Rtes 212 E., 161 N., 1km after golf course.

Nicole and Gérard Théberge
1137, Route 161
Lac-Mégantic G6B 2S1
tel/fax (819) 583-4900

B&B	
single	$50-60
double	$60-75

Open: May 1 to Oct. 31

Number of rooms	4
rooms in semi-basement	2
rooms with private bath	2
shared bathrooms	1

Activities: 🏛 🚣 🚶 🎣 🚴

20. LAC-MÉGANTIC

☀☀☀ | F | E | P | 🚭 | 🐕 | R4

B&B
LA MAISON BLANCHE

Tastefully decorated warm and cosy house, located in the town centre in a quiet residential neighbourhood near the lake, marina and restaurants. Our breakfasts are also very generous; guests benefit from air conditioning in summer.

From Sherbrooke Rte 161, left at 2nd light, Rue Maisonneuve, right on Rue Dollard. From Québec City or Woburn, cross downtown after railway, right on Rue Villeneuve, left on Dollard.

Noreen Kavanagh Legendre
4850, rue Dollard
Lac-Mégantic G6B 1G8
(819) 583-2665

B&B	
single	$60
double	$60

Reduced rates: after Thanksgiving
Open year round

Number of rooms	2
rooms with private bath	2

Activities: 🚤 🚣 🎣 🚴 🏃

21. LAC-MÉGANTIC

★★★ | F | E | P | ⊠

INN
MANOIR D'ORSENNENS

Built in 1891 on the lakeshore, the Manoir D'Orsennens was completely restored and expanded. It offers the comfort of a large hotel with the charm of a small inn, well-equiped rooms, excellent cuisine and a unique décor. Near numerous tourist attractions, guests are greeted with a warm welcome and personalized service. You will definitely want to come back! Packages available. 75km from St-George-de-Beauce, 100km from Sherbrooke. **See color photos.**

From Montréal or Sherbrooke, Hwy 10, Rtes 143 South, 108 East and 161 South. Cross the town, after the bridge, to the right.

Nathalie Michaud
3502, rue Agnès
Lac-Mégantic G6B 1L3
(819) 583-3515
toll free 1-877-583-3515
fax (819) 583-0308
manoirorsennens@
globetrotter.net

	B&B	MAP
single	$81-86	$106-111
double	$100-105	$150-155
triple	$128	$203
quad.	$152	$252
child	$15-20	$23-28

Taxes extra VS MC AM ER IT

Reduced rates: corporatives rates (1 pers.), 50% on the 11th night
Open year round

Number of rooms	12
rooms with private bath	12
shared wc	2

Activities: 🚣 🚶 🎣 🚴 🏃

22. MAGOG

For business or pleasure, for one night or more, come and get back to nature in the peacefulness of our warm, century-old house. Spacious rooms (for 1 to 4 people) with TV. Dining area with fridge and microwave oven at your disposal. Steps away from the town centre, lake and restaurants, and near all cultural and outdoor activities, including shows, cycling, hiking, golf, sailing and skiing, as well as vineyards.

Hwy 10, Exit 118, twd Magog. At the 2nd stop sign, turn left on McDonald and 2nd street right on Des Pins.

B&B
À LA MAISON DREW

Françoise Guézennec and
Michel Meyniel
206, rue des Pins
Magog J1X 2H9
tel/fax (819) 843-8480
www.bbcanada.
com/2700.html
lamaisondrew@sympatico.ca

B&B	
single	$70-85
double	$80-95
triple	$115
quad.	$135
child	$0-15

Taxes extra

Reduced rates: 15% Nov. 1 to May 15
Open year round

Number of rooms	4
rooms with private bath	4

Activities: ⛵ 🏌 🚶 🚲 🎿

23. MAGOG

Imagine an attentive innkeeper, with a house of Gothic Revival architecture in the heart of the village that is part of the heritage tour. We offer bright rooms with romantic names, healthy meals, a fireplace and piano, and welcome you in a warm atmosphere all year-round. Perfect for business meetings, vacations or anniversaries. Available for rent by the month, week or weekend. Welcome!

From Montreal, Hwy 10, Exit 118 twd Magog for 4km. Turn left at the 2nd stop, right on the 1st street, Rue Abbott.

B&B
À L'ANCESTRALE

Monique Poirier
200, rue Abbott
Magog J1X 2H5
tel/fax (819) 847-5555
toll free 1-888-847-5507
www.ancestrale.qc.ca
bbancestrale@hotmail.com

B&B	
single	$55-95
double	$65-105
triple	$85-125
child	$0-20

VS

Reduced rates: 20% 3 nights and more, Oct 1 to May 31
Open year round

Number of rooms	4
rooms with private bath	2
rooms with sink	2
shared wc	1
shared bathrooms	1

Activities: 🏊 🏇 🚗 🚲

24. MAGOG

Looking for a warm ambiance, in a century-old house with period decor, piano, fireplace, dream rooms and whirlpool bath? Then look no further. In the morning, you'll start your day with a lavish, varied breakfast, followed by summer/winter outdoor activities. Packages available—it's all here. Near the lake and the town centre, with the bike path right at our doorstep. Heartfelt welcome.

Hwy 10, Exit 118, Rte 141 South to Magog. At the McDonald's, turn left on Chemin Hatley. Keep left; 1st house on the headland.

B&B
AMOUR ET AMITIÉ

Nathalie and
Pascal Coulaudoux
600, ch. Hatley Ouest
Magog J1X 3G4
(819) 868-1945
toll free 1-888-244-1945
fax (819) 868-4475
www.bbcanada.com
/amouretamitie.html
amouretamitie@sympatico.ca

B&B	
single	$60-95
double	$70-100
triple	$75-115
quad.	$130-135
child	$0-15

Taxes extra

Reduced rates: 10% to 20% Oct. 15 to June 15, 3 nights and more and group
Open year round

Number of rooms	5
rooms with private bath	5

Activities: 🏛 ⛵ 🏌 🚲 🎿

25. MAGOG

☀☀☀☀☀ F E 🚗 P 🐕 R.1 TA

Awaiting you is our elegant Victorian home, its luxuriant yard, a warm atmosphere and gourmet breakfasts with international fine cuisine menus. Lounges, fireplace, sunroom, kitchenette. Within steps: majestic lake, dining, shops, cultural activities, bike path. 8km to Mt Orford park. Well-located to discover Township charms. Package-deals. Bikes to lend. A home away from home! **Ad on back cover.**

From Montréal or Sherbrooke, Hwy 10, Exit 118 twd Magog. After the Magog River, turn left at the flashing light. 3ʳᵈ house on the right.

B&B
À TOUT VENANT

Margaret McCulloch and Marc Grenier
624, rue Bellevue Ouest
Magog J1X 3H4
(819) 868-0419
toll free 1-888-611-5577
fax (819) 868-5115
www3.sympatico.ca
/atoutvenant
atoutvenant@sympatico.ca

B&B	
single	$62-67
double	$72-77
triple	$92-97
quad.	$112-117
child	$10-15

Taxes extra

Reduced rates: Sep.15 to June 15
Open year round

Number of rooms	5
rooms with private bath	5

Activities: 🏛 🍴 🚤 🚣 🎿

---

26. MAGOG

☀☀☀ F E 🚭 🚗 ✕ P 🐕 ♿ R.1 TA

Let yourself be won over by the warm, simple welcome that gives our hundred-year-old house genuine heart. High in originality and flavour, our breakfasts, prepared by a French pastry chef, are a feast for the eyes and the palate. "Cultural and gastronomic" tours to discover the region. Show or outdoor packages. Come share the pleasures that life affords us. **See colour photos.**

From Montreal or Sherbrooke, Hwy 10, Exit 118 to Magog, Rte 141, Rue Merry North. From Quebec City, Hwy 20 West, Hwy 55 South, Hwy 10 West, Exit 118 to Magog.

B&B
AU SAUT DU LIT

Lydia Paraskéva and
Patrick Bonnot
224, rue Merry Nord
Magog J1X 2E8
tel/fax (819) 847-3074
toll free 1-888-833-3074
www.bbcanada.
com/1557.html
ausautdulit@qc.aira.com

B&B	
single	$70-95
double	$80-95
child	$10-20

Taxes extra VS MC IT

Reduced rates: 3 nights and more, weekdays and low season
Open year round

Number of rooms	5
rooms with private bath	5

Activities: 🍴 🎿 🚲 🏃 🚣

---

27. MAGOG

☀☀☀☀ F E 🚭 🚗 P R.05

Pamper yourself in our warm, quiet, non-smoking Loyalist home, located near a historic church and all of Magog-Orford's cultural and outdoor activities. Cozy, inviting rooms illuminated by the cardinal points. Delicious five-course breakfast to delight athletes and epicureans. Bike shed. Show/cruise packages. Welcome.

Hwy 10, Exit 118 toward Magog for 3km, Rue Merry North. Before the church, turn left.

B&B
AU VIRAGE

Louise Vachon and Jean Barbès
172, rue Merry Nord
Magog J1X 2E8
(819) 868-5828
toll free 1-866-868-5828
fax (819) 868-6798
www.bbcanada.com/auvirage
barbesjean@sympatico.ca

B&B	
single	$60-90
double	$65-95

Taxes extra VS IT

Reduced rates: Oct. 15 to May 15
Open year round

Number of rooms	5
rooms with private bath	2
rooms with sink	3
shared wc	1
shared bathrooms	2

Activities: 🍴 🚤 🚣 🚲 🎿

28. MAGOG

Come enjoy a change of scenery and breathe in the fresh country air. Savour an unforgettable five-course breakfast by the fireside or a six-course country dinner on our terrace near the pool. After a walk through our flowery gardens, to the farmhouse or the stream, you will have but one desire: to come back! **Country-style dining p 16. See colour photos.**

From Montreal, Hwy 10, Exit 115 South-Magog/St-Benoît-du-Lac, drive 1.8km. Turn right on Chemin des Pères, twd St-Benoît-du-Lac/Austin. Continue for 6.1km.

INN
AUX JARDINS CHAMPÊTRES

Monique Dubuc and
Yvon Plourde
1575, ch. des Pères, R.R. 4
Magog J1X 5R9
(819) 868-0665
toll free 1-877-868-0665
fax (819) 868-6744
www.auxjardinschampetres.com
auxjardinschampetres
@qc.aira.com

	B&B	MAP
single	$70-90	$112-132
double	$76-96	$158-178
triple	$101-121	$225-245
child	$25	$45

Taxes extra VS MC IT

Open year round

Number of rooms	5
rooms with private bath	1
shared wc	1
shared bathrooms	2

Activities:

29. MAGOG

A place for rest and relaxation par *excellence!* Surrounded by hundred-year-old maple trees, our warm and inviting Victorian house will delight you. Unique decor, 5 rooms with fireplace and air-conditioning. Homestyle cuisine served in the solarium or on the terrace. Vast landscaped garden with spa. Limousine service in an antique car and boating excursions. Café Crème B&B is located two steps away from all the activities: Mont-Orford, the lake, shows, restaurants, etc. **See color photos.**

From Montréal, Hwy 10 East, Exit 118, twd Magog. 2nd stop sign, MacDonalds, left. 2nd street, turn right onto rue Des Pins.

B&B
CAFÉ CRÈME B&B

Annick and Christophe Balayer
235, rue des Pins
Magog J1X 2H8
(819) 868-7222
toll free 1-877-631-7222
fax (819) 868-0050
www.bbcafecreme.com
info@bbcafecreme.com

	B&B
single	$90-105
double	$90-105
child	$40

Taxes extra VS MC

Reduced rates: Nov. 1 to Jan. 31, 15% off, 2 nights and more.
Except for holidays
Open year round

Number of rooms	5
rooms with private bath	5

Activities:

30. MAGOG

Escape to the Eastern Townships! This warm 1880 house will delight you with its creature comforts, guaranteed peace and quiet and sublime breakfasts. Take a nap beneath the apple trees or discover the peacefulness of Lake Memphrémagog or, again, the bustle of the Main Street. **See colour photos.**

From Montréal or Sherbrooke, Hwy 10 Exit 118, twd Magog Rte 141, for 3km. At traffic light, turn left on St-Patrice West, then 1st left Rue Abbott.

B&B
LA BELLE ÉCHAPPÉE

Louise Fournier
145, rue Abbott
Magog J1X 2H4
tel/fax (819) 843-8061
toll free 1-877-843-8061
www.bbcanada.com/echappee
labelleechappee@qc.aira.com

	B&B
single	$45-75
double	$60-90
child	$15

VS MC

Reduced rates: Nov. 1to June 1
Open year round

Number of rooms	5
rooms with private bath	1
rooms with sink	2
shared bathrooms	2

Activities:

31. MAGOG

☀☀☀☀☀ F E 🚫 🐕 🚗 P R.3 TA

Near downtown and Lac Memphre-magog, a quintessential 19th-century Victorian house amidst magnificent gardens. Rustic interior adorned with unique hand-painted objects. Healthy gourmet breakfast, fireplace, bikes, garden spa. Gift certificate. Many packages: rest, massage, reflexology, 2-night co-cooning (Oct-May), ski. Nearby: water sports, fishing, vineyard, horseback riding. Winter discounts.

From Montreal, Hwy 10 East, Exit 118 to Magog, 3km. Opposite the church. From Quebec City, Hwy 20 West, Hwy 55 South, Hwy 10 West, Exit 118...

B&B
LA BELLE VICTORIENNE

Louise De Roy et Jean-Philippe Cambourieu
142, rue Merry Nord
Magog J1X 2E8
tel/fax (819) 847-0476
sans frais 1-888-440-0476
www.bellevic.com
info@bellevic.com

B&B	
single	$70-90
double	$75-95
triple	$115

Taxes extra VS

Reduced rates: 10% 3 nights or more, Nov. 1 to May 31, sunday to thursday
Open year round

Number of rooms	5
rooms with private bath	3
shared bathrooms	1

Activities: 🏊 🎣 🚲 ⛵ ⛷

32. MAGOG

☀☀☀☀☀ F E P 🚗 R.1 TA

Hike, cycle, bird watch or let us take you on our sailboat to discover one of our best kept secrets, Lake Mempremagog. In winter enjoy the Mt. Orford region in a sleigh, a dog sled or on skis. A warm welcome and all the comforts of home await you at La Maison Campbell. We hope our attractive rooms, our cozy fireplace, our café au lait and lovely home cooked breakfasts will make your stay here a memorable one. **Ad on back cover.**

From Mtl or Sherbrooke, Hwy 10, Exit 118 twd Magog. Pass over the Magog river turn left at the flashing yellow light, dir. Ayer's Cliff, keep to the right (becomes Bellevue Street).

B&B
LA MAISON CAMPBELL

Francine Guérin and Louise Hodder
584, rue Bellevue Ouest
Magog J1X 3H2
(819) 843-9000
sans frais 1-888-843-7707
fax (819) 843-3352
www.bbcanada.
com/2701.html
maisoncampbell@sympatico.ca

B&B	
single	$65-75
double	$70-80
child	$0-20

Taxes extra

Reduced rates: Oct. 15 to June 15
Open year round

Number of rooms	5
rooms with private bath	3
shared bathrooms	1

Activities: ⛵ 🚶 🚲 ⛷ 🐕

33. MAGOG

☀☀☀☀☀ F e 🚫 P 🏊 R.01 TA

Peaceful hundred-years-old house in the heart of Magog. Between the pool's clear refreshing water and the cosy fireplace, you will be pleasantly surprised by your attentive hosts' warm welcome. We will turn your dreams of such moments into reality. Package deals available (sports and culture). Near Lake Magog, bike path, downtown and mountain. **Ad on back cover**.

Hwy 10, Exit 118 twd Magog. Rue Merry Nord. After crossing the main street, you are on Rue Merry Sud. We are steps from McDonald's.

B&B
LE MANOIR DE LA RUE MERRY

Sylvie Goulet et Carmel Labbé
92, rue Merry Sud
Magog J1X 3L3
(819) 868-1860
sans frais 1-800-450-1860
www.bbcanada.
com/1560.html
labbejf@sympatico.ca

B&B	
single	$80
double	$80-90
triple	$100-110
quad.	$120-130
child	$20

Taxes extra VS MC IT

Reduced rates: mid-Oct. to mid-May
Open year round

Number of rooms	5
rooms with private bath	5

Activities: 🏊 🎣 🚲 ⛷ 🏃

34. MAGOG, ORFORD ☀☀☀ F

In the quiet of the forest, 5min from Magog, with all its attractions and the lake, the perfect place to relax, for a couple or family. Rooms with queen-size bed, private bathroom, TV. Dinner prepared by "head-chef" Éric. Refined, lavish breakfast. Cross-country skiing, horseback-riding trails, horse sleighs, stable. Nearby: ski resort, bike paths, Mont Orford park, theatre, art centre.

From Montreal, Hwy 10; or Quebec City, Hwy 20 and 55, Omerville Exit 123. At first light, turn right on St-Jacques West; at second stop, turn right on St-Michel and left at the end.

B&B
DOMAINE DE LA FORÊT

Marie-Evelyne Malatchoumy
935, rue St-Michel
Orford J1X 7H4
tel/fax (819) 847-2153
www.bbcanada.
com/domainedelaforet
domaine.de.la.foret
@sympatico.ca

Ope.

Number of rooms
rooms with private bath   I

Activities: 🛶 ⛵ 🚶 🚴 🎿

---

35. ORFORD ☀☀☀☀ F E 🏊 🐕 P R.5

Magnificient country home with rural charm, grange, wooden silo, and large property connected to a golf course. Cosy interior decor with fireplaces, pine accents, parquet floors and solariums. Well-kept rooms of superior comfort with private bathrooms, air conditioning, tv and VCR. Terrace, gardens, heated swimming pool. All this at Orford, between lakes and mountains, for a vacation with class. Gastronomical breakfast. **See coulor photos.**
From Montréal or Sherbrooke, Hwy 10 Exit 118 twd Orford. At the village exit, drive along the golf course. Right on Alfred-Desrochers, 500 m.

B&B
AUBERGE DE LA TOUR

May Brigitte Notari
1837, chemin
Alfred-Desrochers
Orford J1X 6J4
(819) 868-0763
fax (819) 868-4091
www.auberge-de-la-tour.com
franny@
auberge-de-la-tour.com

	B&B
single	$75
double	$85-95
triple	$110-120
child	$15

Taxes extra VS MC AM ER

Open year round

Number of rooms	4
rooms with private bath	4
shared wc	1

Activities: 🚣 🚶 🚴 🏃 🎿

---

36. ORFORD, BONSECOURS ✒ F e 🐕 ❌ P 🏊 R10 TA

Warm welcome. Quiet place for relaxation. Discretion guaranteed. Whether it's to bask in the sun or practise your favourite sports, you'll enjoy an enchanting setting surrounded by trees and greenery, and a splendid panoramic view of Mont Orford. The stay includes golfing, tennis, a swimming pool, a sauna, etc. **Ad end of the guide.**

From Montreal, Hwy 10, Exit 78. Rte 241 North, Rte 220 East. One mile past Lac Bowker, turn left on Chemin Simoneau.

B&B
LE VILLAGE

Robert Quevillon
220, ch. Simoneau,
C.P.26 Bonsecours
Orford J0E 1H0
(450) 532-4077
www3.sympatico.ca/village
village@sympatico.ca

	B&B	MAP
single	$45-90	$70-115
double	$65-110	$115-160
triple	$125	$200
quad.	$140	$240

VS MC

Reduced rates: 20% 3 nights and more
Open year round

Number of rooms	3
room with private bath	1
shared bathroom	1

Activities: 🚣 🚶 🏇 🎿

☀☀☀ | F | E | 🚫 | P | ✕ | TA

e heart of farming
are a Swiss family that
ere for 30 years. In our
staurant we serve Swiss
cooked meals and produce
e-made breads, jams and sau-
s. Take long quiet walks on the
00 acres of land surrounding our
inn. We look forward to meeting
you.

From Montréal, Champlain bridge,
Hwy 10 East, Exit 22 St-Jean-
sur-Richelieu. Hwy 35 South to Rte
133 South (30 min), brown house on
left. Or from US, Interstate 89 North
to Philipsburg, then Rte 133 North,
about 13km on the right.

INN
AUBERGE LA SUISSE

Dora and Roger Baertschi
119, Route 133
St-Pierre-de-Véronne-à-
Pike-River J0J 1P0
(450) 244-5870
fax (450) 244-5181
www.aubergelasuisse.com
reservations@
aubergelasuisse.com

B&B	
single	$55-65
double	$65-75
child	$30

Taxes extra VS MC AM IT

Reduced rates: Feb. 1 to Apr. 30
Open: Feb. 1to Dec. 31

Number of rooms	4
rooms with private bath	4

Activities: 🏛 🍂 👤 🚲 🐎

---

38. PIKE-RIVER

☀☀☀ | F | E | 🚫 | 🚗 | P | 🏊 | 🐕 | R2

One hour from Montréal and 10 min
from Vermont: on the riverbank, an
opulent, flowery B&B invites you for
a restful break in a cosy atmosphere. Hearty Swiss breakfast with
home-made bread and goods from
our farm. Bicycling tours. Near the
wildlife reserve, the Musée Missis-
quoi and the vineyards.

From Montréal, Champlain bridge.
Hwy 10 East, Exit 22 twd St-Jean,
Rte 35 South then Rte 133 twd St-
Pierre-de-Vérone-à-Pike-River. In the
curve, turn left on Chemin des Riviè-
res, 1.5km.

B&B
LA VILLA DES CHÊNES

Noëlle and Rolf Gasser
300, ch. Desrivières
Pike-River J0J 1P0
(450) 296-8848
fax (450) 296-4990

B&B	
single	$50-55
double	$60-75
child	$15

Reduced rates: 10% 3 nights
and more
Open: Feb. 1 to Nov. 30

Number of rooms	4
rooms with private bath	1
rooms in basement	1
shared bathrooms	2

Activities: 🏛 🚣 👤 🚲 🤸

---

39. ST-JOACHIM-DE-SHEFFORD

☀☀☀☀ | F | e | 🚫 | 🐕 | P | 🏊 | R10

On the La Campagnarde bike path,
a warm Canadian house with all
creature comforts: cozy beds, TV in
every room, central air conditioning,
fireplace. Hearty, varied breakfasts
with homemade products served in
the solarium, with a view of the
lake, in a flowery setting. Enjoy
walks on our forest trails, swimming or pedal-boating. Bikes at your
disposal, or a game of bowls...

Hwy 10, Exit 68, Boul. David-
Bouchard North, twd Granby. For
4km after Parc de la Yamaska, turn
left on Chemin Ingram.

B&B
LA BELLE AU BOIS DORMANT

Pauline et Marcel Labelle
623, ch. Ingram
St-Joachim-de-Shefford
J0E 2G0
(450) 539-4039
fax (450) 539-2296
belledormant@videotron.ca

B&B	
single	$55-65
double	$65-75

Open : June 1 to Oct. 31

Number of rooms	2
shared bathroom	1
shared wc	1

Activities: 🏛 👤 🚶 🍂 🚲

40. SHERBROOKE

☀☀☀ F E 🚭 🚗 P R.4

In the heart of a 19th-c. residential district, this superb Second Empire-style house transports you to Provence. A setting of warm coulours with soothing lavender scents. Pastis and olives offered as cokctails on the sun terrace in summer, by the fire in winter. Discover "the charms of the country in the city, the attractions of the city in the country".

From Montréal, Hwy 10. From Québec City, Hwy 20 and 55 Exit 140, Hwy 410 to Boul. Portland, then follow it for 4km. After the Domaine Howard park, turn left on Rue Québec.

B&B
CHARMES DE PROVENCE

Céline Desrosiers and
Alexis Rampin
350, rue du Québec
Sherbrooke J1H 3L8
(819) 348-1147
www.charmesdeprovence.com
charmesdeprovence
@videotron.ca

B&B	
single	$60
double	$75
triple	$100
quad.	$125
child	$15

Open year round

Number of rooms	3
shared wc	1
shared bathrooms	1

Activities: 🏛 🧍 🚶 🚲 ⛷

41. STANSTEAD

☀☀☀ F E 🚗 P R2.5

Dating from 1940, this residence is situated on one of the only border streets in North America. Everything is done to ensure you have a pleasant stay in our peaceful and relaxed environment. Delicious five-course breakfast are served. Located only 5min from Parc Weir (swimming and boat launch). Excursions on Lac Memphrémagog are possible and the property links up with a bike path. There's also a museum, opera house, antique shop and much more. See you soon!

From Montréal, Hwy 10 twd Sherbrooke, Exit 121. Hwy 55 twd Stantead. Vermont, Exit 1 Rte 247 twd Stantead (Beebe plain) 4.5km.

B&B
LA GRENOUILLÈRE DES
TROIS VILLAGES

Francyne and Serge Tougas
25, rue Canusa
Stanstead J0B 3E5
tel/fax (819) 876-5599
stougas@abacom.com

B&B	
single	$55-70
double	$60-75

Taxes extra VS MC AM

Open year round

Number of rooms	3
rooms with private bath	1
shared wc	1
shared bathrooms	1

Activities: 🏛 🛶 🧍 🚲 ⛷

42. WOTTON   `F` `P` `R5` `M4`

Cosy cottage with old-fashioned charm and magnificent view of the lakes. Activities include pedal-boats, canoeing, snowmobiling, hiking through forests and fields. Cross-country skiing, snowshoeing, golf and swimming close by. 4km from Asbestos.

From Montréal, Hwy 20 East, Exit 147. Rte 116 East to Danville, Rte 255 South to Wotton. 4km after crossing Rte 249, turn left on Route des Lacs, drive 2km.

COUNTRY HOME
LA MAISON DES LACS

Monique Mercier
28, chemin des Lacs
Wotton J0A 1N0
(819) 346-3575
pager (819) 573-9478
www.tourisme-cantons.qc.ca/
maisondeslacs

No.houses	1
No. rooms	5
No. people	10
WEEK-SUMMER	$600
WEEK-WINTER	$600
W/E-SUMMER	$300
W/E-WINTER	$300
DAY-SUMMER	$250
DAY-WINTER	$250

Open year round

Activities: 🏛 🐎 ⛷ 🛷 🏃

FARM ACTIVITIES

Farm Stays:

5 FERME AUBERGE D'ANDROMÈDE, Courcelles 48

8 LE CLOS DES PINS, Danville 48

Country-style Dining:

28 AUX JARDINS CHAMPÊTRES, Canton de Magog 16

47 LA CHÈVRERIE DES ACACIAS, Dunham 16

Regional Dining:

44 LES DÉPENDANCES DU MANOIR, Brigham 30

Farm Tour:

44 LES DÉPENDANCES DU MANOIR, Brigham 34

CENTRE-DU-QUÉBEC

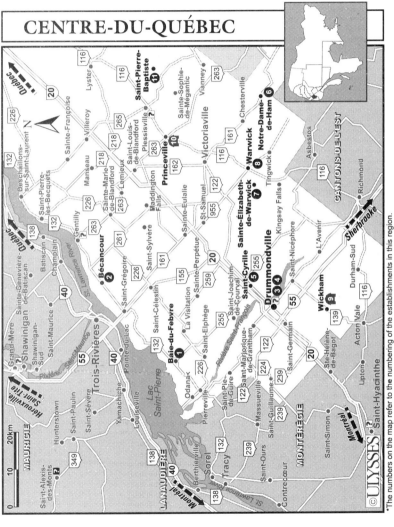

*The numbers on the map refer to the numbering of the establishments in this region.

1. BAIE-DU-FEBVRE

☀☀☀ F e 🚫 🚗 P ✕ R.02 TA

Bask in the charms of a 1920s cottage and revive the past from which the present is formed. For fine gourmets, our *table d'hôte* features local products. The shop offers lace and paper as well as local foodstuffs: pâtés, potted red-deer, goose and duck meat. Up-stairs, a painter offers his works. All passers-by, fill up on small plea-sures at our house, where we take care of every detail and provide every comfort and feasts for the eyes and the palate. **See color pho-tos.**

Hwy. 20, Exit 185, Rte. 255 twd Baie-du-Febvre.

B&B
GÎTE DE L'ARTISANERIE

Francyne and
Raymond Beausoleil
371, rue Principale
Baie-du-Febvre J0G 1A0
(450) 783-6469
fax (450) 783-6431
www.gite-artisanerie.com
gite@gite-artisanerie.com

B&B	
single	$40
double	$54
triple	$74
quad.	$94

VS

Open year round

Number of rooms	5
shared bathrooms	2
shared wc	2
rooms with sink	4

Activities: 👫 🚶 🚴 🛶 ⛷

2. BÉCANCOUR

☀☀☀☀ 🏠 F E ✕ P TA

We are renowned for our welcome, our food and our B&B inside a sumptuous Victorian house. We serve: ostrich, buffalo, caribou, venison, duck, rabbit, beef, seafood and perch. Refined local cuisine. Right nearby: canoeing, tennis, horseback riding, snowmobiling, swimming, fishing, tourist attrac-tions. Hablamos español.

From Montréal or Québec City, Hwy 40. In Trois-Rivières, cross the Laviolette bridge, Rte 132 East. Bécancour Exit. Rue Nicolas Perrot. We are next to the church.

INN
MANOIR BÉCANCOURT

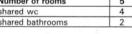

Yvon Beaulieu
3255, Nicolas Perrot
Bécancour G0X 1B0
(819) 294-9068
fax (819) 294-9060
www.bonjourquebec.
com/info/manoirbecancourt
manoirbecancourt
@hotmail.com

	B&B	MAP
single	$35-45	$55-65
double	$50-60	$90-100
child	$15	$35

Taxes extra VS MC

Reduced rates: week days
Open year round

Number of rooms	5
shared wc	4
shared bathrooms	2

Activities: 🏛 🍷 🚣 👫 🚴

3. DRUMMONDVILLE

☀☀☀ 🏠 F E 🚫 🚗 P ♿ 🏊 R1 TA

Prize for Excellence "Special favo-rite" Provincial 2000. "Experience the house from long ago, where both roses and children grow. "Our small" family (11) welcomes you to its table set with home-made bread and jams, fresh eggs, juice and aromatic coffee. Make yourself at home! Halfway between Montréal and Québec City, between Sherbrooke and Trois-Rivières.

Hwy 20, Exit 175 twd Drum-mondville (Boul. Lemire Sud), 300 m from Hwy 20.

B&B
LE GÎTE DES ROSES

Diane and Denis Lampron
215, boul. Lemire, R.R. #6
Drummondville J2C 7X2
(819) 474-4587
fax (819) 474-1500
www.bonjourquebec.
com/info/gitedesroses
info@rose.ca

B&B	
single	$40-60
double	$55-75
triple	$65-85
quad.	$75-95
child	$10

Open year round

Number of rooms	3
shared bathrooms	3
room with private bath	1

Activities: 🏛 🍷 🎿 👫 🚴

4. DRUMMONDVILLE

F E ♿ ✕ 🚗 🐕 P R5 TA

A continually well-kept B&B by the St-François River awaits you. Surrounded by woodlands, greenery and flowers, near a brook. Quiet nights. Complete, refined breakfast on the spot or in the house next door, on the same property. We are 12 minutes from the town centre. Meals upon request.

Hwy 20, Exit 55 twd Sherbrooke, then Rte 139 Exit twd St-Nicéphore. Go through the village twd the airport. Turn right and drive 1.2km.

B&B
MAISON LA COULÉE

Beldora and Daniel Roy
4890, boul. Allard
Drummondville J2B 6V3
(819) 477-4359
fax (819) 477-0672
www.quebecweb.
com/lacoulee/
daniel.roy@dr.cgocable.ca

	B&B	MAP
single	$45-75	$60-90
double	$60-80	$90-110
triple	$110-130	$155-175
child	$10-20	on request

Open year round

Number of rooms	5
rooms with private bath	2
rooms with sink	2
shared bathrooms	2

Activities: 🏛 🍴 🚣 🚶 🚴

5. DRUMMONDVILLE, ST-CYRILLE

☀☀ F e 🚭 P 🐕 R2

Halfway between Montreal and Québec City, 5km from Drummondville. Amidst vast spaces, trees, flowers, water gardens and waterfall. Non-smoking B&B with fireplace and air conditioning. Healthy homemade breakfasts. 4km from Village d'Antan and Légendes Fantastiques, local festivals, health clinic, cross-country skiing and bike path.

Hwy 20, Exit 185, 2km. At the church, turn right on Rte 122, continue for 1km.

B&B
OASIS

Johanna Putzke Beier
3500, Route 122
St-Cyrille-de-Wendover
J1Z 1C3
(819) 397-2917

B&B	
single	$35
double	$45-60
child	$0-10

Reduced rates: 20% 3 nights and more
Open year round

Number of rooms	3
rooms with private bath	1
rooms with sink	1
shared bathrooms	1

Activities: 🍴 🚶 🚴 🐎 🏃

6. NOTRE-DAME-DE-HAM

☀☀☀ F E 🚭 P 🐕 R5

In the heart of the majestic Appalachians, our Victorian house is similar in style to our New England neighbours: antique furniture, warm atmosphere, Swiss-like landscapes. Our knowledge of local history is much appreciated by guests. Our little anecdotes are amusing, and sometimes hard to believe, but we assure they are true!

Jean-Lesage Hwy 20 twd Québec City, Exit 210. At Victoriaville, twd Musée Laurier or S.Q., Boul. Laurier South, Rte 161 South. Notre-Dame-de-Ham, 26km.

B&B
LE GÎTE J.D. TROTTIER

Jeanne D. Trottier
37, rue Principale
Notre-Dame-de-Ham G0P 1C0
tel/fax (819) 344-5640
jdarc@boisfrancs.qc.ca

B&B	
single	$40
double	$55
triple	$70
child	$12

VS MC

Open year round

Number of rooms	3
shared bathrooms	2

Activities: 🏛 🍴 🚶 🚴 🏃

7. STE-ÉLIZABETH-DE-WARWICK ☀☀☀ F e 🏠🚗 P R6 TA

Enjoy the relaxing wide expanses and the quiet countryside. Kitchen garden, orchard and flower gardens surround our home. For more action less than 6 kilometres away, bike along the country road (110km) or enjoy yourselves at the Grands-Chênes theatre in Kingsey Falls. Tempted? Pack your bags, we await you! Packages: cycling, canoeing, theatre.

Hwy 20, Exit 210. Rte 955 to St-Albert, follow signs for Warwick, turn right on 4e Rang, 6km. After the village of Ste-Élizabeth, left on Rte Mondoux, drive 1.5km.

B&B
LE PETIT BALUCHON

Maude, Marie-France and
Jean-René Dumas
305, route Mondoux
Ste-Élizabeth-de-Warwick
J0A 1M0
(819) 358-2406
www.bbcanada.
com/3452.html

B&B	
single	$45
double	$65
child	$10-15

Taxes extra

Open year round

Number of rooms	5
shared bathrooms	2

Activities: 🏛 🍴 🧍 🚲 🐎

8. WARWICK ☀☀☀ F 🐕 P R.5 TA

Located in the heart of Warwick, our bed and breakfast borders on several kilometres of bike paths and snowmobile trails. Also right nearby: golfing, skiing, summer theatre and various festivals. All our rooms have a private bathroom. Upon waking up, the aroma of breakfast beckons you upstairs. Cyclists, snowmobilers and drivers, our home is your home.

Hwy 20, Exit 210, Rte. 122 East, St-Albert, twd Warwick.

B&B
GÎTE LA TOURELLE

Solange Nault
91, rue St-Louis
Warwick J0A 1M0
(819) 358-9555

B&B	
single	$40
double	$50
child	$5

Open year round

Number of rooms	5
rooms in basement	5
rooms with private bath	5

Activities: 🧍 🍴 🚶 🚲 🏃

9. WICKHAM ☀☀☀ F e P ❌ R2.5 TA

A small farm that combines gardens, woodlands and old buildings. Share good times and relaxation in a vast country setting. Spend the night in a cozy bed. Two comfortable rooms in which to sleep, snore and, above all, dream. Dinner by reservation. Many activities nearby. 2km from the "La Campagnarde" bike path. **Country-style Dining p 17, Farm Stay p 49.**

From Montreal, Hwy 20 East, Exit 157 twd Wickham. About 7km past the village of St-Nazaire twd Wickham, turn left on Rte 139. Turn left at the church, drive 1.8km.

B&B
LA FERME DE LA BERCEUSE

Robin Fortin and Réjean Forget
548, Rang 10
Wickham J0C 1S0
(819) 398-6229
(819) 398-6411
fax (819) 398-6496

	B&B	MAP
single	$55	$70
double	$60	$90
Enfant	$9	$15

Taxes extra IT

Open: Mar. 31 to Dec. 23

Number of rooms	2
shared bathroom	1
salle d'eau partagée	1

Activities: 🍴 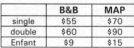 🧍 🚲 🐎

10. PRINCEVILLE

F e 🐕 🚗 P R3 M

Heidi and her grandfather knew about the richness of wide expanses, the beauty of nature. The peace and comfort of "Paradis d'Émy" also makes us embrace nature again. A stone's throw from the farm are the pleasures of skiing, golfing, cycling, snowmobiling. This cozy paradise is a dream come true! **Country home on a farm p 56.**

Between Québec City and Montréal. Hwy 20, Exit 235, for Princeville. Rte 263 South. Drive 15km, turn left on Rang 7 Est. From Rte 116 in Princeville, take the 263 North, 3km, first right onto Rang 7 Est.

COUNTRY HOME
AU PARADIS D'ÉMY

Joceline Desfossés and Normand Jutras
7, Rang 7 Est
Princeville G6L 4C2
(819) 364-2840
fax (819) 364-5426
www.boisfrancs.qc.ca/~emy1
emy1@boisfrancs.qc.ca

No. houses	1
No. rooms	4
No. people	2-14
WEEK-SUMMER	$350-1022
WEEK-WINTER	$350-1022
W/E-SUMMER	$130-370
W/E-WINTER	$130-370
DAY-SUMMER	$75-195
DAY-WINTER	$75-195

Taxes extra

Open year round

Activities: 🐚 🚣 🚶 🏇 🐎.

11. ST-PIERRE-BAPTISTE

F e ♿ 🐕 P 🏊 R6 M6

Lovely house in the Appalachian foothills: natural wood and brick interior. During the cold season, a crackling fire awaits you. Handwoven bedding and rugs. All necessary cooking equipment, 2 bathrooms. On the farm: trails, cross-country skiing, small animals. Nearby: snowmobile trails, swimming at the falls.

From Montréal Hwy 20, Exit 228, from Québec City, Exit 253 to Thetford Mines. Drive 11km past Plessisville, turn left on St-Pierre-Baptiste for 4km. Left at the church 100 m, right on Route Roy; drive 5km. Right Gîte Domaine des Pins.

COUNTRY HOME
DOMAINE DES PINS

Danielle Pelletier and Yvon Gingras
2108, rang Scott
St-Pierre-Baptiste G0P 1K0
(418) 453-2088
fax (418) 453-2760
www.domaine.qc.ca

No. houses	1
No rooms	5
No. people	2-15
WEEK-SUMMER	$325-475
WEEK-WINTER	$400-500
W/E-SUMMER	$250-325
W/E-WINTER	$350
DAY-SUMMER	$250
DAY-WINTER	$275

Taxes extra

Open year round

Activities: 🏛 🐚 🚣 🚶 🛷

FARM ACTIVITIES

Farm Stay:

9 LA FERME DE LA BERCEUSE, Wickham 49

Country-style Dinning :

9 LA FERME DE LA BERCEUSE, Wickham 17

Country home on a farm :

10 AU PARADIS D'ÉMY, Princeville 56

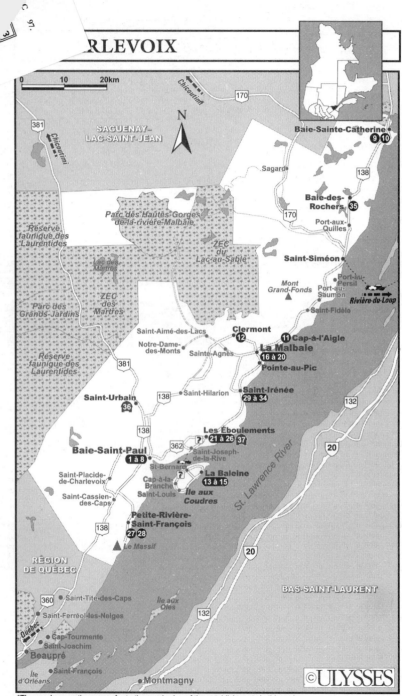

RLEVOIX

0   10   20km

SAGUENAY–LAC-SAINT-JEAN

Chicoutimi

170

381

Chicoutimi

N

Baie-Sainte-Catherine
9 10

Sagard

138

170

Parc des Hautes-Gorges-de-la-rivière-Malbaie

Baie-des-Rochers 35

Port-aux-Quilles

Réserve faunique des Laurentides

ZEC du Lac-au-Sable

Lac des Martres

Saint-Siméon

ZEC des Martres

Mont Grand-Fonds

Port-au-Persil

Port-au-Saumon

Rivière-du-Loup

Parc des Grands-Jardins

Saint-Fidèle

Réserve faunique des Laurentides

Saint-Aimé-des-Lacs

Clermont 12

11 Cap-à-l'Aigle

Notre-Dame-des-Monts

Sainte-Agnès

La Malbaie
16 à 20

381

Pointe-au-Pic

138

Saint-Hilarion

Saint-Irénée
29 à 34

Saint-Urbain
36

132

138

Les Éboulements
? 21 à 26 37

362

Saint-Joseph-de-la-Rive

20

Baie-Saint-Paul
1 à 8

St-Bernard

Saint-Placide-de-Charlevoix

Cap-à-la-Branche

La Baleine
13 à 15

?

Saint-Louis

Île aux Coudres

Saint-Cassien-des-Caps

St. Lawrence River

Petite-Rivière-Saint-François
27 28

138

RÉGION DE QUÉBEC

Le Massif

20

BAS-SAINT-LAURENT

360

Saint-Tite-des-Caps

Île aux Oies

132

Saint-Ferréol-les-Neiges

Québec

Cap-Tourmente

Saint-Joachim

Beaupré

Saint-François

Île d'Orléans

Montmagny

©ULYSSES

*The numbers on the map refer to the numbering of the establishments in this region.

1. BAIE-ST-PAUL

☀☀☀☀ | F | E | 🚭 | 🐕 | P | 🚗 | 🏊 | R.2

An old, colourful house in the heart of artistic Baie-St-Paul. Woodwork, lace, duvet. Wood-burning stove for chilly mornings. Piano, reading room. Terraces and flowery gardens looking out onto the countryside, mountains and the magical seasons. Local and homemade goods at breakfast. Access to kitchen. Packages: skiing, whale-watching, music.

From Québec City, Rte 138 East, 100km. In Baie-St-Paul, Rte 362 East. At the church, turn right on Rue Ste-Anne. At the fork, blue house on the right.

B&B
À LA CHOUETTE

Ginette Guérette and
François Rivard
2, rue Leblanc
Baie-St-Paul G3Z 1W9
(418) 435-3217
www.inns-bb.com/chouette

B&B	
single	$70-75
double	$80-85
triple	$95
child	$5-10

Reduced rates: Apr. 16 to May 17, Oct. 22 to Dec. 22
Open year round

Number of rooms	4
rooms with private bath	4

Activities: 🏛 🛶 🎿 🏂 🏃

---

2. BAIE-ST-PAUL

★★★ | F | e | 🚭 | 🐕 | P | 🚗 | ✕ | TA

Peace, serenity, soft music, hospitality and fine food. A Victorian house with centenary charm nestled beneath the maples in the heart of the village. Fireplace, terrace and garden. Near shops, the Massif and a host of activities, parks, golf, casino, cruise... In summer, MAP plan only. **See colour photos.**

100km from Québec City twd Ste-Anne-de-Beaupré, Rte 138 E. At Baie-St-Paul, Rte 362 E. At church, left on Rue St-Jean-Baptiste. Or from La Malbaie, Rtes 138 or 362 West.

INN
AUBERGE LA MUSE

Evelyne Tremblay and
Robert Arsenault
39, rue St-Jean-Baptiste
Baie-St-Paul, G3Z 1M3
(418) 435-6839
fax (418) 435-6289
toll free 1-800-841-6839
www.lamuse.com
lamuse@charlevoix.net

	B&B	MAP
single	$80-130	$103-153
double	$90-140	$137-187
triple	$120-140	$187 207
quad.	$160	$247
child	$10-20	$25-35

Taxes extra VS MC ER IT

Reduced rates: Apr. 16 to June 15 and Sept. 4 to Feb. 9, except Christmas holidays
Open year round

Number of rooms	12
rooms with private bath	12

Activities: 🏛 🎣 🎿 🏂 🏃

---

3. BAIE-ST-PAUL

☀☀☀ | F | e | 🚭 | 🐕 | P | 🚗 | R.5

Located on one of the most picturesque streets in town, our 100-year-old house, whose garden extends to the Gouffre River, is yours to appreciate. Steps away from good restaurants, art galleries, shops and the exhibition centre. 15 min from "Au Massif de Petite Rivière St-François" ski resort. Hearty breakfasts await.

From Québec City, twd Ste-Anne-de-Beaupré, Rte 138 East, 100km. In Baie-St-Paul, Rte 362 East. At the church, cross the bridge, 1st street on the right.

B&B
AU CLOCHETON

Johanne et Laurette Robin
50, rue St-Joseph
Baie-St-Paul G3Z 1H7
(418) 435-3393
toll free 1-877-435-3393
fax (418) 435-6432
www.quebecweb.com/
gpc/auclocheton

B&B	
single	$45-65
double	$60-80
triple	$80-95
quad.	$110
child	$10-15

MC

Reduced rates: Apr. 2 to May 13, Oct.15 to Dec. 20
Open year round

Number of rooms	4
rooms with sink	4
rooms with private bath	1
shared bathrooms	1

Activities: 🏛 🎣 🎿 🏂 🏃

28 i 29 juin

4. BAIE-ST-PAUL ☀☀☀☀ F E 🚗 P 🐕 R3.5

Come discover one of the loveliest places in Charlevoix! Perched on the mountainside, we offer an exceptional view of the St-Lawrence River, in a peaceful environment... Rooms with panoramic view, private entrance and terrace. Varied, regionally flavoured home-style breakfast. Massif ski package. Located 5min from downtown. Be sure to check out our Web site!

In Baie-St-Paul, Rte 362 East for 3km. At the "Au Perchoir" sign, turn right on Chemin Cap-aux-Rets. After the cross, second house on the left.

B&B
AU PERCHOIR

Jacinthe Tremblay
and Réjean Thériault
443, ch. Cap-aux-Rets
Baie-St-Paul G3Z 1C1
tel/fax (418) 435-6955
www.quebecweb.
com/perchoir
perchoir@sympatico.ca

B&B	
single	$80-105
double	$85-110
triple	$100-125
quad.	$115-140
child	$10-15

Taxes extra VS

Reduced rates: Oct.15 to May 17
Open year round

Number of rooms	3
rooms with private bath	3

Activities: 🏛 ⚘ 🚶 🚴 🎿

---

5. BAIE-ST-PAUL F e 🚗 P R.1 TA

In the heart of tourist activities, away from the hustle and bustle but just steps from art galleries and restaurants, and 15min from the Massif, our house has retained its charm of yesteryear, with its high ceilings and large balcony. Our rooms are decorated in art-related themes. Queen-size beds. Gourmet breakfast by the fire place or on the terrace in summer. Communal living room. Large meeting room available.

From Quebec City, Rte 138 East. In Baie-St-Paul, Rte 362, across from the hospital.

INN
AUX PETITS OISEAUX

Danielle Trussart and
Jacques Roussel
30, boul. Fafard, rte 362
Baie-St-Paul G3Z 2J4
tel/fax (418) 435-3888
toll free 1-877-435-3888
www.quebecweb.com/oiseaux
trussel@charlevoix.net

B&B	
single	$70-95
double	$75-100
triple	$100-115
child	$10

Taxes extra

Reduced rates: Oct. 15 to Dec. 20
Apr. 15 to June 20
Open year round

Number of rooms	7
rooms with private bath	7

Activities: 🏛 ⚘ 🚶 🏊 🏃

---

6. BAIE-ST-PAUL ☀☀☀☀ F E 🐕 🚗 P R2 TA

This 200-year-old house was renowned for its hospitality towards homeless people, and it has kept its shelter charm and vocation. Wake up to the smell of a crackling fire and enjoy a copious breakfast with regional accents. Our home has a lavishly decorated interior. In the rooms, queen-size beds, view of the St. Lawrence River and L'Îsle aux Coudres. Packages and group rates. Near the Massif ski resort. Come visit us!

From Québec City, Rte 138 East. At the tourist info. bureau before Baie-St-Paul, turn right, follow St-Antoine S. at left. Drive 500m, 1st street on right.

B&B
GÎTE LE NOBLE QUÊTEUX

Marie Lou Jacques and
Claude Marin
8, ch. Côte-du-Quêteux
rang St-Antoine Sud
Baie-St-Paul G3Z 2C7
(418) 240-2352
fax (418) 240-2377
www.charlevoix.qc.ca
/noblequeteux
queteux@charlevoix.net

B&B	
single	$60-70
double	$65-75
triple	$80-90
quad.	$95-105

Reduced rates: Nov.1 to Dec. 10,
Apr. 20 to May 11
Open year round

Number of rooms	5
rooms with private bath	2
shared bathrooms	1

Activities: 🏛 ⛷ ⛷ 🏊 🐎

7. BAIE-ST-PAUL

☀☀☀☀ | F | E | 🚭 | P | R.2 | TA

Come discover a prestigious bed and breakfast in the heart of Baie-St-Paul that combines plush comfort and the elegance of houses of yore, with its many rooms, large windows, woodwork, furniture, colours and *objets d'art*. Charming rooms, king/queen-size beds, flowery garden and terrace. Lavish breakfast featuring regional products. A 5min walk from galleries and restaurants; 15min from the Massif.

From Quebec City, Rte 138 East. In Baie-St-Paul, Rte 362 East. At the church, turn right on Rue Ste-Anne.

B&B
GÎTE LES COLIBRIS

Lise Rousseau and
Marc Skinner
80, rue Ste-Anne
Baie-St-Paul G3Z 1P3
(418) 240-2222
toll free 1-888-508-4483
www.charlevoix.net/lescolibris
colibris@charlevoix.net

B&B	
single	$69-100
double	$85-115

Taxes extra VS MC IT

Reduced rates : Nov. 1 to Apr. 30
Open year round

Number of rooms	5
shared bathroom	1
shared wc	1
rooms with sink	2
rooms with private bath	3

Activities: 🏛 🛷 🚶 ⛷ 🎿

8. BAIE-ST-PAUL

☀☀☀ | F | E | 🚭 | P | 🚗 | R.1 | TA

A must for art-lovers, just steps away from the best restaurants, shops, galleries and cultural activities in Baie-St-Paul. Early-20th-century art bed and breakfast with alcove for young people, two living room, fireplace, piano and world music ambiance. Homemade breakfast prepared from regional products. Permanent art exhibition.

From Quebec City, Rte 138 East. In Baie-St-Paul, Rte 362 East. At the church, turn right on Rue Ste-Anne.

B&B
L'ARTOÏT

Jean Perron
50, rue Ste-Anne
Baie-St-Paul G3Z 1P2
(418) 435-4091
fax (418) 240-2813
www.artoit.com
artoit@qc.aira.com

B&B	
single	$50
double	$60
child	on request

Reduced rates: Nov.1 to Dec. 20
Open year round

Number of rooms	3
alcove (child)	1
shared bathrooms	1

Activities: 🏛 🚶 ⛷ 🎿 🍂

9. BAIE-STE-CATHERINE

☀☀☀ | F | e | 🚭 | 🚗 | P | 🐕 | ❌ | R1 | TA

Now swept away by the fury of the waves, now enchanted by the tranquillity of the woods, N.-D. de l'Espace watches over the secret world of whales and our village. Anne-Marie's table d'hôte, regional home cooking. Dogsled, cruise tickets. Prize for Excellence "Special Favorite" Regional 1994-95.

From Québec City, Rte 138 East twd La Malbaie. At bridge, twd Tadoussac. At Baie-Ste-Catherine, watch for blue tourist sign, drive 1km. From Tadoussac, 4km.

B&B
ENTRE MER ET MONTS

Anne-Marie and Réal Savard
476, Route 138
Baie-Ste-Catherine G0T 1A0
(418) 237-4391
fax (418) 237-4252
www.fjord-best.com/entre-
mer-et-monts
entre-mer-et-monts@
fjord-best.com

	B&B	MAP
single	$35-40	$50-55
double	$45-50	$75-80
triple	$65-70	$110-115
child	$15-20	$27.50-30

VS MC

Reduced rates: Nov. 1 to May 31
Open year round

Number of rooms	5
rooms with sink	3
rooms in basement	3
shared wc	1
shared bathrooms	2

Activities: 🛷 🚶 🚶 🚜 🐎

10. BAIE-STE-CATHERINE

☀☀ F 🚗 P 🏊 R.5 TA

Beautifully located in a magnificent bay, near a little church at the heart of a peaceful village, come and immerse yourself in the beautiful countryside. Discover the beauty of the sea. Far from the noise of Rte 138 for peaceful and restful nights. Rooms on the main floor or in the basement. Boat cruise tickets for sale.

From Québec City, Rte 138 E. twd Tadoussac. From the Baie-Ste-Catherine "Bienvenue" (welcome) sign, drive 4km. First road on the left. Watch for the provincial sign on Rte 138.

B&B
GÎTE DU CAPITAINE

Etiennette and Benoit Imbeault
343, rue Leclerc
Baie-Ste-Catherine G0T 1A0
(418) 237-4320
(418) 237-4359

B&B	
single	$40
double	$50
triple	$70
quad.	$90
child	$15-20

VS

Open: May 1 to Oct. 31

Number of rooms	5
rooms in basement	2
shared bathrooms	2

Activities: 🏛 🎿 🚤 🎿 🐎

11. CAP-À-L'AIGLE

★★ F e ✕ 🚗 P TA

The Petite Plaisance inn is a country house from the last century, where life is in harmony with nature and the seasons. Its six charming rooms retain all the charm of the past. A feast for the senses, its table offers all the colours and freshness of simple cuisine with a personal touch. In the heart of Cap-à-l'Aigle, nestled near the peaceful St-Lawrence River, Petite Plaisance encourages you to sample all the essential luxuries! Golf and ski packages. Gift certificates.

From Quebec City, Rte. 138 East twd La Malbaie, Leclerc bridge via Cap-à-l'Aigle.

INN
AUBERGE PETITE PLAISANCE

Bruno McNicoll
310, rue St-Raphaël
Cap-à-l'Aigle G5A 2N7
(418) 665-2653
fax (418) 665-4666
www.quebecweb.
com/petiteplaisance

	B&B	MAP
single	$65	$95
double	$85	$135
triple	$100	$175
child	$15	$25

Taxes extra VS MC

Open year round

Number of rooms	6
room with private bath	1
shared bathrooms	3
shared wc	1

Activities: 🎿 🚴 🎿 🐕

12. CLERMONT

☀☀☀ F e P R1

In the heart of Charlevoix, you will experience a personal warmth and hospitality, as well as our fondness for the country. In the comfort of our large home, your history will fascinate us while ours will enchant you. Come and relax in the gentle warmth of our company.

From Québec City, Rte 138 E. drive 130km to Clermont. From La Malbaie, Rte 138 W., drive 7km to Clermont.

B&B
LA MAISON GAUDREAULT

Jeannine and Antonio
230, boul. Notre-Dame
Route 138
Clermont G4A 1E9
(418) 439-4149
antonio.gaudreault
@sympatico.ca

B&B	
single	$40
double	$50
child	$0-15

Open year round

Number of rooms	5
shared bathrooms	2

Activities: 🏛 🎿 🎿 🚴 🐎

13. ISLE-AUX-COUDRES

☀☀☀ F e 🚗 P R2

Large, peaceful, beautiful and welcoming house where your hosts Rita and Vincent offer you warm hearts and good food. Steps from the river and near cultural and tourist activities. Let yourself be soothed and pampered by the rhythm of the tides in a unique setting.

From Québec City, Rte 138 E. twd Baie-St-Paul. Rte 362 to St-Joseph-de-la-Rive ferry. On the island, left at stop sign, drive 3km.

B&B
GÎTE LA MAISON BLANCHE

Rita and Vincent Laurin
232, rue Royale Est, C.P. 238
Isle-aux-Coudres G0A 3J0
(418) 438-2883

B&B	
single	$50
double	$70

Reduced rates: Oct. 15 to June 15
Open year round

Number of rooms	5
rooms with private bath	1
rooms with sink	4
shared wc	2
shared bathrooms	2

Activities: 🛥 🛶 🏃 🚲 🤸

14. ISLE-AUX-COUDRES

☀☀☀ F 🚗 P R2 TA

Prize for Excellence "Special Favorite" Regional 1997-98. Let yourselves be pampered and charmed by Uncle Wilfrid's house, where we can chitchat in a setting redolent of yesteryear. Cycling, walks, browsing handicraft shops and other activities... will help you digest Isle-aux-Coudriers' typical dish «le p'tit pâté croche».

From Québec City, Rte 138 E. twd Baie-St-Paul. Rte 362 to the ferry. On the island, straight ahead after the stop for 3km, turn right at the 2nd stop, drive 2km.

B&B
GÎTE LA RIVERAINE

Lise Dufour
6, rue Principale
La Baleine, Isle-aux-Coudres
G0A 2A0
(418) 438-2831

B&B	
single	$40-55
double	$55-65
child	$10

Open: May 1 to Oct. 31

Number of rooms	5
rooms with private bath	1
rooms with sink	4
shared bathrooms	2

Activities: 🐚 🛥 🚲 🛶 🤸

15. ISLE-AUX-COUDRES

☀☀☀ F e P 🚗 🐕 R1 TA

Away from the bustle of the city, on an enchanting island. As if time had stopped. Wake up to birds chirping and breakfast on the terrace. Relaxing, large, sunny and flowered living-room.

From Québec City, Rte 138 E. twd Baie-St-Paul. Rte 362 to St-Joseph-de-la-Rive ferry. On the island, right at flashing light, 10km. 500 ft after St-Louis church.

B&B
VILLA DU MOULIN

Louise F. Belley
252, chemin des Moulins
Isle-aux-Coudres G0A 1X0
(418) 438-2649
(418) 665-6126
toll free 1-888-824-6263
www.quebecinformation.com/
villa-du-moulin
villadumoulin@hotmail.com

B&B	
single	$40
double	$55
triple	$75
quad.	$90
child	$10

Open: Apr. 1 to Oct. 31

Number of rooms	5
shared bathrooms	2

Activities: 🏛 🐚 🛥 🛶 🚲

16. LA MALBAIE

★★★ F E ♿ 🚗 P R.2 TA

The very warm, personalized welcome that awaits you here will make your stay a memorable and extraordinarily relaxing one. Whether you're looking for a room with a river view, with a canopy bed and private balcony or with a fireplace and whirlpool bath, we are sure to meet your needs. We offer a hearty, buffet-style breakfast served with care and imagination. Many activities nearby. **See colour photos.**

From Quebec City, twd Ste-Anne-de-Beaupré, Rte 138 East twd La Malbaie, the Casino and Manoir Richelieu.

INN
AUBERGE LA ROMANCE

Louisette and André Pilotte
415, ch. des Falaises
La Malbaie G5A 2V4
(418) 665-4865
fax (418) 665-4954
www.aubergelaromance.com
romance@cite.net

B&B	
single	$129-179
double	$139-189
triple	$164-219
quad.	$199-249
child	$ 25

Taxes extra VS MC AM ER IT

Reduced rates: Dec.1 to June 22 and Sept. 5 to Nov. 30, sunday to thursday, except for holidays
Open year round

Number of rooms	8
rooms with private bath	8

Activities: 🏛 ⛷ 🚶 🚲 🛶

17. LA MALBAIE

☀☀☀ F E 🚗 P 🏊 R4.5 TA

In the mood to hit the casino? It's only 130 seconds away! How about mountains, lakes and attractions? They are all near our residence, where guests are always warmly greeted in a quiet, enchanting setting. Welcome.

Rtes 138 or 362, by the river, the street before or after traffic light at the shopping centre, turn on Rue Laure-Conan and it's the 3rd house on the right.

B&B
GÎTE E.T. HARVEY

Etudienne Tremblay and
Jacques Harvey
19, rue Laure-Conan
La Malbaie, Pointe-au-Pic
G5A 1H8
tel/fax (418) 665-2779
www.bbcanada.
com/2779.html

B&B	
single	$42
double	$47-55
triple	$62-70
child	$15

Reduced rates: 3 nights or more from Oct. 30 to Apr. 30
Open year round

Number of rooms	4
rooms in basement	1
shared wc	1
shared bathrooms	1

Activities: 🏛 🚲 ⛷ 🎿 🐎

18. LA MALBAIE

☀☀☀ F e 🚗 P 🏊 R.5 TA

Our B&B offers rest and relaxation, with its flowery garden, indoor and outdoor fireplaces, outdoor spa, 2-person therapeutic bath, soundproof rooms, TV, small lounge, front and back balconies with view of the river. Not to mention the delicious breakfasts, from orange crepes to Yvonne's brioches.

2km from the casino. Rte 138 E. twd La Malbaie 1st street on your right after the tourist office then left on Rue Laure-Conan. Or Rte 362 to La Malbaie, 2nd street after shopping centre. Left side.

B&B
LA MAISON
DUFOUR-BOUCHARD

Micheline Dufour
18, rue Laure-Conan
La Malbaie G5A 1H8
(418) 665-4982
fax (418) 665-4945
www.charlevoix.qc.ca/
maisondufourbouchard

B&B	
single	$35-45
double	$45-55
triple	$60-70
quad.	$80-85
child	$5-15

Open year round

Number of rooms	4
shared bathrooms	2

Activities: 🛶 🚤 ⛷ 🐎 🚣

19. LA MALBAIE

★ ★ F E ⊘ 🚗 P R1 TA

The ancestral Eau Berge house faces the river and welcomes you with its unique decor. The rooms are particulary comfortable and inviting. Choice of healthy breakfast, or otherwise! Come and be refreshed. Close to the casino and other activities. See you soon.

From Québec City, twd Ste-Anne-de-Beaupré, Rte 138 E. twd La Malbaie. At the traffic lights of the bridge, continue straight. 500m from the shopping centre. On the right across from the "Irving". Or Rte 362 to Pointe-au-Pic, staight beside the river, on the boulevard du Fleuve, at the "Irving" on the left.

INN
L'EAU BERGE

Claudette Dessureault
315, boul. De Comporté
La Malbaie G5A 2Y6
(418) 665-3003
fax (418) 665-2480
www.quebecweb.
com/leauberge

B&B	
single	$65-100
double	$69-110
triple	$90-125
quad.	$145

Taxes extra VS MC

Open : Jan. 20 to Nov. 17

Number of rooms	7
room with sink	1
rooms with private bath	2
shared wc	1
shared bathrooms	2

Activities: 🏛 ⛵ 🛥 🎿 🚶

20. LA MALBAIE, POINTE-AU-PIC

☀☀☀☀ F E 🦌 P 🚗 R.5 TA

Prize for Excellence "Special Favorite" Regional 2000 and 1995-96. Come enjoy peace and comfort in a warm and cozy Austrian house overlooking the winding St. Lawrence River and away from the main road, designed with you in mind. Private entrance, fireplace, balcony, terraces, flowery gardens and varied breakfasts! In the midst of activities, 5 min from the casino.

Québec City, Rte 138 E to La Malbaie. Leclerc bridge: Rte 362 W, 4.4km, left Côteau-sur-Mer. Baie-St-Paul, Rte 362 E to La Malbaie, Pointe-au-Pic. 2km from M. Richelieu golf club, right Côteau-sur-Mer.

B&B
LA MAISON FRIZZI

Raymonde Vermette
55, rue Côteau-sur-Mer
La Malbaie
Pointe-au-Pic G5A 3B6
(418) 665-4668
fax (418) 665-1143
www.inns-bb.com/maisonfrizzi

B&B	
single	$65-70
double	$75-80
triple	$95-100
quad.	$115-120
child	$0-15

Taxes extra VS MC

Reduced rates : Apr.1 to 10 juin, Oct. 9 to Dec. 22 and 10% 3 nights and more, except summer
Open year round

Number of rooms	4
rooms with sink	4
shared bathrooms	2

Activities: 🏛 🛥 🎿 🎿

21. LES ÉBOULEMENTS

★ ★ F E 🦽 🚗 P 🐕 R.5

Up in the heights of Les Éboulements, overlooking the St. Lawrence and l'île aux Coudres and centred among the marvels of Charlevoix, Auberge La Bouclée is a haven of peace for your vacation. Fall in love... An old-fashioned charm that thrills many a heart. For groups, families or sweethearts, young and old, our family welcomes you into its home.

From Baie St-Paul, Rte 362 E. twd La Malbaie/Isle-aux-Coudres, drive about 16km. Right at the flashing light. Left after 500m. Welcome.

INN
AUBERGE LA BOUCLÉE

Ginette and Mario Ouellet
6, route du Port
Les Éboulements G0A 2M0
(418) 635-2531
toll free 1-888-635-2531
www.quebecweb.com/
labouclee

B&B	
single	$52
double	$69-89
triple	$104
quad.	$119
child	$0-15

Taxes extra VS MC ER IT

Reduced rates: Oct.20 to June 20
Open year round

Number of rooms	9
rooms with sink	9
shared wc	1
shared bathrooms	4

Activities: 🏛 🎿 🛥 🎿 🏃

22. LES ÉBOULEMENTS

☀☀ F e ⊠ 🚗 P R5

On arriving, you'll fall under the spell of an open view: the St. Lawrence River lazily stretching before your eyes. You'll then climb the stairs leading to our majestic terrace with panoramic view, where you can leisurely enjoy a refreshing drink along with the enchanting setting of L'Île-aux-Coudres.

From Quebec City, twd Ste-Anne-de-Beaupré, Rte. 138 East twd Baie-St-Paul for about 100km. From Baie-St-Paul, Rte. 362 East twd Les Éboulements for 20km. From La Malbaie, Rte. 362 West for 25km.

INN
AUBERGE LA PENTE DOUCE

Noëlla Desmeules, Michel Pilote
and Éric Léonard
215, rue Principale
Les Éboulements G0A 2M0
(418) 635-1345

	B&B	MAP
single	$45-55	$85-120
double	$55-65	$95-130
child	$10	$20

Taxes extra VS MC IT

Open year round

Number of rooms	4
shared bathrooms	1
shared wc	2
rooms with sink	2

Activities: 🏛 🐎 🎣 🏃 🎿

23. LES ÉBOULEMENTS

★★★ F E 🚭 P 🚗 ⊠ TA

Amidst cultural and sports activities, inn Le Surouêt (southwest wind) offers an unobstructed view of Île-aux-Coudres, a grand decor, luxury rooms with balcony and fireplace, dining room, terrace, tea room, fine cuisine, art gallery and gift shop. All under the same roof for an unforgettable stay. Welcome!

From Baie-St-Paul. Rte 362 E. for 16km. 700m on the right.

INN
AUBERGE LE SUROUÊT

Micheline and Rhéaume Gélinas
195, rue Principale
Les Éboulements G0A 2M0
(418) 635-1401
toll free 1-888- 935-1401
fax (418) 635-1404

	B&B	MAP
single	$82-$102	$110-130
double	$105-125	$160-180
triple	$140	$215
child	$17.50	$27.50

Taxes extra VS MC AM ER IT

Reduced rates: 10 % from Sep. 15 to June 15
Open year round

Number of rooms	5
rooms with private bath	5

Activities: 🏛 🎿 🏃 🏃 🐕

24. LES ÉBOULEMENTS

☀☀☀ F e 🎿 P 🐾 R2

Bicentenary family home located right in the country. Domestic animals. Children welcome! Central location to discover all of Charlevoix's tourist attractions. Come stay with us for a few days; special rates for three days or more. A smile and a big surprise breakfast await you.

From Quebec City, Rte 138. In Baie-St-Paul, at the church, straight ahead toward Les Éboulements, Rte 362 East for about 14km.

B&B
GÎTE DU VACANCIER

Jacqueline Audet
104, Route 362,
Rang St-Joseph
Les Éboulements G0A 2M0
(418) 635-2736
(418) 653-5861
www.inns-bb.com/vacancier

B&B	
single	$45-55
double	$55-70
triple	$70-85
quad.	$75-90
child	$0-15

Reduced rates: 10% Oct. 15 to June 15 and 3 nights and more
Open: June 15 to Dec. 31

Number of rooms	5
rooms with private bath	1
rooms with sink	4
shared bathrooms	2

Activities: 🏛 🐎 🚤 🚶 🚲

25. LES ÉBOULEMENTS ☀☀☀ F e 🚗 P R2

Ancestral house facing Île-aux-Coudres. The village's first hotel in 1930. Decor in the style of yesteryear. Relax on the big porch and admire the mountains and the river that runs between the houses. A paradise to discover, amidst the region's tourist attractions. Varied all-you-can-eat breakfast complemented by little treats lovingly prepared by your hosts.

From Québec City, Rte 138 East to Baie-St-Paul. From Baie-St-Paul, Rte 362 East to Les Éboulements.

B&B
GÎTE VILLA DES ROSES

Pierrette Simard and
Leonce Tremblay
290, rue Principale, C.P. 28
Les Éboulements G0A 2M0
(418) 635-2733

B&B	
single	$40
double	$55
triple	$70
child	$0-15

Reduced rates: Oct. 15 to June 15
Open year round

Number of rooms	5
rooms with sink	4
shared wc	1
shared bathrooms	2

Activities: 🏛 🏊 🚲 🏃 🐎

26. LES ÉBOULEMENTS ☀☀☀ F e P R1.5 TA

Nestled between the mountains and the river, this 200-year-old house offers, calm, reverie and peace of mind. Comfortable familly-size rooms with private bathrooms, antique furniture, a smiling welcome and the delight of home-made pastries and jams make for a veritable Nid-Chouette, or cute little nest!

From Québec City, twd Ste-Anne-de-Beaupré, Rte 138 E. to Baie-St-Paul (about 100km). From Baie-St-Paul, Rte 362 E. to Les Éboulements, drive 20km. Or from La Malbaie, Rte 362 W. for 25km.

B&B
LE NICHOUETTE

Gilberte Tremblay
216, rue Principale
Les Éboulements G0A 2M0
(418) 635-2458
www.chouette.freeservers.
com/nichouette.html
chouette@cite.net

B&B	
single	$40
double	$50
triple	$70
quad.	$90
child	$0-12

VS MC

Open: May 1 to Oct. 31

Number of rooms	3
rooms with private bath	3

Activities: 🏛 ⚓ 🛷 🚶 🏃

27. PETITE-RIVIÈRE-ST-FRANÇOIS ★★★ F e 🚗 P 🚭 🏠 ❌ R1.5 TA

Located by the majestic St. Lawrence River and near the "Le Massif" ski resort, our house is a haven of peace. Enjoy an exhilarating holiday, a good chat, a delicious meal and the luxury of a cosy *courtepointe* or quilt. Come and get to know us. "Bonnes Tables du Québec" directory, 3-star hotel. Panoramic view.
Your hosts,
Alice and Maurice.
See color photos.

From Québec City twd Baie-St-Paul, 90km. Right at Petite-Rivière-St-François sign, for 8km, left on Rue Racine.

INN
AUBERGE LA COURTEPOINTE

Alice and Maurice Bouchard
8, rue Racine
Petite-Rivière-St-François
G0A 2L0
(418) 632-5858
fax (418) 632-5786
www.quebecweb.
com/courtepointe

	B&B	MAP
single	$50	$70
double	$90	$130

Taxes extra VS MC AM ER IT

Open year round

Number of rooms	8
rooms with private bath	8

Activities: 🏛 🚶 ⛷ 🏃

28. PETITE-RIVIÈRE-ST-FRANÇOIS ☀☀☀☀☀ F E 🚫 P R4

Prize for Excellence "Special Favorite" Regional 1996-97. Mountain B&B in the Rivière-du-Sot valley near the Massif ski resort and Baie-St-Paul. Balcony overlooking the river with a view of Charlevoix's "extravagant" landscape. And of course... the VIP treatment...

From Québec City, drive 90km twd Baie-St-Paul. At the Petite-Rivière-St-François sign turn right, 3km. 200m back on the left-hand side of the road.

B&B
TOURLOGNON

Lise Archambault and
Irénée Marier
279, rue Principale
Petite-Rivière-St-François
G0A 2L0
tel/fax (418) 632-5708
toll free 1-888-868-7564
www.quebecweb.
com/tourlognon
irenee@charlevoix.net

B&B	
single	$65-70
double	$80-90
triple	$100-110
child	$15

Taxes extra VS MC

Open year round

Number of rooms	5
rooms with private bath	5

Activities: 🏛 🍁 🏃 ⛷ 🏃

---

29. ST-IRÉNÉE F E 🚗 P R1 TA

Our cosy B&B offers a peaceful haven with a beautiful view of the St. Lawrence River. Your host Danielle welcomes you with open arms. She will make you feel at home, and will ensure that you are pampered with fine cuisine and interesting excursions, such as the "Domaine Forget concerts" or whale cruises. Welcome home!

From Québec City, Rte 138 East for Baie-St-Paul, Rte 362 East for St-Irénée, 25km. From La Malbaie, Rte 362 West about 15km.

B&B
AUX 5 PIGNONS

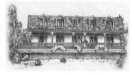

Danielle Papineau
1021 rang Terrebonne
St-Irénée G0T 1V0
(418) 452-8151
www.charlevoix.qc.ca/
aux5pignons
aux5pignons@charlevoix.qc.ca

B&B	
single	$45-55
double	$60-75
triple	$75-95
quad.	$15

Taxes extra VS MC

Open year round

Number of rooms	5
rooms with private bath	2
shared wc	1
shared bathrooms	1

Activities: 🚣 🏃 🏃 🐎 ⛷

---

30. ST-IRÉNÉE F e ♿ 🚗 P R2

After 35 years of living in Saint-Irénée, I had the chance to purchase a classic Charlevoix house set on the edge of a one-of-a-kind beach on the St. Lawrence. Come get away from it all in this extremely relaxing setting.
Lucie Tremblay.

From Québec City, Route 138, about 120km. Route 362 across from the Baie-St-Paul church. Scenic highway to Saint-Irénée, 25km. From La Malbaie, Route 362 West for about 15km.

INN
LA LUCIOLE

Lucie Tremblay
178, chemin Des Bains
St-Irénée G0T 1V0
(418) 452-8283
www.quebecweb.com/luciole
lucie.tremblay2@sympatico.ca

B&B	
single	$50
double	$55-65-85
triple	$75
child	$10

VS

Open year round

Number of rooms	6
rooms with private bath	1
rooms with sink	1
shared bathrooms	2
shared wc	1

Activities: 🏛 🛶 🏃 ⛷

31. ST-IRÉNÉE

☀☀☀☀ F E 🚫 🐕 P R.1 TA

A refined, century-old house, overlooking the river and the beach, where you'll enjoy watching eiders gliding over the St. Lawrence River. Savour our delicious homemade, locally inspired breakfasts in the dining room or on our spacious porch with panoramic view. Relax with the mesmerizing tides and let the melodies of the Domaine Forget, located just steps away, intoxicate you. **See color photos.**

From Quebec City, Rte. 138 East twd Baie-St-Paul, Rte. 362 twd St-Irénée for 25km. From La Malbaie, Rte. 362 West for 15km.

B&B
L'EIDER MATINAL

Annie-Christine Laliberté and Stéphane L'Ecuyer
310, ch. Les Bains
Saint-Irénée G0T 1V0
(418) 452-8259
(418) 452-9222
toll free 1-866-452-9222
www3.sympatico.ca/
eider.matinal/
eider.matinal@sympatico.ca

B&B	
single	$65-90
double	$70-95
child	$15

Taxes extra VS IT

Reduced rates: 3 nights and more
Open year round

Number of rooms	5
rooms with private bath	3
shared bathroom	1
shared wc	1

Activities: 🏛 ⛴ ⚓ 🐎 🏃

32. ST-IRÉNÉE

★★ F E ❌ P TA

Le Rustique stands out from Charlevoix's other bed and breakfasts. Cozily nestled in the heart of St-Irénée, overlooking the river, this beautiful manor house has been welcoming city-dwellers, music-lovers (Domaine Forget concert packages) and seagoing travellers for 10 years. With its warm ambiance, its cuisine and little considerations, this is one of the best places around.

From Québec, Rte 138 to Baie-St-Paul, 90km, Rte 362 to St-Irénée 25km, 500m right at the church. From La Malbaie, Rte 362 West, 15km.

INN
LE RUSTIQUE

Diane Lapointe
102, rue Principale
St-Irénée G0T 1V0
(418) 452-8250

B&B	
single	$45-55
double	$55-75
triple	$75-80
quad.	$85-90

Taxes extra VS MC IT

Reduced rates: May 1 to June 25, Sep. 3 to Oct. 26
Open: May 1 to Oct. 26

Number of rooms	6
shared wc	3
shared bathrooms	2

Activities: 🏛 ⛴ 🐟 🏃 🏇

33. ST-IRÉNÉE

☀☀☀ F e 🚫 🐕 P R3

Between sea and sky, 3km from the Domaine Forget and the Saint-Irénée beach, this lovely blue Canadian house offers a panoramic view of the St. Lawrence River. In a house that combines comfort and conviviality, your hosts invite you to partake of charming, treat-filled breakfasts.

From Quebec City, Rte. 138 twd Baie-St-Paul for 25km. Rte. 362, the Panoramique, twd La Malbaie, 500m past l'Anse-au-Sac.

B&B
LES CHANTERELLES

Michelle Poisson
800, ch. Les Bains
Saint-Irénée G0T 1V0
(418) 452-1099
midoarts@sympatico.ca

B&B	
single	$50
double	$65
triple	$80
child	$10

Reduced rates: May 1 to June 28 and Sep. 8 to Oct. 31
Open: May 1 to Oct. 31

Number of rooms	3
shared bathrooms	2

Activities: 🏛 ⛴ 🏃 🏃 🏇

34. ST-IRÉNÉE

✹✹✹✹ | F | E | 👣 | P | 🚫 | R3

Perched on the high cliffs of St-Irénée and next to the Domaine Forget concert hall, the Manoir offers spacious rooms and a breathtaking view of the St. Lawrence and Charlevoix mountains. 2-km-long seaside promenade in La Malbaie. Superb terrace for breakfast. Packages change with the seasons.

From Québec City, Rte 138 to Baie-St-Paul, then Rte 362 (La Panoramique) to St-Irénée, 25km. From La Malbaie, Rte 362 W., 15km.

B&B
MANOIR HORTENSIA

Jacline Caron
850, chemin Les Bains
St-Irénée G0T 1V0
(418) 452-8180
fax (418) 452-1122
www.manoirhortensia.com
pierre.milot2@sympatico.ca

B&B	
single	$80-125
double	$100-150
child	$20

Taxes extra VS MC IT

Open year round

Number of rooms	5
rooms with private bath	4
shared wc	1
shared bathrooms	1

Activities: 🏛 🛥 👤 🎿 🏃

35. ST-SIMÉON, BAIE-DES-ROCHERS

✹✹✹ | F | e | P | 🏊 | 🐕 | R1 | TA

You are invited to stop over in the hamlet of Baie-des-Rochers where warmth, peace and comfort come together. Nature awaits with the river flowing behind the house. The bay is 3km away, as is the network of hiking trails offering staggering panoramic views of the surroundings.

From Québec City, Rte 138 E. twd Tadoussac. 15km from St-Siméon at the corner store, sign indicating "Gîte de la Baie", turn right.

B&B
GÎTE DE LA BAIE

Judith and Maurice Morneau
68, rue de la Chapelle,
Baie-des-Rochers
St-Siméon G0T 1X0
(418) 638-2821
www.quebecweb.
com/gpc/gitedelabaie
/introfranc.htm

B&B	
single	$35
double	$60
triple	$75
quad.	$85
child	$10

Open: June 1 to Oct. 13

Number of rooms	5
rooms with private bath	2
shared bathrooms	2

Activities: 🐚 🛥 ⛵ 👤 🐎

36. ST-URBAIN

✹✹✹ | F | e | 🚗 | P | R1.3 | TA

Prize for Excellence "Special Favorite" Regional 1999, Tourisme Québec, Regional Prize Hospitality and Customer Service 1999. 20-year-old B&B in the heart of Charlevoix. 10 min from Parc des Grands-Jardins, Mont du Lac des Cygnes, Baie-St-Paul; 30 min from Parc des Hautes-Gorges. Various activities, tickets available. On site: salmon river, picnic area and emu farm. Ancestral house. Large lounge with TV. Varied breakfasts. **See colour photos. Farm Stay p 49.**

From Québec City, Rte 138 East. 10km past Baie-St-Paul, Rte 381 North, 3km.

B&B
CHEZ GERTRUDE

Gertrude and
RaymondeTremblay
706, St-Édouard, rte 381
C.P 293, St-Urbain G0A 4K0
(418) 639-2205
toll free (Canada)
1-866-639-2205
fax (418) 639-1130
www.quebecweb.com/gertrude
raymondetremblay
@videotron.ca

B&B	
single	$40-42
double	$50-65
triple	$65-80
quad.	$80-95
child	$15

Reduced rates: Oct. 16 to May 31
Open year round

Number of rooms	5
rooms with sink	5
shared wc	3
shared bathrooms	3

Activities: 👤 🚲 🏃 🐕 🐎

ESCAPADES À LA FERME

Farm Stay :

36 CENTRE DE L'ÉMEU DE CHARLEVOIX, St-Urbain 49

Regional Dining :

37 LA FERME ÉBOULEMONTAISE, Les Éboulements 31

CHAUDIÈRE-APPALACHES

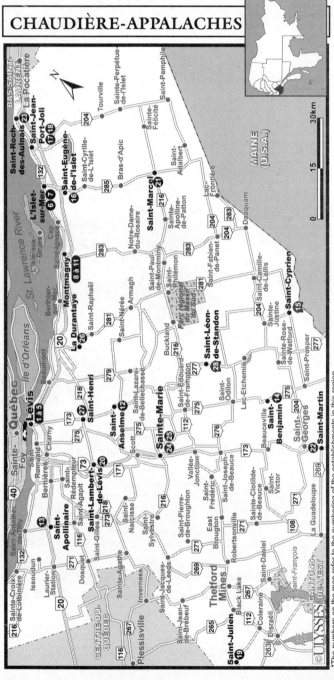

1. LÉVIS

F E P R.5

Overlooking the St. Lawrence River, facing Old Québec, near the ferry. Scenic tours. Enchanting light show, from the residence or terrace. Comfort, relax by the fire. Central air conditioning. Welcome.

From Québec City or Riv.-du-Loup Hwy 20 Exit 327 right on Mgr-Bourget. After 2nd light, drive 1km, left on Champagnat. At 2nd stop right on Des Bosquets. From ferry, in Lévis, right on Côte du Passage, after 1st light left on Champagnat, after 6 stops, left on Des Bosquets.

B&B
ACCUEIL AUX BOSQUETS

Véronique and Émile Pelletier
162, rue des Bosquets
Lévis G6V 6V7
(418) 835-3494
toll free for reservation only
1-888-335-3959
fax (418) 835-0563
accueilauxbosquets
@moncourrier.com

B&B	
single	$35-40
double	$50-60
triple	$70-75
quad.	$85

VS MC

Open year round

Number of rooms	3
rooms with private bath	2
shared bathrooms	1

Activities:

2. LÉVIS

F e P R.5

Located in the heart of Vieux-Lévis, Auberge de la Visitation is a haven of peace in a wooded area next to a monastery. Learn about the history from the builders of Lévis who inhabited this area. Courteous service, cordial atmosphere and numerous activities within walking distance.

Hwy 20, Exit 325 North, straight on Président-Kennedy, 2.5km to St-Georges, turn right, 1km. From the ferryboat, Côte du Passage and St-Georges, turn left, drive 0.3km.

B&B
AUBERGE DE LA VISITATION

Ginette L'Heureux and
Martin Bergeron
6104, rue St-Georges
Lévis G6V 4J8
(418) 837-9619

B&B	
single	$45
double	$55
child	$10

VS MC

Open: May 1 to Sep.30, Oct. 1 to Apr. 30, with reservation except Dec. 24 to Jan. 2

Number of rooms	3
rooms with sink	3
shared wc	1
shared bathrooms	1

Activities:

3. LÉVIS

F E P R.5 TA

Prize for Excellence "Special Favorite" regional 1998. By the ferry leading to the heart of old Quebec City, a traditional bed and breakfast on the most beautiful street in Vieux-Lévis. Superb view of the river and the Château Frontenac. Stained-glass windows, woodwork and high ceilings adorn this stately Victorian house (1890) with period cachet, antiques and modern comfort. Peaceful ambiance and intimacy.

Hwy 20, Exit 325 or Rte 132, or ferry: toward Côte du Passage, Rue Bégin, left on Rue Guénette, Rue Fraser.

B&B
AU GRÉ DU VENT

Michèle Fournier and
Jean L'Heureux
2, rue Fraser
Lévis G6V 3R5
(418) 838-9020
fax (418) 838-9074
www.bonjourquebec.
com/info/augreduvent
augreduvent@msn.com

B&B	
single	$65-75
double	$75-95
triple	$90-110
child	$15

VS

Reduced rates: Nov. 1 to Mar. 31
Open year round (Nov. 1 to Mar.31 on reservation)

Number of rooms	5
rooms with private bath	5

Activities:

4. LÉVIS

☀☀☀ F E 🚭 🚗 P R.1

Great travel enthusiasts, your hosts have prepared comfortable rooms with evocative names. Warm welcome, quiet ambiance, lavish breakfast (homemade specialties). Visit Vieux-Léviss historic houses, restaurants and bistro. Near unique view of Château Frontenac and the St. Lawrence River. Ferry to Vieux-Québec, a world heritage site.

From Montreal, Hwy 20 E., Exit 325 N. Right twd Côte du Passage, left at traffic light, 2.7km. From Riv.-du-Loup, Hwy 20 W., Exit 325 N. Côte du Passage, at the light, straight ahead, 2.7km. From the ferry, right on C. du Passage, 700m.

B&B
GÎTE AU VIEUX BAHUT

France Gingras and
Yvon Lamontagne
116, Côte du Passage
Lévis G6V 5S9
(418) 835-9388

B&B	
single	$55
double	$65
child	$15

Taxes extra

Open year round

Number of rooms	3
shared bathroom	1
shared wc	1

Activities: ⛴ 🦪 🎿 🚲 🎿

5. LÉVIS

☀☀☀ F E 🚭 🚗 P R2 TA

La Maison sous L'Orme is an old renovated home in Vieux-Lévis that has a warm character and a large veranda overlooking Québec City. Located in a peaceful area of town, it has a private living room, food service, generous breakfast and queen beds. A 5min walk from the ferryboat takes you to the heart of Vieux-Québec. Familial suite in the basement, with kitchenette, private entrance, autonomous stay.
Hwy 20, Exit 325 North or Rte 132 or the ferryboat. Follow the signs for the hospital. Before the hospital, Rue Wolfe. 150m, turn right on St-Félix.

B&B
LA MAISON SOUS L'ORME

Anne and André Carrier
1, rue St-Félix
Lévis G6V 5J1
(418) 833-0247
toll free 1-888-747-0247
www.geocities.com/sousorme
sous.orme@qc.aira.com

B&B	
single	$70-80
double	$80-85
triple	$95-100
quad.	$110-115
child	$10

Open year round

Number of rooms	4
rooms with private bath	4

Activities: 🦪 ⛴ 🎿 🚲 🛷

6. L'ISLET-SUR-MER

★★★ F E 🚭 ❌ 🚗 P R1 TA

Near the river, an invitation to relive the history of the Côte-du-Sud in a manor dating from the French regime (1754). Fully renovated, central air conditioning, queen-size beds, TVs. Warm welcome, sunny dining room, hearty breakfast, dinner available, landscaped garden. Packages: Grosse-Île, golf. Activities: ornithology, cycling, theatre, cruise. Steps away from the Musée Maritime.

100km from Quebec City. Hwy 20, Exit 400, Rte 285 North for 2.5km. Rte 132 East for 1km.

INN
AUBERGE LA MARGUERITE

Claire Leblanc and
Louis Boucher
88, des Pionniers Est, rte 132
L'Islet-sur-Mer G0R 2B0
(418) 247-5454
Canada toll free
1-877-788-5454
www.quebecweb.
com/lamarguerite
aubergelamarguerite
@globetrotter.net

	B&B	MAP
single	$66-116	$95-145
double	$80-130	138-188$
child	$15-24	$38-53

Taxes extra VS MC IT

Reduced rates: Nov. 1 to May 15, except for holidays and long weekends
Open year round

Number of rooms	8
rooms with private bath	8
shared wc	1

Activities: 🏛 🦪 ⛴ 🎿 🚲

7. L'ISLET-SUR-MER

☀☀☀ F e 🚫 P 🚗 🐕 R.5 TA

A privileged place for relaxing to the sound of the waves. Charming, very comfortable hundred-year-old house specially decorated for you. Dreamy rooms and dining room on the river. Fancy health/delicacy breakfast. Snow geese in the fall, relaxation, photo-graphy, fresh air, music and hospitality. **Ad end of this region.**

One hour from Québec City or Riv.-du-Loup, 100km, Hwy 20, Exit L'Islet North, Rte 132 East Chemin des Pionniers East for 5km, or Exit St-Jean-Port-Joli North, Rte 132 West, 10km.

B&B
LES PIEDS DANS L'EAU

Solange Tremblay
549, boul. des Pionniers Est
L'Islet-sur-Mer G0R 2B0
(418) 247-5575
fax (418) 247-7772
http://pages.globetrotter.net
/seul/
seul@globetrotter.net

B&B	
single	$40-50
double	$55-75
triple	$80-100
quad.	$110-130
child	$20

Reduced rates: Dec. 1 to Feb. 1
Open year round

Number of rooms	4
rooms in basement	1
rooms with private bath	2
rooms with sink	1
shared wc	2
shared bathrooms	1

Activities: 🏛 🏇 🚶 🛷 🏃

8. MONTMAGNY

★ ★ ★ F E ❌ 🚗 P R.5 TA

This small corner of Europe in the middle of old Montmagny will delight you! Enjoy our warm welcome in this cosy, turn-of-the-century home with Victorian-style rooms. Sample the tasty, authentic cuisine in the quiet ambience of our dining room or stretch out on our sunny terrace. A variety of packages are offered: visiting Grosse-Île, golfing, flying, biking, skiing on a «lunar ground», snowmobiling, relax-ation—and much more. **See colour photos.**

Hwy 20 East, Exits 376 or 378 for the town centre or the scenic Rte 132. Snowmobilers' path 75 and 55.

INN
AUBERGE LA BELLE ÉPOQUE

Carole Gagné
100, rue St-Jean-Baptiste Est
Montmagny G5V 1K3
(418) 248-3373
toll free 1-800-490-3373
fax (418) 248-7957
www.epoque.qc.ca
carole@quebectel.com

	B&B	MAP
single	$77	$99
double	$85	$130
triple	$105	$175
quad.	$125	$220
child	$10	$25

Taxes extra VS MC

Reduced rates: Sept. 15 to May 15, 3rd night free week days, special rates for snowmobilers
Open year round

Number of rooms	5
rooms with private bath	5

Activities: 🏛 🛶 🚶 🛷 🚴

9. MONTMAGNY

☀☀☀ F e 🚫 P R6 TA

Enjoy a wonderful stay at this rest-ful getaway and rediscover peace and quiet while sharing our living environment. A large, luxurious home with fireplace, concert piano, antique furnishings, an island obser-vation tower, sauna, massage and, above all, two loving hosts. Our morning delicacies will prepare you for a fresh start.

1hr from Quebec City or Rivière-du-Loup. Hwy 20, Exit 378, turn left on the service road of the highway, twd Rivière-du-Loup. Right on Chemin Trans-Montagne, left on Chemin Des Sucreries. Exit 378, for 4km.

B&B
AUBERGE LA MAISON BOULET

Hélaine and Maurice Boulet
433, ch. des Sucreries
Montmagny G5V 3R9
(418) 248-2196
fax (418) 248-2286
auberge-la-maison-boulet
@globetrotter.net

B&B	
single	$65
double	$75
child	$15

Taxes extra VS IT

Open year round

Number of rooms	5
shared bathrooms	2
shared wc	1

Activities: 🛶 🚶 🍁 🚴 🛶

10. MONTMAGNY

F e 🚭 🚗 P R1 TA

Only 40 min from Québec City, discover the Snow Goose capital, nature, a superb woodland, a calm and inviting home. Comfortable rooms with fans. Wake up to the birds singing and enjoy a generous breakfast "à la Cécilienne". Golf, cruises to the national historic site of Grosse-Île and to Isle-aux-Grues. World Accordion Jamboree festival and goose hunting. Welcome: make yourselves at home.

From Québec city, Hwy 20, Exit 376, ch. des Poiriers, rte 132 East, cross the bridge of Rivière-du-Sud, continue for 0.5km. The B&B is on the right.

B&B
LA CÉCILIENNE

Doris and Cécile Boudreau
340, boul. Taché Est
route 132
Montmagny G5V 1E1
(418) 248-0165
www.bbcanada.com/
2853.html

B&B	
single	$45
double	$55-60
child	$15

VS

Open year round

Number of rooms	4
shared bathrooms	2

Activities: 🏛 🦆 🚤 🚶 🚲

---

11. MONTMAGNY

☀☀☀ F E 🚭 🐾 🚗 P R.2

We would like to share the charm of our beautiful 200-years-old home with you. Furnished with pieces of period furniture, you will enjoy its peaceful, cheery atmosphere. You can either relax on our large landscaped property or visit the activity centre 4min away. Generous breakfasts served up in a friendly home. A hearty welcome to all.

From Québec City, Hwy 20 East, Exit 376, Chemin des Poiriers, Rte 132 East, 1.1km. At the college, drive twd the centre of town, Rue Fabrique, 0.2km.

B&B
LES DEUX MARQUISES

Danielle Proulx
153, rue St-Joseph
Montmagny G5V 1H9
(418) 248-2178
www.bbcanada.com/4948.html
les2.marquises@globetrotter.net

B&B	
single	$50-55
double	$60-70
child	$15

Open: Mar. 1 to Jan. 31

Number of rooms	4
rooms with private bath	1
rooms with sink	1
shared bathrooms	2

Activities: 🏛 🚤 🚶 🚲 🏃

---

12. ST-ANSELME

☀☀☀☀ F e 🚭 P 🏊 R.5

In the heart of Chaudière-Appalaches, on the doorstep of the Beauce, a dreamy spot decorated to ensure comfort, escape relaxation. Soundproofed rooms, boudoirs, livingroom, fireplace, hot tub, etc. Outdoor fireplace, 40' heated pool, patio, terrace, flowery wooded property. Golf, cycling, skiing. Staying at Douces Évasions is energizing, enriching. Welcome! Room with kitchenette, private bathroom and living room in the basement.

20 min from Québec City. Hwy20, Exit 325 S. twd Lac Etchemin, right at the entrance of St-Anselme.

B&B
DOUCES ÉVASIONS

Gabrielle Corriveau and
Gérard Bilodeau
540, route Bégin, rte 277
St-Anselme G0R 2N0
tel/fax (418) 885-9033
(418) 882-6809
www.quebecweb.
com/evasions
gabycor@globetrotter.net

B&B	
single	$50
double	$65
child	$15

Reduced rates: 10% for 5 nights and more
Open year round

Number of rooms	3
rooms with private bath	1
rooms in basement	1
shared bathrooms	2

Activities: 🦆 🚲 🚤 🚶 🎿

13. ST-APOLLINAIRE

☀☀☀ |F| |e| |🚫| |✕| |P| |🚗| |R3| |TA|

Only 20min from Quebec City, enjoy a stay in our bicentenary house! From the gourmet breakfast to the gastronomic dinner (by reservation), prepared on our antique wood stove, you will share our peaceful haven and a barouche, sleigh or skidoo ride (packages available). 5min from the river (kayak). Near bike paths and skidoo trails, sugar shack, Domaine Joly, golf course...

Hwy 20, Exit 291, Rte 273 North toward St-Antoine-de-Tilly 2.5km, turn right 1.7km.

B&B
NOTRE CAMPAGNE D'ANTAN

Marie-Claude and Donald
412, rang Bois-Franc Est
St-Apollinaire G0S 2E0
(418) 881-3418
fax (418) 881-4393

	B&B	MAP
single	$45	$60-72
double	$55	$85-110
child	$20	$35

Open year round

Number of rooms	2
shared bathrooms	1

Activities: 👤 🚴 🐎 🛷 🏃

---

14. ST-BENJAMIN, BEAUCE

☀☀☀ |F| |e| |P| |R.5| |TA|

In the heart of this lovely backcountry village stands L'Antiquaille, filled with an atmosphere of yesteryear. Come admire our collection of antiques: wood-burning stoves, clawfoot baths, old curios, lace... Breakfast is the hostess' secret! Room with 1925 furniture.

Hwy 20, Exit Hwy 73 South twd St-Georges, Exit 173 South. In St-Odilon, turn right on Rte 275 South twd St-Benjamin.

B&B
L'ANTIQUAILLE

Jacqueline and Catherine
218, rue Principale
St-Benjamin G0M 1N0
(418) 594-8693

B&B	
single	$35
double	$50-55

Open: Apr. 1 to Oct. 30

Number of rooms	4
rooms in basement	1
shared wc	1
shared bathrooms	1

Activities: 🏛 🍷 🚣 👤 🚴

---

15. ST-CYPRIEN

☀☀☀ |F| |e| |✕| |🚫| |P| |R10|

Our B&B is located in the heart of a luxuriant landscape in maple country. Discover: mini farm, organic garden, birds, etc. Healthy breakfast and treats: home-made jams and maple products. Cycling path and skidoo trail right nearby. Packages: health, exploring the maple grove and our saphouse. Hélène (the owner) is a nurse. We are pleased to welcome you. **Farm Stay p 49.**

From Québec City, Hwy 20 East, twd Lac-Etchemin Exit 325, Rte 277 South to Rte 204. Twd Ste-Justine for 7.8km, then right twd St-Cyprien.

B&B
LE JARDIN DES MÉSANGES

Hélène Couture and
Roger Provost
482, route Fortier
St-Cyprien, Barré G0R1B0
tel/fax (418) 383-5777
www.public.sogetel.
net/jardindesmesanges
mesanges@sogetel.net

	B&B	MAP
single	$40	$50
double	$55	$75
triple	$70	$100
quad.	$85	$125
child	$5-15	$15-25

Taxes extra

Open year round

Number of rooms	4
shared bathrooms	3

Activities: 🏛 🍷 👤 🎿 ⛷

16. ST-EUGÈNE-DE-L'ISLET

★ ★ ★ F e P 🛶 ✕ TA

Prize for Excellence "Special Favorite" Regional 1999. Delightful former seigneurial mill will seduce you with its warm ambiance, country decor, gastronomic cuisine. In the heart of a vast estate, the inn boasts remarkable surroundings: river, swimming lake, bird-watching trails. Various packages (golf, cycling, cruise, massage, skiing) also offered. Very romantic! **See colour photos.**

On the south shore, 1 hour from Québec City. At Exit 400 off Hwy 20 E., turn left twd St-Eugène-de-L'Islet, left on Rang Lamartine and left on Route Tortue.

INN
AUBERGE DES GLACIS

Micheline Sibuet and
Pierre Walters
46, route de la Tortue
St-Eugène-de-l'Islet G0R 1X0
(418) 247-7486
toll free 1-877-245-2247
fax (418) 247-7182
www.aubergedesglacis.com
aubergedesglacis@hotmail.com

	B&B	MAP
single	$94-109	$124-139
double	$104-119	$164-179
suites-dbl	$129-149	$189-209

Taxes extra VS MC AM IT

Reduced rates: 3 to 5 nights during the the week and the low season (rates on request)
Open year round

Number of rooms	10
rooms with private bath	10

Activities: 🛶 ⛵ 🧍 🏃

17. ST-JEAN-PORT-JOLI

☀☀☀ F E P R.1 TA

Authentic 200-year-old Canadian home located in the heart of the sculpture capital of Québec and by the St. Lawrence River. In our house it is our pleasure to receive you as a friend. Year-round package for maple grove visits and tastings. **Ad end of this region.**

From Montréal or Québec, Hwy 20 East, Exit 414, turn right, to Rte 132. At Rte 132 turn right, drive 0.5km. Large white house with red roof, 100m past the church.

B&B
AU BOISÉ JOLI

Michelle Bélanger and
Hermann Jalbert
41, rue de Gaspé Est
St-Jean-Port-Joli G0R 3G0
tel/fax (418) 598-6774
auboise@globetrotter.qc.ca

B&B	
single	$45
double	$50-55
triple	$65
child	$10

Taxes extra VS MC

Reduced rates: Sep. 7 to June 15
Open year round

Number of rooms	5
shared bathrooms	3
shared wc	1

Activities: 🏛 🍂 🛶 🧍 🚲

18. ST-JEAN-PORT-JOLI

☀☀☀ F E 🚫 🐕 P 🚗 R.3

Located in the village, a lovely Victorian home of yesteryear set back from the main road. Large plot of land by the river, next to the marina. A peaceful place in an intimate setting. Charming rooms and a lavish breakfast will enhance your stay. Welcome to our home. **Ad end of this region.**

From Montréal or Québec City, Hwy. 20 E., right on Exit 414 to Rte 132. Left on Rte 132 W. for 0.4km, right on Rue de l'Ermitage.

B&B
LA MAISON DE L'ERMITAGE

Johanne Grenier and
Adrien Gagnon
56, rue de l'Ermitage
St-Jean-Port-Joli G0R 3G0
(418) 598-7553
fax (418) 598-7667
www.bbcanada.com/ermitage
ermitage@globetrotter.net

B&B	
single	$50-70
double	$65-85
child	$15

Taxes extra VS MC

Reduced rates: Sep. 8 to June 15
Open year round

Number of rooms	5
rooms with private bath	1
rooms with sink	3
shared bathrooms	2

Activities: 🏛 🍂 🧍 🏃 🛶

19. ST-JULIEN

☀☀☀ F e 🚫 P 🛏 ✕ R15

Prize for Excellence "Special Favorite" Regional 2000 and 1996-97. Nature-lovers, hikers, cyclists and skiers, our cedar-shingled B&B in the Appalaches awaits you. Enjoy peace and quiet, views, "armchair bird-watching" and walks. After a good dinner (available on request), set the world to rights on the terrace or by the fireplace. Various packages. Treat yourself! O' P'tits Oignons, a B&B apart!
From Montreal, Hwy 20, Exit 228. From Quebec City, Exit 253 toward Thetford-Mines. After the detour to Bernierville/St-Ferdinand, Rte 216 West toward St-Julien. Turn right, before the village.

B&B
O' P'TITS OIGNONS

Brigitte and Gérard Marti
917, chemin Gosford,
route 216
St-Julien G0N 1B0
tel/fax (418) 423-2512
www.minfo.net/ptits-oignons/
bgmarti@megantic.net

	B&B	MAP
single	$50-60	$67-77
double	$55-65	$89-99

Reduced rates: 10% 3 nights and more, special rates for 6 nights and more
Open year round

Number of rooms	3
rooms with private bath	1
shared wc	1
shared bathrooms	1

Activities: 🏛 🍃 🧍 🚶 🏇

20. ST-LAMBERT-DE-LÉVIS

☀☀☀ F E 🚫 P 🛏 🚣 🐴 R2.5 TA

20 min from Old Québec City, enjoy the warm, welcoming atmosphere of a country setting. Large landscaped grounds, outdoor pool and flowery patio overlooking the Rivière Chaudière. In winter, relax by a cosy fire. Nearby: cycling, golf, swimming, horseback riding, crosscountry skiing, skidooing and skating. Dogsledding package available upon request.

From Montréal Hwy 20 E.; from Québec City P.-Laporte bridge; from Riv.-du-Loup Hwy 20 W., Hwy 73 S., Exit 115 St-Lambert. Right on Du Pont 1km. Left on des Érables at the church, 1.5km. Right on Dufour.

B&B
LA MAISON BLEUE

Francine and Yvon Arsenault
122, rue Dufour
St-Lambert-de-Lévis G0S 2W0
(418) 889-0545
fax (418) 889-5122
pages.infinit.net/bleue/

B&B	
single	$40
double	$55
child	$10

Open year round

Number of rooms	2
shared wc	1
shared bathrooms	1

Activities: 🍃 🚴 🧍 🎿 🚣 🐴

21. ST-MARCEL

☀☀☀ F e 🚫 ✕ 🚗 P R10 TA

Located in a peaceful town, this 100-year-old presbytery has retained is original charm. There's a museum on the premises, and you can find out how linen and animal fibres are transformed at the various workshops. You can also visit the «Ferme Jouvence», which has some rare animals. Nature area and gourmet restaurant with a healthy menu option on premises. Nonsmoking.

Hwy 20 East, Exit 400, Rte 285 South 33.5km. Left on Rue Taché, 1km. Next to the church.

B&B
L'ANCIEN PRESBYTÈRE

Nicole Bélanger and
Raymond Raby
58, boul. Taché Est
St-Marcel G0R 3R0
tel/fax (418) 356-5060
(418) 356-5663
raby@globetrotter.qc.ca

B&B	
single	$30
double	$40
triple	$55
quad.	$70
child	$5

Taxes extra VS

Open year round

Number of rooms	5
shared bathrooms	2

Activities: 🧍 🚶 🐴 🏂 🚣 🏃

22. ST-MARTIN

✸✸✸✸ F E ⊘ 🐾 P R.25

Built in 1916, La Maison Martin is a large family home with a view of the Chaudière river. Its period charm intact, it offers three rooms, an additional small living room upstairs, 2 magnificent dining rooms and a meeting space that doubles as a tearoom. Enjoy a stay here, in a place with a personal touch that combines the charm of the past and modern comfort. The four-course breakfast is your hostess's secret.

From Quebec City, Hwy 73 S. twd St-Georges and Rte 204 South twd St-Martin/Lac Mégantic. From Montreal, Hwy 10; from Sherbrooke, Rte 108 and Rte 269 twd St-Martin.

B&B
LA MAISON MARTIN

Violette Bolduc and
Serge Thibault
116, 1ʳᵉ Avenue
St-Martin G0M 1B0
(418) 382-3482
st12@globetrotter.net

B&B	
single	$40
double	$55

VS

Reduced rates: 5 $ from Nov. 1 to Mar. 31
Open year round

Number of rooms	3
shared bathroom	1
shared wc	1

Activities: 🏛 🎿 🚶 🛷 🐕

23. ST-ROCH-DES-AULNAIES

✸✸✸ F P 🚗 ✕ R.5 TA

A perfect dream! Fall under the charm of a 200-year-old house on an immense property bordering the St. Lawrence River. Dining room, view of the river, exquisite and copious breakfast. Let time drift by slowly. Marvel at the return of the snow geese, the sunsets, the tides, the winter storms, while keeping warm inside by the fireplace. Meal with reservations. 1 hour from Québec City, 45 min from Riv.-du-Loup **Ad end of this region.**

Hwy 20 Exit 430, left twd Seigneurie des Aulnaies. From Québec City, Rte 132, 15.5km from the St-Jean-Port-Joli church.

B&B
AU SOIR QUI PENCHE

Guy Gilbert
800, ch. de la Seigneurie
St-Roch-des-Aulnaies G0R 4E0
tel/fax (418) 354-7744
www.quebecweb.com/
ausoirquipenche
guygilb@globetrotter.net

B&B	
single	$40-45
double	$45-60
triple	$70
quad.	$80

Open year round

Number of rooms	4
rooms with sink	2
shared wc	1
shared bathrooms	2

Activities: 🎣 🚤 🚶 🎿 🏃

24. STE-MARIE

F E ⊘ ✕ P 🏊 R1 TA

A stately manor on the banks of the Chaudière river. Warm and refined ambiance. Health, golf, romance, show and snowmobile packages. On site: swimming pool, hiking trails, garden, canoes, kayaks, bikes. Weekend tables d'hôte. 20min from bridges to Quebec City. Your hosts Myriam and Jérémy will be delighted to welcome you in this ancestral place. **See color photos.**

From Quebec City, Hwy 73 twd St-Georges. Exit 95, turn right on Rte Cameron and left on Rue Notre-Dame.

B&B
MANOIR TASCHEREAU

Myriam Taschereau
730, rue Notre-Dame Nord
Sainte-Marie G6E 2K9
(418) 387-3671
(418) 561-6618
www.comsearch-can.
com/manoir.htm

	B&B	MAP
single	$45-125	$70-150
double	$60-125	$110-175
triple	$140	$215
child	$10	

Taxes extra VS MC IT

Reduced rates: 1 week and more
Open year round

Number of rooms	5
shared bathroom	1
shared wc	2
room with sink	1
rooms with private bath	2

Activities: 🚶 🎿 🚲 🛷 ⛷

25. STE-MARIE

✹✹✹✹ | F | e | 🚭 | P | TA

Nominated for the Perséides 2000 award, our bed and breakfast offers a panoramic view of Ste-Marie's town centre. In a warm, very relaxing and comfortable ambiance, skiers, golfers and cyclists enjoy the intimacy of a dining room where a hearty, varied breakfast is served. The air conditioning predisposes guests to set out for Quebec City, Montreal or Maine. Reservations are strongly recommended.

From Quebec City, Hwy 73 South, Exit 91 Rte Carter, 3rd street on the right, Taschereau South.

B&B
NIAPISCA

Lise Dufour and Réjean Lavoie
487, boul. Taschereau-Sud
Ste-Marie G6E 3H6
(418) 387-4656
fax (418) 386-1819
www.niapisca.ca.tc
niapisca@hotmail.com

B&B	
single	$60-70
double	$70-80
triple	$90-100

VS MC

Reduced rates: 10% 3 nights and more, Nov. 1 to Dec. 15 and Jan.15 to Apr. 1
Open year round

Number of rooms	3
rooms with private bath	3

Activities: 🏛 🚶 🚲 🏊 ⛷

26. LA DURANTAYE

F E 🚭 🚗 P 🏊 R10 M5 TA

Located on the south shore, 50km east of Quebec City, the lakeside Le Coudrier house, set on a 35,000-sq-ft (3,250m²) wooded property, offers tranquillity, intimacy and lots to do: golf, summer theatre, historical or whale-watching cruises, kayaking, sailing, hiking, horseback riding, cycling, museum, interpretive heritage site, gastronomy, vineyards, bakeries and berry picking.

Hwy 20 East, Exit 345, Rte 281 South. In La Durantaye, turn left on Rue Piémond, right on Chemin du Lac, then left on Rue Côteau des Chênes to the end.

COUNTRY HOME
LE COUDRIER

James Dunnigan
Côteau des Chênes
La Durantaye
mailing adress:
820, rue des Cormiers
St-Nicolas G7A 3Z4
(418) 884-2572
(418) 831-2581

No. houses	1
No. rooms	1-3
No. people	2-6
WEEK-SUMMER	$550-750
WEEK-WINTER	$550-750

Open year round

Activities: 🚤 ⛷ ♠ 🎿 🐎

27. ST-HENRI-DE-LÉVIS

F e P R6 M8 TA

This spacious and well-lit cottage with cathedral roof and stone fireplace welcomes you to a quiet place. Located at the end of a country road, between fields and forest, it offers you the peace of its woodlands. Ambiance inspired by the seasons. Local tours, agrotourism, maple groves...

30 minutes from Vieux-Québec. Hwy 20, Exit 325 S. for Rivière-du-Loup, toward Pintendre, Lac Etchemin, Rte 173 South drive 10km, turn left on Chemin de la Tourbière, 2.5km, turn right, 2km.

COUNTRY HOME
TEMPÉRAMENT SAUVAGE

Sylvie Bouthillette and
Pier Grenier
523, chemin St-Jean-Baptiste
St-Henri G0R 3E0
(418) 882-0558
fax (418) 882-0458
www.cowboys-quebec.
com/temperament.html
tesauvage@globetrotter.net

No. houses	1
No. rooms	2
No. people	4
WEEK-SUMMER	$535-715
WEEK-WINTER	$535-715
W/E-SUMMER	on request
W/E-WINTER	$195-255

MC

Open year round

Activities: 🏛 🚲 🐎 🚤 🏃

FARM ACTIVITIES

Farm Stays:

15 LE JARDIN DES MÉSANGES, St-Cyprien 49

Country-style Dining:

28 FERME LA COLOMBE, St-Léon-de-Standon 18

Farm Tour:

28 JARDINS DES TOURTEREAUX DE LA FERME LA COLOMBE, St-Léon- de-Standon 35

CÔTE-NORD

N

Fermont

MANICOUAGAN

Réservoir Manicouagan

Île René-Levasseur

Mont Babel

Barrage Daniel-Johnson (Manic-5)

Lac Sainte-Anne

Réservoir Manic-3

Réservoir Manic-2

Réservoir Outardes-4

389

Laurieville

Parc régional de Pointe-aux-Outardes
Chûte-aux-Outardes 138

Baie-Comeau

Betsiamites

385

Forestville 138
Sainte-Anne-de-Portneuf

Colombier **7**

4 à 6 Les Escoumins **8 9**

Bergeronnes

11 12 26 Tadoussac **15 à 23**

Sacré-Cœur

Trois-Pistoles

172

FjordSaguenay

SAGUENAY—LAC-SAINT-JEAN

138

DUPLESSIS

Réserve faunique de Sept-Îles–Port-Cartier

Sept-Îles

Gallix

Port-Cartier

Moisie

Les Îles-Caribou

138

Rivière-Pentecôte
Pointe-aux-Anglais

Baie-Trinité

Sainte-des-Monts

Godbout **3 25**

Pointe-Lebel

1 2 24

132

Ste-Flavie
Rimouski

Le Bic

BAS-SAINT-LAURENT

Matane

Métis-sur-Mer

Cap-Chat

Parc de la Gaspésie

La Martre

Réserve faunique de Port-Daniel

GASPÉSIE

Causapscal

132

New Richmond

Carleton

Bonaventure

NEW BRUNSWICK

132

Grande-Vallée

Gaspé

Parc national Forillon

L'Anse-au-Griffon

Percé

Parc de l'Île-Bonaventure-
et-du-Rocher-Percé

Chandler

Newport

132

La Romaine

Kegaska

10 Natashquan

Aguanish

Baie-Johan-Beetz 138

Havre-Saint-Pierre

Mingan

Magpie

Parc national de
l'Archipel-de-Mingan

Sheldrake

Manitou

Rivière-au-Tonnerre

Rivière-Saint-Jean

Longue-Pointe-
de-Mingan

Port-Menier

Parc régional de
l'Archipel des Sept-Îles

Île d'Anticosti

Détroit de Jacques-Cartier

Détroit d'Honguedo

Gulf of
St. Lawrence

ÎLES-DE-LA-
MADELEINE

0   50   100km

Musquaro

*The numbers on the map refer to the numbering of the establishments in this region.

1. BAIE-COMEAU, POINTE-LEBEL

☀☀☀ F e P 🚗 🏊 R2

Calm, cosy and comfortable B&B to discover. Warm family welcome. Nature lovers will cherish the grandeur and beauty of our beach, where the St.Lawrence River meets the Manicouagan; swimming, walks and pool await you. Lavish home-made breakfast. Package deals upon reservation, from November to May. **Country Home p 132.**

From Québec City, Rte 138 E. to Baie-Comeau. 7.5km after Chute-aux-Outardes turn right at the traffic lights. Drive 14km to Pointe-Lebel.

**B&B
AU PETIT BONHEUR**

Carmen Poitras
and Mario Lévesque
1099, rue Granier
Pointe-Lebel G0H 1N0
(418) 589-6476
(418) 589-1294
fax (418) 295-3419

B&B	
single	$35-45
double	$45-55
triple	$65
quad.	$75
child	$10

Open year round

Number of rooms	4
rooms in basement	4
shared wc	1
shared bathrooms	2

Activities: 🐚 🚣 🏃 🚲 🛷

---

2. BAIE-COMEAU, POINTE-LEBEL

☀☀☀ F E 🚗 🐕 P 🏊 R1 TA

Prize for Excellence "Special Favorite" Regional 1996-97. 15 min from Baie-Comeau, between 2 rivers and 200m from a white-sand beach, discover a warm, romantic haven of peace surrounded by greenery! Large terrace and garden, charming rooms, fresh breakfasts! Bring your swimsuit and good mood! We welcome you here to enjoy the four seasons.

From Quebec City, Rte 138 East toward Baie-Comeau. 7.5km past Chutes-aux-Outardes. At the traffic light, turn right and continue for 11.5km. After the church, take the 1st street on your left.

**B&B
LES TOURNE-PIERRES**

Bernadette Vincent
and Jean-Yves Landry
18, rue Chouinard
Pointe-Lebel G0H 1N0
(418) 589-5432
fax (418) 589-1430

B&B	
single	$50-55
double	$60-65
triple	$80-85
child	$20

MC

Reduced rates: Nov. 1 to Apr. 30
Open year round

Number of rooms	5
shared wc	1
shared bathrooms	2

Activities: 🐚 🚣 🏃 🏃 🐎

---

3. BAIE-TRINITÉ

F e ❌ P TA

Old lighthouse: rooms upstairs. 2nd bathroom outside. Also, 7 cottages with bathrooms, by the sea, some of which are log houses. Breakfast service in the main house. Whale-, seal- and gannet-watching. Museum, excursion and fine-cuisine restaurant on site, from mid-June to late August. **Country Home p 132. Ad end of this region.**

From Québec City or from the Matane-Godbout ferry, Rte 138 E., right at the entrance to Pointe-des-Monts, drive 11km. For reception cross footbridge.

**INN
LE GÎTE DU PHARE DE
POINTE-DES-MONTS**

Jean-Louis Frenette
Route du Vieux Phare
Baie-Trinité G0H 1A0
(418) 939-2332
(418) 589-8408
www.pointe-des-monts.com
pointe-des-monts@
globetrotter.net

B&B	
single	$40
double	$49
triple	$58

Taxes extra VS MC IT

Open: June 15 to Sep. 30

Number of rooms	9
rooms with private bath	5
shared wc	2
shared bathrooms	1

Activities: ⛴ 🚣 🏃 🚲 🏛

4. BERGERONNES

F e ✕ 🚗 P TA

Auberge la Bergeronnette is a Victorian-style inn situated in the heart of the village, which lives in harmony with nature. Whale-watching excursions, plane rides, sea kayak expeditions, interpretation centre, bike path and whale observation points from the shore. *Table d'hôte*: game, seafood and fish. Packages available. Taxes and services extra.

24km from Tadoussac on Rte 138 East. 500m from the tourist office.

INN
LA BERGERONNETTE

Anne Roberge and Daniel Brochu
65, Principale C.P. 134
Bergeronnes G0T 1G0
tel/fax (418) 232-6642
toll free 1-877-232-6605
www.bergeronnette.qc.ca
info@bergeronnette.com

	B&B	MAP
single	$40	$60
double	$55	$95
triple	$67.50	$127.50
child	$12.50	$32.50

Taxes extra VS MC AM IT

Reduced rates: Sep.15 to Oct. 31, May 1 to June 15
Open: May 1 to Oct. 31

Number of rooms	8
rooms with sink	6
shared wc	1
shared bathrooms	4

Activities: 🦆 🛥 🛶 🚶 🚲

5. BERGERONNES

☀☀☀ F e 🚗 P R.1

Rock and chat on Petite Baleine's green veranda. The sloping hills unfold in front. Ducks and locals chat on Côte-à-Bouleau hill. One river flows by, then another and another. A smile invites you in. A spirit flows from room to room, breathing the perfumes of yesterday. A piano. A *catalogne* in bed inspires dreams. Sun beams dance across the crystal jam pots as if this were a ball, with Cinderella on the throne. Chicoutai charms our morning table! **See colour photos.**

Near the church.

B&B
LA P'TITE BALEINE

Geneviève Ross
50, rue Principale
Bergeronnes G0T 1G0
(418) 232-6756
(418) 232-2000
fax (418) 232-2001
nross@notarius.net

B&B	
single	$40
double	$50
triple	$70

Open year round

Number of rooms	5
rooms with sink	2
shared wc	2
shared bathrooms	2

Activities: 🏛 🛥 🛶 🚶 🚲

6. BERGERONNES

★ ★ ★ F E ♿ P 🚗 ✕

For a real holiday in whale country, come to the pink granite inn, in the heart of the village. Whale-watching cruises, skidoo, sea kayaking, scuba diving. 5km from Cap Bon-Désir, a whale-watching viewpoint, and only 2km to a prehistory interpretive centre. Regional menu between 6pm and 10pm. Whale watching packages $99 per person. Tx and service extra. TV.

24km from Tadoussac on Rte 138 E. Turn left after the tourist information booth. Follow the signs.

INN
LA ROSEPIERRE

Diane Gagnon
and Richard Bouchard
66, rue Principale, C.P. 116
Bergeronnes G0T 1G0
(418) 232-6543
toll free 1-888-264-6543
fax (418) 232-6215
www.rosepierre.com
rosepierre@rosepierre.com

	B&B	MAP
single	$55-70	$95
double	$65-80	$135
triple	$80-95	$175
quad.	$95-110	$215
child	$15	

Taxes extra VS MC AM IT

Reduced rates: Oct. 1to May 31
Open year round

Number of rooms	10
rooms with private bath	8
shared wc	1
shared bathrooms	1

Activities: 🏛 🛥 🚶 🚶 🚲

7. COLOMBIER

Private beach, showered in the salty waters of St.Lawrence River. A walk by the rocks on the shore will seduce nature lovers. Panoramic view. Comfortable new rooms of superior quality. Suite with front and back balconies. Rooms with private entrance. French, Spanish and some English spoken.

From Québec, Hwy 138 E., 300km. From Tadoussac, 100km. From Forestville, 27km. From the ferry Matane-Baie-Comeau, Hwy 138 W., 70km. From Papinachois Vacation Center, 25km.

B&B
GÎTE ANSE-AU-SABLE

Noëlla Thibault and
Jocelyn Gagnon
104, ch. de l'Anse-au-Sable
Colombier G0H 1P0
(418) 565-3047
(418) 587-3050
fax (418) 587-4808
www.bonjourquebec.
com/info/anseausable
ntibo@quebectel.com

B&B	
single	$65-100
double	$75-125
triple	$150
child	$10

VS IT

Open year round

Number of rooms	3
rooms with private bath	1
shared bathrooms	1

Activities:

8. LES ESCOUMINS

"A stop along the way to discovering the Côte-Nord..." Good beds, good cooking (meals with reservation). Personalized service whether you prefer to relax or explore: the sea, the river or the forest. Whales, salmon and trout are plentiful. Wonderful places for scuba-diving, snowmobiling. The inn is a cosy stop between the river and forest.

From Tadoussac, Rte 138 E., 40km. From Baie-Comeau, Rte 138 West 150km. 2km from the Les Escoumins-Trois-Pistoles ferry.

INN
AUBERGE DE LA BAIE

Esther Gagné
267, Route 138, C.P. 818
Les Escoumins G0T 1K0
(418) 233-2010
fax (418) 233-3378
www.aubergedelabaie.com
aubergedelabaie
@aubergedelabaie.com

B&B	
single	$55-75
double	$65-95
triple	$80-110
quad.	$95-125
child	$5

Taxes extra VS MC AM ER

Reduced rates: Oct. 1to May 31
Open year round

Number of rooms	12
rooms with private bath	12

Activities:

9. LES ESCOUMINS

Recipient of the 1996-97 regional award for hospitality and customer service. Ancestral home rich in memories. Intimate, convivial atmosphere. Flowery, colourful decor. Renowned, refined gourmet fare. View overlooking the river, great for whale-watching. Salt air and endless sandbanks. Ask about our packages!

3hrs from Quebec City, Rte 138 East, 25min from Tadoussac, 2hrs from Chicoutimi, Rte 172, Rte 138 East. From Trois-Pistoles-Les-Escoumins ferry, 2km from the village centre, next to the church.

INN
AUBERGE MANOIR BELLEVUE

Léna St-Pierre
27, rue de l'Église
Les Escoumins G0T 1K0
(418) 233-3325
fax (418) 233-3277
www.manoirbellevue.com
auberge@manoirbellevue.com

	B&B	MAP
single	$45-65	$65-95
double	$60-80	$99-140
triple	$75-95	$139-190
quad.	$80-99	$179-240
child	$10	$25-30

Taxes extra VS MC AM IT

Reduced rates: Oct.15 to June 15, -20% on B&B and -10% on PAM
Open year round

Number of rooms	10
rooms with sink	4
shared bathrooms	2
shared wc	2
rooms with private bath	4

Activities:

10. NATASHQUAN ★ ★ F e ♿ 🐕 🚗 P 🏊 R.5

Twenty feet from the sea, our inn offers relaxation, a warm welcome, personalized service. Fine-sand beaches, sea as warm as in New Brunswick. Footpaths along the river with sea eagles, ducks, birds. In winter: ice fishing, wide-open spaces, freedom. Nature lovers, snowmobilers, skiers, dogsledders, welcome to «plaquebière» (chicoutai) paradise.

Rte 138 East to Natashquan. From Rimouski, Nordik ferry (418) 723-8787. By snowmobile, Trans-Québec 3 trail.

INN
LE PORT D'ATTACHE

Nathalie Lapierre and
Magella Landry
70, rue du Pré
Natashquan G0G 2E0
(418) 726-3569
(418) 726-3440
toll free 1-877-726-3569
fax (418) 726-3767

B&B	
single	$50
double	$65

Taxes extra VS

Open year round

Number of rooms	8
shared bathrooms	3

Activities: 🚣 🏃 🚴 🏊 🎿

---

11. SACRÉ-COEUR F E P 🚗 ❌ 🏊 R1 TA

Share in our family ambiance. "4-season" activities and packages. Québec cuisine also served to our customers staying in our country homes. No charge: visit or care of animals, sugar shack, tennis, pool, hiking trails, game park. Info and reservation service. **Farm Stay p 50, Country Home p 132. For activities, see ads in Côte-Nord and Saguenay-Lac-St-Jean.**

From Tadoussac, twd Chicoutimi, 17km from the intersection of Rtes 138 and 172, and 6km from the Sacré-Coeur church. From Chicoutimi North, Rte 172 S. to the right, 60m before the rest area.

B&B
FERME 5 ÉTOILES

Stéphanie and
Claude Deschênes
465, Route 172 Nord
Sacré-Cœur G0T 1Y0
(418) 236-4833
toll free 1- 877-236-4551
tel/fax (418) 236-4551
www.ferme5etoiles.com
ferme5etoile@ihcn.qc.ca

	B&B	MAP
single	$40	$64
double	$45-50	$88
triple	$55-60	$109
child	$10	$29

Taxes extra VS MC AM IT

Open year round

Number of rooms	4
rooms with sink	2
shared bathrooms	2

Activities: 🚤 🚣 🏃 🛷 🐎

---

12. SACRÉ-COEUR ☼ ☼ ☼ F e P R2 TA

Modern house known for its large spaces, its cleanliness, the warmth and cheer of its residents. Breakfast served in the large solarium with a view of the lake, the geese, the ducks and other farm animals.

From Tadoussac, Rtes 138 E. and 172 N. Or from Chicoutimi North: Rte 172 S. Look for our sign: "Ferme Camil and Ghislaine".

B&B
GÎTE GHISLAINE

Ghislaine Gauthier
243, Route 172
Sacré-Coeur G0T 1Y0
(418) 236-4372

B&B	
single	$40
double	$45
triple	$60
quad.	$65
child	$10-15

Open: June 1 to Oct. 31

Number of rooms	3
rooms in basement	3
shared bathrooms	2

Activities: 🚤 🏃 🚣 🎿 🐕

13. STE-ANNE-DE-PORTNEUF

☀☀☀ F 🚭 P 🚗 R.1 TA

Prize for Excellence "Special Favorite" Regional 2000 and Prov. 94-95.
A warm welcome;
Dreamy rooms;
A well-earned sleep;
A generous breakfast;
Fresh fruit and vegetables;
Tides to behold;
A beach for strolling;
Birds to observe;
An enchanted forest;
Endless trails;
Friendship assured.
Tickets for boat cruises.
From Québec City, Rte 138 E., 288km and 84km from Tadoussac. Or from Matane/Baie Comeau ferry, Rte 138 W., 135km. From Les Escoumins, 33km. From Forestville: 17km.

B&B
GÎTE LA NICHÉE

Camille and Joachim Tremblay
46, rue Principale, route 138
Ste-Anne-de-Portneuf
G0T 1P0
(418) 238-2825
fax (418) 238-5513

B&B	
single	$40
double	$50
triple	$65
child	$10

VS

Reduced rates: Nov 1 to Apr. 30
Open year round

Number of rooms	5
rooms with sink	5
shared wc	1
shared bathrooms	2

Activities: 🏛 🚤 🏂 🛷 🎿

14. STE-ANNE-DE-PORTNEUF

☀☀☀ F e P 🚗 R2 TA

Going to Germina's is like visiting your grandmother. Crepes, jams and giggling fits await you here. Stroll along the sandbank, see the birds, marina, blue whales and a centenary house with coloured past from the times of silent film and grocer's. Welcome to a region as big as the wind, sea and forest.

From Québec City, Rte 138 E., 288km. 3 houses from church. 84km from Tadoussac. Ferries: Escoumins: 33km, Forestville: 17km, Baie-Comeau: 135km, Godbout: 189km, Havre: 505km.

B&B
LA MAISON FLEURIE

Germina and Thérèse Fournier
193, Route 138, C.P. 40
Ste-Anne-de-Portneuf G0T 1P0
(418) 238-2153
fax (418) 238-2793
www.fjord-best.
com/portneuf/fournier.htm
maisonfleurie@moncourrier.com

B&B	
single	$40
double	$50
child	$10

Open year round

Number of rooms	3
shared bathrooms	2

Activities: 🏛 🚤 🏂 🛷 🎿

15. TADOUSSAC

★★ F E P 🚗 R.01 TA

Lovers of nature and grand settings, welcome to our home. Located at the entrance of the village, our inn offers you a warm, intimate reception. Ten pretty rooms with a private bathroom, TV, balcony, lavish breakfast and a view of the Saguenay. Next to the lake, hiking trails, marine mammals and wide-open spaces. Come enjoy the four season with us. Whale-watching ticket service.

From Quebec City, Rte 138 East. After getting off the ferry, 400m to the left.

INN
AUBERGE «MAISON GAGNÉ»

Claire Gagné
139, rue Bateau-Passeur
Tadoussac G0T 2A0
(418) 235-4526
toll free 1-877-235-4526
fax (418) 235-4832
www.fjord-best.
com/maisongagne
maisongagne@ihcn.qc.ca

B&B	
single	$69
double	$79
triple	$89
quad.	$99
child	$10

Taxes extra VS MC AM ER IT

Reduced rates: Sep. 15 to June 15
Open year round

Number of rooms	10
rooms in basement	2
rooms with private bath	10
shared wc	1

Activities: 🚤 🏂 🛷 🎿 🏃

16. TADOUSSAC

☀☀☀ F e 🚫 🚗 P R.3

Far from traffic, next to Parc du Saguenay, 3min from spectacular bay. Old-charm B&B with small, pretty, cozy rooms and friendly, family breakfasts. Delicious varied breakfasts. Everything within walking distance. Stays of 2 to 4 days, whale-watching cruises, bear and beaver watching. In-house info and ticket sales. Welcome to all.

Turn right at the village church, follow "Bord de l'eau", turn right at 1st street, left at "cul-de-sac" sign, 50 m.

B&B
AUX SENTIERS DU FJORD

Elisabeth Mercier and Xavier Abelé
148, ch. Coupe-de-l'Islet
Tadoussac G0T 2A0
(418) 235-4934
fax (418) 235-4252
www.iquebec.com/fjord
elisabethmercier@hotmail.com

B&B	
single	$55
double	$60

Taxes extra VS MC

Reduced rates: Sep.15 to June 15
Open year round

Number of rooms	4
rooms with sink	4
shared bathrooms	2

Activities: 🏛 ⛴ 🧍 🚲 🏃

17. TADOUSSAC

☀☀☀ F 🚗 P 🚫 R.1 TA

Comfortable and intimate rooms in our home. Enjoy magnificent views of the St.Lawrence River and the Saguenay Fjord from our solarium, where buffet breakfast awaits you in the morning. Rest in harmony with nature throughout the day. Tickets for cruises available.

From Québec City, Rte 138 E. Drive 0.5km from the Saguenay ferry. Right on Rue Des Pionniers, drive 0.3km, left on Rue de Forgerons, drive 0.3km. Right on de la Falaise, drive 0.1km.

B&B
GÎTE DE LA FALAISE

Émilienne and Fernand Simard
264, rue de la Falaise,
Tadoussac C.P. 431, G0T 2A0
tel/fax (418) 235-4344
www.fjord-best.com/
gite-falaise
gite-falaise@mail.
fjord-best.com

B&B	
single	$45
double	$55
triple	$70
quad.	$85
child	$10

VS MC

Reduced rates: Apr. and May
Open: Apr. 1 to Oct. 31

Number of rooms	5
rooms with sink	5
rooms in basement	1
shared bathrooms	2

Activities: 🏛 ⛴ 🧍 🧍 🚲

18. TADOUSSAC

☀☀☀ F e 🚗 P R.25 TA

A simple and warm welcome conducive to rest. A tranquil hideaway close to amenities. We will regale you with our generous home-made breakfasts. Whale-watching cruises. We have extensive knowledge of marine mammals. Tickets for sale here.

From Québec City, Rte 138 E. Drive 1.5km along road from Saguenay ferry. Right on Rue Bois-Franc, 300 ft, left on Rue des Bouleaux. We're waiting for you.

B&B
GÎTE DU BOULEAU

Claire-Hélène Boivin and Jean-Yves Harvey
102, rue des Bouleaux,
C.P. 384
Tadoussac G0T 2A0
tel/fax (418) 235-4601

B&B	
single	$45
double	$50-60
triple	$65
quad.	$85

VS MC

Reduced rates: Apr. 1 to June 30
and Sep. 1 to Nov. 30
Open: Apr. 1 to Nov. 30

Number of rooms	5
shared bathrooms	3

Activities: 🏛 ⛴ 🧍 🧍 🚲

19. TADOUSSAC

☀☀☀ F E 🚭 P 🚗 R1

A destination in itself. Welcome to our large, quiet restored house near the village. Soundproof rooms. As biologist and guide, we enjoy acquainting guests with our region. Trails, kayaking, whales, bears, beavers, birds, good advice and tickets on site. In winter: dogsledding, cross-country skiing, snowmobiling and fireplace...

After getting off the ferry, 1st street on the right, 1km from the church, 200m, turn left, past the golf course.

B&B
GÎTE DU MOULIN BAUDE

Virginie Chadenet and
Charles Breton
381, rue des Pionniers,
C.P. 411
Tadoussac G0T 2A0
(418) 235-4765
www.ihcn.qc.ca
/moulinbaude/gite/
moulinbaude@ihcn.qc.ca

B&B	
single	$60
double	$65-75
triple	$90
quad.	$100
child	$10-15

VS MC
Reduced rates: Sep. 5 to July 6
Open year round

Number of rooms	4
rooms with private bath	4

Activities: 🚤 👤 🎿 🐕

---

20. TADOUSSAC

☀☀☀☀ F E 🚭 P 🚗 🐕 R.5

Côte-Nord Excellence Prize 1999. At the top of the village, tasteful, romantic, soundproof rooms with breathtaking view of the St.Lawrence River, fjord, lake, flower garden priv. balcony, queen-size beds. Lux. suite, therap. bath, king-size bed, a.c., TV. Ideal for couple. Hospitality. Copious, varied breakfasts. Bear-/whale-watching, fjord, seaplane tickets.

From the ferry, Rte 138, 1km. Halfway up the hill, at the roadsign, left on Rue des Forgerons, then Rue de la Montagne and Rue Bellevue. Watch for Maison Harvey-Lessard sign.

B&B
LA MAISON
HARVEY-LESSARD

Sabine Lessard and Luc Harvey
16, rue Bellevue
Tadoussac G0T 2A0
in Tadoussac (418) 235-4802
in Québec (418) 827-5505
fax (418) 827-6926
www.dreamcite.
com/harveylessard/

B&B	
single	$80-85
double	$85-89
double suite	$145
child	$20

Open: June 1 to Oct 31

Number of rooms	4
rooms with private bath	4
shared wc	1

Activities: 🚤 ⛵ 👤 🚲

---

21. TADOUSSAC

F P R.1

We are happy to welcome you to our home. Seen from Tadoussac, the Saguenay is breathtaking. Cruises with whale watching. Bus service one kilometre away. Welcome to our home.

From Québec City, Rte 138 E. to the ferry across the Saguenay. Once off the ferry, take the first road on the right.

B&B
MAISON FORTIER

Madeleine B. Fortier
176, rue des Pionniers
Tadoussac G0T 2A0
(418) 235-4215
fax (418) 235-1029

B&B	
single	42 $
double	52 $
triple	67 $
child	10 $

Taxes extra VS

Open year round

Number of rooms	5
rooms with sink	5
shared wc	1
shared bathrooms	3

Activities: 🐋 🚤 ⛵ 👤

22. TADOUSSAC

★★ F E ♿ P 🚗 R.4 TA

Cosy, comfortable hundred-year-old house with view of the Saguenay, on the shores of the lake, in the heart of the village of Tadoussac. 5 rooms with private bathrooms. Rooms with private baths also available in the annex the "Suites de l'Anse". Buffet breakfast served in the Maison Gauthier or in your room. Some rooms are ideal for families. Exceptional off-season rates.

From Québec City, Rte 138 East to the Saguenay ferry at Baie Ste-Catherine. Once off the ferry, 250 m on your left.

INN
MAISON GAUTHIER ET LES
SUITES DE L'ANSE

Lise and Paulin Hovington
159, du Bateau-Passeur
Tadoussac G0T 2A0
(418) 235-4525
(450) 671-4656
fax (418) 235-4897
fax (450) 671-7586
www.charlevoix.qc.ca
/maisongauthier

B&B	
single	$55-75
double	$60-85
triple	$85-100
quad.	$100-115
child	$15

Taxes extra VS MC IT

Reduced rates: May, June, Sept., Oct.
Open: May 1 to Oct. 31

Number of rooms	12
rooms with private bath	12

Activities: 🚤 ⛵ 🚶 🎿 🚲

23. TADOUSSAC

☀☀☀☀ F E P 🚗 🐕 R.4

Located on one of the world's most beautiful bays, our century-old house offers comfortable, warm coloured rooms with double or queen-size beds and private bathrooms; some also have a view of the sea. Varied, lavish, homemade breakfast. Tadoussac-born Paul and his spouse Lise will acquaint you with Tadoussac and the region. Good advice on activities and tickets available on site. **See colour photos.**

From Quebec City, Rte 138 East to Baie-Ste-Catherine. After getting off the ferry, take the first street on your right, Rue des Pionniers.

B&B
MAISON HOVINGTON

Lise and Paulin Hovington
285, rue des Pionniers
Tadoussac G0T 2A0
(450) 671-4656
(418) 235-4466
fax (450) 671-7586
fax (418) 235-4897
www.charlevoix.qc.ca/
maisonhovington

B&B	
single	$55-75
double	$60-100
triple	$115
quad.	$130
child	$15

Taxes extra VS MC IT

Reduced rates: May, June, Sept., Oct.
Open: May 1 to Oct. 31

Number of rooms	5
rooms with private bath	5

Activities: 🚤 ⛵ 🚶 🎿 🚲

24. BAIE-COMEAU, POINTE-LEBEL

`F` `e` `P` 🏠 `M2` `R2` `TA`

Peace, calm and rest await you here. Very relaxing site. On the premises: *jeu de fer*, petanque, pool and beach. You will fall in love with Villa Petit Bonheur! No one leaves 1097 Garnier uncharmed! Carmen and Mario will give you a warm welcome, a custom of the house! **B&B p 124.**

From Québec, Rte 138 E. to Baie-Comeau. 7.5km after Chute-aux-Outardes turn right at the traffic light and head to Pointe Lebel, drive 14km.

COUNTRY HOME
VILLA PETIT BONHEUR

Carmen Poitras and
Mario Lévesque
1097, rue Granier
Pointe Lebel G0H 1N0
(418) 589-6476
(418) 589-1294
fax (418) 295-3419

No .houses	3
No. rooms	1-2
No. People	2-6
WEEK-SUMMER	350-550 $
WEEK-WINTER	300-500 $
W/E-SUMMER	150-180 $
W/E-WINTER	130-160 $
DAY-SUMMER	75-90 $
DAY-WINTER	65-80 $

Reduced rates: Nov. 1 to Apr. 30
Open year round (Nov. 1 to Apr. 30 with reservation only)

Activities: 🦪 🛶 🎿 🛷 🏃

25. BAIE-TRINITÉ

`F` `E` ♿ `P` 🏠 ❌ `R1` `M14` `TA`

7 comfortable chalets right by the sea, most of them loghouses, with kitchenette, bathroom and t.v. The Pointe-des-Monts headland juts out 11km into the Gulf of St.Lawrence. Right on the high seas! You'll see whales, seals and gannets from your kitchen window. Old lighthouse museum, excursions and gourmet restaurant all on site from mid-June to late August. Class. 4-stars oufitter. **Country Inn p 124. Ad end of this region.**

From Québec, Rte 138 E. Entrance to Pointe-des-Monts, 4km before Baie-Trinité (west), secondary road twd old lighthouse parking, 11km.

COUNTRY HOME
LE GÎTE DU PHARE DE
POINTE-DES-MONTS

Jean-Louis Frenette
Route du Vieux Phare
de Pointe-des-Monts
Baie-Trinité G0H 1A0
(418) 589-8408
(418) 939-2332
www.pointe-des-monts.com
pointe-des-monts
@globetrotter.net

No. house	7
No. rooms	1-4
No. people	2-11
WEEK-SUMMER	$390-750
DAY-SUMMER	$62-150

Taxes extra VS MC IT

Reduced rates: ⅓ of the price from May 15 to June 5 and Sep. 6 to Oct. 15
Open: May 15 to Oct. 15

Activities: 🚤 🛶 🏃 🚲

26. SACRÉ-COEUR

★ ★ `F` `E` ♿ `P` 🚗 🏠 ❌ `R1` `M5` `TA`

Share our family ambiance, our 700 acres of farm and forest, access to the fjord, our choice of activities and accommodations with bedding, kitchen and amenities, t.v. and services free of charge. Near Tadoussac and Sainte-Rose-du-Nord. **Farm Stay p 50, B&Bs p 127. For activities: see ads in Côte-Nord and Saguenay-Lac-St-Jean sections.**

From Tadoussac, twd Chicoutimi, 17km from the intersection of Rtes 138 and 172, and 6km from the Sacré-Coeur church. From Chicoutimi-Nord, Rte 172 South to the right, 60m before the rest area.

COUNTRY HOME
FERME 5 ÉTOILES

Stéphanie and
Claude Deschênes
465, Route 172 Nord
Sacré-Cœur G0T 1Y0
(418) 236-4833
tel/fax (418) 236-4551
toll free 1-877-236-4551
www.ferme5etoiles.com
ferme5etoile@ihcn.qc.ca

No. houses	9
No. rooms	1-3
No. people	2-8
WEEK-SUMMER	$410-1125
WEEK-WINTER	$285-910
W/E-SUMMER	$130-370
W/E-WINTER	$90-290
DAY-SUMMER	$59-89
DAY-WINTER	$50-79

Taxes extra VS MC AM IT

Reduced rates: Sep.10 to June 10
Open year round

Activities: 🚤 🛶 🏃 🛷 🐕

FARM ACTIVITIES

Farm Stay:

 FERME 5 ÉTOILES, Sacré-Cœur 50

To ensure your satisfaction

Bed & Breakfast, Country Inns, Country

and City Homes, Farm Stays, Country-Style

Dining, Regional Dining, Farm Excursions :

660 establishments fall into these 7 categories,

and all are accredited and regularly

inspected according to a code of ethics,

a philosophy of personalized

welcome and a consistent standard of quality.

The Fédération des Agricotours du Québec
26 years of hospitality
1975-2001

www.inns-bb.com
www.agricotours.qc.ca

On the north shore of the St-Laurent, halfway between Tadoussac and Minganie, an old lighthouse, the sea, the woods and you...

2 PACKAGES

GREAT MARITIME ADVENTURE

J F M A M **J J** A S O N D

**AT THE GÎTE DU PHARE DE POINTE DES MONTS
3 DAYS AND 2 NIGHTS**

$170 CAN/ per person, double occ.

includes:

• lodging in a log cabin right to the beach

• 2 complete breakfasts

• 3 lunch specials at the Restaurant du Phare

• 2 fine evening meals at the Maison du Gardien (2 choices of table d'hôte)

• 1 afternoon seal-and whale-watching excursion

• tour of the Musée Patrimonial du Vieux Phare

• your very own mountain bike for the length of your stay

A LITTLE ADVENTURE

J F M A M **J J** A S O N D

Package for two includes:

• a fine supper for two
• your rooms in the Maison du Gardien
• breakfast the next morning
• a seal- and whale-watching excursion
• a visit to the 7-story "Musée du Vieux Phare"

$125
per couple!

2 small conditions :
A) be in love or on your way there
B) reserve at least a day in advance

Informatio and photos available :
Le Gîte du Phare de Pointe des Monts
c/o Jean-Louis Frenette

In season :

Chemin du Vieux Phare
C.P. 101, Baie Trinité, Qc
G0H 1A0
(418) 939-2332

Out of season:

1684 Joliet
Baie Comeau, Qc
G5C 1P8
(418) 589-8408

Welcome to the Québec North Shore
10 minutes from Tadoussac

Ferme 5 étoiles

4 seasons
Rental activities
duration : between 2 and 3 hours

Spring-Summer-Fall
★ Beluga, seal and whale watching cruises
★ 4 wheel carts mountain excursions
★ Canoeing on lakes and rivers
★ Sea kayaking on the Saguenay fjord
★ Fishing (gear supplied)
★ Mountain bike and hiking trails
★ Bear and beaver watching
★ Hydroplane
★ Horseriding
★ The life of today's lumberjacks (4 saisons)
★ Museum

Winter
★ Ice fishing
★ Igloo lodging
★ Sliding on air tubes
★ Dogsleding and snowmobile : Initiation and excursion (possibility of many days packages)
★ Sugar shack, maple taffy tasting and traditions
★ Snowshoeing and cross country skiing trails along the Saguenay fjord

Packages

1. «Wild discoveries»
(2 days - 1 night)
One rental activity included (your choice) according to the season :
★ «Goodies» of the farm
★ One night
★ One copious breakfast
★ One traditionnal supper

84$ /pers./bed & breakfast

94$ /pers./country home

2. «Wild exploration»
(3 days - 2 nights)
Two rental activities included (your choice) according to the season :
★ «Goodies» of the farm
★ Two night
★ Two copious breakfast
★ Two traditionnal supper

169$ /pers./bed & breakfast

195$ /pers./country home

3. «A la carte» (3 days and up)
Ask us exactly what you want and we will make your «wilderness» dream come true!

★ Côte-Nord region
★ B&B's and Inns No. 11
★ Country homes No. 26

«Goodies» of the farm free for our clientele :
Guided tours of the farm and the sugar shack, animals daily care (for kids), hiking and cross country skiing trails, outdoor swiming pool, tennis, playground, outdoor fireplace, B.B.Q.

★ Children under 12 with adults : save 20% on adult rates
★ Lodging rates for 2 pers.
★ Taxes are not included with prices
★ Group rates (11 pers. and up)

Visit us at www.ferme5etoiles.com

Phone : (418) 236-4833 • Toll free : 1 877 236-4551 • Fax : (418) 236-4551
FERME 5 ÉTOILES, 465, route 172 Nord, Sacré-Coeur (Québec) G0T 1Y0 • E-mail : info@ferme5etoiles.com

GASPÉSIE

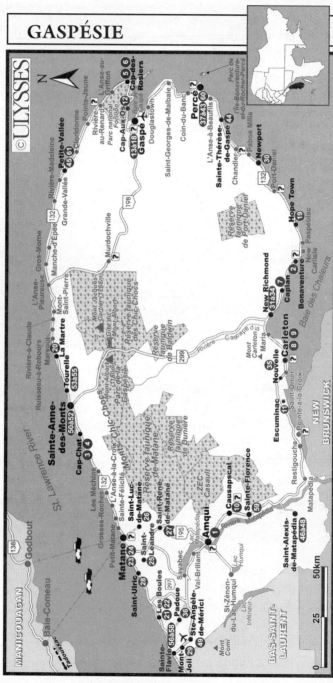

*The numbers on the map refer to the numbering of the establishments in this region.

© ULYSSES

1. AMQUI

☀☀☀ F e 🚭 P R4

Antique-furnished 1920s house on an old 35ha farm, near Lac Matapédia, with a private beach. For nature-lovers, green or colourful landscapes and various activities. A restful stop midway between Quebec City and Percé or New Brunswick. 4km from summer theatre, fishing, canoeing, golf, park with bike paths. Our lavish homemade breakfast and friendly welcome will make you want to come back.

From Mont-Joli, Rte 132 East, 6km past Val-Brillant. From Percé, Rte 132 West 4km past the town of Amqui. On your right, after the campground.

B&B
DOMAINE DU
LAC MATAPÉDIA

Carmelle and Roland Charest
780, Route 132 Ouest
Amqui G5J 2H1
(418) 629-5004
fax (418) 629-6606
http://pages.globetrotter.net
/domainedulac
domainedulac@globetrotter.net

B&B	
single	$45-55
double	$55-65
triple	$80
quad.	$95
child	$15

Reduced rates: Sep. 1 to Oct. 31
Open: June 1 to Oct. 31

Number of rooms	5
rooms with private bath	1
rooms with sink	4
shared wc	1
shared bathrooms	2

Activities: 🦆 🚣 🎣 🚶 🚲

2. BONAVENTURE

☀☀☀ F e 🐕 🚗 P 🏊 R5

For something out of town and out of sight, we offer a colorful atmosphere. A pioneer farm built in 1881 by the famous Bonaventure river, away from the village. Enjoy swimming in the crystalline river, a campfire in the teepee, the terrace, artist workshop, hammock, a communal kitchen, laundromate, bike shed, have a healthy breakfsat with expresso. A great place to drop anchor for a few days. Bring your musical instrument.

At the church, turn on Rue Grand-Pré, drive straight for 5km.

B&B
GÎTE AU FOIN FOU

Hugues Arsenault
204, ch. de la Rivière C.P. 592
Bonaventure G0C 1E0
(418) 534-4413
www.foinfou.qc.ca
foinfou@globetrotter.qc.ca

B&B	
single	$40
double	$55-60
triple	$70
quad.	$85
child	$10

Open: June 15 to Sep. 15

Number of rooms	5
rooms with sink	5
shared wc	1
shared bathrooms	2

Activities: 🏛 🦆 🚣 🐎 🚲

3. CAP-CHAT

☀☀☀ F E 🚭 🏊 P 🚗 ✗ R2

Come join us to the sound of the waves and crying gulls. From our beach, see the whales disappear over the still horizon. At sunset, close your eyes and feel the very soul of Gaspé. Visit the 76-windmill park, the largest vertical-axis windmill and Parc de la Gaspésie. Our 10th year of welcoming guests. Dinner: seafood gratin, by reservation only.

From Québec City, Hwy 20 East, Rte 132 East to Cap-Chat. At west entrance, 3km from the windmill, and 2km from the Centre d'Interprétation du Vent et de la Mer.

B&B
AUBERGE «AU CRÉPUSCULE»

Monette Dion and Jean Ouellet
239, rue Notre-Dame Ouest,
Route 132
Cap-Chat G0J 1E0
tel/fax (418) 786-5751
http://come.to/crepuscule
jeanou@globetrotter.net

B&B	
single	$45
double	$55-65
triple	$75
quad.	$95
child	$15

VS MC IT

Open year round

Number of rooms	5
rooms with sink	3
rooms with private bath	1
rooms in basement	2
shared bathrooms	4

Activities: 🚣 🎣 🚶 🐎 🎿

4. CAP-CHAT, CAPUCINS

Put into port at Baie-des-Capucins, between the Jardins de Métis and Parc de la Gaspésie, to walk along the shore while admiring the windmills of Cap-Chat. In our riverside 1920s house, specially renovated for you, slowly savour dinner with the ebb and flow of the tides, as day gives way to night.

From Quebec City, Hwy 20 East, Rte 132 East twd Capucins. Follow signs for the Centre d'Interprétation, turn left on Rue du Village.

INN
AUBERGE DE LA
BAIE-DES-CAPUCINS

Sylvain Legris and
Bertrand Cloutier
274, rue du Village
Cap-Chat, Capucins G0J 1H0
(418) 786-2749
toll free 1-877-600-2749
capucins@globetrotter.net

	B&B	MAP
single	$65-70	$93-98
double	$75-80	$130-135

Taxes extra VS MC

Open year round

Number of rooms	3
rooms with private bath	3

Activities:

5. CAP-DES-ROSIERS, FORILLON

F e P R.5

Friendly, welcoming B&B near Forillon Park, with its enchanting landscape and animal life. Visit the tallest lighthouse in the country and go on one of our cruises (whale, seal and bird watching). While savouring a copious breakfast, you'll be dazzled by a magnificent view of the sea. Welcome to our home.

From Québec City, Hwy 20 East and Rte 132 East to Cap-des-Rosiers. From Gaspé, Rte 132 to Cap-des-Rosiers; 3km from the entrance to the north part of Forillon Park.

B&B
AUX PÉTALES DE ROSE

Alvine Lebrun
1184, boul. Cap-des-Rosiers
Cap-des-Rosiers G0E 1E0
(418) 892-5031

B&B	
single	$40
double	$55
triple	$70
quad.	$80
child	$10

Reduced rates: May 1 to June 1 and Sep. 15 to Oct. 31
Open: May 1 to Oct. 31

Number of rooms	5
rooms in basement	2
shared bathrooms	2

Activities:

6. CAP-DES-ROSIERS, FORILLON

F e P R.1 TA

Located by the seashore and only 5min from Parc Forillon, our B&B awaits vacationers who are looking for calm and relaxation. You will love our delectable mega-breakfasts including jam, home-made bread and good black coffee. Numerous activities await: marine mammals, ferryboat, kayaking and much more. Less than 2km from the lighthouse. Welcome home!

From Québec, Hwy 20 East and Rte 132 East to Cap-des-Rosiers.

B&B
LA MAISON ROSE

Danielle Slonina
1182 boul. Cap-de- Rosiers,
Route 132 Est
Cap-des-Rosiers G4X 6H1
(418) 892-5602
(450) 666-0303 (Laval)
fax (450) 666-9749 (Laval)

B&B	
single	$45
double	$55-60
triple	$70-75
quad.	$85-90
child	$5-15

Open: July 1 to Sep. 4

Number of rooms	3
rooms with sink	1
rooms with private bath	2
shared bathrooms	1

Activities:

7. CAPLAN ☀☀☀ F E P 🚗 🏖 R1 TA

Located between Bonaventure and Carleton, a memorable B&B overlooking Baie des Chaleurs – one you'll find hard to leave. Trails, beach, flowery gardens, farm animals. 10 minutes from Acadian Museum, Bioparc, adventure boats, golf, 2 salmon rivers, horseback riding. 20 minutes from St-Elzéar cave, British Heritage Centre. Lavish home-made breakfast. In the heart of Baie-des-Chaleurs. Health package: massage and sauna.

From Percé, Rte 132, after the bridge, 3km. In Caplan west side, 1.5km after the church.

B&B
À L'AUBERGE DE LA FERME

Jocelyn Brière
185, boul. Perron Est
Caplan G0C 1H0
(418) 388-5603
www.bbcanada.
com/2931.html
aubferme@globetrotter.net

B&B	
single	$30-35
double	$50
triple	$60-75
quad.	$80-90
child	$0-10

Taxes extra

Open year round

Number of rooms	5
shared wc	1
shared bathrooms	2

Activities: 🐚 🚶 🎿 🚴 🐎

8. CARLETON ★★ F E 🐕 P 🚗 R.1 TA

Located in the midst of activities, between the sea and mountains, just steps from the dock, where each season reveals its charms. Travelling by train or bus? It will be our pleasure to pick you up. Outdoor spa, four-seater bicycles ($), laundry service. Surprise at 4pm. Gourmet breakfasts. Packages available.

From Ste-Flavie, Rte 132 East. In Carleton, turn right at the first light onto Rte du Quai. From Percé, in Carleton, turn left at the second light onto Rte du Quai. At the corner of Rte 132 and Rte du Quai.

INN
AUBERGE LA VISITE SURPRISE

Diane Jodoin and
Martin Leblanc
527, boul. Perron
Carleton G0C 1J0
(418) 364-6553
toll free 1-800-463-7740
fax (418) 364-6500
martinleblanc@sympatico.ca

B&B	
single	$45
double	$55
triple	$70
quad.	$85
child	$5-12

Taxes extra VS MC ER AM

Reduced rates: 10% Nov. 1 to June 1
Open year round

Number of rooms	7
rooms in semi-basement	4
rooms with sink	5
shared bathrooms	3

Activities: 🐚 🚶 🎿 ⛷

9. CARLETON ☀☀☀ F E 🚭 P 🚗 R1 TA

Two Acadians welcome you to their granite Canadian-style house. Spacious rooms, country decor. Large veranda with view of Mont St-Joseph, a few kilometres from the B&B. Children welcome. Near playground, beach, hiking trails, bird-watching tower. 25km from Parc de Miguasha.

From Québec City, Hwy 20 E., Rte 132 E. At the entrance to Carleton, next to "Optique Chaleurs". Entrance on Rue des Érables, 1st house on right. From Percé, 3km from the church, next to Motel l'Abri.

B&B
GÎTE LES LEBLANC

Jocelyne and Rosaire LeBlanc
346, boul. Perron, C.P. 143
Carleton G0C 1J0
(418) 364-7601
(418) 364-3208
fax (418) 364-6333
indleb@globetrotter.net

B&B	
single	$40
double	$50
triple	$60
quad.	$70
child	$10

VS MC

Open: May 1 to Oct. 31

Number of rooms	4
rooms with sink	2
shared bathrooms	2

Activities: 🏛 🐚 🚶 🎿

10. CAUSAPSCAL

☀☀☀ F P R.2

B&B right in the heart of the village of Causapscal. Come relax in a setting typical of the Matapédia valley; it's just like being in a Swiss village. Enjoy a view of the Rivière Matapédia, where you'll see fishermen trying to catch salmon. Just the place for a pleasant stay!

Rte 132 West, Rue d'Anjou first street on the right after the traffic lights, left on Rue Belzile. Or Rte 132 East, Rue d'Anjou (by the «caisse populaire»), left on Rue Belzile.

B&B
LE GÎTE DE LA VALLÉE

Gilberte Barriault
71, rue Belzile
Causapscal G0J 1J0
(418) 756-5226
(418) 756-3072

B&B	
single	$35
double	$45
triple	$60
child	$10

Reduced rates: Nov. 1 to Apr. 30
Open: Jan. 16 to Dec. 14

Number of rooms	3
shared bathrooms	1

Activities: 🦪 🎿 🚶 🛷 🎿

11. ESCUMINAC, MIGUASHA

★★ F E 🚫 ♿ 🏊 🚗 P 🐕 R5 TA

Wanta-Qo-Ti, an experience worthy of its name: serenity. Located between the red cliffs of Miguasha and Baie des Chaleurs, facing the sea, this B&B was once a farm. Come discover this enchanting place. Right next to Parc de Miguasha, to the beaches of Carleton and Fort Listuguj.

From Carleton Rte 132 West to Nouvelle, twd Miguasha-Dalhousie ferry. At the ferry turn right on Rte Miguasha (becomes Pte-à-Fleurant) for 3.2km. From Matapédia Rte 132 East to Escuminac. Right at Parc Miguasha sign, 6.2km.

INN
AUBERGE WANTA-QO-TÍ

Bruce Wafer
77, chemin Pointe-Fleurant
Escuminac G0C 1N0
tel/fax (418) 788-5686
www.bbcanada.com/595.html
bwafer@globetrotter.net

B&B	
single	$40-52
double	$57-75
triple	$81
quad.	$96
child	$0-12

Taxes extra MC IT

Reduced rates: Sep.15 to June 15
Open year round

Number of rooms	7
rooms with private bath	5
shared bathrooms	2

Activities: 🏛 ⛵ 🎣 🛷 🎿

12. FORILLON, GASPÉ

☀☀ F E ♿ 🚗 P R5 TA

A warm family place between sea and mountain offering you an unforgettable stay: the sleep of the just, a gentle wakening followed by an energizing breakfast. Surrounded by the Forillon National Park, enjoy hiking, riding and bike trails, kayaking, swimming and cruises, where nature and history will enchant you. A memorable stopping place with gracious hosts, who await you year-round.

Hwy 20 East and Rte 132 East to Cap-aux-Os. From Gaspé, Rte 132 East to Cap-aux-Os.

B&B
GÎTE BLANCHETTE

Doreen Perry and
Gordon Blanchette
1594, boul. Forillon
Forillon, Gaspé G4X 6L2
tel/fax (418) 892-5782

B&B	
single	$45
double	$55
child	$0-10

Reduced rates: Sept. 15 to June 1
Open year round

Number of rooms	3
shared bathroom	1

Activities: 🏛 🦪 🎿 🏃 🐕

13. GASPÉ

✹✹✹✹ F E 🚫 P 🚗 R.1 TA

Less than 30 minutes from Forillon Park, downtown, 3-storey house, close to one hundred years old, with great view of Baie de Gaspé. Walking distance from restaurants and museum, promenade, cathedral, marina. Cosy rooms and lounge, period decor and ambiance await you. Refined breakfasts to soft music.

From Percé, after the bridge, straight ahead to the first lights. From Forillon, turn right at the first lights. From Murdochville, turn left at the first lights. Everyone, turn left at the 2nd traffic lights, 100 m.

B&B
COUETTE-CAFÉ
LES PETITS MATINS

Noëlline Couture and
Guy Papillon
129, rue de la Reine
Gaspé G4X 1T5
(418) 368-1370
www.bbcanada.
com/petitsmatins
gunoe@cablog.net

B&B	
single	$45-55
double	$55-65
triple	$85

VS MC

Open year round

Number of rooms	3
rooms with sink	1
shared wc	2
shared bathrooms	1

Activities: 🏛 🛶 👣 🚶 🏃

---

14. GASPÉ

✹✹✹✹ F e 🚫 🚗 P R.5

You will feel right at home upon entering the Gîte de Gaspé with Louisette and Gaétan's warm welcome. Enjoy a restful night and breakfast served with products from the family maple grove. Unforgettable! Panoramic view of Parc Forillon and the Gaspé bay from the terrace. Suggested activities.

From Québec City, Hwy 20 East, Rte 132 to Gaspé, toward town centre, Rue Jacques-Cartier up to Rue Wakeham, turn right 75 m, left on Rue Guignion.

B&B
GÎTE DE GASPÉ

Louisette Tapp and
Gaétan Poirier
201, rue Guignion
Gaspé G4X 1L3
(418) 368-5273
fax (418) 368-0119

B&B	
single	$45
double	$60
triple	$75
child	$10

Open: Apr. 1 to Oct. 31

Number of rooms	4
rooms with private bath	3
shared bathrooms	1
rooms in semi basement	1
rooms in basement	2

Activities: 🏛 🛶 🐟 👣 🚶

---

15. GASPÉ

✹✹✹✹ F E 🚫 🚗 P 🐕 R.2

On entering the Gîte Historique l'Émerillon, you'll discover the history of the Gaspésie. Located 30min from the Forillon National Park and 45min from Percé, this bed and breakfast stands in the heart of the Gaspé, overlooking the magnificent bay. Just steps away from restaurants, services and activities (museum, walks, swimming). Each of the four rooms has its own history and charm. As for breakfast, it will introduce you to local and homemade products.

In Percé, turn left at the second light. From Forillon park, turn right at first light and left at second light.

B&B
GÎTE HISTORIQUE
L'ÉMERILLON

Caroline Leclerc and
Olivier Nolleau
192, rue de la Reine
Gaspé G4X 1T8
tel/fax **(418) 368-3063**
(418) 360-3188
www.multimania.
com/emerillon
gaspeg@globetrotter.net

B&B	
single	$50-80
double	$60-80
triple	$75-100
quad.	$75-100

Reduced rates: 15% Oct. 15 to May 1
Open year round

Number of rooms	4
room with private bath	1
shared bathroom	1
shared wc	2

Activities: 🏛 🛶 👣 🚶 🛥

16. GASPÉ

Family house (3 generations). Built in 1922 with period furniture, Honeys' took in sailors during World War II. Enjoy a cocktail on the big porches facing the bay while admiring the superb sunsets. Next to the marina. Gaspesian breakfasts. Picnic on the grounds.

From Percé, right at flashing light after the Gaspé tourist office. From Forillon, left at Gaspé bridge, left at flashing light. From Murdochville, right at the bridge, left at flashing light.

B&B
GÎTE HONEYS

Françoise Lambert Kruse
and Harold Kruse
4, rue de la Marina
Gaspé G4X 3B1
tel/fax (418) 368-3294
www.bbcanada.
com/2866.html
honeys@cgocable.ca

B&B	
single	$50-55
double	$55-60
triple	$75
child	$10

VS

Open: May 1 to Oct. 31

Number of rooms	5
rooms with private wc	2
shared bathrooms	2

Activities: 🏛 ⛴ 🏄 🍴 🚶

17. GASPÉ

Located near Parc National Forillon. A 5min walk from all services, this Canadian-style house will please you with its hosts' welcome and its cleanliness, comfort and tranquillity. Documentation and information on our beautiful region's attractions. Gargantuan breakfast. Washer and dryer available, motorcycle/bicycle garage. See you soon!

Rte 132 or 198 to Gaspé. Rue Jacques-Cartier or Rue de la Reine to the cathedral, where Rue Mgr Leblanc begins opposite the steeple.

B&B
GÎTE LA CANADIENNE

Hélène Pelletier and
Denis Bériault
201, rue Mgr. Leblanc
Gaspé G4X 1S3
(418) 368-3806
fax (418) 368-7390
hberiault@yahoo.com

B&B	
single	$45
double	$55-60

Taxes extra

Open year round

Number of rooms	5
rooms with private bath	5
rooms in semi-basement	5

Activities: 🏛 ⛴ 🏄 🚶

18. GASPÉ

Across from the town of Gaspé, discover a lovely, welcoming period house, with its carved staircase, panoramic view and rich history. Come sample delicious cuisine where seafood holds pride of place. Fresh lobster from the fish tank, terrace, fireplace.

Rte 132 to Gaspé. Located on Boul. York East or Rte 198, across from the town, on the bay, near the tourist office.

INN
L'ANCÊTRE DE GASPÉ

Diane Lauzon and
Ronald Chevalier
55, boul. York Est
Gaspé G4X 2L1
(418) 368-4358
fax (418) 368-4054
www.gaspesie.com/ancetre
ancetre.gaspe
@globetrotter.net

B&B	
single	$65-75
double	$65-75
triple	$80
quad.	$95
child	$10

Taxes extra VS MC AM ER IT

Open: May 1 to Nov. 30

Number of rooms	3
rooms with private bath	1
shared wc	2
shared bathrooms	1

Activities: 🍴 🚶 🏄 🚲 🐎

19. HOPE TOWN, PASPÉBIAC

☀☀☀☀☀ F E 🚫 P 🚗 R4 TA

Prize for Excellence "Special Favorite" Provincial and Regional 1995-96. A dream stay by the sea awaits you in a quiet village located halfway between Rocher Percé and the Matapédia valley. Your visit here will be full of surprises. A trail of larches lined with wild berries leads to the salmon river. Awaken your taste buds with a dinner (lobster in season), by reservation only.

From Québec City, Hwy 20 East, Rte 132 East to Hopetown. From Percé, Rte 132 West to Hopetown, 4km west of the village of St-Godefroi, on the right.

B&B
LA CLÉ DES CHAMPS

Jo-Anne Guimond and
Bernard Gauthier
254, Route 132
Hope Town, Paspébiac
G0C 2K0
tel/fax (418) 752-3113
toll free 1-800-693-3113
www.simarts.com/lacle.html
lacle@globetrotter.net

B&B	
single	$40-45
double	$50-55

Open year round

Number of rooms	3
rooms with sink	1
shared wc	1
shared bathrooms	1

Activities: 🏛 🐚 🔦 🚶 🚲

20. LA MARTRE

☀☀☀ F E 🚫 P 🚗 R6

Prize for Excellence "Special Favorite" Provincial and Regional 1999. Away from the noise of the 132, cheerful ancestral home perched on a hill overlooking the sea and the picturesque village of La Martre. Extraordinary vista. Visit to the lighthouse, museum, archaeological digs. Private forest pavilion for meditation or picnic. Ideal location between two entrances to Parc de la Gaspésie.

From Quebec City, Hwy 20 East, Rte 132 East. 25km east of Ste-Anne-des-Monts, 25km west of Mont-St-Pierre. At the lighthouse, right on Rue de Écoliers, 300m.

B&B
GÎTE L'ÉCUME DE MER

Andréa Neu
21, rue des Écoliers
La Martre G0E 2H0
tel/fax (418) 288-5274
www.bbcanada.
com/3202.html
ecmer@globetrotter.qc.ca

B&B	
single	$50
double	$70
triple	$85
child	$0-15

Open: June 1 to Sep. 30

Number of rooms	4
shared bathrooms	2

Activities: 🐚 🔦 🚶 🚲

21. LES BOULES

★ ★ F e ♿ 🏊 P 🚗 ✕ TA

Secondhand booksellers in Brittany for 20 years, Marie and Raynald decide to return to the Gaspé. They stopped in a charming village, Métis-sur-Mer, and bought the former seaside hotel in a neighbouring village. Their love of peacefulness, good cooking, good books, conviviality and the river make this place a must. Jardins de Métis packages.

At the entrance to the Gaspé, 35km before Matane, 10km past the Jardins de Métis, turn left on Rte de Métis-sur-Mer, drive 6km, by the river.

INN
AUBERGE DU GRAND FLEUVE

Marie-José Fradette and
Raynald Pay
47, Principale, C.P. 99
Les Boules G0J 1S0
tel/fax (418) 936-3332
www.aubergedugrandfleuve.
qc.ca

	B&B	MAP
single	$54-82	$81-109
double	$54-82	$107-135
triple	$80-92	$160-172
quad.	$90-102	$196-208
child	$0-10	depend/age

Taxes extra VS MC IT

Open: Apr. 15 to Oct. 15

Number of rooms	12
rooms with sink	4
rooms with private bath	7
shared wc	2
shared bathrooms	2

Activities: 🐚 🐚 🔦 🚲 🐎

22. LES BOULES

★★ 🖼 F E P 🚗 ❌ TA

Open year round. Near the Jardins de Métis, our inn is licensed and offers refined cuisine. Choose the beauty of nature and the quietness of the countryside. Warm reception, copious breakfasts. Meet the inkeeper, who has lots of tales to tell and activities. Packages available.

Between Rimouski and Matane, following Rte 132, 10km from Jardins de Métis, after blue tourist sign, inland via Rte McNider, 4km, turn on 5e Rang.

INN
L'AUBERGE
«UNE FERME EN GASPÉSIE»

Pierre Dufort
1175, 5ᵉ Rang
Les Boules G0J 1S0
tel/fax (418) 936-3544
www.bonjourquebec.
com/info/fermengaspesie

B&B	
single	$40
double	$60
triple	$70
quad.	$80
child	$10

Taxes extra VS MC

Reduced rates: Sep. 1 to July 1
Open year round

Number of rooms	6
shared bathrooms	3

Activities: 🎿 🚶 🐎 🛷 🐴

---

23. MATANE

★★★ F e 🚭 P 🚗 R1 TA

Former site of the Fraser seigneury, where the Rivière Matane joins the St-Lawrence River. Near the town centre, ancestral house, woodlands, balcony and swings. Participate in a treasure hunt that ends with a welcoming cocktail by the fireplace. Window lace; resplendent with Raymonde and Guy's warm, affable welcome. Gaspésie tourism grand prize for hospitality 1999. 3 stars.

From Quebec City, Hwy 20 East, Rte 132 East. In Matane, Avenue du Phare, after "Tim Horton's," right on Rue Druillette, at no. 148, reception and parking.

INN
AUBERGE LA SEIGNEURIE

Raymonde and Guy Fortin
621, rue St-Jérôme
Matane G4W 3M9
(418) 562-0021
toll free 1-877-783-4466
fax (418) 562-4455
www3.sympatico.ca/mercanti/
seigneurie
mercanti@sympatico.ca

B&B	
single	$50-60
double	$60-80
triple	$85-95
quad.	$100-110
child	$10

Taxes extra VS MC IT

Reduced rates: Sep.15 to June 15
Open year round

Number of rooms	10
rooms with sink	3
rooms with private bath	5
rooms with sink and bath	2
shared wc	1
shared bathrooms	3

Activities: 🏛 🍷 🎿 🚴 🏃

---

24. MATANE

☀☀☀ F E 🚭 P 🚗 R.5 TA

Located right by the sea, our B&B offers an exceptional view! You will be treated to a warm welcome, a comfortable bed, a refined and lavish breakfast, as well as soft and relaxing music. Excellent restaurants in the vicinity. One kilometre from the town centre and the ferry.

On Route 132 in Matane, second house west of the lighthouse (Matane's Tourist Information Centre).

B&B
GÎTE DU PHARE

Josée Landry and
Gilles Blais
984, rue du Phare Ouest
Matane G4W 3M6
(418) 562-6606
fax (418) 562-8876
giteduphare@globetrotter.net

B&B	
single	$40-50
double	$50-60
triple	$70
quad.	$80
child	$10

VS

Open year round: with reservations from Oct. to May

Number of rooms	4
rooms with sink	2
shared bathrooms	2

Activities: 🚣 🎿 🛥 🎿 🏃

25. MATANE, ST-LÉANDRE

✸✸✸✸✸ | F | E | 🚭 | 🏊 | P | R14 | TA

Prize for Excellence "Special favorite" Regional 2000. Charming aeolian mountain village 15min from Matane. Fine home with old-manor-style ancestral decor. In homage to Nelligan, poetry in the rooms, romance by the fire, singing around the old piano. Refinement, cheery mornings, gourmet food. 100 acres of land, forest walks, swimming in the falls, natural spa. Golden retriever, affectionate kittens. Gaspésie tourism grand prize for hospitality 1997.

Rte 132 to Matane. In St-Ulric, south to St-Léandre. Follow the signs.

B&B
LE JARDIN DE GIVRE

Ginette Couture and
Gérald Tremblay,
3263, route du Peintre
Matane, St-Léandre G0J 2V0
tel/fax (418) 737-4411
toll free 1-800-359-9133
www.bbcanada.com/866.html
jardin-de-givre@globetrotter.net

B&B	
single	$40-50
double	$55-65
triple	$75
quad.	$90
child	$15

Taxes extra VS

Reduced rates: 10% 3 nights and more
Open year round

Number of rooms	5
rooms with private bath	2
shared wc	1
shared bathrooms	1

Activities: 🏛 🏄 🚶 🚴 🐎

26. MATANE, ST-LUC

✸✸✸ | F | E | P | 🚗 | 🐕 | R8 | TA

Gaspésie Excellence Prize 1997-98. At 200 m. in altitude, away from Rte. 132, 5 min. from Matane. View over the St. Lawrence River and the region. Therapeutic bath, hearty breakfast, European coffee, near salmon pass, Matane/Baie-Comeau/Godbout ferry. Winter sports, visit the beaver pond, 8km, maple grove, 20km and «parc des origneaux», 28km.

In Matane, opposite Jean Coutu, Ave. Jacques-Cartier to lights, left on Ave. St-Rédempteur, continue for about 7km. Blue "Gîte Le Panorama 1km" signpost, continue for 100m., left on Ch. Lebel, 700m.

B&B
LE PANORAMA

Marie-Jeanne and Hector Fortin
23, chemin Lebel
St-Luc-de-Matane G0J 2X0
tel/fax (418) 562-1100
toll free 1-800-473-3919
www.chez.com/gitepanorama
gitepanorama@chez.com

B&B	
single	$35-40
double	$50-55
triple	$75
quad.	$80
child	$10-15

VS

Reduced rates: Sept. 1 to May 31
Open year round

Number of rooms	4
rooms in semi-basement	2
shared bathrooms	2

Activities: 🚶 🚤 🐎 🎿 🐴

27. MATANE, ST-RENÉ

✸✸ | F | e | 🦽 | 🗡 | P | R10 | TA

Farmhouse fully renovated in the old-fashioned style, located by the road that once led to the village of Saint-Nil. Enjoy a wealth of outdoor activities while living in harmony with nature. Stay in the den of the settler who left his mark on these mountain tops... Your hosts await you. Dinner by reservation only. **Farm Stay p 50.**

From Matane, take southbound Rte 195. At the St-René church, drive 5.5km. Turn left on road to 10e and 11e Rang, then continue for 6.2km.

B&B
GÎTE DES SOMMETS

Marie-Hélène Mercier and
Louis-Philippe Bédard
161, Route 10e and 11e Rang
Saint-René-de-Matane G0J 3E0
(418) 224-3497
gitedessommets
@globetrotter.net

	B&B	MAP
single	$30	$40
double	$50	$70
triple	$75	$105
child	$15	$20

Open year round

Number of rooms	3
shared bathrooms	2
room with private bath	1

Activities: 🏛 🚶 🚶 🎿 🤸

146. GASPÉSIE

28. MATANE, ST-ULRIC

In Matane, see fishers at work, stock up on shrimp and visit the salmon run. In St-Ulric, take in the river's fresh air, watch superb sunsets and wind turbines, unique in Canada. Savour home-made jams, admire our magnificent vegetables and flower gardens, both different every year (winner of many prizes). Rooms with sinks. Welcome all.

From Montréal, Hwy 20 East, Rte 132 East. 45km east of Ste-Flavie and 18km west of Matane. From Gaspé, Rte 132 North. From Matane, drive 18km on Rte 132.

B&B
CHEZ NICOLE

Nicole and René Dubé
3371, Route 132,
St-Ulric-de-Matane
Matane G0J 3H0
tel/fax (418) 737-4896
http://gitenicole.ctw.net

B&B	
single	$35
double	$45-50
triple	$55
quad.	$65
child	$10

Open year round

Number of rooms	3
rooms with sink	3
shared wc	1
shared bathrooms	1

Activities:

29. MONT-JOLI

Our house, located on a plateau 2km from Mont-Joli and 7km from Ste-Flavie, offers a magnificent view of the river. Just minutes from the Jardins de Métis, the Atlantic Salmon Interpretation Centre and good restaurants. Lodging in winter with skiing right nearby. We'll be waiting with a hearty breakfast and traditional accordion music.

From Québec City, Hwy 20 East, Rte 132 East. 2km from Mont-Joli. Or from the Vallée de la Matapédia, before Mont-Joli, 5 min from the shopping centre.

B&B
GÎTE BELLEVUE

Nicole and Émilien Cimon
2332, rue Principale,
route 132
Mont-Joli G5H 3N6
(418) 775-2402
toll free 1-888-551-2402

B&B	
single	$40
double	$50-55
triple	$65
quad.	$75
child	$10

Reduced rates: Sep. 1 to May 31
Open year round

Number of rooms	3
shared bathrooms	2

Activities:

30. NEWPORT

A bed and breakfast to discover! A wealthy merchant's former estate sprawled along the township's most beautiful beach. Old-world charm, enchanting decor and cozy comfort. Nestled between Percé and Bonaventure, it's the ideal spot for a long stay. A dream place for quiet nights and discovery-filled days. Delicious, fresh Gaspésie cooking. Your stay will be a memory to cherish!

From Ste-Flavie, Rte 132 East to Newport. 1.5km west of the church, house facing the islets.

B&B
AUBERGE LES DEUX ÎLOTS

Guylaine Michel and
André Lambert
207, Route 132, C.P. 223
Newport G0C 2A0
(418) 777-2801
toll free 1-888-404-2801
fax (418) 777-4719
www.bbcanada.com/lesdeuxilots
aubergelesdeuxilots
@globetrotter.net

	B&B	MAP
single	$45-60	$65-80
double	$55-70	$95-110
triple	$85	$145
quad.	$100	$180
child	$5-10	$15-20

Taxes extra VS

Reduced rates: Sep.16 to June 14
Open year round

Number of rooms	5
rooms with private bath	2
shared wc	1
shared bathrooms	2

Activities:

31. NEW RICHMOND

✹✹✹ F E 🚫 🏖 P 🚗 R.5 TA

Experience the atmosphere of a cosy Victorian and its exceptional view of Baie-des-Chaleurs. A large veranda facing the sea and the mountains. Spacious and comfortable rooms. The seashore and beach are right nearby! Quiet surroundings, away from route 132.

From Québec City, Hwy 20 East, Rte 132 East to New Richmond. At the intersection of Rte 299, turn right, drive 5km to Boul. Perron. Or from Percé, once in New Richmond, turn left on Boul. Perron.

B&B
AUBERGE L'ÉTOILE DE MER

Diane Bourdages and
Jacques Veillette
256, boul. Perron Ouest
New Richmond G0C 2B0
(418) 392-6246
www.bbcanada.com/3134.html
etoilebb@globetrotter.net

B&B	
single	$45-55
double	$55-65
triple	$75-80
quad.	$85-95
child	$10

Taxes extra VS

Open year round

Number of rooms	5
rooms with private bath	2
shared bathrooms	2

Activities: 🏛 🚣 🚶 🏃 🚲

---

32. NEW RICHMOND

✹✹✹ F e 🚫 P R2 TA

Ancestral house surrounded by flowers, nestled in a peaceful spot in the heart of Baie des Chaleurs. Your cheerful, friendly hostess serves up lavish breakfasts. Enjoy a stroll on the footpath, located a few minutes away, where you can admire a paradise of birds, including eagles, kingfishers and others.

From Quebec City, Hwy 20 East, Rte 132 to New Richmond. At the 3ʳᵈ flashing light, turn right on Chemin St-Edgar, 1.7km, left on Ave. Leblanc, 150m. From Percé, Rte 132 West, at the 1ˢᵗ flashing light, turn left on Chemin St-Edgar, 1.7km, then left on Ave. Leblanc.

B&B
GÎTE DE LA MAISON
LEVESQUE

Vyola A. Levesque
180, Avenue Leblanc
New-Richmond G0C 2B0
(418) 392-5267
toll free 1-888-405-5267
fax (418) 392-6948
www.gitedelamaison
levesque.qc.ca
maison.levesque
@globetrotter.net

B&B	
single	$30
double	$50-55
triple	$65-70
child	$5-10

Reduced rates: Sep. 1 to May 31
Open year round

Number of rooms	3
shared bathrooms	2

Activities: 🐚 🚶 🏃 🚲 🐎

---

33. NEW RICHMOND

✹✹✹ F E 🚫 🏖 P R2 TA

Amidst beautiful white birch on the Baie-des-Chaleurs, our cottage awaits you with a warm welcome. Wooded paths, access to the beach and peaceful surroundings are yours to enjoy.

From Québec City, Hwy 20 East, Rte 132 East to New Richmond. At the intersection of Rte 299, turn right, drive 3.5km to Rue de la Plage and turn right. From Percé, turn left at same intersection.

B&B
GÎTE LES BOULEAUX

Patricia Fallu and
Charles Gauthier
142, rue de la Plage
New Richmond G0C 2B0
(418) 392-4111
fax (418) 392-6048

B&B	
single	$40-50
double	$45-60
triple	$60-75
quad.	$85
child	$5-10

VS

Open year round

Number of rooms	4
rooms with sink	3
rooms in basement	2
shared bathrooms	2

Activities: 🐚 🚣 🚶 🏃 🤸

34. NEW RICHMOND

☀☀☀ | F | P | R2.8

We are located in an attractive little corner of New-Richmond. Relaxation, serenity, home-made breakfasts. The sea and the mountains are also on the menu. Fishing, hiking, cultural and outdoor activities. Our house is your house. I will be waiting for you.

From Québec City, Hwy 20 East, Rte 132 East to New Richmond. Take Chemin Cyr and Boul. Perron East, turn left, drive 2km. From Percé, Boul. Perron, drive 0.4km and turn right.

B&B
LA RELÂCHE

Émilienne Bourdages
108, rue Bellevue, C.P. 36
New Richmond, Cap-Noir
G0C 1C0
(418) 392-6749
fax (418) 392-6359
odini@globetrotter.net

B&B	
single	$35
double	$45-50
triple	$50-60
quad.	$80
child	$5-10

Open year round

Number of rooms	3
shared bathrooms	2

Activities: 🏛 🚣 🎣 🎿 ⛷

---

35. NOUVELLE

☀☀☀ | F | e | 🚭 | 🚗 | P | R1.5 | TA

Located in Baie des Chaleurs, this (1897) village presbytery offers five personalized rooms. Come stay in the romantic Chambre de la Gouvernante or the majestic Chambre de Monseigneur. Rustic decor, warm ambiance, exquisite breakfast with a touch of home, in keeping with the house. Set back from Route 132, 8min from Parc de Miguasha, a world heritage site, and 15min from Carleton.

Rte 132 East or West, in the village centre, set back from Rte 132, next to the church.

B&B
À L'ABRI DU CLOCHER

Sylvie Landry and
Sylvain Savoie
5, rue de l'Église
Nouvelle G0C 2E0
(418) 794-2580
www.bbcanada.
com/alabriduclocher

B&B	
single	$45
double	$55
triple	$75
quad.	$95
child	$10

VS

Open year round

Number of rooms	5
shared bathrooms	2
room with private wc	1
room with sink	2

Activities: 🏛 🚲 🎣 🚶 🚴

---

36. ST-ANTOINE-DE-PADOUE

☀☀☀ | F | e | 🚗 | P | R8.5 | TA

Situated in the backcountry between the sea and the mountain near Matapédia River (15min from Rte 132), Gîte la Villa du Vieux Clocher used to be a presbytery (1910). It's now furnished with period furniture and filled with good humour and conviviality. A variety of activities await. Exquisite Gaspesian breakfasts and cosy room. A dream come true! The next chapter in this adventure story is waiting for you: a town to discover.

From Québec City, Hwy 20 E, Rte 132 E. In front of Jardins de Métis, take the 234 to St-Octave-de-Métis and Padoue.

B&B
GÎTE LA VILLA
DU VIEUX CLOCHER

Marjolaine Fournier
179, rue Beaulieu
Padoue G0J 1X0
(418) 775-9654
toll free 1-877-598-2907
fax (418) 775-3195
marjolaine.fournier@
ri.cgocable.ca

B&B	
single	$40-60
double	$55-75
child	$10

VS

Reduced rates: Oct.1 to May 31
Open year round

Number of rooms	5
rooms with private bath	1
shared bathrooms	3

Activities: 🏛 🎣 🚣 🎿 🚲

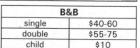

37. PERCÉ

We are located in the centre of the village, behind the church. Everything is very quiet, especially at night. Spacious solarium, large rooms, home-made breakfasts. Here you will be able to park the car, relax and go for a walk. Everything is within reach: Île Bonaventure, Percé rock, mountains, restaurants, boutiques. We are from Percé, live hear year-round and can help you plan your activities.

Rte 132 East to the village of Percé. Take rue du Cap Barré to the last house.

B&B
À L'ABRI DU VENT

Ginette Gagné and
Michel Méthot
44, Cap Barré
Percé G0C 2L0
tel/fax (418) 782-2739

B&B	
single	$45
double	$55
triple	$70
child	$15

VS

Reduced rates: 10$/room from May 15 to July 1 and Sep. 1 to Oct. 15
Open: May 15 to Oct. 15

Number of rooms	5
rooms with sink	4
rooms in basement	2
shared bathrooms	2

Activities:

---

38. PERCÉ

"La Rêvasse" is a dream come true. Why else visit Percé? Oh yes, the rock... The advantage of the B&B at the rock is that it is accessible at both low and high tides. Plus, it is inhabited by very friendly people... Thanks for the Percé welcome!' (*S. Bret, Lyon-France*)
Excursion package: 2 nights, cruise to île Bonaventure, off-track guided tours on the mountains of Percé. 2 people/double $158.[25] with reservation only. **Ad end of this region.**

From Québec City, Hwy 20 East, Rte 132 East to Percé. Near the Palais de Justice, Rue St-Michel.

B&B
À LA RÊVASSE

Brenda Cain and
William Lambert
16, rue St-Michel, C.P. 281
Percé G0C 2L0
(418) 782-2102
tel/fax (418) 782-2980
http://membres.tripod.
fr/revasse/revasse.html
revasse@globetrotter.net

B&B	
single	$40-45
double	$50-60
triple	$70-75
quad.	$85-90
child	$15

Taxes extra

Open: May 1 to Oct. 15

Number of rooms	5
rooms with private bath	1
rooms in basement	1
rooms with sink	4
shared bathrooms	2

Activities:

---

39. PERCÉ

A love story set in a period house, built in the 18th century. Historic estate in the heart of Percé, right on the sea. Pauline Vaillancourt and Jean-François Guité offer you a cozy stay in a dream setting. Take your breakfast on the veranda, facing the sea. Departures for the Percé rock and the isle of birds, a 2min walk. Take advantage of our anniversary rebates. Mentioned in Michelin, AAA, CAA, Ulysses and other guides.

Rte 132, in the village centre, by the sea, look for the large black sign.

INN
AUBERGE AU PIRATE 1775

Pauline Vaillancourt
169, Route 132
Percé G0C 2L0
(418) 782-5055
fax (418) 782-5680
getty@quebectel.com

B&B	
single	$90-150
double	$90-150
triple	$175
quad.	$200
child	$25

Taxes extra VS MC AM ER IT

Reduced rates: 25% 3 nights and more, rates for 1 or 2 people
Open: early June to early Oct.

Number of rooms	5
rooms with private bath	3
shared wc	1
rooms with sink	2
shared bathroom	1

Activities:

40. PERCÉ

☀☀ F E 🐕 🚗 P R2 TA

Lucille and Victor, 9 years old, invite you to their traditional family home situated just outside the affluent town centre of Percé. The setting exudes calm and tranquillity, and this vast landscaped property has a beautiful view of the sea. Generous breakfasts made from local products.

From Gaspé, Rte 132 W. for Percé. Only 3.1km from Percé Tourist information. From Carleton, Rte 132 E. for Percé. It's 12.6km from the Cap d'Espoir caisse populaire.

B&B
CHEZ DESPARD

Lucille Despard
468, route 132 ouest
Percé G0C 2L0
(418) 782-5446

B&B	
single	$35-40
double	$45-50
triple	$60
quad.	$70
child	$7

Reduced rates: Sep.1 to June 20
Open year round

Number of rooms	4
shared bathrooms	2

Activities: 🏛 ⛵ 🚤 🎣 🛶

41. PERCÉ

F E 🚭 🚗 P R.1 TA

A bed and breakfast located in the heart of Percé's natural area, steps away from the famous Percé rock. We offer you the quiet and comfort of the family home. True to the family tradition passed down by Georges, our welcome is founded on Gaspé hospitality, renowned for its human warmth and simplicity. Excursion packages: two nights, tickets for Île Bonaventure, guided tour of the Percé mountains: double occupancy $158.25. **Ad end of this region.**

Rue Principale, Rue Ste-Anne at the corner of the CLSC. Near the church.

B&B
GÎTE CHEZ GEORGES

Brenda Cain and
William Lambert
16, rue Ste-Anne, C.P. 65
Percé G0C 2L0
tel/fax (418) 782-2980
(418) 782-2102
www.percesie.cjb.net
revasse@globetrotter.net

B&B	
single	$45-50
double	$50-55

Taxes extra VS

Open: May 1 to Oct. 31

Number of rooms	4
shared bathrooms	2
rooms with sink	2

Activities: 🏛 ⛵ 🚣 🎣 🛶

42. PERCÉ

☀☀☀ F e 🚗 P R2 TA

Located west of Percé, Nicole and Adelard's house is a haven of peace with a splendid view of the sea and a relaxing patio area. Spacious rooms, bathroom with whirlpool bath, where everything is in place to ensure your well-being. Lavish breakfasts made from homemade products. Fiddle entertainment provided by grandma in the evening. We are told: "Your welcome makes us feel right at home."

2km west of the Percé tourist office.

B&B
GÎTE DU CAP BLANC

Nicole Laflamme and
Adélard Dorion
442, Rte 132 Ouest, C.P. 221
Percé G0C 2L0
(418) 782-2555
fax (418) 782-2662
www.iquebec.
com/giteducapblanc
ndorion@globetrotter.qc.ca

B&B	
single	$50
double	$55-75
triple	$90
quad.	$105
child	$5-15

VS

Reduced rates: Oct. 15 to May 15
Open year round

Number of rooms	5
rooms with private bath	2
rooms with sink	2
shared bathroom	1

Activities: 🛶 ⛵ 🚤 🎣 🛶

43. PERCÉ

✎ F E 🚫 🚲 P ✗ R.25

This century-old house is located on quiet Rue de l'Église. Its location and unique ambiance that testifies to its past ensure peacefulness and tranquillity. Added to that are the view of the rock, the village right nearby, a generous breakfast with homemade treats and trilingual service. And, because Percé rhymes with hospitality, we'll do the rest.

Opposite Rue du Quai, in the village centre, Rue de l'Église to the end.

B&B
LE PRESBYTÈRE

Michel Boudreau
47, rue de l'Église, C.P. 178
Percé G0C 2L0
(418) 782-5557
fax (418) 782-5587
www.perce-gite.com
percegite@yahoo.ca

B&B	
single	$49-69
double	$59-79
triple	$69-89
quad.	$79-99
child	$5-10

VS MC

Open: June 1 to Oct. 15

Number of rooms	5
shared bathrooms	2
room with sink	2

Activities: 🚤 🎣 ⛺ 🐟 🎿

44. PERCÉ, STE-THÉRÈSE

☀☀☀ F e P ✗ R1.5 TA

Enjoy a stay in this picturesque fishing village. Upon entering our B&B, you will be greeted by an old fisherman carved into the door by a St-Jean-Port-Joli artist. Comfortable, well-decorated rooms. Lavish breakfasts in a spacious, Bahutier-style dining room next to the sunny-coloured kitchen. Stay 2 nights and get a free picnick.

15 min from Percé, Rte 132 West. In Ste-Thérèse, halfway between the dock and the church. At the windmill, opposite the Bria restaurant.

B&B
GÎTE DU MOULIN À VENT

Jeannine Desbois
247, Route 132, C.P. 10
Ste-Thérèse-de-Gaspé
G0C 3B0
(418) 385-4922
tel/fax (418) 385-3103

B&B	
single	$35
double	$50-60
child	$10

Open: May 1 to Sep. 30

Number of rooms	4
shared bathrooms	2

Activities: 🏛 🚤 🎣 🎿 🚴

45. PETITE-VALLÉE

★★ F e 🏊 P 🚲 ✗ R5 TA

On a long headland, set back from Route 132 and one hour (70km) from Forillon Park, our centenary house opens its doors to offer you a family welcome and traditional cuisine, featuring fish and seafood. Glassed-in dining-room with superb sea view. Dinner and theatre or concert packages available. **Country Home p 157. See colour photos.**

From Québec, Hwy 20 East, Rte 132 East to Petite-Vallée. At the entrance to the village, take the first street on the left, Longue-Pointe. At the fork, stay left.

INN
LA MAISON LEBREUX

Denise Lebreux
2, rue Longue Pointe,
Petite-Vallée G0E 1Y0
(418) 393-2662
tel/fax (418) 393-3105
www.lamaisonlebreux.com
lamaisonlebreux
@globetrotter.net

	B&B	MAP
single	$40-45	$55-65
double	$50-60	$80-100
triple	$70	$115-130
quad.	$80	$140-160
child	$7-10	$15-20

Taxes extra VS IT MC

Open year round

Number of rooms	8
rooms with sink	4
shared bathrooms	3

Activities: 🐟 🏛 🎿 🚤 🎣

46. ST-ALEXIS-DE-MATAPÉDIA ☀☀☀ F E 🏊 🚫 P 🚗 R1.5 TA

Enjoy a unique stay on a natural plateau. Original, peaceful, radiant house with flowers, vast wood-lands, large heated in-ground pool beneath a dome. Activities, vistas, wildlife observation, maple groves, canoeing, fishing. A perfect stop-over on the way to New Brunswick and Îles-de-la-Madeleine. Very warm welcome.

Located 85km from Carleton. In Matapédia, after the bridge, turn right toward St-Alexis for 10km; at the stop sign, straight ahead for 1.4km. 100km from Amqui; take the St-Alexis-bound bridge, via St-Benoît, 10km.

B&B
BOIS D'AVIGNON

Laura Chouinard
171, rue Rustico
St-Alexis-de-Matapédia
G0J 2E0
(418) 299-2537
tel/fax (418) 299-2111
toll free 1-877-767-8027
www.gitecanada.com/
boisdavignon
boisdavi@globetrotter.qc.ca

B&B	
single	$44
double	$52
triple	$60
quad.	$70
child	$9

Taxes extra

Reduced rates: Oct. 1 to June 1
Open year round

Number of rooms	3
shared bathrooms	2
shared wc	1

Activities: 🎣 🚴 🛶 🎿 🏃

47. ST-ALEXIS-DE-MATAPÉDIA ☀☀☀ F E 🧵 🚗 P R.5

An unparalleled detour. Warm wel-come. Ancestral house with cozy comfort, original decor and gourmet fare. Picturesque site, for nature- and animal-lovers. Thrills and chills guaranteed when observing our wild black bears. "Magical stolen moments in bear country... thank you Daniel!" (Conti, Italy)

9km from Matapédia. Turn left at the stop sign. From Amqui, twd St-Alexis bridge, drive 5km along un-paved road; at the stop sign, con-tinue straight ahead on Rue Principale.

B&B
GÎTE J.A.DUFOUR

Luce Bossé and Daniel Dufour
170, rue Principale, C.P. 100
Saint-Alexis-de-Matapédia
G0J 2E0
(418) 299-3040
fax (418) 299-3140
www.gitescanada.com/
jadufour
j.a.dufour@globetrotter.net

B&B	
single	$40
double	$55
child	$10

Open year round

Number of rooms	5
shared bathroom	2

Activities: 🏛 🛶 🎿 🏃

48. ST-ALEXIS-DE-MATAPÉDIA ✎ F E ♿ 🚗 P R1 TA

Holiday on a farm? Why not! Brac-ing, edifying vacation: in dairy farm, woods, rivers, small, equip-ped house with wood-panelled inte-rior. Fishing, canoeing, swimming, cycling, hunting, ice fishing, maple grove, wilderness camping, sweat lodge, campfire, Acadian history. On way into Baie des Chaleurs and N.-B. Warm welcome. By reserva-tion. RVs welcome. 10min from Matapedia and Restigouche River.

From Mont-Joli to Matapédia, St-Alexis bridge, Rang St-Benoît, 6km. From Carleton to Matapédia, Matapédia bridge. 16km, right on Rang St-Benoît.

B&B
LA P'TITE MAISON
DES LEBLANC

René Leblanc
153 A, rang St-Benoit
St-Alexis-de-Matapédia
G0J 2E0
tel/fax (418) 299-2106
tel/fax (418) 299-2443
maisonleblanc
@moncourrier.com

B&B	
single	$35
double	$50
triple	$65
child	$8

Reduced rates: 10% 2 nights and more, special rates on week days
Open year round

Number of rooms	3
shared bathroom	1

Activities: 🏛 🛶 🏃 🎿 🚴

49. STE-ANGÈLE-DE-MÉRICI

☀☀☀ F E 🐴 🚗 P 🏊 R.5 TA

14km from St-Flavie and the St. Lawrence River, in the heart of the village of Ste-Angèle, nature centre of the Métissienne region. In-ground pool; cozy, comfortable rooms; hearty breakfast any time. 10 to 20km from Mont Comi, Jardins de Métis, salmon fishing on the Métis river 300 m, Ste-Luce beach, De La Pointe golf course, Mont-Joli airport. Rimouski: 48km. Free stay for children under 6 year old.

Hwy 20 and Rte 132 East. In Ste-Flavie, twd Mont-Joli. 12km past Mont-Joli. In the village of Ste-Angèle, turn right onto Boul. de la Vallée.

B&B
LA GUIMONTIÈRE

Jeanne-Mance Guimont
515, av. Bernard Levesque
Ste-Angèle-de-Mérici G0J 2H0
(418) 775-5542

B&B	
single	$40
double	$55
triple	$75
quad.	$95
child	$0-10

Reduced rates: Sep.15 to June 15
Open year round

Number of rooms	5
shared bathrooms	2

Activities: 🚣 🚶 🎿 🐕

---

50. STE-ANNE-DES-MONTS

☀☀☀ F e P 🐴 R1 TA

Why Ste-Anne-des-Monts? Well, of course to discover the magnificent Parc de la Gaspésie, Mont Albert and Mont Jacques Cartier. Golf, Explorama, and a warm welcome from the locals. 10% reductions for stays of three days or more. Rooms in the basement have a separate entrance.

From Québec City, Hwy 20 East, Rte 132 East to Ste-Anne-des-Monts. Turn left before the bridge. At the stop sign turn left on 1st Avenue.

B&B
CHEZ MARTHE-ANGÈLE

Marthe-Angèle Lepage
268, 1ʳᵉ Avenue Ouest,
C.P. 3159
Ste-Anne-des-Monts G0E 2G0
tel/fax (418) 763-2692

B&B	
single	$38-40
double	$53-55
triple	$68-70
quad.	$80
child	$10-15

Reduced rates: 10% 3 nights and more
Open year round

Number of rooms	5
rooms with sink	3
rooms in basement	3
shared bathrooms	3

Activities: 🚣 🚶 🛷 🎿 🏃

---

51. STE-ANNE-DES-MONTS

✎ F E 🚫 ♿ 🐴 🚗 P 🚢 R.5 TA

Perched atop a seaside cliff, with private access to the strand, at the gates of the majestic Chic-Chocs Mountains. We offer several nature packages. Moose-watching, sailing, interpretation of the marine world and more. Stay in one of our two spacious, very private rooms. Star-gaze from your pillow and be lulled by the mesmerizing tides. "Monts Gîte et Mer": nature, a bed and breakfast, the seashore. **See ad on front inside cover.**

Rte 132 East to Tourelle, 0.5km east of the church.

B&B
MONTS GÎTE ET MER

Andrée Poisson and
Mario Bellemare
218, 1ʳᵉ Avenue Est
Ste-Anne-des-Monts G0E 2G0
(418) 763-5308
toll free 1-800-903-0206
fax (418) 763-5398
http://site.voila.fr/montsgite
info@giselebenoit.com

B&B	
single	$45-55
double	$55-75
triple	$85
quad.	$95
child	$5

Taxes extra VS MC IT

Reduced rates: 10% Oct. 15 to May 15 or 3 nights and more
Open year round

Number of rooms	4
rooms with private bath	3
shared wc	1
shared bathroom	1

Activities: 🏛 🚤 🚣 🚶 🏃

52. STE-ANNE-DES-MONTS

❋❋❋ F e P 🚗 🎿 R1 TA

Our guests cherish our merry breakfasts of favourite treats like homemade bread, jams and pancakes; the quiet location near the park and the sea, far from Route 132; and the soothing sea breeze. Guests tell us our warm welcome makes them feel like family. Welcome!

From Quebec City, Hwy 20 East, Rte 132 East, at junction of Rte 299 (Rte du Parc) for 1km. Turn left on 2nd street after the bridge; or heading east from the church, 1km, on the right.

B&B
SOUS LA BONNE ÉTOILE

Denis Béchard
30, 5ᵉ Rue Est, C.P. 1132
Ste-Anne-des-Monts
G0E 2G0
(418) 763-3402
fax (418) 763-3456

B&B	
single	$40
double	$55
triple	$70
quad.	$85
child	$10-15

VS

Reduced rates: Nov. 1 to May 31
Open year round

Number of rooms	4
rooms with sink	1
rooms in semi-basement	4
shared bathrooms	2

Activities: 🏛 ⛷ 🚶 🎿 🏃

53. STE-ANNE-DES-MONTS, TOURELLE

❋❋❋ F E P 🚗 R.5

At the heart of the Gaspé peninsula, outdoor terrace from which to admire marine mammals, superb sunsets and fishing village. Discover Parc de la Gaspésie, Mont Albert, Mont Jacques-Cartier, Explorama, walking by the river. Two rooms with private bathrooms. Copious breakfast. 10% reduction for 3 nights or more. Welcome.

From Québec City, Hwy 20 East, Rte 132 East to Tourelle. From the rest area, drive 0.2km, turn left, white house.

B&B
AU COURANT DE LA MER

Bibiane Miville and
Rino Cloutier
3, rue du Fleuve, C.P. 191
Tourelle G0E 2J0
tel/fax (418) 763-5440
For reservation only:
1-800-230-6709
from 5 pm to 11 pm
www.iquebec.com/
au-courant-de-la-mer/
aucourantdelamer
@iquebec.com

B&B	
single	$40-55
double	$55-65
triple	$67-70
quad.	$80
child	$10-15

VS

Reduced rates: 10% 3 nights and more
Open: Apr. 1 to Oct. 31

Number of rooms	5
rooms with private bath	2
shared bathrooms	2
shared wc	1
rooms in basement	1

Activities: 🚶 🛷 🛶 ⛷

54. STE-ANNE-DES-MONTS, TOURELLE

❋❋❋ F e 🚫 P R5 TA

Enjoy the peace and rustic decor of our B&B. Lovely rooms with bathroom for your comfort. Savour our delicious homemade jams. Take advantage of our flowery terrace, with a view of the river. Owner Jean-Guy will share his passion for Parc de la Gaspésie with you!

Hwy 20 East and Rte 132. 1hr from Matane. From the Tourelle church, drive 4km along the 132. From Gaspé: 215km, 2.5hrs.

B&B
GÎTE DE LA NOUVELLE-
FRANCE

Danielle Martin and
Jean-Guy Brisebois
203, boul. Perron, rte 132
Ste-Anne-des-Monts, Tourelle
G0E 2J0
(418) 763-3338
martin.dani@globetrotter.net

B&B	
single	$55
double	$60
triple	$85
child	$12

VS

Open year round

Number of rooms	4
rooms with private bath	4

Activities: 🚶 🚶 🐎 🏃 🐎

55. STE-ANNE-DES-MONTS, TOURELLE ☼☼☼ F e 🚗 P R3.5 TA

Welcome to our house at the foot of a lovely mountain by the "sea". You can walk along the shore to Tourelle and watch the fishermen in the harbour. Our breakfasts, complete with crepes and a selection of home-made preserves, go over big with guests – as does our Gaspé-style table talk. You'll feel right at home in our house.

From Québec City, Hwy 20 East, Rte 132 East to Tourelle. Drive 2km past the church (we are located 8 min from the intersection of the 299 - Parc de la Gaspésie Sainte-Anne-des-Monts).

B&B
GÎTE DE LA TOUR

Pierre Paul Labrie
151, boul. Perron Est C.P. 183
Tourelle G0E 2J0
tel/fax (418) 763-2802

B&B	
single	$35
double	$50
triple	$60
child	$5-10

VS

Open: June 15 to Sept. 30

Number of rooms	3
shared bathrooms	2

Activities: 🏛 🏃 🎿 🏂 ⛷

56. STE-FLAVIE ☼☼☼ F e 🚭 🏊 P 🚗 R.1 TA

Magnificent site, facing the majestic St. Lawrence River. Vast landscaped grounds. Small covered bridge across the river to the falls and the lake, where you can feed the trout. Welcome to snowmobilers; warm reception, memorable decor, lavish breakfasts. Jardins de Métis, 5km; art centre, 0.7km; snowmobiling, 1.5km. Family-size room available.

From Quebec City, Hwy 20 East, Rte 132 East to Ste-Flavie. Continue to 571 Route de la Mer.

B&B
AUX CHUTES

Nicole R. and Jocelyn Bélisle
571, route de la Mer
Ste-Flavie G0J 2L0
(418) 775-9432
toll free for reservation only
1-877-801-2676
fax (418) 775-5747
www.bbcanada.
com/1866.html

B&B	
single	$40-50
double	$50-65
triple	$65-80
quad.	$80-95
child	$10-15

VS MC

Reduced rates: 10% 3 nights and more from Otc. 15 to Apr. 15
Open year round

Number of rooms	5
room with private bath	1
shared wc	1
rooms with sink	4
shared bathrooms	2

Activities: 🏛 🎣 🚣 🏃 🛷

57. STE-FLAVIE ☼☼☼ F E 🚭 P 🚗 R.2

Come and experience traditional Gaspé hospitality in an ancestral home rich with the echoes of four generations of the same family. Magnificent sunsets over the St-Laurent will cast a spell. 6km from the famous Métis gardens and just a few steps from excellent restaurants.

Take Rte 132 East twd Gaspé, 24km beyond Rimouski, and 0.4km beyond the tourist information centre of Ste-Flavie.

B&B
LA MARÉE BLEUE

Jacqueline Paquet and
Peter Innis
411, route de la Mer
Ste-Flavie G0J 2L0
(418) 775-7801
www.bbcanada.
com/lamareebleue
innisp@globetrotter.net

B&B	
single	$45-50
double	$50-55
child	$10

VS IT

Reduced rates: Sep.1 to May 31
Open year round

Number of rooms	4
shared bathrooms	2

Activities: 🏛 🎣 🐎 🏃 🚲

58. STE-FLAVIE

☀☀☀ F e P 🚗 🍽 R1 TA

I await you by the river at the gateway to the Gaspé region amongst the charm and comfort of a wooden house. Here, the day starts with the sound of waves lapping on the shore, warms up with the pleasant company and comes to a close with the colourful spectacle of the sunset.

From Québec City, Hwy 20 East, Rte 132 East to Ste-Flavie. 5km past the church, driving east along the shore. From Gaspé, Rte 132 West. 60km from Matane.

B&B
LA QUÉBÉCOISE

Cécile Wedge
705, route de la Mer,
route 132 Est
Ste-Flavie G0J 2L0
(418) 775-2898
(418) 775-3209
fax (418) 775-9793

B&B	
single	$40
double	$50-55

Reduced rates: Oct. 1 to May 31
Open year round

Number of rooms	3
shared wc	1
shared bathrooms	1

Activities: 🏛 ⚓ 🚤 🎣 🚶

59. STE-FLORENCE

☀☀ F e 🚫 🚗 P R1.5 TA

Situated away from the hustle and bustle, this ancient house used to be my grandparents' home. You will enjoy a refreshing sleep here. Behind the house, there's a stream, where you fish the trout or appreciate its natural surroundings. In front, there's a spectacular view of Rivière Matapédia, where fisherman catch large salmon. Delicious breakfasts served up with a smile.

From Québec City, Hwy 20, to Mont-Joli Rte 132 for Ste-Florence. In the town, at the railway crossing, turn right, 1km.

B&B
GÎTE DU VIEUX MOULIN

Réjeanne Doiron
314, Beaurivage nord C.P. 85
Sainte-Florence G0J 2M0
(418) 756-6208
www.multimania.com/
vieuxmoulin
vieux_moulin@hotmail.com

B&B	
single	$40
double	$50
child	$5

Reduced rates: Oct.15 to Apr. 30
Open year round

Number of rooms	4
shared bathrooms	2

Activities: 🎣 🚶 🚲 🛷 🏃

60. PERCÉ

F E 🚭 **P** 🏊 **R1** **M1**

La Maison Laberge is a typical Gaspé house located on Cap Mont-Joli. The house affords magnificent panoramas of the ledge known as the Trois Sœurs, which overlooks Cap Barré. To the east, the massive wall that is the Rocher Percé can be seen rising up behind Cap Mont-Joli. **B&B in Bas-St-Laurent section, p 71 n° 24.**

From Québec City, Hwy 20 East, Rte 132 East. Located above the village on the cap Mont-Joli, on the ocean side.

COUNTRY HOME
LA MAISON LABERGE

Bertrand Daraiche and
Thérèse Ng Wai
232, Route 132 Est
Percé G0C 2L0
(418) 782-2816
(514) 393-1417
fax (514) 393-9444
www.total.net/~chq
chq@total.net

No. houses	1
No. rooms	2
No. people	6
WEEK-SUMMER	$700
DAY-SUMMER	$125

Open: June 1 to Sep.30

Activities: 🏛 ⛴ 🚤 🎿 🚴

61. PETITE-VALLÉE

★★ **F e** ✗ **P** 🚗 🏊 **R5** **M1** **TA**

On the coast, magnificent fully equipped chalets offer you the rest you want. You will go to sleep and wake up to the sound of the waves and watch the sun set or rise over the sea. This is what awaits you here! Domestic animals are accepted for an additional fee. **Country Inn p 151. See colour photos.**

From Québec, Hwy 20 East, Rte 132 East to Petite-Vallée. At the entrance to the village, first street on the left, Longue Pointe. At the fork, stay left.

COUNTRY HOME
LA MAISON LEBREUX

Denise Lebreux
2, Longue Pointe
Petite-Vallée G0E 1Y0
(418) 393-2662
tel/fax (418) 393-3105
www.lamaisonlebreux.com
lamaisonlebreux
@globetrotter.net

No. houses	4
No. rooms	1-2
No. people	4-6
WEEK-SUMMER	$550-620
WEEK-WINTER	$450-520
DAY-SUMMER	$80-90
DAY-WINTER	$65-75

Taxes extra MC VS IT

Reduced rates: Sep.16 to June 15
Open year round

Activities: 🚣 🏛 🎿 🚤 🚤

FARM ACTIVITIES

Farm Stay:

27 GÎTE B&B DES SOMMETS, St-René-de-Matane 50

ÎLES-DE-LA-MADELEINE

Réserve écologique de l'Île Brion

Gulf of St. Lawrence

La Grosse Île

Grosse-Île

Réserve nationale de faune de la Pointe-de-l'Est

Havre de la Grande-Entrée

199

Grande-Entrée

Île de la Grande Entrée

199

Île aux Loups

Pointe-aux-Loups

Dune-du-Sud

Île du Cap aux Meules

Île du Havre aux Maisons

Fatima

199

Havre-aux-Maisons

Les Caps

❶

Cap-aux-Meules

[?]

La Vernière

L'Étang-du-Nord

Anse aux Étangs

L'Île d'Entrée

Gulf of St. Lawrence

Île d'Entrée

Baie de Plaisance

199

Baie du Havre aux Basques

Dune de Sandy Hook

Île du Havre Aubert

La Grave

Havre-Aubert

L'Étang-des-Caps

Basin

L'Anse-à-la-Cabane

Souris (P.E.I.)

Montréal

0   5   10 km

©ULYSSES

*The numbers on the map refer to the numbering of the establishments in this region.

1. FATIMA

✸✸✸ F e ⊘ 🚗 P R1.5

Enjoy the hospitality of a real "Madelinot" family. Quiet, wooded area, near services, in a residential district on the island of Cap-aux-Meules. Comfortable rooms, 1km from the beach. Hearty breakfasts for which we are now famous. Lounge with TV. Outdoor terrace at your disposal. Warm welcome, friendly atmosphere. Our home is your home; we await you.

From the ferry, Rte 199 East, Chemin Marconi to Chemin les Caps. In Fatima, near the church, take Chemin de l'Hôpital. Turn left on Chemin Thorne.

B&B
GÎTE BLANDINE ET THOMAS

Blandine and Thomas Thorne
56, chemin E. Thorne
Fatima G0B 1G0
(418) 986-3006
fax (418) 986-6126
www.ilesdelamadeleine.
com/b + b/

B&B	
single	$50
double	$60
triple	$70
quad.	$80
child	$10

Open: May 1 to Oct. 31

Number of rooms	4
shared bathrooms	2
shared wc	1

Activities: 🐚 ⚓ 🚶 🚲 🐎

Petite Auberge Les Bons Matins Bed & Breakfast

À BON MATIN, rue Argyle, Montréal, région de Montréal

AUBERGE LA MARÉE DOUCE, Pointe-au-Père, Bas-Saint-Laurent

AUBERGE LA SOLAILLERIE, Saint-André, Kamouraska, Bas-Saint-Laurent

AUBERGE DE L'EIDER, Sainte-Luce-sur-Mer, Bas-Saint-Laurent

AUBERGE LES PIGNONS VERTS, Austin, Cantons-de-l'Est

AUBERGE DU JOLI VENT, Lac-Brome, Foster, Cantons-de-l'Est

MANOIR D'ORSENNENS, Lac-Mégantic, Cantons-de-l'Est

AUX JARDINS CHAMPÊTRES, Magog, Cantons-de-l'Est

AUBERGE DE LA TOUR, Orford, Cantons-de-l'Est

CAFÉ CRÈME B&B, Magog, Cantons-de-l'Est

LA BELLE ÉCHAPPÉE, Magog, Cantons-de-l'Est

AU SAUT DU LIT, Magog, Cantons-de-l'Est

GÎTE DE L'ARTISANERIE, Baie-du-Febvre, Centre-du-Québec

AUBERGE LA MUSE, Baie-Saint-Paul, Charlevoix

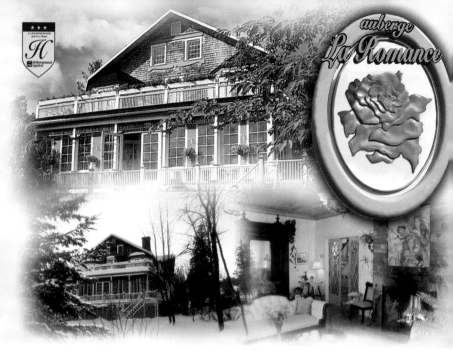

AUBERGE LA ROMANCE, La Malbaie, Charlevoix

AUBERGE LA COURTEPOINTE, Petite-Rivière-Saint-François, Charlevoix

L'EIDER MATINAL, Saint-Irénée, Charlevoix

CHEZ GERTRUDE, Saint-Urbain, **Charlevoix**

AUBERGE DES GLACIS, Saint-Eugène-de-l'Islet, Chaudière-Appalaches

MANOIR TASCHEREAU, Sainte-Marie, Chaudière-Appalaches

RESTAURANT - AUBERGE

La Belle Époque

AUBERGE LA BELLE ÉPOQUE, Montmagny, Chaudière-Appalaches

MAISON HOVINGTON, Tadoussac, Côte-Nord

LA MAISON LEBREUX, Petite-Vallée, Gaspésie

CHALETS DES PINS, Rawdon, Lanaudière

LA VILLA DES FLEURS, Repentigny, Lanaudière

LE PROVINCIALAT, Lac-Nominingue, Laurentides

Auberge
Villa Bellerive

LAC-NOMININGUE

AUBERGE VILLA BELLERIVE, Lac-Nominingue, Laurentides

L'AUBERGE À LA CROISÉE DES CHEMINS, Mont-Tremblant, La Conception, Laurentides

GÎTE ET COUVERT LA MARIE-CHAMPAGNE, Mont-Tremblant, Lac-Supérieur, Laurentides

AUBERGE LA PETITE CACHÉE, Mont-Tremblant, Laurentides

AUBERGE LAC DU PIN ROUGE, Saint-Hippolyte, Laurentides

LES JARDINS DU "LORD" WILDE (WILDE'S HEATH B&B), Mont-Tremblant, Saint- Jovite, Laurentides

LES JARDINS DE LA GARE, Val-Morin, Laurentides

Auberge Charme des Alpes

AUBERGE CHARME DES ALPES, Val-David, Laurentides

AUBERGE DE LA GARE, Sainte-Adèle, Laurentides

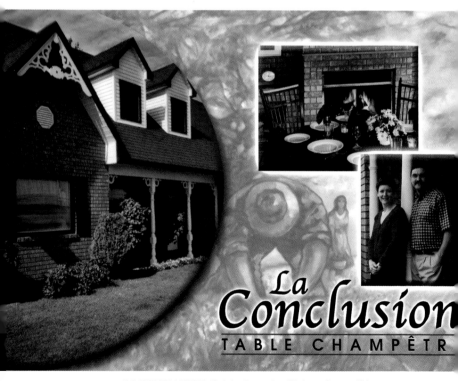

LA CONCLUSION, Sainte-Anne-des-Plaines, Laurentides

AUBERGE ROCHE DES BRISES, Saint-Joseph-du-Lac, Laurentides

GÎTE LA BELLE AU BOIS DORMANT, Grand-Mère, Mauricie

MAISON EMERY JACOB, Saint-Tite, Mauricie

AUBERGE LA JARNIGOINE, Chambly, Richelieu, Montérégie

L'air du Temps

AUBERGE L'AIR DU TEMPS, Chambly, Montérégie

LA MAISON DUCHARME, Chambly, Montérégie

AUX RÊVES D'ANTAN, Saint-Marc-sur-Richelieu, Montérégie

FERME JEAN DUCHESNE, Promenade à la ferme, Saint-Pie, Montérégie

LA VICTORIENNE, rue Notre-Dame est , Montréal, région de Montréal

PIERRE ET DOMINIQUE, Carré Saint-Louis , Montréal, région de Montréal

FERME DE BELLECHASSE, Gatineau, Outaouais

LES JARDINS DE VINOY, Vinoy, Chénéville, Outaouais

LA MAISON ANCESTRALE THOMASSIN, Québec, Beauport, région de Québec

AUBERGE CHEMIN DU ROY, Deschambault, région de Québec

B&B MAISON LESAGE, chemin Saint-Louis , Québec, région de Québec

HAYDEN'S WEXFORD HOUSE , rue Champlain, Québec, région de Québec

AUX TROIS BALCONS, rue Saunders , Québec, région de Québec

B&B LES CORNICHES, Québec, Sillery, région de Québec

GÎTE DU PARC, rue Fraser, Québec, région de Québec

CHALETS-VILLAGE MONT-SAINTE-ANNE, Mont-Sainte-Anne, Saint-Férréol, région de Québec

LE GÎTE DES ÉQUERRES, Saint-Gabriel-de-Valcartier, région de Québec

AUBERGE DE LA FERME ST-ADOLPHE, Stoncham, Saint-Adolphe, région de Québec

AUBERGE PRESBYTÈRE MONT LAC VERT, Hébertville, Saguenay-Lac-Saint-Jean

AUBERGE LA MAISON LAMY, Métabetchouan, Saguenay-Lac-Saint-Jean

LES GÎTES MAKADAN, Normandin, Saguenay-Lac-Saint-Jean

LANAUDIÈRE

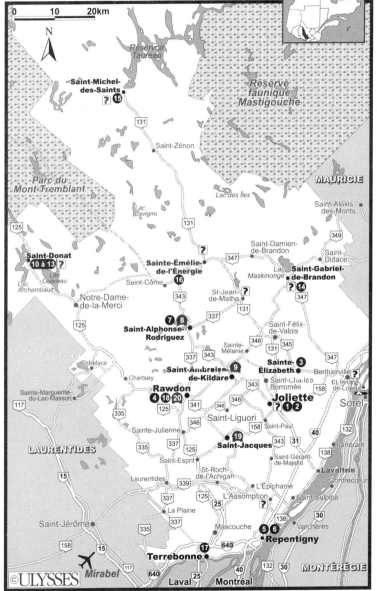

0   10   20km

N

Réservoir
Taureau

Réserve
faunique
Mastigouche

**Saint-Michel-
des-Saints**
? 15

131

Saint-Zénon

*Parc du
Mont-Tremblant*

Lac
Lavigne

Lac des Îles

MAURICIE

Saint-Alexis-
des-Monts

125

349

Saint-
Didace

347

Saint-Damien-
de-Brandon

Saint-Donat
10 à 13 ?

Lac
Ouareau

Lac
Archambault

**Sainte-Émélie-
de-l'Énergie**
16

Saint-Côme

Notre-Dame-
de-la-Merci

343

125

St-Jean-
de-Matha

?

131

Lac
Maskinongé

**Saint-Gabriel-
de-Brandon**
? 14

347

**Saint-Alphonse-
Rodriguez**
7 8

337

348

Saint-Félix-
de-Valois

131   345

Sainte-
Mélanie

337   343

**Saint-Ambroise-
de-Kildare**
9

Entrelacs

Chertsey

Rawdon
4 18 20

125

341

343

Sainte-
Élizabeth
3

Saint-Charles-
Borromée

Berthierville

St-Ignace-
de-Loyola

?

158

Joliette
? 1 2

Sorel

Sainte-Marguerite-
du-Lac-Masson

117

335

346   346

Saint-Liguori

Sainte-Julienne

335   337   125

346

158   Saint-Paul

40

132

LAURENTIDES

15

Saint-Esprit

Saint-Jacques
19

343   31

Saint-Gérard-
de-Majella

Lanoraie

138

Lavaltrie

Contrecoeur

Laurentides

339

St-Roch-
de-l'Achigan

337   125   25

L'Assomption

L'Épiphanie

?

Saint-Sulpice

La Plaine

138

30

Saint-Jérôme

335   337

Mascouche

5 6
Repentigny

Verchères

158   15

117

Terrebonne
17

640

©ULYSSES   *Mirabel*

640   25   **Laval**   **Montréal**

40   132   30   **MONTÉRÉGIE**

*The numbers on the map refer to the numbering of the establishments in this region.

1. JOLIETTE

F e 🛏 P 🐕 R.5 TA

Prize for Excellence "Special Favorite" Regional 1997-98. Enjoy comfort, human warmth, breakfast, the terrace, flowery garden and the soul of this hundred-year-old house. Located near the town centre, the amphitheatre, art museum, golf courses, bike paths, skating rink or boating on the river. Bikes available.

From Montréal or Québec city, Hwy 40, Exit 122 to Joliette. In Joliette, left on Rue Salaberry, facing the tourist office, to Boul Base-de-Roc, turn left.

B&B
GÎTE AUX P'TITS OISEAUX

Céline Coutu
722, boul. Base-de-Roc
Joliette J6E 5P7
(450) 752-1401
fax (450) 759-7836

B&B	
single	$45-50
double	$55-60-70
triple	$75
quad.	$100
child	$10

VS

Open year round

Number of rooms	3
rooms with private bath	1
rooms in basement	1
shared bathrooms	1

Activities: 🏛 🍴 ⚓ 🚶 🚴

2. JOLIETTE

F e 🚫 P R4

Rest and relaxation await you at our friendly, down-to-earth B&B, where you will enjoy a scrumptious breakfast. Take a walk in our enchanting garden or huddle around a bonfire. Numerous activities nearby: music, golf (0.5km), bike path, amphitheatre (2km), Joliette (5km), art museum (6km). Indoor pool open May-Sep. Skating rink in winter. Visit to the greenhouses and guided tours of Joliette ($).

Hwy 40, Exit 122, Hwy 31 Exit 7 for St-Paul, first street on your right, 2.4km.

B&B
LA PETITE MONET

Francine and
Claude Coulombe
3306, boul. Base-de-Roc
Joliette J6E 3Z1
tel/fax (450)759-5798

B&B	
single	$55
double	$70
child	$15

Open year round

Number of rooms	2
rooms in semi basement	1
room with private bath	1
shared bathrooms	2

Activities: 🏛 🚶 🚴 🎿

3. JOLIETTE, STE-ÉLISABETH

☀☀☀ F E P R4

Lanaudière Excellence Prize 1999. One hour from Montréal, a few minutes from Joliette, in a country setting. We welcome travelers from near and far. From here, a 30- to 60- minute drive takes you to the heart of a region of varied landscapes and flavours. A grand welcome and excellent breakfasts. Sampling of maple products.

One hour from Montréal, Hwy 40, exit 122, Hwy 31 and Rte 131 N. At Notre-Dame-de-Lourdes, twd Ste-Elisabeth, drive for 1.5km.

B&B
CHEZ MARIE-CHRISTINE

Micheline and Michel Adam
3120, rang Du Ruisseau
Ste-Élisabeth J0K 2J0
(450) 759-9336

B&B	
single	$50
double	$65
child	$15

Open: May to Nov.

Number of rooms	3
shared wc	1
shared bathrooms	1

Activities: 🏛 🍴 🛶 🚶 🚴

4. RAWDON

F E P R.1 TA

A memorable stay in this Victorian house is offered to wilderness lovers, history buffs, skiers and golfers alike. Enjoy the mansard roofed bedrooms, the 5-course breakfast on the gallery or in the garden, and a guide for your cultural, gastronomic or sporting activities. My goal is your enjoyment! Mimi. Prize for Excellence "Special Favorite" Regional 1995-96.

From Montréal, Hwy 25 N. In St-Esprit, Rte 125 N. In Ste-Julienne Rte 337 N. to Rawdon. From Mirabel, Hwy 15 N., exit Rte 158 E. to Ville des Laurentides, Rte 337 N... From Dorval, Hwy 40 E., 640 W., 25 N...

B&B
GÎTE DU CATALPA

Micheline Trudel
3730, rue Queen
Rawdon J0K 1S0
(450) 834-5253
www3.sympatico.ca/catalpa/
catalpa@sympatico.ca

B&B	
single	$40-55
double	$60-75
triple	$95-100
quad.	$120
child	$15

Taxes extra VS

Open year round

Number of rooms	5
rooms with private bath	1
shared bathrooms	2

Activities:

5. REPENTIGNY

F E P R.2

Located at the entrance to Repentigny, on the outskirts of Montreal where you can enjoy many activities, including theatre, cinema, cross-country skiing, walking, cycling and golf. Whether you've been outside or comfortably nestled inside, you can relax in our spa with a seawater bath, sauna and a massage. Our warm and cozy rooms will wrap you in the arms of Morpheus.

From Montreal or Quebec City, Hwy 40, Exit 96 East twd Charlemagne, after the 4th light. Or Rte 138 twd Repentigny. After the bridge, left at the light; 4th house on the right.

B&B
LA MAISON DE MORPHÉE

Suzanne Le Brun and
Claude Mercier
221, rue Notre-Dame-des-Champs
Repentigny J6A 3B4
(450) 582-2303

B&B	
single	$45-55
double	$55-65
triple	$90
quad.	$110

Open year round

Number of rooms	4
rooms with private bath	2
shared bathroom	1

Activities:

6. REPENTIGNY

F E P R.5 TA

Large, modern air-conditioned house near the St. Lawrence River. 30 min from Mirabel and Dorval airports; 15 min from the Biodome and the Olympic Stadium. Kitchen, parking, in-ground pool, fireplace. Accommodations for 12 people. Room with private entrance. **See color photos.**

From Mirabel, Hwy 15 South, 640 East to Repentigny, left on l'Assomption, right on Perrault, left on Gaudreault. From Dorval, 520 East, 40 East, Charlemagne Exit 96 East...138, Claude David, Boul. l'Assomption, right on Perrault.

B&B
LA VILLA DES FLEURS

Denise Cloutier and
Claude Neveu
45, rue Gaudreault
Repentigny J6A 1M3
(450) 654-9209
fax (450) 654-1220
www3.sympatico.ca
/lavilladesfleurs
lavilladesfleurs@sympatico.ca

B&B	
single	$30-40-50
double	$40-50-60
triple	$60-70
quad.	$70-80-90
child	$10

VS AM

Open year round

Number of rooms	4
rooms with sink	3
rooms with private bath	1
shared bathrooms	2

Activities:

7. ST-ALPHONSE-RODRIGUEZ

☀☀☀☀ F E 🐾 🚫 P R2.5 TA

In an exceptional setting, overlooking Lac Pierre, this "Swiss chalet" transports you to heaven! A marvellous place for relaxation, offering a warm welcome, delicious hearty breakfast, fireplace and communal kitchen. 500m from the beach. Nearby: hiking, skiing, snowmobiling, golfing, horseback riding, music, theatre.

From Montreal, Hwy 40 East, Exit 122 toward Joliette, Rte 343 North. In St-Alphonse, turn right at Lac Pierre, left on N.-Dame, drive past the church, take Chemin Lac Pierre North for 2km, Rue Promontoire.

B&B
LA PETITE CHARTREUSE

Christiane Merle
771, rue Promontoire
St-Alphonse-Rodriguez
J0K 1W0
(450) 883-3961
sans frais 1-866-464-5315
www.petitechartreuse.com
info@petitechartreuse.com

B&B	
single	$45-55
double	$60-70
triple	$75-85
quad.	$100

Reduced rates: Nov., Apr. and May
Open year round

Number of rooms	3
rooms with sink	1
shared bathrooms	2

Activities: 🚣 ⛷ 🚶 🛷 🎿

8. ST-ALPHONSE-RODRIGUEZ

✒ F E ♿ 🐾 P ✕ R5

We offer a stay with plenty of activities included. Located in the mountains, our ranch can accommodate you with several packages: horseback riding, fishing, a day outdoors. Western and family atmosphere. Comfortable rooms, some with whirlpool bath; massotherapist available. Generosity of heart and food; we enthusiastically await you in our little paradise! **Farm Stay p 50. Ad at and of guide.**

From Montreal, Hwy 25 N, right at Rte 337 Exit, Rte 343 N. Or Hwy 40 E, Exit 122 twd Joliette, Rte 343 N. In St-Alphonse-Rodriguez, follow the

INN
RANCH 4 SAISONS

Michelle and Steven Jordan
651, Rang 4
St-Alphonse-Rodriguez
J0K 1W0
(450) 883-0933
toll free 1-877-883-0933
www.ranch4saisons.com

MAP	
single	$115
double	$230
child	$85

Taxes extra VS MC AM IT

Open year round

Number of rooms	8
room with private bath	1
shared bathroom	3

Activities: 🏹 🐎 🚣 🚶 ⛷

9. ST-AMBROISE-DE-KILDARE

☀☀☀☀ F E 🚫 🚤 P 🏊 R2 TA

A weekend at school? Why not if it is located on a farm with 400 sheep and offers: rooms with private bathrooms, communal kitchen, meeting room, heated in-ground pool and fine cuts of meat. Discover our breeding facilities, our region and wool fleece; we enthusiastically await you. **Country-style Dining p 19.**

From Montréal, Hwy 40 East, Exit 122, Hwy 31 North. Rte 158 West, 1km, right on Rte 343 North, 15km to St-Ambroise. Left at flashing yellow light on Rang 5, 2km. Pink-and-white farmhouse on the left!

B&B
BERGERIE DES NEIGES

Desneiges Pepin and
Pierre Juillet
1401, Rang 5
St-Ambroise-de-Kildare
J0K 1C0
tel/fax (450) 756-8395
www.bergeriedesneiges.com
info@bergeriedesneiges.com

B&B	
single	$59
double	$69
child	$15

Taxes extra VS MC

Open year round

Number of rooms	5
rooms with private bath	5

Activities:  🛷 🚶 🚲 ⛷

10. ST-DONAT

☀☀☀ F E ♿ 🐕 🚗 P ⛱ R1 TA

Charm, warmth and comfort await you at this Canadian house right on Lac Archambault, across from the village and a 5 minute's walk via Parc des Pionniers. Private beach, fishing dock, pedal boat, canoe and bike supplied. Motor-boat rental. Mt-Tremblant Park: 12km away; Mt-Garceau: 3km away; snowmobile trail: 50 metres away; a few metres from cross-country ski trail; golf course: 4km away.

From Montréal, Hwy 25 North or 15 North, Exit 89 to St-Donat, left on Ave. du Lac, right on Chemin Bilodeau, right on Chemin La Marguerite.

B&B
AU PETIT CHÂTEAU DU LAC

Johanne Bertrand
59, chemin la Marguerite
St-Donat J0T 2C0
(819) 424-4768

B&B	
single	$55-65
double	$65-75
child	$15-20

Open: Dec. 1 to Mar. 31 and from May 15 to Oct. 15

Number of rooms	4
shared bathrooms	1
rooms with private bath	2

Activities: 🚤 🎿 🛷 ⛷ 🏃

---

11. ST-DONAT

F E P R1 TA

New, very sunny B&B with 5 spacious, soundproof rooms. Surrounded by lakes, 8 kilometres from Mont-Tremblant park. Lovely village with shops, bars and restaurants. Snowmobile paradise. Specials for groups and extended stays. "Meal" packages. Reduced rates for downhill skiing.
Your hosts, *Louise and Jean.*

From Montréal, Rte 125 North or Hwy 15 North, Exit 89, Rte 329 North to St-Donat. At the lights, in the centre of town, turn right on Allard street, 1km from church.

B&B
HALTE AUX PETITS OISEAUX

Sylvie Bouchard and
Jean L'Espérance
631, rue Allard
St-Donat J0T 2C0
(819) 424-3064
fax (819) 424-4367
www.st-donat.com/halte/

B&B	
single	$45
double	$65
triple	$90
quad.	$115
child	$10

Taxes extra VS MC AM

Reduced rates: Oct. 30 to Nov. 30 and Mar. 30 to May 30
Open year round

Number of rooms	5
rooms with private bath	5

Activities: 🚤 🎿 🛷 ⛷

---

12. ST-DONAT

F e 🚗 P R.1 TA

Near many sports: winter and summer, I have 4 rooms for you, tv, sink, all the conveniences. Comfortable house with wrap-around veranda, close to a large clean lake, with clean beach and park for children. Warm welcome.

From Montréal, Hwy 25 and Rte 125 North to St-Donat. Or Hwy 15 North, Exit 89, Rte 329 North to St-Donat. At the flashing light, Rte 125 North. After the traffic light in the centre of town, at the second stop, left on Rue Bellevue.

B&B
LA MAISON ROBIDOUX

Annie Robidoux
284, rue Bellevue
St-Donat J0T 2C0
tel/fax (819) 424-2379
www.bonjourquebec.
com/info/lamaisonrobidoux

B&B	
single	$45
double	$60-65
triple	$80
quad.	$100
child	$10-15

VS MC

Reduced rates: 3 nights and more
Open year round

Number of rooms	4
rooms with sink	4
shared wc	1
shared bathrooms	2

Activities: 🎿 🐎 🛷 🏃 🐎

13. ST-DONAT

☀☀☀☀☀ F e 🚭 🚗 P 🏊 R2 TA

Steps away from Mt-Garceau, 10km from Mont-Tremblant park, our lakeside bed and breakfast offers one room with queen-size bed, sofa bed and TV, and a suite with living room, private bathroom, fireplace, TV and fridge. On site: swimming, pedal-boat, exterior fireplace. Small families welcome.

From Montreal, Hwy 25, Rte 125 North to St-Donat or Hwy 15 North, Exit 89, Rte 329 North to St-Donat. At the flashing light, Rte 125 North. At the traffic light in the centre of the village, turn right on Rue Allard, 2km. At the end, turn left, 1km.

B&B
LA MAISON SUR LE LAC

Line and Denis Boivin
103, chemin Lac Blanc
St-Donat J0T 2C0
(819) 424-5057
fax (819) 424-1795
www.st-donat.com/maison

B&B	
single	$50-60
double	$60-70
triple	$80-90
quad.	$100-110
child	$0-20

VS

Reduced rates: 7th night free
Open year round

Number of rooms	2
rooms with private bath	1
shared bathrooms	1

Activities: 🏃 🛶 🎣 🚶 ⛷

14. ST-GABRIEL-DE-BRANDON

☀☀☀ F E 🚭 🎿 🚗 P 🏊 R1

Prize for Excellence "Special Favorite" Regional 2000. Andante! Lento... Here everything is music! The gentle touch of the wind off the lake, the warmth of the hearth for peace and quiet, the spa's caresses for relaxation, Princesse's sweet purring, this B&B's special treats for pleasure! Need a little rest? We are waiting for you!

From Montréal, Hwy 40 East, Exit 144, right on Rte 158 for 2km, right on Rte 347 North, right twd St-Gabriel, drive about 30km.

B&B
L'ANDANTE

Lise Vézina and
Claude Perrault
480, rue Maskinongé
St-Gabriel-de-Brandon J0K 2N0
(450) 835-7658
www.bbcanada.com/andante
andante@pandore.qc.ca

B&B	
single	$40-45
double	$50-60

Open year round

Number of rooms	4
shared bathrooms	2

Activities: 🐚 🚣 🚴 🏊 🏃

15. ST-MICHEL-DES-SAINTS

☀☀☀☀ F e 🚗 P 🏊 R1 TA

Crowning the summit of Mont-Roberval, this big country house with chapel was once the home of the founder of Saint-Michel-des-Saints. Several lounges, fireplace, piano, sumptuous period decor, panorama over magnificent Lac Toro, forest trails, swimming pool, river and waterfall... A haven of peace near activities.

2 hours from Montréal: Hwy 40, Exit 122, Hwy 31 twd Joliette and Rte 131 North. In Saint-Michel-des-Saints: left at bowling alley onto Rue Provost and right on Rue Laforest to the end.

B&B
LE GÎTE SAINT-MICHEL

Robert Burelle
1090, rue Laforest
St-Michel-des-Saints J0K 3B0
(450) 833-6008
toll free 1-888-843-6008
www.gitesaintmichel.qc.ca
memo@gitesaintmichel.qc.ca

B&B	
single	$50-60
double	$70-80
triple	$90
child	$10-15

VS

Open year round

Number of rooms	5
shared bathrooms	3

Activities: 🚣 🎣 🚶 🏃 🐕

16. STE-ÉMÉLIE-DE-L'ÉNERGIE ★★★ F E ♿ P 🚗 ⛵ ✕ TA

A log house on a private lakeside property by the Noire river, with activities and equipment included in our prices. The chef-owner offers gourmet fare of game, steak and seafood. A snowmobiling resort with an indoor Jacuzzi and sauna. Hiking trails with panoramic views, observation of bears and deer in season.

From Montreal, Hwy 40, Exit 122, Hwy 31 twd Joliette and Rte 131 North. In Ste-Émélie, turn right at the flashing light, drive 11.3km to St-Zénon.

INN
AUBERGE DU VIEUX MOULIN

Sylvie and Yves Marcoux
200, ch. du Vieux Moulin
Ste-Émélie-de-l'Énergie J0K 2K0
(450) 884-0211
toll free 1-866-884-0211
fax (450) 884-0702
www.aubvieuxmoulin.com
info@aubvieuxmoulin.com

	B&B	MAP
single	$80	$110
double	$100	$150
triple	$115	$175
quad.	$130	$200
child	$5	$12

Taxes extra VS MC IT

Open year round

Number of rooms	12
rooms with private bath	12

Activities: 🚤 🎿 🚶 🐕

17. TERREBONNE ▢ F E 🚭 🚗 P R.25 TA

Set in vast woodlands, our large house awaits lovers of cultural activities, music, history, genealogy and ornithology, who enjoy the company of country folk. We are a few minutes' walking distance from old Terrebonne, Île des Moulins and public transportation. Quiet, restful place.

Hwy 440 or 640 to Hwy 25, Exit 22 Boul des Seigneurs, turn right at 1st street; on St-Michel, east of Chemin Gascon (Moody).

B&B
LE MARCHAND DE SABLE

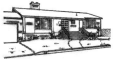

Paule and Jacques Tremblay
658, rue St-Michel
Terrebonne J6W 3K2
(450) 964-6016
fax (450) 471-7127
www.bonjourquebec.
com/info/lemarchanddesable
lemarchandde
sable@videotron.ca

	B&B
single	$45
double	$50-60
triple	$75

Open year round

Number of rooms	2
rooms with sink	2
shared wc	2
shared bathrooms	1

Activities: 🏛 🍂 🚶 🚴

18. RAWDON

F E ✕ P 🏊 R7 M7

Our little hideway opens wide it's arms to greet you! 1h north of Montreal, you will be confortably accomodated in our carefully equiped homes. In an enchanting setting, ideal for relaxation. Private lake, beach and many four season activities. Packages available. Discover our gourmet room!
See you soon. **See color photos.**

From Montreal, Hwy 25 North and 125 North .turn right on Vincent Massey and drive 1.5km. From Dorval, Hwy 13 North, exit 13 North, exit Hwy 440 East, Hwy 25 North...

COUNTRY HOME
CHALETS DES PINS

Carole Halbig and
Philippe Richomme
5749, rue Vincent Massey
Rawdon J0K 1S0
(450) 834-3401
fax (450) 834-1377
www.chaletsdespins.qc.ca
info@chaletsdespins.qc.ca

No. houses	4
No. rooms	1-4
No. people	1-10
WEEK-SUMMER	$700-1 005
WEEK-WINTER	$700-1 005
W/E-SUMMER	$260-620
W/E-WINTER	$260-620
DAY-SUMMER	$130-310
DAY-WINTER	$130-310

Taxes extra VS IT

Reduced rates: Jan. 8 to Feb. 23 and Mar. 14 to June 22 and Sept. 4 to Dec. 14
Open year round

Activities: 🎿 🐎 🚲 🛷 ⛷

FARM ACTIVITIES

Country-style Dining:

9 BERGERIE DES NEIGES, St-Ambroise-de-Kildare 19

19 BERGERIE VOYNE, St-Jacques-de-Montcalm 19

Farm Tour:

20 ARCHE DE NOÉ, Rawdon 36

Farm Stay:

8 RANCH 4 SAISONS, St-Apphonse-de-Rodriguez 50

LAURENTIDES

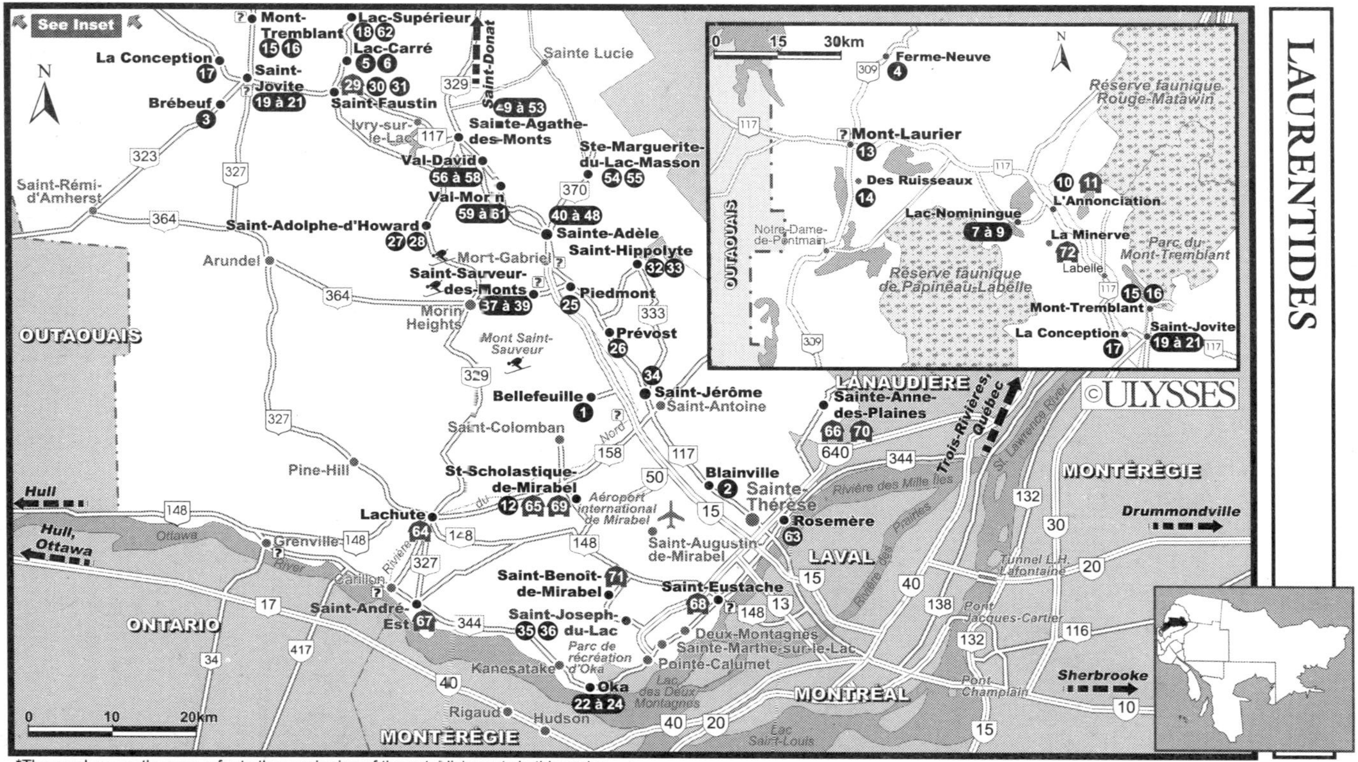

See Inset
La Conception
17
Mont-Tremblant
15 16
Saint-Jovite
19 à 21
Brébeuf
3
Lac-Supérieur
18 62
Lac-Carré
5 6
29 30 31
Saint-Faustin
Saint-Donat
Sainte Lucie
49 à 53
Sainte-Agathe-des-Monts
Ivry-sur-le-Lac
Val-David
56 à 58
Val-Morin
59 à 61
Ste-Marguerite-du-Lac-Masson
54 55
40 à 48
Sainte-Adèle
Saint-Hippolyte
32 33
Saint-Rémi-d'Amherst
Saint-Adolphe-d'Howard
27 28
Arundel
Mont-Gabriel
Saint-Sauveur-des-Monts
37 à 39
Piedmont
25
Morin Heights
Prévost
26
Mont Saint-Sauveur
34
Saint-Jérôme
Saint-Antoine
Bellefeuille
1
Saint-Colomban
OUTAOUAIS
Pine-Hill
St-Scholastique-de-Mirabel
12 65 69
Aéroport international de Mirabel
Blainville
2
Sainte-Thérèse
Rosemère
63
Lachute
64
Hull
Hull, Ottawa
Grenville
Ottawa River
Carillon
Rivière du Nord
Saint-Augustin-de-Mirabel
LAVAL
Saint-Benoît-de-Mirabel
71
Saint-Eustache
68
Saint-André-Est
67
Saint-Joseph-du-Lac
35 36
Deux-Montagnes
Sainte-Marthe-sur-le-Lac
Pointe-Calumet
Parc de récréation d'Oka
Kanesatake
Oka
22 à 24
Lac des Deux Montagnes
ONTARIO
Rigaud
Hudson
MONTÉRÉGIE
MONTRÉAL
Lac Saint-Louis
LANAUDIÈRE
Sainte-Anne-des-Plaines
66 70
Trois-Rivières, Québec
St. Lawrence River
Rivière des Mille Îles
Rivière des Prairies
MONTÉRÉGIE
Drummondville
Sherbrooke
Tunnel L.H. Lafontaine
Pont Jacques-Cartier
Pont Champlain
0 10 20km
©ULYSSES
0 15 30km
Ferme-Neuve
4
Mont-Laurier
13
Des Ruisseaux
14
OUTAOUAIS
Notre-Dame-de-Pontmain
Lac-Nominingue
7 à 9
Réserve faunique Papineau-Labelle
Réserve faunique Rouge-Matawin
10 11
L'Annonciation
La Minerve
72
Labelle
Parc du Mont-Tremblant
15 16
Mont-Tremblant
La Conception
17
Saint-Jovite
19 à 21

*The numbers on the map refer to the numbering of the establishments in this region.

1. BELLEFEUILLE

☀☀☀ F 🚫 🏊 🐕 P R12

Panoramic mountain location, 20min from Mirabel airport. Cross-country skiing at your doorstep, forest walks, private lake and healthy breakfasts. We are reserving a warm welcome, tranquillity, intimacy and comfort just for you... massage service available.

From Montréal or Mirabel, Hwy 15 North, Exit 43 West, Bellefeuille.Rue De Martigny becomes De la Montagne and Blvd. Lasalette. After the traffic lights and the church, right on Rue St-Camille, drive 4.8km.

B&B
GÎTE FLEURS DES BOIS

Monique F. Morin
and Rémi Gagnon
1331, rue St-Camille, R.R. #2
Bellefeuille J0R 1A0
(450) 438-7624

B&B	
single	$40-45
double	$55-60
triple	$85
child	$15

Taxes extra

Open: Jan. 5 to Dec.15

Number of rooms	5
rooms with private bath	2
shared wc	2
shared bathrooms	1

Activities: 🚤 ⛷ 🚴 ⛷ 🏃

---

2. BLAINVILLE

☀☀ F e 🚫 P 🚗 R1 TA

15 min from Mirabel, to fight the inconveniences of jet lag, we offer you the comfort and quietness of our home. At the foot of the Laurentides and 30 min from Montréal, it is a pleasant stop for cyclists. Biking, skiing and walking trails nearby.

From Mirabel, Hwy 15 South, Exit 31 twd St-Janvier. Right Rte 117, 3km. Right Rue Notre-Dame, left Rue J. Desrosiers. From Montréal, Hwy 15 North, Exit 25. Left Rte 117 for 3km, left 98th Ave.

B&B
LE GÎTE DU LYS

Francine Beauchemin
1237, rue Jacques-Desrosiers
Blainville J7C 3B2
(450) 437-4948
fax (450) 437-3658
gitedulys@videotron.ca

B&B	
single	$35
double	$45-55

Open year round

Number of rooms	3
rooms in basement	3
shared bathrooms	1

Activities: 🚤 🚴 🚣 ⛷ 🏃

---

3. BRÉBEUF

☀☀☀ F e 🚫 🐕 🏊 P R7 TA

Discover a charming inn situated just a stone's throw from Mont-Tremblant. Listen to the sound of the babbling river or gaze at a lingering sunset. In the morning, savour a breakfast prepared with seasonal ingredients. The hospitality and picturesque setting will make you want to come back year after year to «l'Été Indien».

From Montréal, Hwy 15, Rte 117 North. After St-Jovite, Exit 323 Brébeuf. Left at the lights 323 South. At Brébeuf, left before the bridge. From Ottawa, Rte 323 North for St-Jovite. At Brébeuf, turn right after the bridge.

B&B
AUBERGE L'ÉTÉ INDIEN

Johanne Pépin and
Luc Lemay
157 A, route 323
Brébeuf J0T 1B0
toll free 1-877-429-6622
(819) 429-6622
fax (819) 429-6922
www.eteindien.qc.ca
info@eteindien.qc.ca

B&B	
single	$60-70
double	$75-85
triple	$100
quad.	$115
child	$10

Taxes extra VS MC

Reduced rates: 3 nights and more
Open: Dec. 1 to Oct. 15

Number of rooms	4
rooms with private bath	1
shared wc	1
shared bathrooms	2

Activities: 🚤 ⛷ 🚴 🚣 ⛷

4. FERME-NEUVE

F E X P R8 TA

A quiet, cozy house with tremendous charm, artistic woodwork and full of windows. A picture-postcard landscape, 106 acres of fields, forest and a little river. Delicious, lavish cuisine. 20 minutes from the beaches of the Baskatong Reservoir, the devil's mountain and the Windigo Falls.

From Montréal, Hwy 15 North, then Rte 117. In Mont-Laurier, 309 North. In Ferme-Neuve, past the church, left at the ball park, left on Montée Gravel, 8km.

INN
AUBERGE AU BOIS
D'MON COEUR

Louison Morin
183, rang 4, montée Gravel
Ferme-Neuve J0W 1C0
(819) 587-3383
(819) 623-7143

	B&B	MAP
single	$45	$60-70
double	$60	$90-110
triple	$70	$115-145
quad.	$80	$140-180
child	$5	$15

Open year round

Number of rooms	4
shared bathrooms	2

Activities: 🏛 ⛵ 🛶 👤 👤

---

5. LAC-CARRÉ

☀☀☀ F E P 🚗 R.1 TA

"La Licorne", or The Unicorn, symbolizing freedom, invites you to share in its wonders and landscapes. After a day of cycling on the linear park 50 metres away, relax in our garden to the sound of waterfalls or go for a refreshing swim in the lake in front of the B&B. In winter, after skiing, relax in front of a fire. Mt Blanc 1km away, Tremblant 20km, good restaurants in St-Jovite 10km. Atkm 69.5 of the bike path.

From Montréal, Hwy 15 N. and Rte 117 N. After Ste-Agathe, 20km, Lac-Carré Exit, at the stop, right for 1km.

B&B
LA LICORNE

Patricia and Robin
1690, rue Principale
Lac-Carré J0T 1J0
(819) 688-3030
fax (819) 688-5020
www.boreale.net/licorne
lalicorne@sympatico.ca

B&B	
single	$40-50
double	$60-70
triple	$85
quad.	$90

VS

Open: Dec. 1 to Apr. 15,
May 1 to Oct. 31

Number of rooms	4
shared bathrooms	2

Activities: 🛶 👤 🚲 🏊 🏃

---

6. LAC-CARRÉ

☀☀☀ F E X P 🚗 🐕 R1 TA

10km from St-Jovite and 18km from Mt-Tremblant, our octogenarian house is a haven of peace for nature lovers. 50m from the linear park (bicycle and snowmobile) and 1km from Mont-Blanc, our B&B lets you relax on the beach of the lake, on the terrace or by the fire upon your arrival. Come morning, you will enjoy our now-famous hearty breakfast. Dinner on reservation. Gift certificates available.

From Montréal, Hwy 15 North and Rte 117 North. After Ste-Agathe drive 18km. Exit Lac-Carré. At 1st stop sign turn right, drive 1.5km, right on Rue de La Gare.

B&B
GÎTE DE LA GARE

Johanne Mathon
362, rue de La Gare
St-Faustin, Lac-Carré
J0T 1J0
tel/fax (819) 688-6091
toll free 1-888-550-6091

B&B	
single	$50-55
double	$60-65

VS MC IT

Open year round

Number of rooms	5
shared bathrooms	2

Activities: 👤 🚲 🛶 🏊 🏃

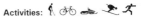

7. LAC-NOMININGUE ★★★ F E 🐾 ⊠ 🚗 P 🏊 TA

We offer packages (nature, relaxation and Belgian gastronomy) so that you may share our passion for this beautiful part of the country. Activities: canoeing, pedal-boating, in-line skating and snowmobiling... The kitchen and rooms with therapeutic bath will enchant you. Réal Pelletier (La Presse): "It's good, beautiful and warm. What more can you ask for from an inn!"

From Montreal, Hwy 15 North, Rte 117. Past L'Annonciation, at the flashing light, Rte 321 South. After 8.8km, right on Chemin des Tilleuls, drive 200m. By bike, at Km 141.5 of the Le P'tit Train du Nord bike path.

INN
AUBERGE-RESTAURANT
«CHEZ IGNACE»

Yolande Louis and
Ignace Denutte
1455, ch. des Tilleuls
Lac-Nominingue J0W 1R0
(819) 278-0689
toll free 1-877-278-0677
fax (819) 278-0751
www.ignace.qc.ca
info@ignace.qc.ca

	B&B	MAP
single	$60-75	$70-95
double	$75-90	$100-138
triple	$110	$160-175
child	$10	$20

Taxes extra VS MC AM IT

Reduced rates: Mar. 15 to May 15 and Oct. 15 to Dec. 15, 3 nights and more 10% off
Open year round

Number of rooms	5
rooms with private bath	5

Activities: 🧍 🚴 🎣 🏃 🐎

8. LAC-NOMININGUE ★★★ F e ♿ ⊠ 🚗 P 🏊 TA

Located on the shores of Lac Nominingue and the Linear Park, Auberge Villa Bellerive is a renovated historic inn that is popular with cyclists and snowmobilists. Enjoy a coffee on the pier or in the dining room, which serves delectable six-course dinner. A terrace garden and a heated spa will delight you, even in winter, and the variety of our rooms will fulfill all of your desires. Discover our fine cuisine and cordial welcome. **See color photos.**

Hwy 15 and 117 North. After L'Annonciation, at the flashing light, 321 South, 9km.km 142 Le P'tit Train du Nord bike path.

INN
AUBERGE VILLA BELLERIVE

Cécile L'Heureux and
Yvon Massé
1596, ch. des Tilleuls
Lac Nominingue J0W 1R0
toll free 1-800-786-3802
(819) 278-3802
fax (819) 278-0483
www.villabellerive.com
villabellerive@hotmail.com

	B&B	MAP
single	$60	$75-85
double	$75-125	$118-168
triple	$90-100	$165-195
quad.	$95-110	$200-240
child	$15	---

Taxes extra VS MC AM IT

Reduced rates: Mar. 15 to May 15, Oct. 15 to Dec.15
Open year round

Number of rooms	12
rooms with private bath	12

Activities: 🚣 🧍 🎣 🏃 🐎

9. LAC-NOMININGUE ☀☀☀ F E 🚭 P 🚗 ⊠ R1 TA

A 20-room century-old house on a protected religious, ancestral site at the edge of the woods. Discover the history of the Laurentians' colonization while enjoying outdoor activities in our wide-open, unspoilt spaces. Relaxing, novel ambiance, cooking with garden-fresh produce, in season, non-smoking. "At the Provincialat, guaranteed peace and quiet." (*La Presse*, 5/26/90). Regional winner of the 1999 Grand Prix du Tourisme. Cycling packages. **See colour photos.**

Rte 117, Rte 321, Chemin Tour du Lac to Rue St-Ignace, turn left, then right on Rue Sacré-Coeur.

INN
LE PROVINCIALAT

P. Seers and G. Petit
2292, Rue Sacré-Coeur
Lac-Nominingue J0W 1R0
(819) 278-4928
toll free 1-877- 278-4928
fax (819) 278-3517
www.provincialat.com
provincialat@qc.aira.com

	B&B	MAP
single	$50-55	$70-75
double	$65-95	$105-135
triple	$75-105	$135-165
quad.	$125-135	$205-215
child	$20	$35

Taxes extra VS MC

Reduced rates: Oct.15 to June 15, taxes included 3 nights and more
Open year round

Number of rooms	5
rooms with private bath	2
rooms with sink	1
shared bathrooms	2

Activities: 🧍 🚴 🎣 🏃 🐎

10. L'ANNONCIATION

☀☀☀ | F | E | 🚳 | 🚗 | P | 🏊 | R5

Nestled in the heart of the Upper Laurentians and located along a quiet road near the bike path (shuttle available), the magnificent Rouge river and Mont Tremblant (30min). The white roughcast house harbours an artist's studio. A poetic trail is laid out on the 78-acre (31.5ha) property. Canoe and art-workshop packages.

From Montreal, hwy 15 North, Rte. 117 North. Past L'Annonciation, turn left at the flashing light, Rte. 321 South, turn right on Chemin Laliberté.

INN
GÎTE DE LA BÊTE PARESSEUSE

Lise Létourneau
55, ch. Laliberté
L'Annonciation J0T 1T0
(819) 275-3363
fax (819) 275-1798
www3.sympatico.ca/
beteparesseuse
beteparesseuse
@netcourrier.com

B&B	
single	$40
double	$60
child	$15

Open year round

Number of rooms	3
shared bathrooms	2

Activities: 🚶 🏃 🚴 🧍 ⛷

---

11. L'ANNONCIATION

☀☀☀ | F | e | P | ✖ | R5

We cleared this patch of mountainside land so that our small herd could graze and we could set up house comfortably. Former teachers, your hosts are genuine, unpretentious people who enjoy sharing the happiness of living with their guests according to old-fashioned values. A warm welcome awaits you. **Country-style Dining p 20 and Farm Stay p 50.**

From Montréal, Hwy 15 North and Rte 117 to L'Annonciation. Drive 4.3km past the hospital, and turn left on Chemin Laliberté. First house on the right.

B&B
LA CLAIRIÈRE DE LA CÔTE

Monique Lanthier and
Yves Bégin
16, chemin Laliberté
L'Annonciation J0T 1T0
(819) 275-2877

B&B	
single	$35-50
double	$50-65

Open: Dec. 1 to Mar. 31 to
May 1 to Oct. 31

Number of rooms	4
rooms in basement	3
shared wc	2
room with private bath	1
shared bathrooms	1

Activities: 🚣 🧍 🚴 🛷 ⛷

---

12. MIRABEL

☀☀☀ | F | E | 🚳 | P | 🏊 | R5 | TA

First-prize winner of the Commerce Fleuri 2000 award Mirabel area, located 8km from the airport and 5min from: golf clubs, horse-riding centres, sugar shacks, snowmobile trails, restaurants and environmental centre. Our three rooms will delight you. A lavish breakfast is served in a unique setting. Our bed and breakfast is an unforgettable journey into a bygone romantic era.

Hwy 15, Exit 35 West, twd, Ste-Scholastique.

B&B
GÎTE PARLEZ-MOI D'AMOUR

Raymonde Grenier and
Yves Pariseau
9861, rue de Belle Rivière
Mirabel J7N 2X8
(450) 258-4666

B&B	
single	$55-75
double	$65-85
triple	$90-100

Open year round

Number of rooms	3
shared bathroom	1
shared wc	1

Activities: 🧍 🍴 🧍 🐎 🛷

13. MONT-LAURIER

☀☀☀ F e P R.1 TA

Memorable stay. Friendly welcome, considerations, cosy bed, lounge at your disposal: chats, reading, soft music, TV. Not to mention the breakfast!!! "As appetizing to the eyes as to the belly." Near the linear park. Welcome to our home with magnificent woodwork.

From Montréal, Hwy 15 N., Rte 117 to Mont-Laurier. We're on Boul A. Paquette, which is the extension of Rte 117. The inn is on your right.

B&B
AUBERGE DE LA MAISON GRENIER

Pauline Boisvert
335, boul. A. Paquette
Mont-Laurier J9L 1K5
tel/fax (819) 623-6306

B&B	
single	$40
double	$55
triple	$70
child	$5

Taxes extra VS MC

Open year round

Number of rooms	5
rooms with sink	1
shared bathrooms	2

Activities: 🏛 🎿 🚲 🚤 🏃

14. MONT-LAURIER, DES RUISSEAUX

☀☀ F e 🚗 P R12 TA

Once upon a time... there were dreams and passions you'll discover immediately on arrival! Nordic dogs, horses, rooms set up above the ranch, in a decor of cedar and old beams. Unique, picturesque ambiance. We welcome you as friends and serve breakfast in the main house.

From Montreal, hwy 15 and Rte. 117 North. In Mont-Laurier, Rte. 309 South. After 7km, turn left on Chemin Ferme Rouge, drive 5km.

B&B
RÊVE BLANC

Nathalie and
Jean-François Tuveri
707, ch. Ferme-Rouge
Des Ruisseaux J9L 3G3
(819) 623-2628
fax (819) 623-4518
www.reveblanc.com
reveblanc@sympatico.ca

B&B	
single	$40
double	$55
child	$15

Taxes extra VS MC

Reduced rates: 20% 3 nights and more
Open year round

Number of rooms	4
shared bathroom	2
shared wc	1

Activities: 🦪 🎿 🐎 ⛷ 🚤 🐕

15. MONT-TREMBLANT

★★★ F E 🚭 ♿ 🚗 P 🏊 R.1 TA

The warmth of a log house within your reach. Ten spacious rooms, each with its own rustic charm to welcome you. Newly built, it boasts a television, therapeutic bath, balcony and a view of magnificent Mont-Tremblant. Lounge with fireplace to warm you in winter, pool to refresh you in summer. Excellent breakfast. Prices higher in winter. **See colour photos.**

From Montréal, Hwy 15 North, Rte 117 North for 1.5km. After St-Jovite, turn right on Montée Ryan to Lac Tremblant, turn left twd the village. 1km on the left.

INN
AUBERGE LA PETITE CACHÉE

Manon Millette and
Normand Chalifour
2681, ch. Principal C.P. 1009
Mont-Tremblant J0T 1Z0
(819) 425-2654
toll free 1-888-475-2654
fax (819) 425-6892
www.petitecachee.com
manon@petitecachee.com

B&B	
single	$70-100
double	$89-130
triple	$115-135
child	$15

Taxes extra VS MC AM IT

Reduced rates: May, June, Oct., Nov.
Open year round

Number of rooms	10
rooms with private bath	10

Activities: ⛵ 🎿 🚲 ⛷ 🏃

16. MONT-TREMBLANT ★★★ F E 🕭 P 🚗 🛥 🐕 R1 TA

Sylvie and Pierre have been welcoming guests to their large log house, located 1km from Mont-Tremblant, for 10 years now. Located amidst cross-country-skiing trails and bike paths, this warm inn is graced with nine cozy rooms, some with a fireplace. Deer watching in winter, access to a private beach in summer, gourmet breakfast year-round! Large living room with fireplace. Prices higher in winter. Check out our Web site.

From Montreal, Hwy 15 N, Rte 117 N. Past St-Jovite, right at the light Montée Ryan to the end. Left at the stop, Rue Pinoteau at the next stop.

INN
AUBERGE LE LUPIN

Sylvie Senécal and
Pierre Lachance
127, rue Pinoteau
Mont-Tremblant J0T 1Z0
(819) 425-5474
toll free 1-877-425-5474
fax (819) 425-6079
www.lelupin.com
lelupin@lelupin.com

B&B	
single	$75-104
double	$95-124
triple	$130-149
child	$15

Taxes extra VS MC AM ER IT

Reduced rates: May 18, June 21 and Oct. 15 to Dec. 21
Open year round

Number of rooms	9
rooms with private bath	9
shared wc	1

Activities: 🚶 🏃 🚴 🎿 🎿

17. MT-TREMBLANT, LA CONCEPTION ★★★ F E 🚭 ✕ 🛏 P 🚗 R6 TA

Located on the shores of the Rouge river, a few minutes from the "Le P'tit Train du Nord" bike path and the ski slopes of Mont Tremblant. Cozy, comfortable rooms. Breakfast included in the price of our rooms. We serve dinner. SAQ liquor permit. **See colour photos.**

From Montreal, Hwy 15 North, Rte 117 North. 6.5km past the Montée Ryan traffic light. La Conception Exit; at the stop sign, continue straight ahead for 6.5km. Turn left at the stop sign, drive 1km.

INN
L'AUBERGE À LA
CROISÉE DES CHEMINS

Carole Laplante, Claude
Lapointe and Odile Malépart
4273, chemin des Tulipes
Mt-Tremblant, La Conception
J0T 1M0
(819) 686-5289
toll free 1-888-686-5289
fax (819) 686-9205

B&B	
single	70-90
double	$70-100
triple	$95-125
quad.	$120-150
child	$15

Taxes extra VS AM IT

Reduced rates: Nov. 1 to Dec. 15, May 15 to June 15
Open year round

Number of rooms	9
rooms with private bath	7
shared wc	2
shared bathrooms	1

Activities: 🚶 🏃 🚴 🎿 🎿

18. MONT-TREMBLANT, LAC-SUPÉRIEUR ☀☀☀ F E 🐕 🛥 P 🚗 R2.5 TA

At the entrance to Mont-Tremblant park, and the northern mountain, a magnificent Canadian house embraced by nature. Linear park 2.5km away. Skiing and cycling. Snowmobile package. Pool, terrace, relaxation by the fireplace. Dinner by reservation. Enjoy family breakfasts and the *joy de vivre* of your hosts. Family-size suite with kitchenette for an independent stay. **See colour photos.**

From Montreal, Hwy 15 North, Rte 117 North, St-Faustin/Lac-Carré Exit. Turn right at the stop sign, 2.3km, follow signs for Mt-Tremblant park, 2.5km along chemin Lac-Supérieur.

B&B
GÎTE ET COUVERT
LA MARIE-CHAMPAGNE

Marie-France
and Denis Champagne
654, chemin Lac-Supérieur
Lac-Supérieur J0T 1J0
(819) 688-3780
fax (819) 688-3758
gite.mariechampagne
@expresso.qc.ca

B&B	
single	$40-50
double	$60-70
triple	$80
quad.	$100
child	$15

VS AM

Open: Dec. 1 to Oct. 31

Number of rooms	4
rooms with private bath	4

Activities: 🛥 🚶 🚴 🛷 🎿

19. MONT-TREMBLANT, ST-JOVITE

☀☀☀ | F | E | 🏊 | 🚗 | P | R2 | TA

Get away from it all in our B&B that offers very modern comfort in the style of yore. You'll be amazed by our exquisite breakfasts, overflowing with fresh fruit. Just steps away from a vast choice of activities. Located 8km from Mont Tremblant and Mont Blanc. Linear park 500m away (cycling, snowmobiling), cross-country skiing. Our motto: to welcome you back.

From Montreal, Hwy 15 and 117 North. Turn right at the first exit for St-Jovite, continue for 100m. Turn right at the first intersection, Montée Kavanaugh, 1.8km.

B&B
GÎTE LA TREMBLANTE

France Renault
1251, montée Kavanagh
Mont-Tremblant, St-Jovite
JOT 2H0
(819) 425-5959
toll free 1-877-425-5959
fax (819) 425-9404
www.st-jovite.com/tremblante
tremblante@st-jovite.com

B&B	
single	$50-60
double	$60-70
triple	$75-85

Taxes extra VS MC

Open year round

Number of rooms	4
rooms with private bath	4

Activities: 🚶 🏃 🚴 🏊 🏃

20. MONT-TREMBLANT, ST-JOVITE

☀☀☀ | F | E | 🚭 | P | 🚗 | R.5 | TA

Situated 500m from the Linear Park Le P'tit Train du Nord and 10min from Mont-Tremblant, Le Second Souffle is a Canadian-style home in the hilly St-Jovite region. Sports, cultural and gastronomic activities are a stone's throw from the B&B. There are five rooms, each with their own private bath-room and unique décor. Unforgettable breakfasts served in a laid-back, friendly ambience.

From Montréal, Hwy 15 and Rte 117 North. At St-Jovite, Rue Ouimet and then immediately turn onto Rue Kavanagh, drive 500 m.

B&B
LE SECOND SOUFFLE

Monique and
Jean-Marie Leduc
815, montée Kavanagh
St-Jovite JOT 2H0
tel/fax (819) 429-6166
www.bbcanada.com
/secondsouffle

B&B	
single	$65
double	$75
triple	$95
child	$15

Taxes extra VS MC

Reduced rates: low season
Open year round

Number of rooms	5
rooms with private bath	5

Activities: 🚶 🏃 🚴 🏊 🏃

21. MONT-TREMBLANT, ST-JOVITE

☀☀☀☀ | F | E | 🏊 | P | 🐕 | R3 | TA

Secluded in the Laurentian mountains, less than 10min from Mont-Tremblant, Wilde's Heath is a magnificent Victorian mansion. Furnished with late-19th-century antiques, Wilde's Heath confirms that a life of luxury is still to be had in St-Jovite. Enjoy breathtaking panoramas and kiss all your troubles goodbye. Breakfast served in bed. **See colour photos.**

From Montreal, Hwy 15 North and Rte 117. Past St-Jovite, turn left at the viaduct toward Brébeuf, take Rte 323 for 1.6km and look for the "Wilde's Heath B&B" sign.

B&B
WILDE'S HEATH B&B

«Lord» Daniel H.Wilde
268, Route 323
St-Jovite JOT 2H0
(819) 425-6859
toll free 1-888-846-5555
fax (819) 425-7636
www.wildesheath.com

B&B	
single	$130-280
double	$150-300

Taxes extra VS AM IT

Reduced rates: 20% Dec. 1 to Nov. 14 and May1 to June 23
Open year round

Number of rooms	4
rooms with private bath	4

Activities:  🚣 ⛵ 🚶 🚴 🎿

22. OKA

A complete change of scenery 40 min from Mirabel, 45 min from Montréal. Enchanting site on a lake and around a pool. Bicycle path. Parc Oka nearby. In summer, water sports and golf available. In winter, cross-country skiing, ice-fishing, and snowmobilling.

From Mirabel, Hwy 15 South, exit onto Hwy 640 West to the end. Right on Rte 344 West to Oka, left on Rue Olier. Right on St-Sulpice, 8.5km from the end of Rte 640 West. 8.5km from the end of Rte 640 West.

B&B
LA MAISON DUMOULIN

Francine Leblond
53, rue St-Sulpice
Oka J0N 1E0
(450) 479-6753
fax (450) 479-1723

B&B	
single	$40-50
double	$50-60
child	$10

Open year round

Number of rooms	4
shared bathrooms	2

Activities:

---

23. OKA

Near the Mirabel and Dorval airports, Oka is a village located in the heart of nature, which is magnificent year-round. You will be cordially welcomed by our family, in our warm and comfortable house. Enjoy breakfasts for which we are famous! Guests are greeted at the airport. We didn't participate at the voluntary classification program.

From Mirabel, hwy 15 South, Exit 20 West, Rte. 640 West. From Montreal, hwy 15 North, Exit 20 West, or hwy 13 North to the end. Hwy 640 West to the end, Rte. 344 West twd Oka for 10km, turn left on Rue Ste-Anne.

B&B
LE CLOS DES LILAS

Sabine Le Boulengé and
Martin Goulet
14, rue Ste-Anne
Oka J0N 1E0
tel/fax (450) 479-8214
closdeslilas@sympatico.ca

B&B	
single	$45
double	$60
child	$10

Open year round

Number of rooms	3
shared bathroom	1
rooms with sink	2

Activities:

---

24. OKA

In the charming village of Oka, just steps away from the ferry, Lac des Deux-Montagnes, small shops, the bike path, the park and its superb beach, we welcome you as you are year-round in the spirit of friendship. Exquisite, delicious breakfasts. Comfort and relaxation guaranteed.

From Montreal, hwy 15 North or 13 North, Exit 640 to the end, Rte 344 West for 10 min. From Mirabel, hwy 15 South, hwy 640 to the end, Rte 344 West for 10min.

B&B
LE ZIBOU

Fabienne Mourin and
Éric Lebailly
119, rue des Cèdres
Oka J0N 1E0
tel/fax (450) 479-6407
zibou@videotron.ca

B&B	
single	$45
double	$60
triple	$75
child	$15

Reduced rates: 10% Nov. 1 to Mar. 31
Open year round

Number of rooms	3
shared bathroom	1
shared wc	1

Activities:

...ONT

...is a majestic cocoon in the mountains offering tranquillity and relaxation. Situated near St-Sauveur, it's in the heart of vibrant cultural and sporting events. Our rooms have a scenic view, jacuzzis, fireplaces and terraces. You will be impressed by our gourmet breakfasts. Come to La Chrysalide. A great time guaranteed!

From Montréal Hwy 15 North, turn right at Exit 58, Rte 117 North. Right at first light onto Ch. de la Gare. After the bridge, keep right on Ch. de la Rivière. Turn left at the 2nd stop sign onto Ch. des Grands Ducs. We are at the end of the private road.

B&B
LA CHRYSALIDE

Ginette Paré and Lauréan Martin
237, chemin des Grands Ducs
Piedmont J0R 1K0
(450) 227-0944
fax (450) 277-6930
www.bbcanada.com/chrysalide
laurean.martin@sympatico.ca

B&B	
single	$55-90
double	$65-100
triple	$80-115
child	$10

VS

Reduced rates: 10% 3 nights and more and Apr., May, Nov., 7th night free
Open year round

Number of rooms	5
rooms with private bath	3
shared wc	1
shared bathrooms	1

Activities: 🏛 🍴 🎿 🚲 🎿

---

26. PRÉVOST

Located 5min from St-Sauveur and 15min from Mirabel, a relaxing place for non-smoking adults. Patio, panoramic view, solarium with Jacuzzi, music, TV. Healthy breakfast. 1km from linear park (200km) for cycling. Transportation available. Just 5min from the lake, golf, tennis, flea market, antique dealers. Partial wheelchair access.

Hwy 15 North, Exit 55, on Rue Louis-Morin. Turn right on Rue Morin, cross the bridge. Turn left on Rue de la Station. 1km past Rte 117's traffic lights, turn left on Montée Sauvage, then right on Du Sommet and right on Voie Lactée.

B&B
À LA MONTAGNE
CHEZ MADELEINE ET PIERRE

Madeleine Sévigny
and Pierre Lavigne
1460, Voie Lactée, C.P. 92
Prévost J0R 1T0
(450) 224-4628
fax -daytime- (450) 224-4628
www.bbcanada.com/2074.html
chez_madeleine_et_pierre
@hotmail.com

B&B	
single	$40-55
double	$55

Open: June 1 to Oct. 15

Number of rooms	2
shared wc	1
shared bathrooms	1

Activities: 🏛 🍴 🚣 🚲 🐎

---

27. ST-ADOLPHE-D'HOWARD

Prize for Excellence "Special Favorite" Regional 2000. A white, stone-built turreted house on the lake, surrounded by mountains. Come in and luxuriate in the peace and quiet. Cozy rooms for the laziest of nights. Near the fire: books, games, soft couch. As for breakfast? Wow! Aube Douce: "a charming place."

From Montreal, Hwy 15 North, Exit 60, Rte 364 West to Rte 329 North. Drive 10km, turn left on Montée Lac Louise, 1.5km, right on Gais Lurons, left at the first stop sign.

B&B
AUBE DOUCE

Michèle Ménard and
Gilles Meilleur
22, chemin de la Québécoise
St-Adolphe-d'Howard J0T 2B0
(819) 327-5048
toll free 1-877-527-5851
fax (819) 327-5254
www.bbcanada.
com/2767.html

B&B	
single	$55-80
double	$60-80
triple	$80-105
child	$0-10

Open year round

Number of rooms	4
rooms with private bath	4

Activities: 🍴 🚣 🚲 🎿 🏃

28. ST-ADOLPHE-D'HOWARD

 F E

Located 8km from Sainte-Agathe facing Lac Saint-Joseph, come experience some of the greatest pleasures in life. Meticulously decorated rooms, private bathrooms, living room with balcony and view of the lake. Sumptuous breakfast served in the spacious dinning-room. A great place to rejuvenate yourself and practice aquatic or winter sports. Welcome to our friendly home.

From Montréal, Hwy 15, Exit 60 Rte 364 to Morin-Heights, Rte 329 to Saint-Adolphe, 3km after the town.

B&B
CHEZ BÉCASSINE

Nicole Sénécal and Maurice Roy
2875, chemin du Village
Saint-Adolphe-d'Howard
J0T 2B0
(819) 327-5029
toll free 1-888-822-5029
fax (819) 327-3513
www.angelfire.com/mt/
chezbecassine/index.html
chezbecassine@hotmail.com

	B&B
single	
double	
child	$

Taxes extra VS IT

Reduced rates: Nov. 1 to Dec. 15, Apr. 1 to May 15
Open year round

Number of rooms	4
rooms with private bath	4
shared wc	1

Activities:

Not available

---

29. ST-FAUSTIN

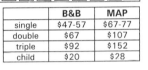 F E P R8

Discover the sheperd's way of life; simplicity, nature, culture. Vast domain to explore as to contemplate. Lovely rooms annexed to the barn's calmess. Meals served in a family-style atmosphere in our intimate log house. National Silver laureate Grands prix du tourisme 2000. An enchanting experience. **Farm Stay p 51. Farm tour p 39.**

From Montreal, Hwy 15 North. In St-Faustin, 2km after Mt-Blanc, left on Chemin la Sauvagine for 7km. From St-Jovite, Rte 327 South twd Arundel for 2km. Left on Chemin Paquette for 6km.

B&B
FERME DE LA
BUTTE MAGIQUE

Diane, Maud and children
1724, chemin de la Sauvagine
St-Faustin J0T 1J2
tel/fax (819) 425-5688
www.citeweb.net/bmagique
fermedelabuttemagique
@hotmail.com

	B&B	MAP
single	$47-57	$67-77
double	$67	$107
triple	$92	$152
child	$20	$28

Reduced rates: 10% 2 nights and more (B&B), except holidays
Open year round

Number of rooms	3
shared wc	1
shared bathrooms	1

Activities:

---

30. ST-FAUSTIN

 F E P R1 TA

Special mention "Success 1999" "Our beautiful Inns of yesteryears". Superb antique-laden Victorian ancestral house facing Mont-Blanc, 2min from Route 117, at the entrance to Mont-Tremblant park, 1km from the lake and bike path (P'tit Train du Nord). 6 rooms, including one family-size room and one private four-person studio. Delicious cuisine served on the terrace in summer, by the fire in winter. Enticing ski and cycling packages.

From Montreal, Hwy 15 North twd Ste-Agathe, Rte 117 for 16km, St-Faustin Exit, left on Rue Principale, Rue de la Pisciculture.

INN
LA BONNE ADRESSE

Odette Bélanger and
Jean-Marie Noël
1196, rue de la Pisciculture
St-Faustin J0T 1J3
(819) 688-6422
toll free 1-877-688-6422
fax (819) 688-5052
www.bonjourquebec.
com/info/labonneadresse
bonneadresse@sympatico.ca

	B&B	MAP
single	$50-70	$70-90
double	$65-100	$105-140
triple	$95-125	$155-185
quad.	$110-130	$190-210
child	$15	$25

Taxes extra VS MC IT

Open: Dec. 15 to Nov. 1

Number of rooms	6
rooms with private bath	4
shared bathrooms	1

Activities:

31. ST-FAUSTIN, LAC-CARRÉ

F E 🚭 🐕 P R1 TA

Warm and relaxed welcome in a recently renovated century-old house with period atmosphere. Ideal location facing Mont-Blanc and 15min from Mont Tremblant, 1km from the "Le P'tit Train du Nord" bike path, near Parc du Mont-Tremblant. Packages: ski, wilderness and/or gastronomy. Near many outdoor-sports opportunities. Hearty breakfast with homemade products.

From Montreal, hwy 15 North, Rte. 117 North, St-Faustin Exit, turn left at the second stop.

B&B
L'ENTREMONT

Manon and David Bruchez
1119, rue de la Pisciculture
St-Faustin, Lac-Carré J0T 1J3
(819) 688-6662
toll free 1-888-928-6662
www.entremont.net
info@entremont.net

B&B	
single	$55-65
double	$65-75
triple	$85
quad.	$105
child	$10

Taxes extra VS MC IT

Open year round

Number of rooms	5
room with private bath	1
shared bathroom	2

Activities: 🏊 🚶 🚲 🎿 🏃

---

32. ST-HIPPOLYTE

★ ★ F E P ✗ 🏊 R4 TA

Facing the lake, in the mountains rife with lush flora. Imagine the scene at dusk when the sun paints its canvas! Dining room with terrace, unparalleled view. Innovative, lavish fine cuisine. Discover edible flowers. Charming, comfortable rooms. Private beach, free watercraft, grade-A water. No motorboats allowed. Rest assured. 1st prize «Villages Fleuris». A true paradise! **See colour photos.**

Hwy 15 N., Exit 45 twd St-Hippolyte, left at 1st light for 16km to Rte 333 N. Turn left at the church, drive 4km, keep to the right, inn is 300 m further.

INN
AUBERGE LAC DU PIN ROUGE

Nicole Bouffard and
Yvan Trottier
81, chemin Lac-du-Pin-Rouge
St-Hippolyte J8A 3J3
(450) 563-2790
toll free1-800-427-0840

	B&B	MAP
single	$51-75	$84-108
double	$65-90	$129-151
triple	$88-119	$175-208
child	$20	à la carte

Taxes extra VS MC

Reduced rates: up to 25%
Open: May 18 to Oct. 9

Number of rooms	8
rooms with private bath	4
rooms with sink	4
shared wc	3
shared bathrooms	2

Activities: 🏊 🚶 🚲 🏇

---

33. ST-HIPPOLYTE

☀☀☀ F e 🚭 🎿 🚗 P R2 TA

A quiet place at 45min of Mtl. Terrace with panoramic view. Water garden with water fall. Fire place and living room. Shared kitchenette. We offer massages, seaweed wrapping and other body cares on reservation. Swimming in the lake, free pedal boat rides. At 6km from linear park "Le p'tit train du nord".

Hwy 15, Exit 45, direction St-Hypolite. 1st light at left rte 333, 9,3 km. Left on Du lac Écho road, 50km , right on Desjardins St., 1km, right on 88th Ave., left at the stop sign.

B&B
L'ÉVEIL SUR LE LAC

Huguette Péloquin and
René St-Vincent
214, 92e avenue
St-Hippolyte J8A 1V1
(514) 865-9485
toll free 1-888-224-9716
www.eveilsurlelac.cjb.net
eveil@aei.ca

B&B	
single	$43-50
double	$60-65
child	$10

VS MC

Reduced rates: 5$ Sept. 10 to June 20, 10% 3 nights and more
Open year round

Number of rooms	3
shared bathrooms	2

Activities: 🛶 🏊 🚲 🎿 🏃

34. ST-JÉRÔME

Ten min from Mirabel airport and 30 min from Dorval, generous and considerate hospitality à la québécoise. Nice ambience, gourmet breakfast. Gérard, a history professor, is proud to tell you about his Québec! Located at 100 metres from the bicycle path "Le P'tit train du Nord".

Hwy 15 North, Exit 43 East twd downtown. After the bridge, right on Rue Labelle. At the lights, left on Rue du Palais (cathedral), left on Melançon street, 2nd light. B&B is 1 block away on the left.

B&B
L'ÉTAPE CHEZ MARIE-
THÉRÈSE ET GÉRARD LEMAY

Marie-Thérèse and
Gérard Lemay
430, rue Melançon
St-Jérôme J7Z 4K4
(450) 438-1043

B&B	
single	$45
double	$55
triple	$75
child	$15

Reduced rates: 5 nights and more
Open year round

Number of rooms	3
shared wc	1
shared bathrooms	2

Activities: 🏛 ♦ ⚓ 🚶 🚲

35. ST-JOSEPH-DU-LAC

Like a nest overhanging mountains and apple trees, at the foot of the vineyards, is a unique place that combines a vinery and award-winning wines, only steps away from a singular gastronomic experience with a French twist. And after reception, what could be better than sipping porto by the fire before retiring for the night? **See color photos.**

25min from Montreal, hwy 13 or 15 North, hwy 640 West, Exit 2, left on chemin Principal, 4.7km.

INN
AUBERGE ROCHE DES BRISES

Gina Pratt and Bryan Harvey
2006, rue Principale
St-Joseph-du-Lac J0N 1M0
(450) 472-2722
(450) 472-8756
fax (450) 473-5878
www.rochedesbrises.com
info@rochedesbrises.com

	B&B	MAP
single	$90-100	$130-140
double	$110-120	$190-200

Taxes extra VS MC IT

Reduced rates: 10% Nov. and Feb.,
3 nights and more
Open year round

Number of rooms	5
rooms with private bath	5

Activities: ♦ ⚓ 🚲 🐎 🏃

36. ST-JOSEPH-DU-LAC

Surrounded by a forest, gardens and apple trees, our bed and breakfast welcomes you to share good times and gourmet breakfasts. Quiet, invigorating, comfortable stay in rooms with panoramic views and private bathrooms. Pool, hiking and cycling on 30 acres (12ha). Located 5min from Parc d'Oka (package) and Oka ferry (hwy 401 or 417), 15min from Mirabel and 35min from Dorval.

From Montreal, hwy 13 or 15 North, 640 West twd Oka, Exit 2, St-Joseph-du-Lac, turn left, 4km past the church.

B&B
GÎTE DES JARDINS
DE LA MONTAGNE

Jocelyne Dion and
Richard Gravel
2371, ch. Principal
St-Joseph-du-Lac J0N 1M0
(450) 623-0574
fax (514) 856-2595
pages.infinit.net/jardinsm
jardins@videotron.ca

B&B	
single	40-50 $
double	50-60 $
triple	65-75 $
child	10 $

Reduced rates: Oct.15 to Dec.15 and Mar. 15 to May 10
and 10% 3 nights and more
Open year round

Number of rooms	3
rooms with private bath	3

Activities: 🏖 ⚓ 🚲 🏊 🏃

37. ST-SAUVEUR-DES-MONTS ★★ 🏠 F E 🏊 P 🚗 R2

Winner of the *Grand Prix du Tourisme Laurentides*: welcome and customer service 1997. Facing ski hills, 2km from town. Enchanting decor, tranquillity, attention and discretion. Heated pool, central air conditioning, flowered terrace, 2 rms with fireplaces, including one semi-basement suite. Many recreational/tourist activities nearby. But above all, relaxation, comfort and a warm welcome. Gourmet breakfast.

From Montréal, Hwy 15 N. left at Exit 60, at Rte 364 W. turn right, 3rd set of lights, left on Rue Principale, 2km.

INN
AUBERGE SOUS L'ÉDREDON

Josée Guertin and Mario Amyot
777, rue Principale
St-Sauveur-des-Monts
J0R 1R2
(450) 227-3131
www.bonjourquebec.com/info/
aubergesousledredon

B&B	
single	$59-89
double	$79-109
triple	$94-124
child	$10-15

Taxes extra VS MC

Reduced rates: Apr., May, Nov., and 10% 3 nights and more
Open year round

Number of rooms	7
rooms with private bath	5
rooms in semi-basement	1
shared bathrooms	1

Activities: 🛶 ⛷ 🎿 🚴 ⛷

---

38. ST-SAUVEUR-DES-MONTS ☀☀☀ F E 🚭 P 🚗 🏊 ✕ TA

Lovely charming house. Cosy air conditioned non-smoking haven, peaceful setting in a very picturesque Laurentian Village. Fireplace, view of ski hills. Beautiful gardens and outdoor pool. Private bathrooms. Luxury suite with double whirlpool. Packages available: ski, dogsled, snowmobile, golf, biking, water slides, etc. Very warm ambiance, well travelled hosts speaking various language. Candlelight gourmet breakfast. Welcome!

From Montréal Hwy 15 N., left at Exit 60. Right onto Rte 364 W. At 2nd light, right on Rue de la Gare. Left on Rue Principale 0.4km.

B&B
«AUX PETITS OISEAUX...»

Mireille and Benny
342, rue Principale
St-Sauveur-des-Monts J0R 1R0
(450) 227-6116
toll free 1-877-227-6116
fax (450) 227-6171
www.bbcanada.
com/auxpetitsoiseaux
auxpetitsoiseaux@
sympatico.ca

B&B	
single	$60-100
double	$65-125
triple	$90-145
quad.	$150-200
child	$10-20

Taxes extra VS MC AM

Reduced rates: Week days Apr., May , Oct., Nov., 3 nights and more except summer and holidays
Open year round

Number of rooms	5
rooms with private bath	3
shared bathroom	1
rooms in basement	2

Activities: 🛶 🤸 🚶 🚴 ⛷

---

39. ST-SAUVEUR-DES-MONTS ☀☀☀☀ 🏠 F E 🚭 🚗 P R.1

A charming B&B in the heart of Laurentian Mountains. Our ancestral home welcomes you with romantic bedrooms (two with fireplaces) and gourmet breakfasts. Stone fireplace in the common room. Minutes from boutiques, fine restaurants, ski and golf resorts. Smoke-free. "A peaceful haven where your dreams have a good chance of coming true." *Le Bel Âge*

From Montréal, Hwy 15 North, turn left at Exit 60, turn right at Rte 364, turn right at the 3rd light onto Rue Principale.

B&B
LE BONNET D'OR B&B

Michelle McMillan and
Glen Bonney
405, rue Principale
St-Sauveur-des-Monts J0R 1R0
(450) 227-9669
toll free 1-877-277-9669
www.bonjourquebec.
com/info/bonnetdor
bonnetdor@qc.aibn.com

B&B	
single	$80-115
double	$90-125
triple	$140

Taxes extra VS MC

Open year round

Number of rooms	5
rooms with private bath	5

Activities: 🛶 🚴 ⛷ 🤸

40. STE-ADÈLE

★★★ | F | E | ♿ | P | 🚗 | ✕ | R.3 | TA

Charming inn with country-style decor in the heart of the village! Fireplace, dining room. Many activities nearby. Packages: jaunt, health, lovers, snowmobiling, skiing, dogsledding, theatre, golf, cruise. Shuttle service. Some luxury rooms with double therapeutic bath, fireplace, TV, queen-size bed. Hearty breakfast to brighten up your mornings.

From Montréal, Hwy 15 North, Exit 67; at 4th lights, turn right onto Chemin Pierre-Péladeau. From Ste-Agathe, Hwy 15 South, Exit 69, left at first stop sign, right at next stop sign onto Chemin Pierre-Péladeau.

INN
AUBERGE AU NID DOUILLET

Martin Leduc
430, chemin Pierre-Péladeau
Ste-Adèle J8B 1Z4
(450) 229-6939
toll free 1-800-529-6939
fax (450) 229-6651
www.auniddouillet.com

	B&B	MAP
single	$65-95	$85-115
double	$75-135	$119-179
triple	$95-145	$159-199
quad.	$105-155	$199-219
child	$0-15	$0-30

Taxes extra VS MC AM ER IT

Reduced rates: Apr., May, and Oct. week days, 10% 2 nights and more
Open year round

Number of rooms	16
rooms in basement	2
rooms with private bath	16

Activities: 🎿 🤸 🐕 🐎 🏂

---

41. STE-ADÈLE

☀☀☀ | F | E | 🚭 | 🏊 | 🚗 | P | R.5

Our little love nest is tucked away between Montréal and Tremblant, amidst all the cultural and outdoor activities. Total relaxation is guaranteed. Friendly hosts, a night by the fire. In the morning, a big breakfast awaits in the solarium, where you can admire the birds, flowered garden, stream and heated pool. Enjoyable days and nights await. Spoil yourself.

From Montréal, Hwy 15 N., Exit 67, Rte 117, Boul Ste-Adèle for 2km. 25 min from Mirabel airport.

B&B
BONNE NUIT BONJOUR

Gillian Lee and Timothy Eccles
1980, boul. Ste-Adèle
Ste-Adèle J8B 2N5
tel/fax (450) 229-7500
toll free 1-888-229-7500
www.bonnenuitbonjour.com
bonnenuitbonjour
@qc.aibn.com

	B&B
single	$55-65
double	$90-100
triple	$110
quad.	$130
child	$20

Taxes extra VS MC IT

Open year round

Number of rooms	5
rooms with private bath	5

Activities: 🍷 🎿 🚲 ⛷ 🤸

---

42. STE-ADÈLE

☀☀☀ | F | e | 🚭 | 🚗 | P | R.4 | TA

Located near the bike and cross-country skiing path, Auberge de la Gare is a Victorian-style house from the *belle époque*. This rustic property is furnished with antiques, which complement the meticulous décor. We offer two different breakfasts, living room with fireplace, billiard table, reading room and more. Numerous sports activities, hydroplane, new concert theatre, cinema, art gallery, waterfall. Shuttle buses to the airports and excellent restaurants in the area. Terrace and Belgian specialities. **See colour photos.**

From Montréal, Hwy 15 North, Exit 69, 370 East 4km.

B&B
AUBERGE DE LA GARE

Geneviève Ostrowski and
Michel Gossiaux
1694, ch. Pierre-Péladeau
C.P. 2587
Ste-Adèle J8B 1Z5
(450) 228-3140
toll free 1-888-825-4273
fax (450) 228-1089
www.laurentides.
com/membres/006a.html

	B&B
single	$57-62
double	$65-70

Taxes extra VS MC IT

Open year round

Number of rooms	5
rooms with sink	5
shared wc	2
shared bathrooms	2

Activities: 🍷 🚲 🤸 🐎

43. STE-ADÈLE

☀☀☀ | F | E | 🐾 | 🏊 | P | 🚗 R6 | TA

A home away from home! Our domain built on the mountainside is an oasis of peace and tranquillity! Warmth, relaxation and comfort blend together to offer you an unforgettable stay. Dream breakfasts that will fulfil you! Swimming pool on the premises. Parks, hikes, bikes path, ski resorts a stone's throw away. Golf, theatre and massage packages available.

From Montréal, Hwy 15 North, Exit 67. Right at the traffic lights Rue St-Joseph. At the stop sign, turn left on Rue Rolland, drive 3km.

B&B
AUBERGE DES SORBIERS B&B

Lise Fournier and Alain Parpal
4120, rue Rolland
Ste-Adèle J8B 1C7
(450) 229-3929
www.sorbiers.com
info@sorbiers.com

B&B	
single	$60-70
double	$70-80
triple	$105

VS

Reduced rates: 3 nights and more in Mar., Apr. and from Nov. 1 to Dec. 15
Open year round

Number of rooms	4
rooms with sink	2
rooms with private bath	2
shared bathrooms	1

Activities: 🏊 🎿 🚴 🎿 🏃

44. STE-ADÈLE

☀☀☀ | F | E | 🚭 | 🚗 | P | R.3 | TA

High above the valley! On mountainside, quiet area, near the lake and the city beach, ski Chanteclerc and many restaurants. Central air-conditioned inn, European charm, private balconies, V.I.P. suites. Splendid views! Stone fireplace, guests' living room, large indoor sauna and spa, outdoor snowbath! Learn German at breakfast!

From Montréal, Hwy 15 N. Exit 67, Rte 117, Blvd Ste-Adèle, left at the 4th light at Rue Morin, 0.3km, then turn left onto Rue Ouimet, drive 0.2km. 4th house on your left at the end of the street.

B&B
AUBERGE LA GIROUETTE
DES B&B

Helga Büchel Bélanger
941, rue Ouimet
Ste-Adèle J8B 2R3
tel/fax (450) 229-6433
toll free 1-800-301-6433
www.bbcanada.com/1536.html
la.girouette@securenet.net

B&B	
single	$55-90
double	$65-110
triple	$105-135
quad.	$120-160
child	$0-15

Taxes extra VS MC IT

Reduced rates: Apr., May and Nov.
Open year round

Number of rooms	5
rooms with pivate bath	5

Activities: 🚣 🎿 🚴 🎿 🏃

45. STE-ADÈLE

★★★ | F | E | 🍽 | 🚗 | P | R.1 | TA

Large and majestic, this authentic Victorian house offers you the pleasure of staying in one of the beautiful homes of yesteryear. Period cachet, gourmet breakfasts, country fare, huge fireplace, extensive woodlands. Located by the linear park, near winter and summer activities. Exclusive use of the inn available for conferences, weddings and anniversaries.

Hwy 15 North, Exit 67. At the light, turn right on Rue St-Joseph, right on Rue Rolland and right on Rue St-Jean. Next to the church.

INN
AUBERGE LE CLOS ROLLAND

Sylvie Nardone and
Jean-François Benoît
1200, rue St-Jean
Ste-Adèle J8B 1E6
(450) 229-2797
toll free 1-888-409-2797
fax (450) 229-2791
www.bbcanada.
com/leclosrolland
aubergeclosrolland@qc.aira.com

	B&B	MAP
single	$60-80	$85-105
double	$70-90	$120-140
triple	$80-100	$155-175
quad.	$90-110	$165-185
child	$0-10	$10-25

Taxes extra VS MC IT

Reduced rates: 10% Apr. to June, Nov. week days, and 3 nights and more
Open year round

Number of rooms	9
rooms with private bath	6
shared bathroom	1
shared wc	1

Activities: 🏊 🚣 🚴 🎿 🏃

46. STE-ADÈLE

★ ★ F E ✕ ☒ P TA

Halfway between Montreal and Tremblant, a small-hotel-style inn with an in-house restaurant offering excellent, renowned cuisine. Rustic rooms with air conditioning. Lounge with fireplace. Conference room for small groups (approx. 15 people). Located 0.5km from "Le P'tit Train du Nord" linear park, hiking in forest on site. Packages: massage, golf, theatre, dogsledding. Near skiing and snowmobiling.

From Montreal, hwy 15 North, Exit 69, turn right on Rte. 370 East, drive about 4km.

INN
AUBERGE RESTAURANT
LA BRUYÈRE

Nathalie Charbonneau and
Michel Bruyère
1406, ch. Pierre-Péladeau
Ste-Adèle J8B 1Z4
(450) 229-4417
toll free 1-800-535-4417
http://pages.citenet.net/
users/ctmz2736
aub-la-bruyere@citenet.net

	B&B	MAP
single	$50-60	$63-73
double	$63-73	$89-99
triple	$77-87	$116-126
child	$0-14	

Taxes extra VS MC AM ER IT

Open year round

Number of rooms	11
rooms with private bath	11

Activities: 🦪 🎿 🚶 🚴 🎿

47. STE-ADÈLE

☀☀☀ F E P 🚗 ✕ R.5 TA

Our place is a private estate located 5min from all activities in the Laurentians, and you are our welcome guests. Fireplace, piano, living room, air conditioning, outdoor spa in summer... in short, everything for your relaxation. Hearty breakfasts. Other meals by reservation. A convivial place where you'll want to return, whether to have fun, to work or to celebrate... with family or friends.

From Montreal, Hwy 15 North, Exit 69 toward Ste-Marguerite, for about 7km.

INN
AUX PINS DORÉS

Carmen Champagne and
René Tremblay
2251, chemin Pierre-Péladeau
Ste-Adèle J8B 1Z7
(450) 228-4556
toll free 1-877-228-4556
fax (450) 228-1881
members.tripod.com/~pins
pins_dores@lycosmail.com

B&B	
single	$50-60
double	$60-75
triple	$90
quad.	$105
child	$0-10

Reduced rates: 2 nights or more during weeks except summertime and school holidays.

Open year round

Number of rooms	4
rooms with private bath	1
shared bathrooms	2

Activities: 🦪 🎿 🚴 🎿 🏃

48. STE-ADÈLE

F E 🚭 ✕ 🚗 P R.2 TA

Let yourself be amazed by this Swiss chalet and its treasures: antiques, stone fireplace, cozy rooms and an unforgettable breakfast. Offering a panoramic view of the Laurentian Mountains, facing the water slides and an interprovincial snowmobile trail (packages available), just steps away from the town centre and its summer theatres, and 30min from Mont Tremblant. Dinner available by reservation.

Hwy 15 North, Exit 67, turn left at the village exit.

B&B
GÎTE DES AMÉRIQUES

Laurence and Claude Albert
1724, boul. Ste-Adèle
Ste-Adèle J8B 2N5
tel/fax (450) 229-9042
www.bbcanada.
com/4550.html
amerique@citenet.net

B&B	
single	$35-55
double	$50-65
triple	$80
quad.	$95
child	$0-10

MC

Reduced rates: 10% 3 nights and more
Open year round

Number of rooms	4
shared bathrooms	2
shared wc	2

Activities: 🎿 🚶 🚴 🎿 🏃

49. STE-AGATHE-DES-MONTS ★★★ F E P R.1

On the shore of Lac des Sables, our Inn has 5 luxurious thematic rooms, which include whirlpools for two, chimneys, balconies, sound systems, air conditioned, private bathrooms and breakfast served in the privacy of your own room. Massages available on the premises. Free use of our canoes, pedal-boats and bikes. Snowmobiling and other winter sports are nearby. 1 hour from Mtl and 35 min from Tremblant. Call us to know more about our promotions. **Ad end of guide.**

From Montréal, Hwy 15 N., Exit 86. Rte 117 N., 3rd light, left on Rue Principale, left on Ste-Lucie and left on Larocque.

INN
AUBERGE AUX NUITS DE RÊVE

Carol McCann
14, rue Larocque Ouest
St-Agathe-des-Monts
J8C 1A2
tel/fax (819) 326-5042
toll free 1-888-326-5042
www.reve.ca
auberge@reve.ca

B&B	
single	$110-145
double	$110-145

Taxes extra VS MC

Open year round

Number of rooms	5
rooms with private bath	5

Activities:

50. STE-AGATHE-DES-MONTS ★★★ F E P R1 TA

Special Mention «Our beautiful Inns of yesteryear» success 1999. Imagine a beautiful 100-year-old house where comfort is a living tradition. A fire burning in the hearth, Swedish massages. The colours of the changing seasons. The peaceful contentment of gathering twilight. 1 hour from Montréal, 35 min from Tremblant: 12 rms, including 8 with fireplace and whirlpool bath. **Ad end of guide.**

From Montréal, Hwy 15 N. Exit 86. Rte 117 N., at 5th lights turn left on Rue Préfontaine, right on Chemin Tour-du-Lac.

INN
AUBERGE DE LA TOUR DU LAC

Jean-Léo Legault
173, chemin Tour-du-Lac
Ste-Agathe-des-Monts
J8C 1B7
toll free 1-800-622-1735
(819) 326-4202
fax (819) 326-0341
www.delatour.qc.ca

B&B	
single	$73-103
double	$88-118
child	$15

Taxes extra VS MC AM ER IT

Reduced rates: Apr. and Nov.
Open year round

Number of rooms	12
rooms with private bath	12

Activities:

51. STE-AGATHE-DES-MONTS ★★★ F E P R2 TA

Discover a haven of peace where refinement and hospitality are only matched by the splendour of breathtaking scenery (nine rooms facing the lake). Appreciate the warmth and quiet that pervades Le Saint-Venant and brightens up the divine breakfasts. Located 1hr from Montreal, the inn is also just steps away from the village and many activities.

From Montreal, Hwy 15 North, Exit 83, turn left at the stop sign, drive 2km along Rte 329 South. Turn right at the stop sign, drive 500m along Rte 329 North, turn left on private road.

INN
AUBERGE «LE SAINT-VENANT»

Kety Kostovski and Benoît Meyer
234, rue Saint-Venant
Ste-Agathe-des-Monts J8C 2Z7
toll free 1-800-697-7937
(819) 326-7937
fax (819) 326-4848
www.st-venant.com
venant@intlaurentides.qc.ca

B&B	
single	$80-130
double	$86-136

Taxes extra VS MC AM

Reduced rates: 20% Apr. and Nov.,
10% Jan. 6 to Mar. 31
Open year round

Number of rooms	9
rooms with private bath	9

Activities:

52. STE-AGATHE-DES-MONTS

☀☀☀☀☀ F E 🚫 🐕 🚗 P 🏊 R2 TA

Situated in the heart of a picturesque, quaint little village, Au Nid D'Hirondelles was built pieces on pieces. The Canadian-style decor with two fireplaces creates the atmosphere of a bygone era. In harmony with Mother Nature, we celebrate her changing seasons. After a night of restful sleep, you will be served a copious breakfast. Located between Mont-Tremblant and St-Sauveur, it's the ideal spot for sports enthusiasts and nature lovers.

From Montréal, Hwy 15 North to the end, drive 1km. Turn right on Chemin Mt-Castor, 1.5km.

B&B
AU NID D'HIRONDELLES

Suzanne and Michel Grève
1235, des Hirondelles
Mont-Castor
Ste-Agathe-des-Monts J8C 2Z8
(819) 326-5413
toll free 1-888-826-5413
fax (819) 326-3839
www.nidhirondelles.qc.ca
gite@nidhirondelles.qc.ca

	B&B	MAP
single	$70-80	$90-100
double	$80-95	$120-135

Taxes extra VS MC

Open year round

Number of rooms	5
rooms with private bath	5

Activities: 🚶 🚴 🎿 🏃 🐕

---

53. STE-AGATHE-NORD

F E 🍴 🐕 🚗 P R5 TA

Relive the turn of the century in our manor. Built for Count d'Ivry in 1902, its original woodwork and stone fireplaces have been preserved. Nature and many outdoor activities are just outside your doorstep. There's swimming in Lac Manitou, as well as biking and snowmobiling on the P'tit Train du Nord path (1km). Discount for Mont-Blanc ski resort. A breakfast made with seasonal products is served up by your friendly hosts.

From Montréal, Hwy 15 North. When the highway ends and links up with Rte 117, first street on your left, Chemin Renaud.

INN
MANOIR D'IVRY B&B

Isabelle Taverna, Daniel Potvin, Isabelle Giroux, Pascal Potvin
3800, chemin Renaud
Ste-Agathe-Nord J8C 2Z8
(819) 321-0858
www.manoirdivry.com
manoirdivry@ste-agathe.net

	B&B
single	$45-50
double	$55-60
triple	$75
quad.	$90
child	$5-10

Taxes extra VS

Reduced rates: Price for group, 5$ off/night, 3 nights and more
Open year round

Number of rooms	9
shared wc	1
shared bathrooms	3

Activities: ⛴ 🚤 🚶 🚴 🎿

---

54. STE-MARGUERITE-DU-LAC-MASSON

☀☀☀ F e ✕ P 🏊 R5 TA

A rural atmosphere, spacious house and soothing landscape await you at the Au Phil de l'Eau inn. And not only that, but refined cuisine with the flavours of Quebec and beyond, a lakeside terrace, private beach, fireplace and activities for all tastes, including golf, canoeing, skiing, cruises, theatre and skating... All this less than an hour from Montreal.

Hwy 15 North, Exit 69, Rte 370 East for 8km. At the "Les 2 Roses" house, turn left on Chemin Guénette, continue for 4.5km.

B&B
AUBERGE AU PHIL DE L'EAU

Murielle Godin and
Philippe Gauzelin
150, ch. Guénette
Ste-Marguerite-du-Lac-Masson
J0T 1L0
(450) 228-1882
fax (450) 228-8271
www.auphildeleau.com
aubergeauphildeleau@yahoo.com

	B&B	MAP
single	$45-60	$63-95
double	$55-70	$91-140
triple	$85	$139-190
quad.	$100	$172-240
child	$15	

Taxes extra VS

Reduced rates: 15% 4 nights and more, 20% 7 nights and more
Open year round

Number of rooms	5
shared wc	1
shared bathrooms	2

Activities: 🚤 🦆 🚶 🛶 🎿

55. STE-MARGUERITE-DU-LAC-MASSON ✹✹✹ F E 🚭 P 🚗 🐕 R1 TA

"The tranquillity of the forest, the beautiful setting, the sun-lit house, the warmth of two hearths, such warm-hearted people, an extra-special breakfast. The place had it all." Here you will find the contentment of a pleasant, informal home. Near St-Sauveur and Ste-Adèle, between Montréal and Mont Tremblant. 2km from the "Bistrot Champlain".

From Montréal, Hwy 15 North, Exit 69. Rte 370, 10.5km. After the cemetery and Sommet Vert, left on Lupin. Left on Rue Des Rapides, to the end of the street.

B&B
GÎTE DU LIÈVRE

Chantal Belisle and Patrice Richard
34, rue du Lièvre
Ste-Marguerite-du-Lac-Masson
J0T 1L0
tel/fax (450) 228-4131
toll free Mtl (514) 823-4582
pages.citenet.net/
users/ctmx0131
gite_du_lievre@citenet.net

B&B	
single	$60
double	$65
triple	$80
quad.	$95

Open year round

Number of rooms	3
rooms with private bath	1
shared bathrooms	1

Activities: ● 🛷 🚴 🏃 🐎

---

56. VAL-DAVID ★★★ F e ♿ ✕ 🏖 🚗 P R.5 TA

Come discover our charming little inn, located deep in the country, in an exceptional wooded area by the river. Cozy and gastronomic comfort await you here. On site, sure-fire canoeing or cycling adventure, or relaxation by the pool. Package for every season. Be on the lookout, our visitors such as the beaver and the moose can surprise you! Welcome to a world apart! **See color photos.**

Hwy 15 North, Exit 76, Rte 117 North. After the Val David light, turn right on chemin de L'Île.

INN
AUBERGE CHARME DES ALPES

Beatrice and Laurent Loine
1459, rue Merette, ch. de L'Île
Val-David J0T 2N0
(819) 322-3434
(819) 323-0099
fax (819) 322-5478
www.auberge
charmedesalpes.com
info@
aubergecharmedesalpes.com

	B&B	MAP
single	$75-95	$95-115
double	$85-145	$125-185
triple	$105-165	$165-225
quad.	$135-185	$215-265
child	free	$5-15

Taxes extra VS MC IT

Reduced rates: 2 nights and more
Open year round

Number of rooms	12
rooms with private bath	12
shared wc	1

Activities: 🛷 🎿 🚴 🐎 🛷

---

57. VAL-DAVID ✹✹✹ F e 🚭 P R.5

Warm house with charm of yesteryear, main floor made of unhewn-timber, fireplace, veranda, garden. Family atmosphere; spacious, well-ventilated rooms; comfortable king-size bed. And what can we say about our breakfasts? Succumb to new flavours! Across from the linear park for cycling, cross-country skiing...

From Montréal, Hwy 15 North, Exit 76, Rte 117 North. In Val-David: right at 2nd lights onto Rue de l'Eglise, right on Rue de la Sapinière, 2nd block on the left.

B&B
LA CHAUMIÈRE AUX
MARGUERITES

Fabienne and Marc Girard
and their daughter Jéromine
1267, rue de la Sapinière
Val-David J0T 2N0
(819) 322-2043

B&B	
single	$60
double	$60
child	$0-10

VS

Reduced rates: 2 nights and more
Open year round

Number of rooms	2
shared bathrooms	1

Activities: 🏛 🚶 🚴 🎿 🏃

58. VAL-DAVID   ★ ★ F e 🚭 P 🚗 ✕ TA

Old-station-style inn on the summer bike path/winter ski trail (*"P'tit train du nord"*). Terrace on the Rivière du Nord. Ideal for lovers. Rooms on the river or trail. Transport to anywhere on the path (15-passenger minibus). Treks organized: cross-country ski, snowmobile, dogsled, bike, canoe, visits around Québec. At our restaurant: Québec beers and traditional food.

1 hr from Montréal, Hwy 15 N. or Rte 117 N., Exit 76 Val David, then take the 1st street on the left for 600 m.

INN
LE RELAIS DE LA PISTE

Anne-Marie and Thierry Chaumont
1430, de l'Académie
Val-David J0T 2N0
(819) 322-2280
fax (819) 322-6658
www.relaisdelapiste.com
lerelais@polyinter.com

	B&B	MAP
single	$68	$86
double	$75	$120
triple	$90	$155
quad.	$105	$190
child	$15	$30

Taxes extra VS AM IT

Reduced rates: 20% Oct. 15 to Dec. 20, Mar. 20 to May 15
Open year round

Number of rooms	6
rooms with private bath	6

Activities: 🚶 🚲 🐎 🎿 🏃

59. VAL-MORIN   ☀☀☀ F E ♿ 🚭 🏊 🚗 ✕ P TA

Near the P'tit Train du Nord linear trail for biking or skiing excursions. We also organize canoe trips throughout Québec. Large salon with foyer to have a coffee or read. Guests love our copious breakfasts and suppers. Les Florettes is located in a pleasant landscaped spot near a lake without a dock for motorboats.

From Montréal, Hwy 15 North, Exit 76, Rte 117 North, right on Rue Curé-Corbeil, at the stop sign, right on Rue Morin, left on 7e Avenue until the end, then left on Rue de la Gare.

B&B
LES FLORETTES

Micheline Boutin and Jacques Allard
1803, rue de la Gare
Val-Morin J0T 2R0
(819) 322-7614
toll free 1-888-775-7614
fax (819) 322-3029
escapade@polyinter.com

B&B	
single	$45-60
double	$65-80
child	$16

Taxes extra VS MC

Reduced rates: 10% 2 nights and more
Open year round

Number of rooms	5
rooms with private bath	1
shared bathrooms	2

Activities: 🛶 🚶 🚲 🎿 🏃

60. VAL-MORIN   ★ ★ F E 🚭 P 🐕 R2 🏊 TA

Recipient of the Laurentians tourism grand prize 2000 and Prize for Excellence "Special Favorite" Regional 1999. Former general store and post office. A heritage gem. A privileged site by the linear park and Lac Raymond. Free pedal-boating, canoeing and cycling. Relax on the large lakeside porches. Enjoy our 5-course breakfast and a memorable stay. Gift certificate. **See colour photos.**

From Montreal, Hwy 15 North, Exit 76. Rte 117 North for 0.5km, turn right on Curé-Corbeil to the end. Turn right on Rue Morin, 0.5km. Turn left at 1ˢᵗ stop sign, to the end.

INN
LES JARDINS DE LA GARE B&B

Françoise and Alain
1790, 7ᵉ Avenue
Val-Morin J0T 2R0
tel/fax (819) 322-5559
toll free 1-888-322-4273
http://pages.infinit.net/
racetr/jardin.html

	B&B	MAP
single	$60-85	$80-105
double	$80-110	$120-150

Taxes extra VS MC IT

Reduced rates: Oct. 15 to Dec. 15, Apr. 1 to May 15
Open year round

Number of rooms	8
rooms with private bath	2
rooms with sink	2
shared wc	1
shared bathrooms	2

Activities: 🏛 🛶 🚶 🚲 🏃

61. VAL-MORIN

F E ⊘ P R2 TA

In the Laurentians, discover Lise & Camil's eden on a quiet lake surrounded by hills. In summer, take a deep breath while canoeing on the lake with loons and beavers. In winter, relax by an impressive fireplace after a day of ski. 3 large rooms on lakeside, 2 with fireplace and private terrace.

Hwy 15 North Exit 76 rte 117 North. Follow signs to Ski Far Hills. After Cross-country ski center, go straight ahead for 1.7km. Keep right on ch. Lac Lasalle twd cul-de sac.

B&B
NID D'AMOUR

Lise and Camil
6455, chemin du Lac Lasalle
Val-Morin J0T 2R0
tel/fax (819) 322-6379
toll free 1-888- 4321-NID
www.nidamour.qc.ca
nidamour@hotmail.com

B&B	
single	$90-120
double	$90-120

VS MC

Reduced rates: 2 nights and more (lake side)
Open year round
(except during the Christmas Holidays)

Number of rooms	4
rooms with private bath	4

Activities:

62. LAC-SUPÉRIEUR, MONT-TREMBLANT

`F` `E` `🦽` `P` `R1` `M.4` `TA`

Hypnotized by the wind in the trees and an unforgettable view of the mountains. This carefully decorated home (1930) offers relaxation by the fireplace and access to nature; beach, lake, river. 7min from the two largest sites, park and ski resort of Mont-Tremblant. A few steps away: Hiking trails, biking, cross-country skiing and 5 beautifull studios wich will also charm you.

Hwy 15 North, Rte 117 North, St-Faustin Exit. Right at stop sign, 2.3km, follow Mt-Tremblant Park and ski resort signs, continue for 9.5km.

COUNTRY HOME
CHALETS ET STUDIOS
LE VENT DU NORD

Géraldine and Jean Christie
1954, ch. du Lac Supérieur
Lac-Supérieur J0T 1P0
(819) 688-6140
fax (819) 688-3196
www.leventdunord.qbc.net
ventdunord@sympatico.ca

No. houses	6
No. rooms	1-4
No. people	1-14
WEEK-SUMMER	$350-1 225
WEEK-WINTER	$490-2 450
W/E-SUMMER	$140-600
W/E-WINTER	$170-750

Taxes extra VS MC IT

Reduced rates: Jan. 5 to Feb. 15, Mar. 26 to Apr. 1
Open year round

Activities: 🏊 🚶 🎿 ⛷ 🎿

63. ROSEMÈRE

`F` `E` `🐕` `🚗` `P` `🛶` `R.01` `M.03` `TA`

Century house of the French-Canadian sculptor Louis-Philippe Hébert. This magnificient home has all the modern comforts. For business meetings or family get-togethers, it can accommodate 8 people. Reflecting of our recent past, it invites you to its peaceful surroundings on the banks of the 1000 Islands River. 20 min from Montréal, 5 min from Laval. **See colour photos.**

Hwy 15 North, Exit 19. Right at stop sign, left at first light, 1.5km on Grande-Côte. Right on Blvd Labelle, 0.5km. Right, reception at 125 Blvd Labelle (Hôtel Le Rivage).

COUNTRY HOME
LA MAISON DE L'ENCLOS

Christianne and Pierre Verville
463, Île Bélair Ouest
Rosemère
J7A 2G9
(450) 437-2171
toll free 1-888-437-2171
fax (450) 437-3005

No. houses	2
No. rooms	1-4
No. people	2-8
WEEK-SUMMER	$1 043-2 450
WEEK-WINTER	$1 043-2 450
W/E-SUMMER	$300-700
W/E-WINTER	$300-700
DAY-SUMMER	$150-350
DAY-WINTER	$150-350

Taxes extra VS MC AM ER IT

Open year round

Activities: 🏛 ♣ 🏊 🚤 🚶

FARM ACTIVITIES

Farm Stays:

11 LA CLAIRIÈRE DE LA CÔTE, L'Annonciation 5C

29 FERME DE LA BUTTE MAGIQUE, St-Faustin 5

Country-style Dining:

64 AU PIED DE LA CHUTE, Lachute 2C

65 AUX DOUCEURS DE LA RUCHE, Mirabel, St-Scholastique 2

11 LA CLAIRIÈRE DE LA CÔTE, L'Annonciation 2C

66 LA CONCLUSION, Ste-Anne-des-Plaines 2

67 LA FERME DE CATHERINE, St-André Est 22

68 LE RÉGALIN, St-Eustache 22

69 LES RONDINS, Mirabel, Lachute 2

Regional Dining:

70 BASILIC ET ROMARIN, St-Anne-des-Plaines 3

Farm Tour:

71 INTERMIEL, St-Benoît, Mirabel 38

72 FERME ÉCO-FORESTIÈRE LA MINERVE, La Minerve 3

29 FERME DE LA BUTTE MAGIQUE, St-Faustin 3

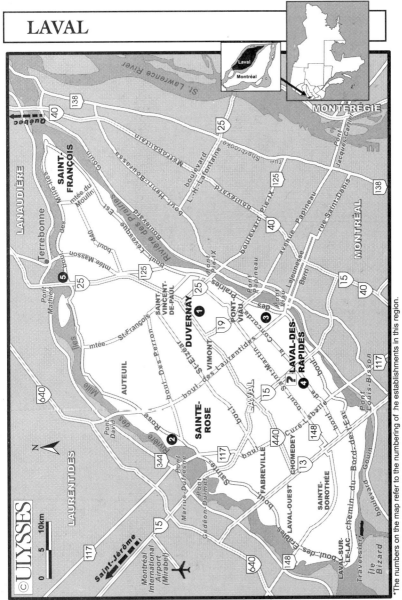

LAVAL

MONTÉRÉGIE

Laval
Montréal

© ULYSSES

0 5 10km

N

Montréal
International
Airport
(Mirabel)

Saint-Jérôme

LAURENTIDES

LANAUDIÈRE

Terrebonne

SAINT-FRANÇOIS

St. Lawrence River

Québec

138

40

25

boulevard des Prairies

boul. Lévesque Est

mtée du Moulin

boul. Henri-Bourassa

Métropolitain

Sherbrooke

rue

boulevard Pie-X

L-H.-Lafontaine

boul. Lévesque

Rivière des Prairies

125

138

125

40

MONTRÉAL

Pont Jacques-Cartier

rue Saint-Denis

avenue Lajeunesse

Berri

boulevard Pie-X

Pont Pie-X

Pont Papineau

Pont Viau

boulevard Papineau

15

40

117

Pont Louis-Bisson

117

Pont Mathieu

Pont David

mtée. Masson

Pont des Îles

mtée. St-François

boul. Des-Prairies

boul. Ste-Rose

boul. des Laurentides

DUVERNAY

SAINT-VINCENT-DE-PAUL

VIMONT

PONT-VIAU

LAVAL-DES-RAPIDES

LAVAL

AUTEUIL

SAINTE-ROSE

Pont Marius-Dufresne

Pont Gédéon-Ouimet

Rivière des Mille Îles

boul. Rossi

117

344

117

440

148

13

15

640

640

148

25

25

19

5

1

2

3

4

2

boul. de la Concorde

boul. Cure-Labelle

boul. Saint-Martin

boul. Industriel

LAVAL-OUEST

FABREVILLE

CHOMEDEY

SAINTE-DOROTHÉE

LAVAL-SUR-LE-LAC

Traversier

Île Bizard

boulevard Gouin

chemin du Bord-de-l'Eau

boul. Sainte-Croix

sep.

sep.

sep.

*The numbers on the map refer to the numbering of the establishments in this region.

1. DUVERNAY EST

It is with great pride and joy that I invite you into my home in the countryside—and with a typically warm Gaspesian welcome. You will sleep peacefully in our cosy bedrooms. Located near conveniences and large centres. Sumptuous breakfast waits for you! "The flavour of Gaspé at the gateway to the metropolis."

Hwy 440, Exit 16 to Boulevard Lévesque East to Des Sapins, 1ˢᵗ street on your right, Des Cèdres.

B&B
LE GÎTE LA GASPÉSIENNE

Yvette Anglehart Grenier
85, rue des Cèdres
Duvernay Est, Laval
H7A 2V7
(450) 665-8475

B&B	
single	$45
double	$55
child	$10

Open year round

Number of rooms	3
shared wc	1
rooms in basement	2
shared bathrooms	1

Activities:

2. LAVAL

Welcome to business people and those curious about the village of Vieux-Ste-Rose in Laval, located 30min from Montreal and the Laurentians. We have had guests from 27 countries stay with us. Guests truly feel they are on vacation here, chatting leisurely over breakfast in front of the Milles-Îles wildlife sanctuary. See you soon!

Hwy 15 North or South, Exit 16, right on Blvd. Ste-Rose, continue for 2.5km. Left on Rue des Patriotes (at the corner of the Vieux-Ste-Rose restaurant), continue for 0.9km.

B&B
GÎTE DU BORD DE L'EAU

Louise Trudeau
495, rue des Patriotes
Laval H7L 2L9
(450) 625-3785
fax (450) 625-8235
www.bbcanada.
com/3402.html
gite_d_eau@hotmail.com

B&B	
single	$47
double	$62
triple	$82
quad.	$102
child	$5-10

Reduced rates: 5$ off/night for 4 nights and more, anytime
Open year round

Number of rooms	1
rooms with private bath	1

Activities:

3. LAVAL

For tourists and business people, near the metro, the Cosmodôme and the Laval convention centre, with the park and bike path leading straight to the old port right at our doorstep. Our rooms include a magnificent suite with private bathroom and whirlpool bath. Our breakfasts are a pleasure to savour, whether inside or in a secluded garden with a pond. Free parking.

Hwy 15, Exit 7, go left on Blvd. Cartier to the end, left on St-Hubert and right on Blvd. Lévesque.

B&B
GÎTE DU MARIGOT

Chantal Lachapelle
128, boulevard Lévesque Est
Laval H7G 1C2
(450) 668-0311
fax (450) 668-5624
www3.sympatico.ca/
gitedumarigot/index.htm
gitedumarigot@sympatico.ca

B&B	
single	$45-60
double	$60-70
triple	$75-85
child	$5-10

Taxes extra VS

Open year round

Number of rooms	4
rooms with private bath	2
rooms with sink	2
shared bathrooms	1

Activities:

4. LAVAL

B&B
L'ABRI DU TEMPS

Comfortable house located 3km from Montreal, near the Henri-Bourassa metro station. Shuttle service for those taking public transportation. Warm welcome, hearty breakfast to your liking and at your convenience. Children welcome. Living room, patio, BBQ, refrigerator, pantry, swimming pool, flowery terrace, large garden, swing.

From Montréal, Hwy 15 North, Exit 7, Boul. des Prairies East. From Mirabel, Hwy 15 South, Exit 7, eastbound Boul. des Prairies. After 13 blocks, left on Boul. Bon-Pasteur.

Marguerite and Raoul St-Jean
2, boul. Bon Pasteur
Laval-des-Rapides
H7N 3P9
tel/fax (450) 663-5094

B&B	
single	$47
double	$57-60
triple	$75
child	$15

Reduced rates: 15% after 7 consecutive nights
Open year round

Number of rooms	3
shared bathrooms	2
shared wc	1

Activities: 🏛 ☞ 🧍 🏃 🚴

5. LAVAL

B&B
NOTRE MAISON SUR LA RIVIÈRE

Facing Île-des-Moulins, Notre Maison sur la Rivière is sheltered by ash trees and watched over by herons. The babbling river, arts and culinary pleasures nearby will entice you to come visit our stone house, which has a fireplace and relaxing atmosphere. Our breakfasts are full of pleasant surprises. You will want to make this your first visit of many.

From Montréal, Boulevard Pie IX, Rte 25, Exit 20, turn right onto Boulevard des Milles-Îles, 1st stop sign, turn left on Rue Guglia, 1st street turn right Dessureaux.

Viviane Charbonneau and
Serge Gaudreau
6125, rue Dessureaux
St-François, Laval H7B 1B1
(450) 666-4095
fax (450) 666-6383
www3.sympatico.ca/
viviane.serge/
viviane.serge@sympatico.ca

B&B	
single	55-60 $
double	65-75 $

Taxes extra VS

Open year round

Number of rooms	2
rooms with sink	2
shared wc	1
shared bathrooms	1

Activities: 🏛 🍴 🚤 🧍 🐎

MAURICIE

© ULYSSES

La Tuque

Lac Wawagamac

Carignan

155

Rivière-aux-Rats

Grande-Anse

Lac Mékinac

155

Rivière-Matawin

Saint-Joseph-de-Mékinac

Notre-Dame-des-Anges

RÉGION DE QUÉBEC

Réserve faunique du Saint-Maurice

Saint-Roch-de-Mékinac

Sainte-Thècle

363

Saint-Ubalde

354

Parc national de la Mauricie

155 **159**

153

❸ Saint-Tite

Saint-Adelphe

Réserve faunique Mastigouche

Grandes-Piles
4 à 6

Hérouxville
❼ ❽

159

Saint-Stanislas

Sainte-Anne-de-la-Pérade

138

Lotbinière

❷ **❸ Grand-Mère**

Saint-Mathieu

Shawinigan • Shawinigan-Sud **⓰ ⓱**

Ste-Geneviève-de-Batiscan

❶

⓮ ⓯

132

Deschaillons

226

155

55

157

359

Batiscan

Saint-Pierre-les-Becquets

351

Saint-Maurice

Champlain

Sainte-Françoise

218

265

Saint-Paulin

Saint-Louis-de-France

40

Cap-de-la-Madeleine
❷

132

Manseau

20

153

Saint-Sévère

Trois-Rivières
18 à 21

Bécancour

Sainte-Marie-de-Blandford

263

350

Pointe-du-Lac
22 à 24

155

Saint-Louis-de-Blandford

Louiseville
9-10 **11** **25**
40

Nicolet

55

261

Princeville

138

Lac Saint-Pierre

132

CENTRE-DU-QUÉBEC

162

Baie-du-Febvre

Saint-Wenceslas

161

Sainte-Eulalie

116

LANAUDIÈRE

Berthierville
St-Ignace-de-Loyola

Pierreville

226

Sainte-Perpétue

155

20

Victoriaville

138

Saint-Elphège

259

161

Sorel
Tracy **132**

122

255

N

0   10   20km

1. BATISCAN

Located by the St-Lawrence River, on the Chemin du Roy, an inn with a decor of old awaits you. Steps away from a superb little-known beach, near Parc de la Batiscan. Less than 40min from Parc de la Mauricie, Village du Bûcheron, Cité de l'Énergie and Les Forges du St-Maurice. Winter activities: snow-shoeing, dogsledding, ice fishing, snowmobiling, cross-country skiing, sugar shack.

Between Montreal and Quebec City, Hwy 40, Batiscan Exit toward Rte 361 South, Rte 138 West. 4km from the highway.

B&B
LE ST-ÉLIAS

Guylaine and Marcel
951, Principale rte 138
Batiscan G0X 1A0
(418) 362-2712
fax (418) 362-2081
www.quebecweb.com/elias
guylaine.marcel
@tr.cgocable.ca

	B&B	MAP
single	$47-51	$62-66
double	$57-61	$87-91
child	$15	

VS IT

Reduced rates: 5% 2 nights, 10% 3 nights and more
Open year round

Number of rooms	4
shared bathrooms	2

Activities: 🏛 🦆 ⚓ 👤 🚲

---

2. CAP-DE-LA-MADELEINE

Magnificent Victorian wooden man-sion located right on the St-Law-rence River, with a private sandy beach and an exceptional view of the river and its boats. Enchanting, peaceful garden, 1.5km from a golf course and the Sanctuaire Notre-Dame-du-Cap. Kayaking on the river. Outdoor whirlpool. Warm ambiance.

From Montreal, Hwy 40, Exit 205. Follow the signs for the Sanctuaire. Once in front, turn right on Rue Notre-Dame, drive 1.5km.

B&B
GÎTE DU CHEMIN DU ROY

Lucie Fontaine and
Jérôme Francoeur
382, rue Notre-Dame
Cap-de-la-Madeleine G8T 4E2
(819) 374-7997
fax (819) 374-8951
rodak@cgocable.ca

B&B	
single	$53-61
double	$57-70
triple	$67-80
child	$5

Taxes extra VS MC IT

Open year round

Number of rooms	5
rooms with private bath	3
shared bathroom	1
shared wc	1

Activities: 🏛 🚤 ⚓ 👤 🚶

---

3. GRAND-MÈRE

Come as you are and share the plea-sure of reliving a page of history with us, in large and comfortable rooms. Our beautiful Victorian house, having painstakingly pre-served its charms, stands proudly and majestically 20min from Cité de l'Énergie and the national park, and less than 15min from three magnifi-cent golf courses. **See color photos.**

From Quebec City, Hwy 40 West, Exit 220 twd Grand-Mère, 0.5km from the bridge. From Montreal, Hwy 40 East, Hwy 55 North Exit, Exit 223, all the way down 5ᵉ Ave. Circle the park and turn on 3ᵉ Ave.

B&B
GÎTE LA BELLE AU
BOIS DORMANT

Valérie, Lucie or
Pierre Dumont
20, 3ᵉ Avenue
Grand-Mère G9T 2T3
(819) 538-6489
fax (819) 538-4145
www.knightsoft.ca/belle
minivalou@hotmail.com

B&B	
single	$60-80
double	$65-85
child	$10

Open year round

Number of rooms	3
shared bathrooms	1
shared wc	1
rooms with private bath	1

Activities: 👤 🚶 🐎 🎿 🏃

4. GRANDES-PILES

★★★ F e 🚭 ♿ ✕ 🚗 P 🏊 TA

"Le Bôme, some Mauricie balm to bask in". Snug inside an ancestral home, you will discover a friendly inn with cozy, comfortable rooms during your stay. The French-Italian-flavoured cuisine is a must. The singular landscape of mountains scored by the St-Maurice river will draw you to its national park. This 3-star inn boasts a spa, sauna and tennis court.

Halfway between Montréal and Québec City. Hwy 40 to Trois-Rivières, Hwy 55 North and Rte 155 twd La Tuque. Lac St-Jean, 10km past Grand-Mère, follow roadsigns to the inn.

INN
AUBERGE-LE-BÔME

Matilde Mossa and
Jean-Claude Coydon
720, 2ᵉ Avenue
Grandes-Piles G0X 1H0
toll free 1-800- 538-2805
(819) 538-2805
fax (819) 538-5879
www.auberge-le-bome.qc.ca
auberge-le-bome@infoteck.qc.ca

	B&B	MAP
single	$80-115	$115-150
double	$85-135	$155-185
triple	$105-140	$215-260
child	$15	$30

Taxes extra VS MC IT

Open year round

Number of rooms	10
rooms with private bath	10

Activities: 🚶 🏃 🛷 ⛷ 🐎

---

5. GRANDES-PILES

☀☀☀ F E ✕ 🚗 P 🏊 TA

Relive the region's history and enjoy a clear view of the St-Maurice River at our warm, ancestral B&B. Comfort, human warmth, patios, rooms with TV, delicious breakfasts, suggestions for activities, itineraries, guide service. 15min from the national park. Four-seasons packages: meals, cruise, snowmobiling, etc. Observation of black bears, moose, red-headed vulture. *Hablamos español*! **See ad on back inside cover.**

Halfway between Quebec City and Montreal, Hwy 40, Hwy 55 North and Rte 155 North twd La Tuque/Lac-St-Jean. In the village, left at Garage Crevier.

B&B
À LA CAPITAINERIE
DU PASSANT

Anie Desaulniers and
Mario Therrien
740, 3ᵉ Avenue
Grandes-Piles G0X 1H0
(819) 533-1234
toll free 1-877-213-1234
fax (819) 538-2966
http://site.voila.fr/gite
croisieres.des.piles@qc.aira.com

B&B	
single	$55-80
double	$55-80
triple	$75-95
quad.	$90-110
child	$10

VS

Reduced rates: Nov. 1 to Mar. 30, 3 nights or more
Open year round

Number of rooms	3
shared bathrooms	2
rooms with private bath	2

Activities: 🛶 🚶 🛷 ⛷ 🐎

---

6. GRANDES-PILES

☀☀☀ F E 🎿 P 🏊 R1 TA

The cradle of rafting, Grandes-Piles is one of the most beautiful villages in Quebec, nestled between the river and the mountain. In our century-old house, an unobstructed view of the St. Maurice welcomes you in our comfortable rooms with shower and sink, and a large veranda with fireplace. After an excellent breakfast, enjoy a cruise or visit the national park, the Musée du Bûcheron or Cité d'Énergie...

Hwy 55 North, Rte. 155 North twd La Tuque. 10km past Grand-Mère. At the Garage Crevier, turn left, 2nd street on the right.

B&B
AU REPOS DU DRAVEUR

Martine and Nick Muller
762, 3ᵉ Avenue
Grandes-Piles G0X 1H0
(819) 533-5385

B&B	
single	$55-65
double	$65-75
triple	$75-85
quad.	$85-95
child	$10

Open year round

Number of rooms	3
shared wc	1
rooms with sink and shower	2
room with private bath	1

Activities: 🚤 🚶 🏃 🐎 🛶

7. HÉROUXVILLE

A B&B designed for young and old alike. Share in the simplicity and *joie de vivre* of our family enterprise in a farming environment. Let yourself be charmed by the special language of animals in a country setting, and rediscover human warmth and well-deserved rest and relaxation. Air-conditioned house and outdoor pool. Several tourist attractions nearby. **Farm Stay p 51.**

From Montreal or Quebec City, Hwy 40. In Trois-Rivières, Hwy 55 North. At the end of Hwy 55, Exit Rte 153 North. In Hérouxville, cross the railway and drive 2km.

B&B
ACCUEIL LES SEMAILLES

Christine Naud and Nicolas Dion
1460, rang Saint-Pierre
Hérouxville GOX 1J0
(418) 365-5190
christine_nicolas@hotmail.com

	B&B	MAP
single	$40	$50
double	$50	$70
child	$12	$17

Open year round

Number of rooms	5
shared bathrooms	2

Activities:

8. HÉROUXVILLE

Next to Parc de la Mauricie, a Que-bec house amidst flowers, lush gardens and stretches of water. A home away from home, with wood-work and cozy, attractively decorated rooms. Warm family atmosphere, very Québécois breakfasts. Reasonably priced "winter packages" (tax included) such as snow-mobiling, ice fishing, dogsledding, snowshoeing and hockey. Indoor/outdoor fireplace. Welcoming you is a pleasure.

Hwy 20 or 40, Hwy 55 N. via Trois-Rivières. At the end of Hwy 55, Exit Rte 153 North. In Hérouxville, at the light, street next to the church.

B&B
MAISON TRUDEL

Nicole Jubinville
and Yves Trudel
543, rue Goulet
Hérouxville GOX 1J0
(418) 365-7624
fax (418) 365-7041
www.maison-trudel.qc.ca
maison-trudel-quebec
@concepta.com

B&B	
single	$40
double	$55
triple	$85
child	$15

VS

Open year round

Number of rooms	4
shared bathrooms	3

Activities:

9. LOUISEVILLE

The Carrefour is not only a presti-gious B&B but also one of the most cultural in Québec. Our Queen-Anne house is the only official historic one in the village. Sumptuously furnished and decorated, it offers the utmost in comfort. Each of its four rooms is more opulent than the next. Discover its garden, as well.

From Montréal or Québec, Hwy 40, Exit 166 or 174 to Rte 138 twd downtown Louiseville. Corner Rte 349 and 138.

B&B
GÎTE DU CARREFOUR

Réal-Maurice Beauregard
11, av. St-Laurent Ouest
Louiseville J5V 1J3
tel/fax (819) 228-4932
www.bonjourquebec.
com/info/giteducarrefour

B&B	
single	$50
double	$65

Open year round

Number of rooms	4
shared wc	1
room with private bath	1
shared bathrooms	2

Activities:

10. LOUISEVILLE

☀☀☀ | F | e | 🚗 | P | R1

Built in 1858, the Victorian-era La Maison de l'Ancêtre has retained its architectural charms of yesteryear. Conveniently located 1km from the town centre, it offers guests a tasteful decor with quality furnishings in a peaceful oasis. Lavish breakfast complemented by homemade goods. Your hosts' warm, heart-felt welcome awaits.

From Montréal, Hwy 40, Exit 166. Rte 138 East, 3.5km. Rte 349, Rue Notre-Dame North, 1km. From Québec City, Hwy 40, Exit 174. Rte 138 West, 4.9km, Rte 349, Rue Notre-Dame North, 1km.

B&B
LA MAISON DE L'ANCÊTRE

Julienne Leblanc
491, rue Notre-Dame Nord
Louiseville J5V 1X9
(819) 228-8195

B&B	
single	$45-55
double	$50-60
triple	$65-75

Open year round

Number of rooms	3
shared bathrooms	2

Activities: 🚶 🎿 🚴 ⛷ 🐕

11. LOUISEVILLE

☀☀☀ | F | e | 🚗 | ✕ | P | R1 | TA

Comfortable, peaceful Victorian farmhouse (1880). A romantic trip back in time. Quality and harmony, it has been called "a corner of paradise..." (La Presse) 10km from Ste-Ursule waterfalls, Lac St-Pierre. 6 years old, 6 prizes for excellence. **Farm Stay p 51, Country-style Dining p 24, Country Home p 56 and 205, Farm Excursion p 40.**

From Montréal or Québec City, Hwy 40, Exit 166. Rte 138 East, drive 2.4km to Rte 348 West. Left twd St-Ursule, drive 1.5km, 1st road on the right.

B&B
LE GÎTE DE LA SEIGNEURIE

Michel Gilbert
480, chemin du Golf
Louiseville J5V 2L4
(819) 228-8224
fax (819) 228-5576
www.bbcanada.
com/3448.html
m.gilbert@infoteck.qc.ca

	B&B	MAP
single	$45-70	$65-90
double	$60-90	$100-130
triple	$85	$145
quad.	$100	$180
child	$20	$30

Taxes extra

Open year round

Number of rooms	5
rooms with sink	2
rooms with private bath	1
shared bathrooms	2

Activities: 🏛 🚣 🎿 🚶 🚴

12. ST-MATHIEU-DU-PARC

F | E | P | 🐾 | R5 | TA

Welcome to our haven of peace and harmony. 7km from Parc de la Mauricie. You're invited to l'Herbarium, a picturesque residence, enchanting and grandiose decor, amidst lakes, mountains, flower gardens. Friendly welcome, relaxing atmosphere, delicious breakfast. Picnics and hiking on site.

From Montréal, Hwy 40 East, Hwy 55 North, Exit 217. Rte 351 North, 12km. Right on Ch. St-François, 4km. Left on Ch. Principal, 1km. Right on Ch. St-Paul, 0.5km.

B&B
L'HERBARIUM

Anne-Marie Groleau
1950, chemin St-Paul
St-Mathieu-du-Parc G0X 1N0
(819) 532-2461

B&B	
single	$40-50
double	$55-65
triple	$75
child	$10

Open year round

Number of rooms	3
shared wc	1
shared bathrooms	1

Activities: 🚶 🚣 🎿 🚴 ⛷

13. ST-TITE

⚜⚜⚜ F e 🚭 🐕 🚗 P 🏊 R.03 TA

Prize for Excellence "Special Favorite" Regional 1999. In St-Tite, a town with western cachet, discover our wooden Victorian house (1907) renowned for its warm welcome, cozy decor and lavish breakfasts. Nearby: Parc de la Mauricie, Village du Bûcheron, Cité de l'Énergie, maple grove, seaplane, dogsled. Swimming pool on site. Lucie and Réal welcome you. **See colour photos.**

From Quebec City or Montreal, Hwy 40. In Trois-Rivières, Hwy 55 North, Exit Rte 153 North. In St-Tite, 500m left of the "caisse populaire."

B&B
MAISON EMERY JACOB

Lucie Verret and Réal Trépanier
211, rue Notre-Dame
St-Tite G0X 3H0
(418) 365-5532
toll free 1-877-600-5532
fax (418) 365-3957
www.maisonemeryjacob.qc.ca
emeryjac@globetrotter.net

B&B	
single	$40
double	$55
triple	$75
child	$10

VS AM

Open year round

Number of rooms	4
shared wc	1
shared bathrooms	2

Activities: 🚤 👤 🚲 🎿 🐎

---

14. STE-ANNE-DE-LA-PÉRADE

⚜⚜⚜ F e 🐕 🍽 🚗 P TA

An ancestral house where time has stopped. Stay in a historic monument with documents and furniture dating from 1702. Part of the heritage tour. Magnificent formal garden. An invitation to relive history in our museum-house -- all these are sure to enhance your stay. Good fishing opportunities. Dinner served on the premises.

On the Chemin du Roy, Rte 138, 2hrs from Montreal, 1hr from Quebec City, via Hwy 40, Exit 236, 2km east of the church.

INN
À L'ARRÊT DU TEMPS

Serge Gervais and René Poitras
965, boul. de Lanaudière
Chemin du Roy
Ste-Anne-de-la-Pérade
G0X 2J0
tel/fax (418) 325-3590

	B&B	MAP
single	$40-50	$55-65
double	$50 60	$80-90
triple	$65-75	$110-120
child	$15	on request

Taxes extra VS MC AM ER IT

Open year round

Number of rooms	3
shared wc	1
rooms with sink	2
shared bathrooms	2

Activities: 🏛 👤 🚶 🚲 🚤

---

15. STE-ANNE-DE-LA-PÉRADE

⚜⚜⚜⚜ F E 🍽 P TA

On the Chemin du Roy, between "smelt" river and the forgotten *"marigotte"*, the timeless old Manoir Dauth offers a world of delightful packages: fishing, snowmobiling, dogsledding, sightseeing, croquet, cycling, mouthwatering cuisine and sweet dreams in a canopy bed.

Between Montréal (2 hours) and Québec City (1 hour) on Chemin du Roy (Rte 138), 100 m from the church. Via Hwy 40, Exit 236, right at 1st stop, left at 2nd stop, then 200 m.

INN
AUBERGE DU
MANOIR DAUTH

Lise Garceau and
Yvan Turgeon
21, boul. de Lanaudière
C.P. 111
Ste-Anne-de-la-Pérade
G0X 2J0
tel/fax (418) 325-3432
www.bbcanada.com/3193.html
manoir.dauth@tr.cgocable.ca

	B&B	PAM
single	$40-60	$53-73
double	$52-72	$78-98
triple	$64-84	$103-123
quad.	$76-96	$128-148
child	$10	$20

Taxes extra VS MC ER IT AM

Reduced rates: 3 nights and more
Open year round

Number of rooms	5
rooms with private bath	1
shared wc	2
shared bathrooms	2

Activities: 🏛 🚲 🚤 🎿 🐎

16. SHAWINIGAN-SUD

✹✹✹ [F] [E] [🐕] [🛶] [P] [🏊] [R1] [TA]

Pamper yourself at two artists' cozy refuge. Retire to your apartments, born of a dream. Discover Cité de l'Énergie, breathe in fresh air in the national park. Private living room with fireplace, bathrooms with shower or whirlpool bath, garden with swimming pool, breakfast on the terrace. All that's missing... is you.

From Trois-Rivières, Hwy 55 North, Exit 211 twd Shawinigan-Sud. After Cité de l'Énergie, first exit on the right, Blvd. du Capitaine Veilleux, 2km, left on Rue Lacoursière (119ᵉ Rue), right at 2ⁿᵈ stop onto Rue Adrienne-Choquette, right on Rue Albert-Dufresne.

B&B
LES P'TITS POMMIERS

Michelle Fortin and Jean-Louis Gagnon
2295, rue Albert-Dufresne
Shawinigan- Sud G9P 4Y6
(819) 537-0158
toll free 1-877-537-0158
fax (819) 537-4839
www.bbcanada.
com/3460.html
pommiers@yahoo.com

B&B	
single	$45
double	$55
child	$10

VS

Open year round

Number of rooms	3
rooms in semi-basement	3
shared bathrooms	2

Activities: 🛶 ⛷ 🚶 🚴 🛷

---

17. SHAWINIGAN-SUD

✹✹✹ [F] [e] [🚗] [P] [R4] [TA]

At the gate of the Cité de l'Énergie, the country in the city. Four rooms overlooking the St-Maurice: calm nights, tantalizing breakfast. Writer Adrienne Choquette once lived here; her words echo through Time. Pleasant old-fashioned decor; always pleasant and warm.

From Montréal or Québec City, Hwy 55 N. At Trois-Rivières, Hwy 55 N. Exit 211 twd Cité de l'Énergie, Rte 157. After bridges, right at the overpass Boul. du Capitaine. At the end, before the hill, go left on Ch. St-Laurent.

B&B
LE TEMPS DES VILLAGES

Reynald Roberge
155, chemin Saint-Laurent
Shawinigan-Sud G9P 1B6
tel/fax (819) 536-3487
reynald.roberge
@sh.cgocable.ca

B&B	
single	$50-60
double	$60-70
child	$10

Open year round

Number of rooms	4
shared wc	1
shared bathrooms	1

Activities: 🏛 ⛷ 🚶 🎿 ⛸

---

18. TROIS-RIVIÈRES

[F] [E] [🚭] [🍽] [P] [TA]

Our beautiful Victorian inn is nestled in the centre of town, on the way into historic Trois-Rivières, on a secluded, shady street. Rich oak woodwork, bevelled doors, gilding and lovely moulding, handed down from the old aristocracy. The elegant dining room, with its lustrous chandelier, lacework and old lamps is open to the public. Parking and air conditioning.

Hwy 40 Exit Trois-Rivières downtown. To Notre-Dame. Left on Rue Radisson.

INN
AUBERGE DU BOURG

Monic and Jean-Marc Beaudoin
172, rue Radisson
Trois-Rivières G9A 2C3
(819) 373-2265
(819) 379-9198

	B&B	MAP
single	$50-70	$65-85
double	$60-80	$90-110

Taxes extra VS MC AM IT

Open year round

Number of rooms	4
rooms with sink	2
rooms with private bath	2
shared wc	2
shared bathrooms	1

Activities: 🛶 ⛷ 🚶 🚴 🛷

19. TROIS-RIVIÈRES

☀☀☀ F e 🚫 🚗 P R.3 TA

Family property! Grandpa Beau would be proud, his house welcomes so many people! Spacious, attractively decorated home whose attic rooms bring back wonderful childhood memories. You'll enjoy a generous breakfast complemented with garden-fresh vegetables. Near all tourist attractions and the university.

From Québec City, Hwy 40 West, Exit 199 to the town centre, right on Rue Ste-Marguerite for 2km. From Montréal, Hwy 40, Exit 199. At 2nd light, left on Rue Ste-Marguerite for 2km.

B&B
CHEZ GRAND'PAPA BEAU

Carmen and Yvon Beaudry
3305, rue Ste-Marguerite
Trois-Rivières G8Z 1X1
(819) 693-0385
www3.sympatico.ca/voir/gite
grandpapa_beau@altavista.net

B&B	
single	$40
double	$50
triple	$65
quad.	$80
child	$10

VS

Open year round

Number of rooms	4
shared bathrooms	2

Activities: 🏛 ⛴ 🎿 🚶 🚴

20. TROIS-RIVIÈRES

☀☀☀☀ F E 🚤 P 🏊 R.1 TA

A must on the shores of the St-Laurent. Comfort, safety in an upscale decor. Gardens, pool and air conditioning. Renowned for its welcome and gastronomic breakfast. Good place for family get-togethers or with friends. One French guide commented: "In short, an excellent place for the price".

From Hwy 55, Exit 181, Rue Notre-Dame, left Rte 138 East, about 1km. At McDonald's, turn right on Rue Garceau. Right on Rue Notre-Dame.

B&B
GÎTE SAINT-LAURENT

Yolande and René Bronsard
4551, Notre-Dame
Trois-Rivières Ouest G9A 4Z4
tel/fax (819) 378-3533
www.iquebec.com
/bbsaint-laurent
rene.bronsard@sympatico.ca

B&B	
single	$50
double	$65

Taxes extra VS

Open year round

Number of rooms	4
rooms with sink	4
shared wc	2
shared bathrooms	1

Activities: 🏛 🍷 ⛴ 🎿 🚴

21. TROIS-RIVIÈRES

☀☀ F e 🚫 🚤 P R.7

Delightful English-style house, located in Vieux-Trois-Rivières, steps away from the town centre and the harbour park. Near Parc National de la Mauricie. Come share our charming house and lavish breakfasts with us. A warm welcome awaits you.

Hwy 40, Exit 201, twd Blvd. des Chenaux, turn right, drive 1.6km, turn right on Rte 138 West or Rue St-Maurice, drive 0.8km. At the 4th light, at the church, turn left on Rue St-François-Xavier, drive 0.7km.

B&B
MAISON WICKENDEN

Diane Houle and Yoland Ferland
467, rue St-François-Xavier
Trois-Rivières G9A 1R1
tel/fax (819) 375-6219

B&B	
single	$45-50
double	$55-60
triple	$70-75
child	$10

VS

Reduced rates: Nov. 1 to May 1
Open year round

Number of rooms	3
rooms with sink	2
room with private bath	1
shared wc	1
shared bathrooms	2

Activities: 🏛 ⛴ 🚤 🎿 🚴

22. TROIS-RIVIÈRE, POINTE-DU-LAC ★ ★ F e P TA

Enjoy the peace and joy of living by the St. Lawrence River. Outdoor activities: golf, cruises, canoeing, cycling, hiking with or without a guide, cross-country skiing, snowshoeing, snowmobiling, ice fishing. Pick-up at the airport and on-site car rental. Gourmet French cuisine. Equipped meeting or reception room. Families welcome.

From Montreal, Hwy 40 East, Exit 187, Rte 138 East, 7km. From Quebec City, Hwy 40 West and 55 South, Notre-Dame Exit, Rte 138 West, 5km.

INN
AUBERGE BAIE-JOLIE

Françoise and Jean-Marie Roux
709, rue Notre-Dame, rte 138
Pointe-du-Lac G0X 1Z0
(819) 377-2226
fax (819) 377-4221
www.baie-jolie.com
auberge@baie-jolie.com

	B&B	MAP
single	$45	$65
double	$65	$100
triple	$80	$130
quad.	$95	$160
child	$10	$20

Taxes extra VS MC IT

Reduced rates: 3 nights and more
Open year round

Number of rooms	12
rooms with private bath	12

Activities:

---

23. TROIS-RIVIÈRES, POINTE-DU-LAC ☼☼☼ F E P R.2 TA

10km from old Trois-Rivières and its harbour park, enchanting site right on the shores of the St. Larence River and Lac St-Pierre. Large shaded park, picnic tables, Numerous winter and summer activities. Excursions organized. Generous and varied breakfast. Fully equipped studio for independent stays. Discounts for long stays and groups.

From Montréal, 130km, Hwy 40 E., Exit 187. Rte 138 E., 7km. From Mirabel, Hwy 15 S., 640 E., 40 E. From Québec City, 130km Hwy 40 W. and 55 S., Exit Notre-Dame, Rte 138 W., 5km.

B&B
GÎTE BAIE-JOLIE

Barbara and Jacques Piccinelli
711, Notre Dame, route 138
Pointe-du-Lac G0X 1Z0
tel/fax (819) 377-3056
toll free 1-877-271-4341
jacques.piccinelli@
baie-jolie.com

B&B	
single	$40-50
double	$55-65
triple	$85-105
quad.	$100-120
child	$10

VS

Reduced rates: Oct.15 to May 31
Open: Dec. 1 to Oct. 31

Number of rooms	3
rooms with private bath	3

Activities:

---

24. TROIS-RIVIÈRES, POINTE-DU-LAC ☼☼☼ F e P R2

Prize for Excellence "Special Favorite" Regional 2000 and 1997-98. This B&B in the country side is just 10min from Trois-Rivières. Enjoy calm, rest, a warm welcome and unforgettable gourmet breakfasts in our secluded Canadian house. Enchanting decor, flowery gardens, living room, air conditioning, fireplace, therapeutic bath, indoor pool, year-round.Inexpensive dream stay.

From Montreal, Hwy 40 East, Exit 187. Rte 138 East, 7km, left on Rue des Saules (at the end). From Quebec City, Hwy 40 West, Hwy 55 South, Notre-Dame Exit, Rte 138 West, 5km. Right on Rue des Saules.

B&B
SOLEIL LEVANT

Léonie Lavoie and
Yves Pilon
300, av. des Saules
Pointe-du-Lac G0X 1Z0
tel/fax (819) 377-1571
toll free 1-877-8-SOLEIL
www.bonjourquebec.
com/info/gitesoleillevant
gitesoleillevant@qc.aira.com

B&B	
single	$45
double	$60-70
triple	$85
child	$15

Reduced rates: 2 nights and more
Open year round

Number of rooms	3
shared bathrooms	2

Activities:

25. LOUISEVILLE

F | e | 🚗 R1 | M1.5 | TA

Heritage home located on a farm surrounded by thousands of flowers. Take advantage of the gardens and tend your own! Ideal place to get into gardening or learn more. Gardening library. All-season guided excursions: hiking, canoeing, fishing, biking, snowshoeing, dogsledding... Ste-Ursule waterfalls, Lac St-Pierre. **Farm Stay p 51, B&B p 200, Country-style Dining p 24, Farm Excursion p 40, Country Home on a farm 56.**

From Montréal or from Québec City, Hwy 40, Exit 166. Rte 138 E., 2.4km to Rte 348 W. Left twd Ste-Ursule 1.5km. 1st road on the right.

COUNTRY HOME
LA MAISON DU JARDINIER

Michel Gilbert
480, chemin du Golf
Louiseville J5V 2L4
(819) 228-8224
fax (819) 228-5576
www.bbcanada.
com/3448.html
m.gilbert@infoteck.qc.ca

No. houses	1
No. rooms	3
No. people	4
WEEK-SUMMER	$400
WEEK-WINTER	$400
DAY-WINTER	$100

Taxes extra

Open year round

Activities: 🏛 🛶 🎿 🚲 🏃

FARM ACTIVITIES

Farm Stay:

7 ACCUEIL LES SEMAILLES, Hérouxville 51

11 FERME DE LA SEIGNEURIE, Louiseville 51

Country-style Dining:

11 LA TABLE DE LA SEIGNEURIE, Louiseville 24

Farm Tour:

11 LES JARDINS DE LA SEIGNEURIE, Louiseville 40

Country Home on a Farm :

25 LA MAISON DU JARDINIER 56

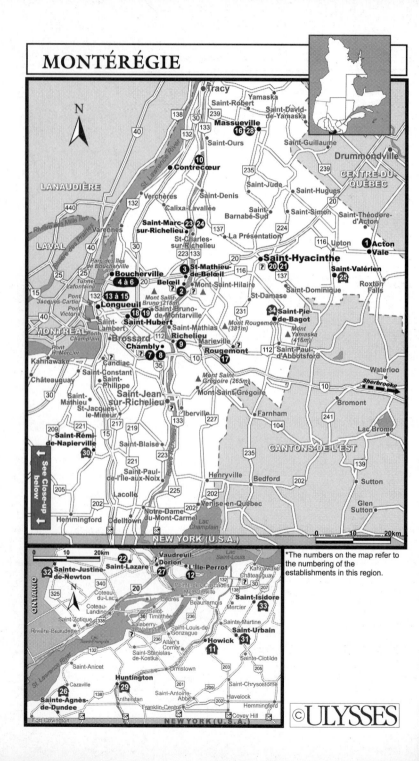

MONTÉRÉGIE

Tracy
Saint-Robert
Yamaska
Saint-David-de-Yamaska
Massueville **16 28**
Saint-Ours
Saint-Guillaume
Drummondville
10 Contrecœur
Saint-Jude
Saint-Hugues
CENTRE-DU-QUÉBEC
Verchères
Calixa-Lavallée
Saint-Denis
Saint-Barnabé-Sud
Saint-Simon
Saint-Théodore-d'Acton
LANAUDIÈRE
Saint-Marc-sur-Richelieu **23 24**
St-Charles-sur-Richelieu
La Présentation
Upton
1 Acton Vale
LAVAL
Parc des îles de Boucherville
Boucherville **4 à 6**
3 St-Mathieu-de-Beloeil
Beloeil
Mont-Saint-Hilaire
Saint-Hyacinthe **20 21**
Saint-Valérien **25**
Roxton Falls
Tunnel Lafontaine
Longueuil **13 à 15**
Mont Saint-Bruno (218m)
2
St-Damase
Saint-Dominique
MONTREAL
Saint-Lambert
18 19 Saint-Bruno-de-Montarville
Saint-Hubert
Saint-Mathias
Mont Rougemont (381m)
34 Saint-Pie-de-Bagot
Mont Yamaska (416m)
Brossard
Chambly **7 8**
Richelieu **9**
Marieville
Saint-Paul-d'Abbotsford
Kahnawake
Candiac
35
Rougemont **17**
Châteauguay
Saint-Constant
Saint-Philippe
Saint-Jean-sur-Richelieu
Mont Saint-Grégoire (265m)
Waterloo
Sherbrooke
Saint-Mathieu
St-Jacques-le-Mineur
Iberville
Mont-Saint-Grégoire
Farnham
Bromont
Lac Brome
Saint-Rémi-de-Napierville **30**
Saint-Blaise
CANTONS-DE-L'EST
Saint-Paul-de-l'Île-aux-Noix
Lacolle
Henryville
Bedford
Sutton
Hemmingford
Odelltown
Notre-Dame-du-Mont-Carmel
Venise-en-Québec
Lac Champlain
Glen Sutton
NEW YORK (U.S.A.)
0   10   20km

Vaudreuil-Dorion
Lac Saint-Louis
22 Saint-Lazare
Sainte-Justine-de-Newton **32**
27
L'Île-Perrot **12**
Kahnawake
Châteauguay
ONTARIO
Coteau-du-Lac
Pointe-des-Cascades Melocheville
Les Cèdres
Beauharnois
Saint-Isidore **33**
Coteau-Landing
Saint-Timothée
Mercier
Sainte-Martine
Saint-Zotique
Rivière-Beaudette
Salaberry-de-Valleyfield
Saint-Louis-de-Gonzague
Saint-Urbain **31**
Allan's Corner
Howick **11**
Saint-Stanislas-de-Kostka
Sainte-Clotilde
Huntington **29**
Ormstown
Saint-Anicet
Cazaville
Sainte-Agnès-de-Dundee **26**
Athelstan
Saint-Antoine-Abbé
Havelock
Hemmingford
Fort Covington
Franklin-Centre
Covey Hill
NEW YORK (U.S.A.)

*The numbers on the map refer to the numbering of the establishments in this region.

©ULYSSES

1. ACTON VALE

Between Montréal and Québec City, in cycling country, 2km from "La Campagnarde" path, 8km from La Dame de Cœur theatre, across from a golf course, what more could you ask for! Breakfast on the veranda. Take advantage of golf and cycling packages. It's about the simple pleasure in welcoming people from far and wide.

Hwy 20, Exit 147, right on Rte 116 for 17km. Or, Hwy 55, Rtes 139 and 116. Across from the golf course.

B&B
AUBERGE AUX P'TITS OIGNONS

Denise Morin and
Jacques McCaughan
1011, Route 116 Ouest
Acton Vale J0H 1A0
(450) 549-5116
fax (450) 549-6116
www.bbcanada.com/
1086.html
auberge@ntic.qc.ca

B&B	
single	$40-50
double	$55-65
triple	$70-80
quad.	$85
child	$10

VS MC

Open year round

Number of rooms	4
rooms with private bath	1
rooms in basement	3
shared wc	1
shared bathrooms	2

Activities:

---

2. BELOEIL

The Richelieu valley will win you over... 20 minutes from Montréal, stop and enjoy the peace and cozy charm of our ancestral home (1846) on the banks of the Rivière Richelieu, in the heart of Vieux Beloeil. Admire the beauty of Mont St-Hilaire. Copious breakfast; lace, china and silver.

Hwy 20, Exit 112, Rte 223 South, for 2.3km. Next to presbytery and church. From Rte 116, Rte 223 North, 0.8km.

B&B
BEAUX BRUNELLES

Fernande Vézina and
Raymond Chrétien
1030, rue Richelieu
Beloeil J3G 4R2
(450) 467-4700
fax (450) 467-4668
www.bbcanada.
com/beauxbrunelles
beauxbrunelles@convitech.ca

B&B	
single	$45-50
double	$60-65
triple	$75-80
quad.	$80-90
child	$0-10

Open year round

Number of rooms	5
shared bathrooms	2

Activities:

---

3. BELOEIL, ST-MATHIEU

20 min from Montreal. Snowshoe hiking on Mt-St-Hilaire, ski Mont St-Bruno; a stone's throw from summer theatres. In the country, 6km from Vieux Beloeil. With spacious rooms, our air conditoned ancestral house (1905) beneath the trees awaits you. Different breakfasts served in the warmth of our kitchen graced with a wood-burning stove.

From Montréal or Québec City, Hwy 20, Exit 109. On Rue St-Jean-Baptiste go north twd St-Mathieu-de-Beloeil, drive for 1km. Right on first street Ruisseau Sud for 3.8km.

B&B
LA MAISON DU GAZEBO

Monique and
Georges Blanchard
2054, ch. du Ruisseau Sud
St-Mathieu-de-Beloeil J3G 2C9
(450) 464-2430
fax (450) 464-4541
www.bbcanada.com/
maisondugazebo
gazebo@zoo.net

B&B	
single	$40-65
double	$55-65
triple	$70-80
child	$10

Reduced rates: 7th night free
Open year round

Number of rooms	3
shared wc	2
shared bathrooms	1

Activities:

4. BOUCHERVILLE

☀☀☀ F E 🚭 🐕 🚗 P ⛵ R1 TA

Located 15min from Montreal, this cozy home, warm and passionate like it's owner, awaits you. Doris is bilingual, has a good ear, and gives good directions. This air conditioned B&B offers queen size beds, inground pool, inspiring garden and terrace and just like home ambiance. Bike avalaible.

From Montreal, pont-tunnel L-H-Lafontaine, Hwy 20 Exit 92, turn left on blvd. Mortagne (or right from Quebec City). Drive 4km, turn left on Etienne Brûlé, right on Duluth.

B&B
CHEZ FLEUR DO

Doris Hupé
919, rue Duluth
Boucherville J4B 6Y5
(450) 449-5659
fleurdo.freeservers.com

B&B	
single	$50
double	$65
triple	$80
child	$10

Open year round

Number of rooms	3
shared wc	1
shared bathrooms	2

Activities: 🎿 🛶 🚶 🚲 🚣

5. BOUCHERVILLE

✎ F e 🚭 🐕 🚗 P ⛵ R.5 TA

Located 15min from Montreal, near services. Quiet area facing a bike path. Large, air-conditioned rooms with private bathrooms and TV. In the summer, you can enjoy a lavish breakfast by the pool on our superb covered terrace. Large parking lot. Warm welcome from your hosts Johanne and Michel year-round. Welcome. See you soon.

From Montreal, take the L.-H. Lafontaine tunnel. Hwy 20, Exit 92, turn left on Boul. Mortagne, drive 3km. From Quebec City, Hwy 20, Exit 92, Boul. Mortagne East for 3km.

B&B
LA BOUCHERVILLOISE

Johanne and Michel Leverne
605, boul. de Mortagne
Boucherville J4B 5E4
tel/fax (450) 449-6237
(514) 817-1579
pages.infinit.net/boucherv
bouchervilloise@videotron.ca

B&B	
single	$50
double	$65
triple	$80
child	$10
VS

Open year round

Number of rooms	3
shared wc	1
room in basement	1
rooms with private bath	3

Activities: 🚣 🎿 🚲 🏊 🏃

6. BOUCHERVILLE

☀☀☀ F e 🚭 P R.5 TA

Prize for Excellence "Special Favorite" Regional 2000 and finalist for Provincial. Just 15 min from the sights of Montréal. Friendly atmosphere, we like to chat with people. Bicycles and tandems available for free; bike paths; bus to the Métro. Generous breakfasts, air conditioning and a small souvenir for everyone.

From Montréal by Louis-H. Lafontaine tunnel or from Québec City, Hwy 20, Exit 90 twd Varennes. Rte 132 East Exit 18, Montarville. Turn left to Boul. Fort St-Louis, turn left and drive 1.2km.

B&B
LE RELAIS DES ÎLES PERCÉES

Colette and Raymond LeBlanc
85, rue des Îles Percées
Boucherville J4B 2P1
tel/fax (450) 655-3342
www.bbcanada.com/318.html
lerelais@total.net

B&B	
single	$40
double	$55
triple	$70
child	$10
VS

Open year round

Number of rooms	3
rooms in basement	2
shared bathrooms	2

Activities: 🏛 🛶 🎿 🚲 🏊

7. CHAMBLY

☀☀☀☀ | F | e | P | 🚗 | R.2 | TA

Recipient of the Lauréat Grand Prix du Tourisme Montérégie 2000 and the provincial "Réussite" award of excellence 1999. Located 20min from Montreal, 1914 Victorian house with magnificent woodwork, period mouldings, fireplace and French doors. Breakfast on the veranda with a view of the mountains that merge with the water. Boat dock. Near all the city's services and activities. Group dinners only. Air conditioned. **See colour photos.**

From Montreal, Hwy. 10, Exit 22, Blvd. Fréchette to the end. Follow the signs. Next to St-Joseph's church.

B&B
AUBERGE L'AIR DU TEMPS

Lucie Chrétien and
Daniel Desgagné
124, Martel, Chambly J3L 1V3
(450) 658-1642
toll free 1-888-658-1642
fax (450) 658-2830
www.airdutemps.qc.ca
hote@airdutemps.qc.ca

B&B	
single	$65
double	$69-79
triple	$104
quad.	$129

Taxes extra VS AM

Open: year round except Nov.

Number of rooms	5
rooms with private bath	5

Activities: 🛶 🚤 🚶 🚴 🏇

8. CHAMBLY

☀☀☀☀☀ | F | E | 🏊 | P | 🚗 | R.2 | TA

This old Fort Chambly officer's residence, transformed into a luxurious manor, offers a panoramic view, a superb ambiance and exceptional comfort. Make it a base to visit Montréal (20 min) and the Valley of Forts, and let yourself be serenaded by the songs of the rapids or the flames of the 3 fireplaces. Spacious rooms with TV and modem access. Gastronomic breakfast. Free access to our outdoor tennis club. Rated 3 diamonds by the AAA (CAA). **See colour photos.**

Hwy 10 (Exit 22), Rte 112 or Rte 223, follow the signs for Fort Chambly. The Maison Ducharme is next to the guardhouse.

B&B
LA MAISON DUCHARME

Danielle Deland and
Edouard Bonaldo
10, rue de Richelieu
Chambly J3L 2B9
(450) 447-1220
toll free 1-888-387-1220
fax (450) 447-1018
www.maisonducharme.ca
maison.ducharme@mlink.net

B&B	
single	$90-105
double	$110-125
triple	$135-150
child	$25

Taxes extra VS MC

Reduced rates: Oct. 15 to May 18
Open year round

Number of rooms	4
rooms with private bath	4

Activities: 🛶 🚶 🚴 ⛷ 🏃

9. CHAMBLY, RICHELIEU

☀☀☀☀ | F | E | 🚭 | ✕ | P | 🛶 | R.3

Located on the banks of the Richelieu river, in a Victorian house, the La Jarnigoine inn offers guests the peacefulness of the countryside, just a few kilometres from Montreal. In the evening, take advantage of our refined *table d'hôte* featuring local products and traditional French cuisine. By reservation only. **See color photos.**

Hwy 10, Exit 29, Rte. 133 twd Richelieu, turn left on Rte. 112 and left at the 1st street. Or Hwy 20, Exit 113, Rte. 133, turn right on Rte. 112 and left at the 1st street.

INN
AUBERGE LA JARNIGOINE

Sébastien Bélair and
Roger René Villeneuve
1156, 1ʳᵉ Rue
Richelieu J3L 3W8
(450) 658-8031
(514) 573-0689
www.bbcanada.
com/lajarnigoine
jarnigoi@dsuper.net

B&B	
single	$50-70
double	$70-110

Taxes extra VS IT

Open year round

Number of rooms	3
room with private bath	1
shared bathroom	1

Activities: 🏛 🚤 🚶 🛶 🚴

10. CONTRECOEUR

☀☀☀☀ F e 🚫 🚗 P 🏊 R.1

Are you looking for an escape from the hectic pace of life today? Do you want to have a great time and be pampered? Then succumb to the allure of our charming B&B, which offers a friendly and cosy ambiance, and a kitchen full of exciting flavours. Imagine listening to music by candlelight, lounging in a hammock, relaxing in a pool, reading in a garden, going on a pedal-boat trip to some islands, or cycling on a country road. Let all your worries trickle off you like water off a duck's back.

From Montréal, Hwy 20 and 30 East, Exit 158, Rte 132 East, 1.6km.

B&B
LES MALARDS

Hélène Delisle
4741, rue Marie-Victorin
Contrecoeur J0L 1C0
(450) 587-5581
(514) 953-2307
www.bbcanada.com
/lesmalardsbb
les.malards@enter-net.com

B&B	
single	$50-70
double	$65-85
triple	$105
quad.	$125

Taxes extra VS MC

Reduced rates: 20% 3 nights and more, Feb. to May, Oct. and Nov.
Open year round

Number of rooms	4
rooms with sink	2
room with private bath	1
shared bathrooms	2

Activities: 🦆 🛶 🚶 🚴 🏃

---

11. HOWICK

f E 🚫 🏊 P 🚗 🐕 R3

Welcome to our 150-acre 5th-generation dairy farm. Enjoy feeding small animals, campfire, take a hay ride, cycle or relax by our inground pool. Non-smokers please. A delicious home-baked breakfast is served! We have been receiving guests for more than 12 years. Smoke free B&B. **Farm Stay p 52.**

From Montréal, Hwy 20 West, Mercier bridge, Rte 138 West, Rte 203 twd Howick (about 40km). Cross the bridge, turn left on Rue Lambton. Take English River Road, 2km.

B&B
HAZELBRAE FARM

Gloria and John Peddie
1650, English River Road
Howick J0S 1G0
(450) 825-2390

B&B	
single	$30
double	$50
child	$5-9

Open year round

Number of rooms	3
rooms with private bath	1
shared wc	1
shared bathrooms	2

Activities: 🏛 🎣 🚶 🚴 🏃

---

12. ÎLE PERROT

☀☀☀ F E 🐕 🚗 R4 TA

Situated on Lac Deux-Montagnes in the middle of the wilderness, our B&B offers a beautiful view facing the north: Oka, the L'Îsle aux Tourtes bridge and some small colourful islands. It also offers peace and tranquillity with a large landscaped property and some magnificent places to relax by the water's edge.

Hwy 20 West, right at the first light when you arrive on Île Perrot, after the train track, drive 1.6km. Turn right on Roy. Last house by the water.

B&B
GÎTE DE L'ÎLE

Nicole Frappier
10, rue Roy
Île Perrot J7V 8W3
(514) 425-0965
(514) 592-2248

B&B	
single	$60
double	$75

Open year round

Number of rooms	2
shared bathrooms	2

Activities: 🏛 🦆 🛶 🎣 🚶

13. LONGUEUIL

☀☀☀ F E 🚭 P R.1 TA

On the South Shore, 10 minutes from downtown Montreal, on a quiet street near the metro in the heart of Vieux Longueuil, a welcoming house invites you to come relax in a warm ambiance. Come as you are and enjoy its charming rooms and good breakfast.

From Montréal, Jacques-Cartier bridge, keep left, Rte 132. From Hwy 20, Exit 8, right on Rue St-Charles, right on Quinn at the Esso, 100 m. Ste-Élizabeth, on the left.

B&B
À LA BRUNANTE

Louise Bélisle
480, rue Ste-Elisabeth
Longueuil J4H 1K4
(450) 442-7691
www.bbcanada.
com/4682.html
guy.marion@sympatico.ca

B&B	
single	$45-55
double	$55-69
triple	$84
child	$10

Open year round

Number of rooms	2
rooms with sink	1
shared bathrooms	2

Activities: 🛥 🧍 🚶 🚴 🏃

14. LONGUEUIL

☀☀☀☀ F E 🚗 R.01 TA

Upscale B&B surrounded by restaurants located in the heart of Vieux-Longueuil and a few minutes from Montreal, the metro and the river shuttle. Romantic, air-conditioned rooms with private bathroom and entrance. Let yourself be charmed by our flowery garden and waterfall in the middle of an oasis. Your hosts live upstairs to better respect your privacy. See you soon!

From Montreal, Jacques-Cartier Bridge, St-Charles Exit. Behind city hall.

B&B
À L'OASIS DU VIEUX-LONGUEUIL

Ginette and Luc Desbiens
316, rue de Longueuil
Longueuil J4H 1H4
(450) 670-9839
fax (450) 670-6638
http://pages.infinit.net/loasis
luc.ginette@videotron.ca

B&B	
single	$60-75
double	$65-80

Reduced rates: Nov. 1 to May 1
Open year round

Number of rooms	2
rooms with private bath	2

Activities: 🦆 🧍 🚶 🚴 🏃

15. LONGUEUIL

☀☀☀ F e ♿ 🚗 🐕 R.2 TA

Come take advantage of a poetic ambience in a warm century-old house in the heart of Vieux Longueuil. Succulent breakfasts served on the terrace in the summer. Close to downtown Montréal by Métro or the ferry. Reductions for stays of 3 nights and more.

From Montréal, Jacques-Cartier Bridge, keep left, Exit Rte 132 or Hwy 20 immediately right, Exit Rue St-Charles. From Rte 132, Exit 8. Rue St-Charles and right on Rue St-Jean. Located behind Longueuil Town Hall.

B&B
LE REFUGE DU POÈTE

Louise Vézina
320, rue de Longueuil
Longueuil J4H 1H4
(450) 442-3688

B&B	
single	$45-50
double	$50-60
triple	$60-70
child	$10

Reduced rates: 5$ night, 3 nights and more
Open year round

Number of rooms	3
rooms with sink	1
rooms with private bath	1
shared bathrooms	1

Activities: 🏛 🛥 🧍 🚴 🏃

16. MASSUEVILLE, ST-AIMÉ

✎ F E 🐕 ✕ 🚗 P ⛵ R3.5

Discover an ancestral house surrounded by stately trees and flower gardens overlooking the Yamaska river. In this beautiful, quiet place, admire works of art and savour excellent country fare. Come discover the Sorel-islands archipelago, its theatre and festivals, museums and interpretive centre. We will be happy to welcome you.

From Montreal, Hwy 20 twd St-Hyacinthe, Exit 130 North. In Massueville, turn left on Rue Royale. Drive 3.5km.

B&B
L'ENSORCELAINE

Odette Langlois and
Yves De Celles
279, rang du Bord-de-l'eau
Massueville, St-Aimé
J0G 1K0
(450) 788-2283

	B&B	MAP
single	$55	$75
double	$65	$105
child	$10	$20

Open year round

Number of rooms	3
room with private bath	1
shared bathroom	1
shared wc	1
rooms with sink	2

Activities: 🏛 🚤 🛶 🎣 🚩

17. ROUGEMONT

☀☀☀ F e 🐕 🚗 P R.1 TA

Located next to the summer theatre, this country house offers warmth, quiet, comfort and serenity in a unique setting. Breakfast in the solarium with a view of the flower garden and water garden. Near local tourist activities; 3 golf courses, bike path, theatre, etc. "A stopping place in apple country."

Hwy 20, Exit 115; Rte. 229 South twd St-Jean-Baptiste; 1km past the village, turn left on Rte 229 twd Rougemont. Or Hwy 10, Exit 37 twd Marieville; turn right twd Rougemont, Rte. 112, left on Rte. 229 South, and left at the end onto Rang de la Montagne.

B&B
UN TEMPS D'ARRÊT

Denise Landry and
Jacques Collette
350, rang de la Montagne
Rougemont J0L 1M0
(450) 469-2323
fax (450) 469-3615
www.untempsdarret.com
untempsdarret@hotmail.com

B&B	
single	$55-65
double	$60-75

Reduced rates: 20% 3 nights and more
Open year round

Number of rooms	3
shared bathroom	1

Activities: 🎣 🚶 🚴 🏃

18. ST-HUBERT

☀☀☀ F e P 🚗 R.5 TA

Prize for Excellence "Special Favorite" Regional 1997-98. Located 7km south of Montreal, 35min from Dorval; easy access to major highways. Within reach of all activities in Montreal, Chambly and Montérégie, including the Biodome, festivals, the casino, etc. Wake up to our home specialties. Receiving you will be a pleasure.

From Montreal, Hwy 20 East, Exit Hwy 30 West. Or Hwy 10 East, Exit Hwy 30 East, Exit 115, Rte 112 West (Blvd. Cousineau) for 3.7km. Left on Rue Prince Charles, right on Rue Primot, left on Rue Latour.

B&B
AUX DEUX LUCARNES

Ginette and
Jean-Marie Laplante
3310, rue Latour
St-Hubert J3Y 4V9
(450) 656-1224
fax (450) 656-0851
www.bbcanada.com/
2345.html
auxdeuxlucarnes@
sympatico.ca

B&B	
single	$40-50
double	$60-70

VS

Reduced rates: Oct. 15 to Apr.15 for long stays
Open year round

Number of rooms	5
rooms with sink	3
rooms with private bath	1
shared bathrooms	2

Activities: 🎣 🚶 🚴 🏃

19. ST-HUBERT

✹✹✹ | F | e | 🚭 | P | R.7

A base for all your activities in Montérégie: cycling, golfing, Parc Safari, cruise, summer theatre, festival, museum, etc. For a short or long stay, it will be our pleasure to welcome you to the quietness of the suburbs. Right near Montréal, a few kilometres from the highways. Simple & quiet ambiance.

From Montréal via the Champlain bridge, Boul. Milan to Brossard, change to Gaétan Boucher in St-Hubert, left on Rue Normand, right on Rue Harding. In Québec City, via Hwy 10, 20, 30.

B&B
CHEZ GRAND-MAMAN
JACQUELINE

Jacqueline Castonguay
4545, rue Harding
Saint-Hubert J3Y 2K5
(450) 676-8667

B&B	
single	$40-50
double	$50
triple	$65
quad.	$80
child	$5-10

Open year round

Number of rooms	2
rooms with private bath	1
rooms in basement	1
shared bathrooms	1

Activities: 🏛 ⚓ 🚴 🎿 🏃

20. ST-HYACINTHE

✹✹✹✹ | F | E | 🚭 | 🏊 | P | 🚗 | 🐕 | R.2 | TA

Montérégie Excellence Prize 1996-97. An English garden hidden in the heart of the town. 1km from the convention centre and agriculture campus. In summertime the spa, the plant and water gardens offer complete relaxation. Antiques, paintings and books will warm you up in winter. Scrumptious home-made breakfasts on the menu. Come and share our house! Montérégie Excellence Prize 1996-97.

From Montréal or Québec City, Hwy 20, Exit 130. Boul. Laframboise to the arch. Rue Bourdages turn right, Rue Bourassa turn right, Rue Raymond, turn left.

B&B
LE JARDIN CACHÉ

Carmen and Bernard Avard
2465, avenue Raymond
St-Hyacinthe J2S 5W4
(450) 773-2231
fax (450) 773-9099
www.bbcanada.
com/lejardincache
jardincache@sympatico.ca

B&B	
single	$40-50
double	$55-65

Taxes extra VS MC

Reduced rates: corporate rates and Oct. 1 to May 31
Open year round

Number of rooms	3
shared bathrooms	2

Activities: 🦪 🍷 🚶 🚴 🏇

21. ST-HYACINTHE

✹✹✹ | F | E | 🚭 | P | 🚗 | R.8 | TA

Let yourselves be pampered in our warm and peaceful nest, located in a quiet neighbourhood. Romantic decor. Delicious breakfast in the solarium. Rest area filled with birdsong near the water garden and amidst flowers. Little considerations guaranteed. Golf, horseback riding, canoeing and pedal boating only a 5-minute drive away.

Hwy 20, Exit 123, twd St-Hyacinthe, drive 7km. Turn right at the 1st lights, Boul. Laurier. Left at the 2nd lights, Rue Dieppe, 2nd street turn right.

B&B
LE NID FLEURI

Suzanne and Gilles Cournoyer
5985, rue Garnier
St-Hyacinthe J2S 2E8
(450) 773-0750
www3.sympatico.ca/nid.fleuri
nid.fleuri@sympatico.ca

B&B	
single	$40-50
double	$50-60

VS

Reduced rates: Sep. 15 to Dec. 15 and Apr. 1to May 31
Open: Apr. 1 to Dec 15

Number of rooms	3
shared wc	1
shared bathrooms	1

Activities: 🦪 🍷 🚶 🚴 🏇

22. ST-LAZARE-DE-VAUDREUIL

☀☀☀☀☀ F E 🚭 🐾 P 🚗 R1 TA

Near Dorval, at the gates of Montreal, between the road to Ottawa (Hwy 40) and the one to Niagara Falls (Hwy 20), treat yourself to a delightful combination of nature, comfort and gastronomy. In a country setting, with a bike path at our doorstep, mix business and pleasure, activities and relaxation. Massage available on site.

Hwy 20 and/or Hwy 40, St-Lazare-bound Exit 22 to Chemin Ste-Angélique.

B&B
HALTE DE RESSOURCEMENT

Lise Bisson
2565, ch Ste-Angélique
St-Lazare-de-Vaudreuil
J7T 2K6
(514) 990-7825
fax (450) 455-1786
ressourcement.citeglobe.com
ressourcement@citeglobe.com

B&B	
single	$50-70
double	$65-85
triple	$85-105
quad.	$105-125
child	$10-15

VS MC AM

Reduced rates: 10% Oct. 30 to May 1, except Dec. 15 to Jan. 15
Open year round

Number of rooms	4
rooms with private bath	1
shared bathrooms	2
rooms with sink	2

Activities: 🍷 🏊 🎿 🚴 🏃

23. ST-MARC-SUR-RICHELIEU

☀☀☀ F E 🚭 🛏 P 🐾 R1 TA

A beautiful Victorian-style, century-old house that once served as the village hotel and the MP's house. The three large and very comfortable rooms offer a view of the magnificent Richelieu river. We have a warm welcome and lavish breakfasts in store for you. Less than 30min from Montreal and near many gourmet restaurants, golf courses and excursions to the villages of the Vallée des Patriotes. Looking forward to receiving you. **See colour photos.**

Hwy 20, Exit 112, Rte. 223 North.

B&B
AUX RÊVES D'ANTAN

Cécile and André Bergeron
595, rue Richelieu
Saint-Marc-sur-Richelieu
J0L 2E0
(450) 584-3461
http://pages.infinit.net/antan
bandre@videotron.ca

B&B	
single	$45-50
double	$55-60
triple	$65-70

Open year round

Number of rooms	3
shared bathrooms	2

Activities: 🍷 🎿 🚴 🐎 🚣

24. ST-MARC-SUR-RICHELIEU

☀☀☀☀ F E P R.2 TA

Less than 30 min from Montréal, the enchantment begins by following the Richelieu River and the small country roads, continues in the theatres, restaurants and art galleries, and ends in the warm ambiance of our house. We offer guests three spacious rooms with private bathrooms and a most delicious breakfast. You'll be back...

Take Exit 112 off Hwy 20 and follow the 223 North.

B&B
LE VIREVENT

Johanne Jeannotte
511, rue Richelieu
Saint-Marc-sur-Richelieu
J0L 2E0
(450) 584-3618
http://virevent.com
info@virevent.com

B&B	
single	$40
double	$60
triple	$75
quad.	$90

Open year round

Number of rooms	3
rooms with private bath	3

Activities: 🏛 🍷 🚴 🐎 🚣

25. ST-VALÉRIEN

Your host, a veterinarian, will greet you with a warm welcome and will share his passion for animals, plants and nature with you. Located on the border of Montérégie and the Eastern Townships, La Rabouillère is a unique farm. You can dine at the farm (reservations required). Pool, jacuzzi, play area. Near summer theatre, bike path, zoo and downhill skiing. **Country-style Dining p 26 Farm Excursion p 43, Farm Stay p 52.**

From Montréal, Hwy 20, Exit E.141 twd St-Valérien. Once in town, turn right at the 2nd, 1.3km. From Québec, Hwy 20 West, Exit 143 twd St-Valérien...

B&B
LA RABOUILLÈRE

Pierre Pilon, Denise Bellemare and Jérémie Pilon
1073, rang de l'Egypte
St-Valérien J0H 2B0
(450) 793-4998
fax (450) 793-2529
www.rabouillere.com
info@rabouillere.com

B&B	
single	$50-70
double	$60-80
triple	$75-95
child	$15

Taxes extra VS IT

Open year round

Number of rooms	3
shared bathrooms	2

Activities:

---

26. STE-AGNÈS-DE-DUNDEE

Peaceful country setting, flowery gardens, spacious house with colonnades and balconies reminiscent of Louisiana. 15km from Dundee border to New York, 5km from Lac St-François National Wildlife Reserve and Droulers (prehistoric Iroquois village) archaeological site. Bicycles on loan, golf courses, lake, water skiing, snowmobiling. Lunch or dinner table d'hôte by reservation. Looking forward to your visit. **Farm Stay p 52.**

Rte 132 from Valleyfield to Cazaville, turn left on Montée Cazaville and right on Chemin Ridge.

B&B
LE GÎTE CHEZ MIMI

Émilienne Marlier
5891, chemin Ridge
Ste-Agnès J0S 1L0
(450) 264-4115
toll free 1-877 264-4115

B&B	
single	$45
double	$55
triple	$65
quad.	$80
child	$10

Taxes extra VS MC

Open year round

Number of rooms	3
rooms with sink	2
shared bathrooms	1

Activities:

---

27. VAUDREUIL-DORION

Our bed and breakfast offers a superb view of Lac des Deux Montagnes and its sailboats. Nearby: shopping centre, restaurant and museum. Come unwind in our pool with patio area and relax in our lounge. A lavish breakfast featuring homemade products will round off your stay. We look forward to welcoming you.

From Montreal, Hwy 40 West, Exit 35; at the traffic light, turn right on Rue St-Charles, drive 1km. At the convenience store, turn right on Chemin de l'Anse, drive 0.4km, third house on the left.

B&B
GÎTE DE L'ANSE

Denise and Gilles Angell
154, chemin de l'Anse
Vaudreuil-Dorion J7V 8P3
(450) 424-0693

B&B	
single	$45
double	$55-65
child	$5-10

Open: May 1 to Oct. 31

Number of rooms	2
shared bathrooms	2

Activities:

28. MASSUEVILLE, ST-AIMÉ

1hr from Montréal. House in farming country. Comfort, fireplace. By the Yamaska river. Canoe. 20min from Odanak Indian reserve, Sorel Islands cruise, Gibelotte and Western festivals. Admire Canada geese and snow geese. Golfing, skidooing, Cyclo-Québec path at our door. **City home p 226 n° 26.**

From Montréal, Hwy 20 twd St-Hyacinthe, Exit 130 North, right at 3rd light onto the 235 North. In Massueville, left on Royale, 2km. From Sorel, 132 East, before Yamaska bridge at the flashing light right on Rang Bord de l'Eau, 8km.

COUNTRY HOME
MAISON BOIS-MENU

Nicole Larocque and
Gaétan Boismenu
387, rang Bord-de-l'Eau
Massueville, St-Aimé J0G 1K0
(450) 788-2466
www.chez.com/boismenu
boismenu@chez.com

No. houses	1
No. rooms	4
No. people	8
WEEK-SUMMER	$400
WEEK-WINTER	$400
W/E-SUMMER	$200
W/E-WINTER	$200
DAY-SUMMER	$100
DAY-WINTER	$100

Open year round

Activities:

 # FARM ACTIVITIES

Farm Stays:

25 LA RABOUILLÈRE, St-Valérien 52

26 CHEZ MIMI, Ste-Agnès-de-Dundee 52

11 HAZELBRAE FARM, Howick 52

Country-style Dining:

29 DOMAINE DE LA TEMPLERIE, Huntingdon 25

30 FERME KOSA, St-Rémi-de-Napierville 25

31 LA BERGERIE DU SUROÎT, St-Urbain 26

25 LA RABOUILLÈRE, St-Valérien 26

32 LA SEIGNEURIE DE NEWTON, Ste-Justine-de-Newton 27

Farm Tour:

25 LA RABOUILLÈRE, St-Valérien 43

33 LES ÉLEVAGES RUBAN-BLEU, St-Isidore 41

34 FERME JEAN DUCHESNE, St-Pie 42

MONTRÉAL REGION

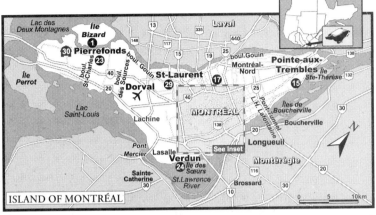

ISLAND OF MONTRÉAL

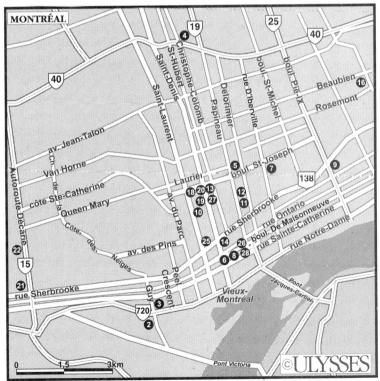

©ULYSSES

*The numbers on the map refer to the numbering of the establishments in this region.

1. ÎLE BIZARD

☀☀ F E 🚫 🐾 🚗 P R4

Situated on a peaceful, rustic island, Gîte Île Bizard is a modern and comfortable B&B with two spacious bedrooms. Vibrating bed in one room, and whirlpool in the other. Breakfasts on the terrace. Come for a visit! It won't be your last!

From Montréal, Hwy 20 or Hwy 40 West, Exit Boul. St-Jean North. Left on Boul. Pierrefonds, right on Jacques Bizard (bridge). Left at 1st light on Rue Cherrier, right on Rue de L'Église, to the end of the street, at "Le Bizard" stop turn left. From Mirabel, Hwy 15 South and 40 West...

B&B
GÎTE ÎLE BIZARD

Osithe Paulin
1993, rue Bord du Lac
L'Île-Bizard H9E 1P9
(514) 620-0766
fax (514) 620-2384
www.bbcanada.com/3069.html
osithepaulin@hotmail.com

B&B	
single	$50
double	$60
triple	$75
quad.	$90
child	$6-12

Reduced rates: Sep.1 to May 31
Open year round

Number of rooms	2
rooms with private bath	1
rooms in semi basement	1
shared bathrooms	1

Activities: 🏛 🚤 🏊 🏃 🚴

2. MONTRÉAL

F e P R.1

Historic Victorian house with a private garden facing a cosy park. 3 min walk from Métro, 5 min drive from downtown and Old Montréal. Outdoor market and many antique dealers in the area. Free private parking and easy access from highway. Bicycles available. Full breakfast. Shared or private bathrooms.

Atwater exit on Ville-Marie expressway (720). Take St-Antoine (one way) until you meet Rue Agnès, left. From Champlain bridge, Exit Atwater. Straight on Atwater after the tunnel, to St-Antoine...

B&B
À BONHEUR D'OCCASION

Francine Maurice
846, rue Agnès
Montréal H4C 2P8
tel/fax (514) 935-5898
www.bbcanada.com/526.html

B&B	
single	$50-55-75
double	$70-75-95
triple	$90
child	$10

Taxes extra

Reduced rates: Nov. 1 to Dec. 15, Jan. 15 to Apr. 15
Open year round

Number of rooms	5
rooms with private bath	2
shared bathroom	2

Activities: 🏛 🚤 🐟 🏃 🚴

3. MONTRÉAL

☀☀☀ F E 🚫 P R.1 TA

Right downtown, a large sunny house with southern decor, period furniture, a garden and terraces. Suites with whirlpool bath and wood-burning fireplace. Rooms with phone, voice mail, modem hookup, TV, hair dryer, makeup mirror, bathrobes, goosedown duvet, etc. 50m from the metro. "A gem." says Michel Vastel of *Le Soleil*. **See color photos.**

Ville-Marie Hwy (720 Est), Rue Guy Exit. At 1st lights, right on René-Lévesque; at 2nd lights, right on southbound Rue Guy, 1st street on the left after Hotel Days Inn. Lucien-L'Allier metro station.

B&B
À BON MATIN

1393, av. Argyle
Montréal H3G 1V5
(514) 931-9167
toll free 1-800-588-5280
fax (514) 931-1621
www.bonsmatins.com

B&B	
single	$89-119
double	$89-119
triple	$109-139
quad.	$129-159
child	$10

Taxes extra VS MC AM ER IT

Open year round

Number of rooms	5
rooms with private bath	5

Activities: 🏛 ⛷ 🚤 🐟 🚴

4. MONTRÉAL

☀☀☀ F e 🏊 P R.1 TA

Located in a residential neighbourhood, on a quiet street, we offer a warm welcome, family atmosphere and copious breakfast. Free parking, flowered terrace with pool, T.V. in room. Near services (0.1km), buses, Crémazie Métro, highways, bicycle path and olympic pool (0.8km).

Easy access from Dorval and Mirabel airports. From Dorval, rte 520 East twd Hwy 40 East, Exit 73, Rue Christophe-Colomb north, 1km. Rue Legendre, right and drive 0.2km to Ave. André-Grasset, turn left. First street turn right. From Mirabel, Hwy 15 South twd 40 East, sortie 73...

B&B
À LA BELLE VIE

Lorraine and M.Camille Grondin
1408, rue Jacques Lemaistre
Montréal H2M 2C1
(514) 381-5778
fax (514) 381-3966
www.bbcanada.com/3399.html
alabellevie@hotmail.com

B&B	
single	$50
double	$65
child	$10

Open: Jan 15 to Dec. 15

Number of rooms	2
shared bathroom	1

Activities: 🏛 🛶 ⛷ 🚴 🏃

5. MONTRÉAL

☀☀☀ F E 🚫 🚗 R.2 TA

A park and a flowery garden surround a B&B offering an incomparable welcome. Easy parking. Here will you find everythings a B&B has to offer: comfort, discrete environment, varied breakfasts, information. Everything to make your stay a memorable one... when one has a lucky star!

From the Jacques-Cartier bridge, Boul. De Lorimier North, right on Boul. St-Joseph, right on Rue Bordeaux. From Dorval Rte 520 East twd Hwy 40 East, Exit Papineau twd South, 15th traffic light, left on Boul. St-Joseph, left at next traffic light, Rue Bordeaux.

B&B
À LA BONNE ÉTOILE

Louise Lemire and
Christian Guéric
5193, rue de Bordeaux
Montréal H2H 2A6
(514) 525-1698
fax (514) 525-7656
www.bbcanada.com/
1947.html

B&B	
single	$55
double	$65
triple	$85

Open year round

Number of rooms	2
shared bathroom	1

Activities: 🏛 🛶 ⛴ 🛶 🚴

6. MONTRÉAL

F e 🚫 R.2

The next best thing to home. Steps from Berri-UQAM metro, bus terminal, old port, museums, restaurants. Ancestral home, roof-top terrace, huge rooms, living room, good breakfasts. Low-season: extended-stay rates. See you soon...

From the terminus, walk one street to the east. By Métro, Berri-UQAM, exit Place Dupuis. By car, Hwy Ville-Marie (720), Berri Exit, right on Ontario, right on St-André, right on de Maisonneuve, right on St-Christophe.

B&B
À L'ADRESSE DU CENTRE-
VILLE

Nathalie Messier and
Robert Groleau
1673, rue St-Christophe
Montréal H2L 3W7
(514) 528-9516
fax (514) 528-2746
www.bbcanada.com/657.html
adresvil@dsuper.net

B&B	
single	$55-65
double	$70-80
triple	$90-105

Reduced rates: Nov. 1 to Mar. 31
Open year round

Number of rooms	5
shared bathroom	2

Activities: 🏛 🛶 ⛴ 🏃 🚴

7. MONTRÉAL

F E 🚫 P R.5

In the heart of the Plateau Mont-Royal—a very popular district teeming with cultural activities, shops and restaurants—our bed and breakfast is located on a quiet street where guests are guaranteed a safe and peaceful stay, with a gourmet breakfast and attentive service. Free parking available for cars and bikes.

Hwy 720, Exit 7, Rue De Lorimier North, turn right on Rue Gilford, 2nd street, Rue Parthenais. Or Hwy 40, Exit 74, Rue Iberville South, turn right on Rue St-Joseph, 3rd street, Rue Parthenais. Mont-Royal metro.

B&B
À LA GLOIRE DU MATIN B&B
MORNING GLORY

Geneviève Ouellette
4776, rue Parthenais
Montréal H2H 2G7
tel/fax (514) 590-0797
www.arvox.com/
bbgloiredumatin
bbgloiredumatin@arvox.ca

B&B	
single	$60-80
double	$75-95
triple	$110
quad.	$125
child	$15

Reduced rates: 15% Nov.1 to Apr. 30
Open year round

Nombre de chambres	4
room with private bath	1
shared bathrooms	2
rooms with sink	3

Activities: 🏛 🛥 🚶 🚴 ●

8. MONTRÉAL

F E ♿ R.5 TA

At the Berri-UQAM metro, in the heart of downtown Montreal and local activities, enjoy the quiet comfort of a warm house fully renovated for your convenience: spacious, soundproof rooms, kitchenette available and separate eating area for your personal use. Gracious welcome and lively, lavish breakfasts.

Berri-UQAM metro, Place Dupuis exit. From the airport, Hwy Ville-Marie (720), Berri North Exit, turn right on Rue Ontario, right on Rue St-André, right on De Maisonneuve and right on St-Christophe.

B&B
AU GÎT'ANN

Anne and Nicolas Messier
1806, rue St-Christophe
Montréal H2L 3W8
(514) 523-4494
(514) 525-3938
fax (514) 879-3236
www.bbcanada.com/879.html
augite@cam.org

B&B	
single	$55-75
double	$70-90
triple	$90-110
quad.	$120

Reduced rates: Nov. 1 to Mar. 31
Open year round

Nombre de chambres	3
room with private bath	1
shared bathroom	1

Activities: 🏛 🛥 ● 🚴 🏃

9. MONTRÉAL

☀☀☀ F E 🚫 🐕 P R.1 TA

Finalist 2000 and Prize for Excellence "Special Favorite" Regional 1999. Meet Denis the real montrealer and Sasha, the "public relation director" (gentle dog). The front door is the city; There is the Olympic Park, Botanical Garden, Biodome, Pie-IX subway, the backyard is country with a large outside terrace surrounded with trees, inside it is homey, luxurious (private bathroom, color TV). Must try french toast, croissant & home jelly.

From Dorval, 520 E., 40 E., Exit 76, Boul Pie-IX S., 4km. From Mirabel, 15 S., 40 E., Exit 76. From downtown, east on Sherbrooke, right on Boul. Pie-IX South.

B&B
AU GÎTE OLYMPIQUE

Denis Boulianne
2752, boul.Pie-IX
Montréal H1V 2E9
(514) 254-5423
toll free (CAN and USA)
1-888-254-5423
fax (514) 254-4753
www.dsuper.net/~olympic
olympic@dsuper.net

B&B	
single	$75-85
double	$95-105
triple	$115-125
child	$15

Taxes extra VS MC AM

Reduced rates: low season and long stay
Open year round

Number of rooms	5
rooms with private bath	5
rooms in semi-basement	3

Activities: ● 🛥 🚶 🚴 🏃

10. MONTRÉAL

F E 🚫 R.1 TA

Victorian house with age-old woodwork on a quiet street facing Square St-Louis. Ten minutes' walking distance from downtown and Old Montreal, in the heart of the Latin Quarter. Lavish breakfasts and warm welcome.

From Dorval, Hwy 20 and Rte 720 East, Boul. St-Laurent North Exit. After 1km, turn right on Ave. des Pins, right on Ave. Laval. Sherbrooke metro station, Rigaud St. exit.

B&B
AUX PORTES DE LA NUIT

Christiane and Philippe Boscher
3496, av. Laval
Montréal H2X 3C8
(514) 848-0833
fax (514) 848-9023
www.bbcanada.com/
767.html
auxportesdelanuit
@videotron.ca

B&B	
single	$60-90
double	$70-100
triple	$85-125
quad.	$145
child	$10

Open year round

Number of rooms	5
shared bathrooms	1
rooms with private bath	3

Activities: 🏛 🍴 ⛴ 🚶 🚲

11. MONTRÉAL

✎ F E 🚫 🐕 R.2 TA

A little piece of paradise... On the menu: enchantment and R&R. A very colourful, singular bed and breakfast! Charming, intimate ambiance. Will you sleep in the Mango, or the Mexicaine? Memorable, healthy breakfast. Massotherapy package, bike rental. Facing Parc Lafontaine, in the Plateau, the second-best neighbourhood in North America. Easy parking. On a quiet street, 10min from everything! *Hablamos español.*

Voyageur terminus: 3min by taxi. From Sherbrooke metro: Bus 24 East; Rue Papineau, north.

B&B
AZUR

Caroline Misserey and
Genya St-Arnaud
1892, rue Gauthier
Montréal H2K 1A3
(514) 529-6364
www.genya.homestead.com
genyya@yahoo.com

B&B	
single	$55-65
double	$70-80
triple	$105
quad.	$125

VS

Open year round

Number of rooms	2
shared bathroom	1

Activities: 🏛 ⛴ 🚣 🍴 🚲

12. MONTRÉAL

F E P R.5 TA

Our old house facing Lafontaine park and surrounded by greenery has been entirely renovated; Botanical Gardens, Olympic Park and summer theatres are nearby. Copious breakfast, cosy and modern comfort. Refined atmosphere, original works of art. An oasis of peace and tranquillity. Private parking.

From Dorval, twd Montréal Hwy 40 E., Exit Papineau S., drive 5km. From Métro Papineau, bus #45 N., 2nd stop after Sherbrooke.

B&B
CHEZ FRANÇOIS

François Baillergeau
4031, rue Papineau
Montréal H2K 4K2
(514) 239-4638
fax (514) 596-2961
www.bbcanada.
com/2838.html

B&B	
single	$70-75
double	$90-120
triple	$100-130
child	$10

Taxes extra VS

Open year round

Number of rooms	5
rooms with private bath	3
rooms with sink	1
shared bathroom	1

Activities: 🏛 🍴 ⛴ 🚶 🚲

13. MONTRÉAL

☀☀☀ F e R.1 TA

Prize for Excellence "Special Favorite" Regional 2000. We are located on a quiet, tree-lined street, right by a lively avenue of shops and restaurants, that's great for strolling, and close to the metro to explore the city. Our B&B offers an atmosphere where time stands still and you can fully enjoy a comfortable stay and the morning's lavish breakfasts.

From the Jacques-Cartier bridge, Rue De Lormier. Left on Rue Sherbrooke, right on Rue Émile-Duployé, left on Rue Rachel, right on Rue Boyer. From Mont-Royal metro, turn right at the exit. Right on Rue Boyer.

B&B
GÎTE LA CINQUIÈME SAISON

Jean-Yves Goupil
4396, rue Boyer
Montréal H2J 3E1
(514) 522-6439
fax (514) 522-6192
http://cinquiemesaison.
multimania.com
cinquieme.saison
@sympatico.ca

B&B	
single	$55
double	$70

Taxes extra VS MC IT

Open year round

Number of rooms	5
shared wc	1
shared bathroom	1
shared showers	1

Activities: 🏛 🦆 ⛴ 🚣 🚴

14. MONTRÉAL

☀☀☀ F e 🚭 R.1 TA

A few min from the Old Montréal market, St-Denis and Ste-Catherine, the yellow house right in the midst of Montréal's cultural, social and tourist activities. This ancestral house's unique character and tranquillity will add to your stay. Good advice on activities, restaurants, entertainment.

Hwy 20, Rte 132, Jacques-Cartier bridge twd Rue Sherbrooke, left on Ontario, drive 1.2km, right on St-Hubert.

B&B
LA MAISON JAUNE

Sylvain Binette and
François Legault
2017, rue St-Hubert
Montréal H2L 3Z6
(514) 524-8851
fax (514) 521-7352
www.maisonjaune.com

B&B	
single	$50-55
double	$65-75
triple	$80-90
quad.	$95-105

Taxes extra

Reduced rates: Nov. 1 to Apr. 30
Open year round

Number of rooms	5
shared wc	2
shared bathroom	2

Activities: 🏛 🦆 ⛴ 🚣 🚴

15. MONTRÉAL

☀☀☀ F E 🚭 🏊 P R1 TA

Prize for Excellence "Special Favorite" Regional 1996-97. Located by the St. Lawrence River, 25min from downtown, this 1900 house will charm you with its garden, flowers and in-ground swimming pool. Lavish breakfast on the terrace. The country right in the city. Private parking. Children welcome. **See colour photos.**

From Dorval, Rte 520 E, Hwy 40 E, Exit 87, Tricentenaire to Notre-Dame, turn right, 200 m. From Mirabel, Hwy 15 S, 40 E, Exit 87... From Hwy 20, Lafontaine tunnel, 1st Exit, twd East. Drive south: Notre-Dame, twd East.

B&B
LA VICTORIENNE

Aimée and Julien Roy
12560, rue Notre-Dame Est
Montréal H1B 2Z1
(514) 645-8328
fax (514) 645-1633
www.bbcanada.
com/3372.html

B&B	
single	$40
double	$55
triple	$70
child	$0-5

Open: May 1 to Oct. 15

Number of rooms	3
rooms with sink	1
shared bathroom	2

Activities: ⛴ 🚣 🚶 🚴

16. MONTRÉAL

☀☀☀ | F | E | 🚭 | 🏊 | R1 | TA

This is the place for comfort and a warm welcome at a low price. Close to the Olympic tower, L'Assomption metro and 10 min from the botanical garden. Breakfasts are made with fresh, quality ingredients and you can have as much as you like. Pool, bikes available, free laundry.

From Mirabel Hwy 40 East, Boul. Lacordaire South Exit. Drive down to Boul. Rosemont and turn right, continue to Rue Lemay (2nd street, turn right). From Dorval, Hwy 520 East to Hwy 40 East...

B&B
«LE 6400»
COUETTE ET CAFÉ
BED & BREAKFAST

Lise and Jean-Pierre Durand
6400, rue Lemay
Montréal H1T 2L5
(514) 259-6400

B&B	
single	$45-50
double	$60-65

Reduced rates: Nov. 1 to Apr. 30
Open year round

Number of rooms	2
shared bathroom	1

Activities: 🚤 ⛵ 🎣 🚶 🚲

---

17. MONTRÉAL

☀☀☀ | F | E | 🚭 | P | R.2 | TA

Right near a vast park, our large and sunny room with private entrance and parking awaits you. It provides easy access to expressways and airports while offering you a guaranteed haven of peace with healthy breakfasts and private garden. Come enjoy the metropolis in a warm and intimate ambiance.

From Dorval, 520 East, Hwy 40 East, Exit 73 Ave. Papineau North. From Mirabel, Hwy 15 South, 440 East, 19 South, Ave. Papineau South. We are 0.6km east of Ave. Papineau, via Prieur (two blocks south of Gouin Blvd.).

B&B
LE CLOS DES ÉPINETTES

Diane Teolis and Léo Lavergne
10358, rue Parthenais, app. 1
Montréal H2B 2L7
(514) 382-0737
www.bbcanada.
com/3181.html
leclos@vl.videotron.ca

B&B	
single	$65
double	$75
triple	$95
quad.	$105
child	$5-10

Open year round

Number of rooms	1
rooms with private bath	1
rooms in semi-basement	1

Activities: 🏛 🎣 🚶 🚲 🏃

---

18. MONTRÉAL

☀☀☀ | F | E | 🐕 | R.05 | TA

Lovely Victorian house (marble fireplace) a stone's throw from festival sites, restaurants, museums, shops. Quiet and centrally located historic district. Relaxed ambiance with a soothing decor, home-made jams and rooms tempting one to take a nap. Friendly young hosts respectful of everyone's space. Make yourselves at home!

From Mirabel or Toronto, Hwy 40 East, St-Denis Exit, 6km. Right on Des Pins, right on Laval. From Québec City, Hwy 20, Rte 132, J.-Cartier bridge, left on Sherbrooke, right on St-Denis, left on Des Pins, right on Laval.

B&B
LE ZÈBRE

Jérôme Delville and
Alain Boulanger
3767, avenue Laval
Montréal H2W 2H8
(514) 844-9868
www.bbcanada.
com/2728.html
lezebrebb@yahoo.com

B&B	
single	$60
double	$75
triple	$95

Open: Apr. 1 to Dec. 15

Number of rooms	3
shared bathroom	2

Activities: 🏛 🍷 🚤 ⛵ 🚲

19. MONTRÉAL

☀☀ F E ⊘ R.1 TA

Square Saint-Louis is a peace of the countryside downtown. Everything is within walking distance: museums, exhibitions, restaurants, shopping, Old Montréal, etc. After a long day, relax in the park filled with birdsong. At breakfast, we eat, chat, laugh and start all over again! **See colour photos.**

From Dorval, Hwy 20 East, then Hwy 720 East, Boul. St-Laurent North Exit. Continue for 1km, then right on Ave. des Pins, right on Ave. Laval, left on St-Louis square. Or Sherbrooke metro station, Rigaud exit.

B&B
PIERRE ET DOMINIQUE

Dominique Bousquet
and Pierre Bilodeau
271, Carré St-Louis
Montréal H2X 1A3
(514) 286-0307
www.bbcanada.com/928.html
pierdom@sympatico.ca

B&B	
single	$40-55
double	$70-85
triple	$100
quad.	$115
child	$15

Open year round

Number of rooms	3
rooms with sink	2
shared bathroom	1

Activities: 🏛 ⚲ 🚶 🚲 ⚡

20. MONTRÉAL

☀☀ F E ⊘ 🐕 P R.1

In the heart of the Latin Quarter (restaurants-nightclubs-theatres-boutiques). Easy parking. Garden, hammocks. Quiet, safe street. 2 min from Métro. Near the bike path, international events: Jazz Festival, Just For Laughs, World Film Festival. 6-person suite. Superb lovers' suite. Family or group rooms (2 to 6 people).

Airports: Voyageur bus terminus, Métro Mont-Royal. By Car: twd downtown. Berri is parallel to St-Denis (2 streets to the east). 4272 Berri is between Mont-Royal and Rachel.

B&B
SHÉZELLES

Lucie Dextras and
Lyne St-Amand
4272, rue Berri
Montréal H2J 2P8
(514) 849-8694
cell. (514) 943-2526
fax (514) 528-8290
www.bbcanada.com/2469.html
shez.masq@sympatico.ca

B&B	
single	$45-95
double	$65-110
triple	$85-125
quad.	$150

Reduced rates: 10% 7 consecutives nights and more
Open year round

Number of rooms	4
rooms with private bath	1
shared bathroom	1

Activities: 🏛 ● ⚆ 🌊 🚲

21. MONTRÉAL, NOTRE-DAME-DE-GRÂCE

☀☀☀ F E ⊘ 🚗 P R1

Pretty Victorian House located in the heart of the Monkland village in N.D.G. Close to the restaurants and boutiques. 15min from Dorval airport via Hwy 20 or 40. Convenient access to downtown attractions by Metro (Villa Maria station). Our rooms are comfortable and well-furnished. Hingston House is filled with warmth.

From Dorval airport, Côte-de-Liesse East and Décarie South, Hwy 15, Exit Sherbrooke West turn right, right on Hingston.

B&B
MAISON HINGSTON 4335

Hélène Groulx
4335, rue Hingston
Notre-Dame-de-Grâce
Montréal H4A 2J8
(514) 484-3396
fax (514) 369-0263
www.bbcanada.com/4281.html
maisonhingston@hotmail.com

B&B	
single	$65
double	$75

Open year round

Number of rooms	2
shared bathrooms	1

Activities: 🏛 ⚆ 🌊 ⚲ 🚲

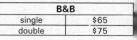

22. MONTRÉAL, NOTRE-DAME-DE-GRÂCE

F E ⊗ P R.25 TA

"Ulysse" Grand Prize winner for housing 2000 and Grand Prize winner in 1999 for its warm welcome and professional service. Picturesque Victorian manor, luxurious air conditioned rooms with total comfort, king/queen size beds, and the warmth of antique furnishings. Only steps away from the cafes and shops of Monkland Village, near the Decary Hwy leading to Dorval Airport and the downtown core, and near the Villa Maria subway station.

Decary Hwy, Côte Saint-Luc, head West to Somerled, left, right on Harvard.

B&B
MANOIR HARVARD

Robert Bertrand
4805, avenue Harvard
Notre-Dame-de-Grâce,
Montréal H3X 3P1
(514) 488-3570
fax (514) 369-5778
www.bbcanada.com/1963.html
alrc@sympatico.ca

B&B	
single	$165
double	$175
triple	$185
quad.	$20

Taxes extra VS MC IT

Open year round

Number of rooms	4
rooms with private bath	4

Activities: 🏛 ⛴ 🚶 🎿 🚲

23. PIERREFONDS

☀☀☀☀ F E ⊗ P 🚗 R.1 TA

Air-conditioned, renovated ranch house in west-end Montréal, close to Dorval airport, accessible from downtown via Rtes 40 or 20. Free off-the-street parking. Cozy bedrooms, spacious meeting rooms, piano, fireplaces, screened veranda, well-kept grounds. Healty & hearty breakfast. A restful place to return to.

Coming from Dorval Airport, Hwy 20 West, 7km, until Boul Saint-Jean, Exit 50 N., proceed on St-Jean for 7km, then left on Boul Pierrefonds, 1.4km, turn left again at Rue Paiement.

B&B
GÎTE MAISON JACQUES

Micheline and Fernand Jacques
4444, rue Paiement
Pierrefonds H9H 2S7
(514) 696-2450
fax (514) 696-2564
www.maisonjacques.qc.ca
gite.maison.jacques
@qc.aira.com

B&B	
single	$49-58
double	$69-78
triple	$99
quad.	$120
child	$6-15

MC AM VS *Taxes extra*

Reduced rates: 7% seniors and 4 nights and more
Open: Jan. 31 to Nov. 30

Number of rooms	3
rooms with private bath	3
rooms in basement	1

Activities: 🐚 🍂 🚶 🏇

24. VERDUN

☀☀ 🔒 F E ⊗ P R.7 TA

Sunny and peaceful with private entrance and parking just 10 min from downtown (museums, festivals, theatres). Close to beautiful park along St. Lawrence River banks (cycling, hiking, rafting, in line skating). Quick access to airports and regional activities via Hwys. Discount on 4 nights and more.

From Dorval, Hwy 20 East, Hwy 15 South. From the south, Champlain bridge to Hwy 15 North, La Vérendrye Exit, turn left at 6th light onto Stéphens, left on Beurling and left on Rolland.

B&B
PACANE ET POTIRON
CAFÉ COUETTE

Nathalie Ménard and
Jean-Pierre Bernier
1430, rue Rolland
Verdun H4H 2G6
(514) 769-8315
www.bonjourquebec.
com/info/pacaneetpotiron
jpb_nm@hotmail.com

B&B	
single	$50-70
double	$70-95
child	$15

VS

Reduced rates: 10% Oct. 15 to Dec. 10 and Jan. 15 to Apr. 15
Open year round

Number of rooms	2
shared bathroom	1

Activities: ⛴ 🍂 🎿 🏃

25. MONTRÉAL

★★★ F e 🏠 R1 TA

Beautifully furnished apartments in a prime, central location! Fully equipped kitchen. Daily, weekly or monthly rentals. Balcony, television, radio, telephone, pool and air conditioning. Great view of the city. Near festivals, Palais des Congrès, shopping centre, universities and hospitals. Parking. Great value for your dollar.

Metro Place-des-Arts, Jeanne-Mance exit, bus #80, get off at the 2nd bus stop, walk right. By car, situated downtown four streets west of Boul. St-Laurent and 1st street north of Sherbrooke between Milton and Prince-Arthur.

CITY HOME
APPARTEMENTS MEUBLÉS
MONTRÉAL CENTRE-VILLE

Bruno Bernard
3463, rue Ste-Famille
Office 008
Montréal H2X 2K7
(514) 845-0431
fax (514) 845-0262
www3.sympatico.ca/app
app@sympatico.ca

No. apt.	10
No. rooms	studio-1
No. people	1-4
WEEK-SUMMER	$500-700
WEEK-WINTER	$500-700
W/E-SUMMER	$170-300
W/E-WINTER	$170-300
DAY-SUMMER	$85-150
DAY-WINTER	$85-150

Taxes extra VS MC AM

Reduced rates: Oct. 21 to June 1
Open year round

Activities: 🏛 ● 🐎 🏃 🚴

26. MONTRÉAL

F E 🐎 🚗 P R.2 M.5

In the heart of the "Cité des Ondes" (TVA, Radio-Can., Télé-Qué.) and the Gay Village. Private parking. Comfort, sound system, cable TV, whirlpool, washer/dryer, dishwasher. Ground-floor loft, open area, access to a terrace. 20min walk: Old Montreal, St-Denis Street, Place des Arts; 10min: UQAM, between Papineau and Berri métros. **See ad at end of the guide. Country home p 216 n° 28.**

Beaudry Métro, north, turn right on De Maisonneuve, left on Visitation, right on Logan. From the airports, Voyageur Terminus shuttle to Beaudry Métro. By car, Rue Ste-Catherine, turn left on Beaudry.

CITY HOME
CONDOTELOGAN

Gaétan Boismenu
1472, rue Logan, Montréal
correspondance:
78 ouest boul. St-Joseph
Montréal H2T 2P4
(514) 849-6780
(514) 528-9120
fax (514) 849-9011
www.chez.com/condotelogan
condotelogan@chez.com

No. apt.	1
No. rooms	1
No. people	2
WEEK-SUMMER	$650
WEEK-WINTER	$650
W/E-SUMMER	$290
W/E-WINTER	$290
DAY-SUMMER	$160
DAY-WINTER	$160

Open year round

Activities: 🏛  🐎 ● 🚴

27. MONTRÉAL

F E R.01 M.01

Big second-floor loft located in the popular Plateau district. Quiet, sunny and modern. TV, fax machine, VCR, washer/dryer, telephone. One bedroom, large living room, equipped kitchen, two bathrooms, whirlpool bath. Near restaurants, cafés and shops. 2min from the Mont-Royal Métro, 100m from a bike path, 15min from downtown and its festivities. Perfect for lecturers, business people and visitors.

One block south of the Mont-Royal Métro. 10min from the Voyageur bus station, 20min from Dorval Airport.

CITY HOME
LOFT L'ESCALE

Kara Brahim
4336, rue Berri app.2
Montréal H2J 2P8
(514) 849-6860
(514) 219-4619
fax (514) 985-9885

No. houses	1
No. room	1
No. people	1-6
WEEK-SUMMER	$875-1050
WEEK-WINTER	$650-850
W/E-SUMMER	$330-425
W/E-WINTER	$280-325
DAY-SUMMER	$165-220
DAY-WINTER	$135-170

Reduced rates: Nov. to Apr. 30
Open year round

Activities: 🏛  🏃 🚴

28. MONTRÉAL

`F` `E` `⊘` `P` `R.1` `M.1` `TA`

Nice, big 4-room apartment in south-central Montreal, the media and arts district known as "the Village", where the population is the most diverse of any Canadian city. Private entrance, phone, whirlpool bath, stove, fridge, microwave oven, TV, patio door, terrace, garden. View of the city, trees and sky. Safe, quiet and comfortable.

Ville-Marie Hwy (720) twd downtown, Exit Vieux-Port/Vieux-Mtl/St-Laurent/Berri twd Berri. Left on Rue Berri, right on Rue Ste-Catherine, left on Rue Wolfe.

CITY HOME
MAISON GRÉGOIRE

Christine Grégoire
1766, rue Wolfe
Montréal H2L 3J8
(514) 524-8086
www.gregoire.qc.ca
maison@gregoire.qc.ca

No. houses	1
No. rooms	2
No. people	4-5
WEEK-SUMMER	$875-1000
WEEK-WINTER	$650-850
W/E-SUMMER	$330-400
W/E-WINTER	$270-325
DAY-SUMMER	$165-200
DAY-WINTER	$135-170

VS ER

Reduced rates: Nov.1 to Apr. 30
Open year round

Activities: 🏛 ⛵ 🧍 🚲 🏃

---

29. ST-LAURENT

`F` `E` `⛷` `⊘` `🚗` `P` `R.4` `M.2` `TA`

Lovely 3½ (living room, kitchen, bathroom). Spacious, quiet, fully equipped, with bedding, dishes, iron, hair dryer, telephone, cable TV, VCR, sound system, microwave oven. Residential district. Near Marcel Laurin park, Raymond Bourque arena, shopping centres and restaurants. 5min from Côte-Vertu metro, 10min from Dorval airport. Garden, laundry. Parking. Personalized welcome.

Hwy 40, Exit 67, Marcel Laurin North, about 1.5km. Left on Lucien Thimens. At the stop sign, left on Boul. Alexis-Nihon, right on Rue Hufford and left on Rue Sigouin.

CITY HOME
STUDIO MARHABA

Assia and Ammar Sassi
2265, rue Sigouin
St-Laurent H4R 1L6
(514) 335-7931
(514) 744-9732
fax (514) 335-2117
studiomarhaba@videotron.ca

No. houses	1
No. rooms	1
No. people	1-3
WEEK-SUMMER	$350-500
WEEK-WINTER	$250-350
W/E-SUMMER	$100-180
W/E-WINTER	$60-140
DAY-SUMMER	$60-100
DAY-WINTER	$40-80

Reduced rates: Nov.1 to Apr. 30
Open year round

Activities: 🏛 🧍 🧍 🚲 🏃

FARM ACTIVITIES

Farm Tour:

30 FERME ÉCOLOGIQUE DU PARC-NATURE DU CAP-SAINT-JEAN, Pierrefonds 44

OUTAOUAIS

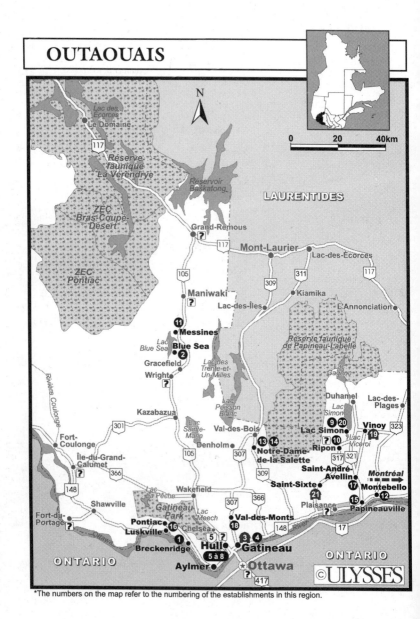

*The numbers on the map refer to the numbering of the establishments in this region.

1. AYLMER, BRECKENRIDGE

✺✺✺ | F | E | 🚭 | P | R1 | TA

Our split-level home offers you comfort, tranquillity and a warm welcome. Take the time to enjoy nature in the magnificent woods bordering the Outaouais River. 20 min to the Parliament and Ottawa's other tourist attractions. Bicycle storage available. Generous breakfast.

From Montreal, Hwy 417, in Ottawa Exit 123 (Island Park Drive) follow Island park, cross Champlain bridge to chemin Aylmer left. At the Aylmer city Hall, right on Eardley Street for 5km. Left on Terry Fox twd the river, right on Cedarvale.

B&B
MAISON BON REPOS

Denyse and Guy Bergeron
37, rue Cedarvale
Aylmer J0X 2G0
(819) 682-1498
tel/fax (819) 684-6821
www.bbcanada.
com/3276.html
denise.bergeron2
@sympatico.ca

B&B	
single	$40-50
double	$50-60

Open year round

Number of rooms	3
rooms with private bath	2
shared bathrooms	1

Activities: 🏊 🎿 🚶 🚴 🎿

---

2. BLUE SEA

✺✺ | F | E | 🚭 | P | R1.5 | TA

"The smile and warm welcome you take pleasure in offering us enhances the charm and setting of this magnificent bed and breakfast. The aromas of a lovingly prepared breakfast make us loth to leave." The Blue Sea lake and the linear park offer you a host of activities.

From Ottawa/Hull, Hwy 5 North and Rte. 105. In Gracefield, turn left at the flashing light. From Montreal, Hwy 15 North; in St-Jovite, Rte. 117 North In Grand-Remous, turn left on Rte. 105 South twd Maniwaki. In Messines, turn right at the flashing light, drive 7km.

B&B
CHEZ NAP

Claire and Conrad Bénard
4, ch. de La Gare
Blue Sea J0X 1C0
(819) 463-0246
www.lino.com/~cheznap
cheznap@iroseau.com

B&B	
single	$45-50
double	$55-65
triple	$80

Taxes extra

Open year round

Number of rooms	3
shared bathroom	1
shared wc	1

Activities: 🏊 🎿 🚶 🚴 🛷

---

3. GATINEAU

✺✺✺ | F | E | 🚭 | 🚗 | P | R5

A very comfortable bed and breakfast with large rooms and country charm, 12min from downtown Ottawa/Hull, casino, museum, bike path and golfing. Hearty breakfast near the fireplace or on the covered terrace. **Farm Stay p 53. See color photos.**

From Montreal, Hwy 40 twd Ottawa, Hwy 417, Mann Exit, King Edward twd Hull, Hwy 50 East, Paiement North Exit, drive 1.5km and turn left on Rue Bellechasse. Or Rte. 148, Hwy 50 to Masson, Paiement North Exit, turn left on Bellechasse.

B&B
FERME DE BELLECHASSE

Jacques Sauvé
115, ch. de Bellechasse
Gatineau J8T 4Y6
(819) 568-3375
(613) 769-7542
fax (819) 568-1112
www.bbregistry.com/ca
/ferme-de-bellechasse.htm
jsauve@sba.ca

B&B	
single	$60-90
double	$75-110
triple	$90-130
quad.	$105-150
child	$15-20

Open year round

Number of rooms	4
room with private bath	1
shared bathrooms	2
shared wc	1

Activities: 🏛 ⛵ 🎿 🚴 🎿

4. GATINEAU

☀☀ F E 🐕 P 🏊 R1 TA

Warm and peaceful B&B; breakfast in gazebo, inground swimming pool, resting areas. On a hill, view on Gatineau, Hull and Ottawa; 15min from parliament, casino, Musée des Civilisations, bike baths, Gatineau park and golf course. Tourist information available on site.

From Hwy 417, Exit Nicholas to Hull, Hwy 50 East, Exit Maloney, left on Main, left on Magnus, right on Craik. From Montréal, Rte 148, right on Main, etc. From Maniwaki, Hwy 5 S., Hwy 50 East...

B&B
LA MAISON SUR LA COLLINE

Josée and Jean-Pierre Allain
520, rue Craik
Gatineau J8P 5N7
(819) 663-3185
toll free 1-866-663-3185
fax (819) 663-7108
www.bbcanada.com/1376.html
allain@magma.ca

B&B	
single	$55-65
double	$60-70

VS MC

Open year round

Number of rooms	2
rooms with private wc	1
shared bathrooms	2

Activities: 🏛 🍴 🚣 🏃 🚲

5. HULL

☀☀☀ F a 🚭 P R.5

Prize for Excellence "Special Favorite" regional 2000 and **1995.** Recommended by La Presse in 1994, 1997. Small, well-decorated, century-old Victorian house located a few minutes' walk from Ottawa: Parliament, museums, market, etc. Access to beautiful cycling paths. A 5min drive to the casino. Hearty breakfast. Parking. Air conditioned.

From Montreal, Rtes 148 and 550, Hull West Exit, Boul. Maisonneuve Exit, left on Verdun, left on Champlain. Or from Montreal, Hwy 417, Mann Exit (which turns into King Edouard), Cartier McDonald Bridge, Boul. Maisonneuve Exit.

B&B
À COUETTE ET CROISSANT

Anne Picard Allard
330, rue Champlain
Hull J8X 3S2
(819) 771-2200
fax (819) 771-4920
www.couette-et-
croissant.qc.ca

B&B	
single	$55-60
double	$65-70
triple	$90
child	$15

VS

Open : Apr. 1 to Oct. 31

Number of rooms	3
room with private bath	1
room in basement	1
shared bathroom	1

Activities: 🏛 🍴 ⛴ 🚲 🏃

6. HULL

☀☀☀ F e 🚭 🚗 P R1 TA

An invitation to relax in a calm spot, near Gatineau Park, bike paths and walking trails. Country charm in the city. Warm welcome. Comfortable rooms and delicious breakfasts. Living room with fireplace, piano and TV. A few min from Ottawa, the casino and museums. Make yourself at home.

From Queensway, Mann Exit twd Hull and Hwy 5 N.; Mt-Bleu Exit. Right on Boul. Mt-Bleu, on the hill go left. Take Rue des Bouleaux, turns into des Ormes. From Mtl, Rte 148, Hwy 5 N... Mann Exit.

B&B
AU PIGNON SUR LE PARC

Fernande Béchard-Brazeau
63, rue des Ormes
Hull J8Y 6K6
(819) 777-5559
fax (819) 777-0597
brazeau-a@sympatico.ca

B&B	
single	$50-55
double	$60-65
triple	$85
quad.	$100
child	$10-15

Open year round

Number of rooms	3
rooms in basement	1
shared bathrooms	2

Activities: 🏛 🍴 🚣 🏃

7. HULL

☀☀☀ F E ⊘ P 🚗 R1 TA

Comfort and tranquility just minutes from Ottawa (museums) and the casino; 2 min from Parc de la Gatineau, bike paths. Attentive service. Finely decorated, air-conditioned house with living room, fireplace. Breakfast on the terrace, by magnificent woodlands and a golf course. Bike shed. Welcome!

Hwy 417, Mann Exit, then King Edward twd Hull, Hwy 5 North, Hautes-Plaines Exit 8, left on Rue du Contrefort, right on Du Versant. From Montréal, Rte 148 West. In Hull, Hwy 5 North...

B&B
AU VERSANT
DE LA MONTAGNE

Ghyslaine Vézina
19, rue du Versant
Hull J8Z 2T8
(819) 776-3760
fax (819) 776-2453
www.bbcanada.
com/3577.html
auversant@sympatico.ca

B&B	
single	$50-55
double	$60-65
triple	$85
quad.	$100
child	$10

VS

Open year round

Number of rooms	3
rooms in semi-basement	1
shared bathrooms	2

Activities: 🏛 🚶 👣 🚲 🏃

8. HULL

☀☀☀ F E ⊘ 🐕 P R1 TA

By Gatineau Park, a few minutes from downtown Hull and Ottawa. Welcome to our home with modern-classical decor and family ambiance. You will enjoy comfort, quiet and hearty breakfasts while abandoning yourselves to tourist activities such as: museums, outdoors, etc. See you soon! Families welcome.

From Ottawa or Rte 148 via Montréal, Hwy 5 North, St-Raymond Exit toward Rte 148 West, right on Ch. Pink, left on Rue des Peupliers, left on Rue Atmosphère, right on Rue Astrolabe.

B&B
MANOIR DES CÈDRES

Christiane and Yvon Charron
5, rue de l'Astrolabe # 1
Hull J9A 2W1
(819) 778-7276
fax (819) 778-6502
yvonc3r@infonet.ca

B&B	
single	$60
double	$70
triple	$75
quad.	$100
child	$15

Open year round

Number of rooms	2
shared wc	1
rooms in basement	2
shared bathrooms	1

Activities: 🏛 👣 🚶 🚲 🏃

9. LAC-SIMON, CHÉNÉVILLE

☀☀☀ F E 🐕 ✕ P 🏊 R1 TA

Are you looking for a getaway? Come rejuvenate yourself in the countryside in a picturesque setting offering a stunning panoramic view of the lakes and mountains year-round. Fine sand private beach. Our rooms, generous breakfasts, *table d'hôte* meal plan and the magnificent view will delight you. **Country home p 236.**

From Montréal, Rte 148 West or from Ottawa Rte 148 East to Papineauville and Rte 321 North. At Chénéville, Rte 315 West for 1.3 km. Turn right onto Chemin Tour-du-Lac and drive 1.5 km, then turn left onto Chemin Marcelais.

B&B
DOMAINE AUX CROCOLLINES

Thérèse Croteau et
Franz Collinge
642, chemin Marcelais
Lac-Simon, Chénéville J0V 1E0
tél/fax (819) 428-9262
www.lacsimon.com/
lacsim/menu/hebergements
/crocolines/index.html
dom.aux.crocollines@orbit.qc.ca

	B&B	MAP
single	$45	$65
double	$65	$104
triple	$80	$138
child	$15	$25

Reduced rates : 3 nights and more
Open year round

Number of rooms	2
rooms with sink	2
shared wc	1
shared bathrooms	1

Activities: 🛷 👣 ⛵ 🏃 🐎

10. LAC-VICEROI (CANTON DE RIPON)

F E R5 TA

Stately residence with turrets, period furniture, grand piano and organ. Family or gourmet cooking. Family-size room for 4 people. All our activities are free: canoeing on the river in front, trout fishing, dogsledding, tennis. Packages for our summer theatre.

From Montréal, Rte 148 W. From Ottawa-Hull, Hwy 50 and Rte 148 E. At Papineauville, Rte 321 N, 27 km. At 4 lanes, left on Rte 317. After the bridge, right on Ch. des Guides, 1.6 km, right at the sign, 0.09 km.

B&B
CHÂTEAU ÉPI D'OR

Claire and Charles Dussault
29, chemin Périard
Ripon J0V 1V0
(819) 428-7120
fax (819) 428-2514

	B&B	MAP
single	$40	$48
double	$50	$65
child	$10	$15

Taxes extra VS MC

Open year round

Number of rooms	4
rooms with private bath	4
shared bathrooms	1

Activities:

11. MESSINES

F E TA

Prize for Excellence "Special Favorite" Regional 1999. Located in a peaceful, enchanting setting in Haute-Gatineau, our inn has a tranquil atmosphere that will envelop you in a pleasant sense of well-being. The fine cuisine served in our restaurant is among the best in the region.Golf,cross-country skiing on Trans-Canadian path. 3 rooms with therapeutic bath.

From Ottawa/Hull, take Hwy 5 N. and Rte 105 twd Maniwaki. Left at the flashing light in Messines. From Montréal, Hwy 15 N., Rte 117 N., in St-Jovite to Grand-Remous. Left on Rte 105 South, to Maniwaki...

INN
MAISON LA CRÉMAILLÈRE

Andrée and André Dompierre
24, chemin de la Montagne
Messines J0X 2J0
(819) 465-2202
toll free 1-877-465-2202
fax (819) 465-5368
www.lacremaillere.qc.ca
la.cremailliere@ireseau.com

	B&B
single	$50-70
double	$65-85
child	$15

Taxes extra VS MC IT

Open year round

Number of rooms	5
rooms with private bath	3
rooms with sink	1
shared wc	3
shared bathrooms	2

Activities:

12. MONTEBELLO

F E R1 TA

Spacious rooms, inspired breakfasts, a grand living room with fireplace. A place to stop and unwind! Near Château Montebello, Manoir Papineau and Oméga Park. In the heart of nature, it is a haven of peace. Enjoy the spa with an on-sight professionnal massage therapist and personal body care. Inground pool, canoeing, paddle-boat, ice skating, tobogganing, snowshoeing.

From Montréal, Ottawa-Hull-bound Hwy 40 West; Hawkesbury Exit, Rte 148 West, 2 km before Montebello. From Ottawa-Hull, Hwy 50 and Rte 148 East to Montebello; 2 km east of the village.

B&B
JARDINS DE RÊVES

Michelle Lachance
1190, Côte du Front
Montebello J0V 1L0
(819) 423-1188
fax (819) 423-2084
www.bbcanada.
com/2878.html
jardinsdereves@sympatico.ca

	B&B
single	$75
double	$85-110
child	$20

Taxes extra VS MC IT

Open year round

Number of rooms	5
rooms with private bath	5

Activities:

13. NOTRE-DAME-DE-LA-SALETTE ☀☀☀ 🏠 F E ⊘ 🚗 P ✗ R17 TA

Located in the country, our place offers you the comfort and tranquillity you're looking for. After a great night's sleep, you'll appreciate our delicious breakfast. Upon request, we can also make you lunch or dinner to your taste. We offer several packages to enhance your stay in our lovely region: sports, cultural and outdoor.

From Montréal, Rte. 148 West. From Hull/Ottawa, Hwy 50 East, Exit Rte 309 twd Buckingham, Rte. 309 North, Buckingham Exit, drive 17km.

B&B
AUX 2 LUCARNES

Colette and Marcel Savoie
29, Route 309
Notre-Dame-de-la-Salette
J0X 2L0
(819) 766-2772
fax (819) 766-2141
www.bonjourquebec.
com/info/aux2lucarnes
aux2lucarnes@sympatico.ca

	B&B	MAP
single	$45-65	$65-85
double	$55-75	$95-115
child	$15	$25

Taxes extra VS

Reduced rates: 10% Oct.1 to Apr.30, 3 nights and more and senior citizen anytime
Open year round

Number of rooms	3
shared bathroom	1
shared wc	1

Activities: 🏛 ⛵ 🚣 ⛷ 🏃

14. NOTRE-DAME-DE-LA-SALETTE ☀☀☀ F E ✗ P ♒ R.5 TA

Looking for peace and tranquillity? That is just what our B&B offers. Located by a river surrounded by mountains. Our farm animals graze on our 9-acre park. 15min from the B&B, «Club Vacances Royal» awaits you with various outdoor activities.

2.5 hours from Montréal, take Hwy 40 West twd Ottawa-Hull; take the Hawksbury Exit to Cumberland. Take the ferry at traffic light then Rte 309 twd Buckingham. After Buckingham, drive 27 km and cross the bridge at left.

B&B
DOMAINE DE LA MAISON BLANCHE

Doreen Desjardins and
Jean-Georges Burda
Notre-Dame-de-la-Salette
C.P. 185, J0X 2L0
(819) 766-2426
fax (819) 766-2429
www3.sympatico.ca/
maison.blanche

B&B	
single	$60
double	$70
triple	$85
child	$0-15

Open : Jan.15 to Dec. 20

Number of rooms	4
shared wc	1
shared bathrooms	2

Activities: 🦆 🚣 ⛷ 🏃 🛷

15. PAPINEAUVILLE, MONTEBELLO F E ♒ P R.5 TA

Our 150-year-old house will charm you. Peaceful environement. Just 5km from Chateau Montebello, 65km from Hull/Ottawa. Homemade jams, outdoor pool. Nearby you will find: golf, horseback riding, rafting, cross-country skiing, ice-fishing. Golf packages available. This B&B does not participate in the volontary classification program.

Halfway between Montréal and Hull-Ottawa by Rte 148. From Montréal to Papineauville, right on Rue Joseph Lucien Malo at the corner with the Ultramar garage.

B&B
À L'ORÉE DU MOULIN

Suzanne Lacasse
170, rue Joseph Lucien Malo
Papineauville, Montebello
J0V 1R0
tel/fax (819) 427-8534
www.aloreedumoulin.qc.ca
moulin.lacasse@sympatico.ca

B&B	
single	$50
double	$65
triple	$90
child	$15

VS

Open year round

Number of rooms	4
shared bathrooms	2

Activities: 🏛 🦆 ⛷ 🐎 🏃

16. PONTIAC, LUSKVILLE

☀☀☀ | F | E | 🚭 | 🐾 | P | R2 | TA

Recipient of the Grand Prix du Tourisme de l'Outaouias 2000 and the 1998 regional "Coup de Coeur" award of excellence. Located 25min from Ottawa, near Gatineau Park, a log house with a fieldstone fireplace. On site: museum, bikes, canoes, showshoes, reflexology, *reiki*, wildlife observation, canoe-building workshop, historical-style canoe excursions on the Ottawa River. Exquisite breakfast.

From Hull, Chemin de la Montagne North, drive 17km, turn right on Chemin Crégheur.

B&B
AU CHARME
DE LA MONTAGNE

Thérèse André and Armand Ducharme
368, chemin Crégheur
Pontiac, Luskville J0X 2G0
(819) 455-9158
fax (819) 455-2706
www.bbcanada.com/740.html
aucharmedelamontagne
@videotron.ca

B&B	
single	$45-60
double	$55-70
triple	$80-90
child	$15

VS

Open year round

Number of rooms	3
shared bathrooms	2
rooms with sink	3

Activities: 🛶 🚲 🧍 🐎 🏃

---

17. ST-ANDRÉ-AVELLIN

☀☀☀☀ | F | E | P | R.5 | TA

Hundred-year-old house on the heritage tour in the historic heart of the village. Victorian period furniture. 4 cosy romantic rooms. Solarium. Restaurants, shops, attractions and services close by. The charm and simplicity of days gone by... Friendly welcome.

From Montréal, Rte 148 West or from Ottawa-Hull Hwy 50 and Rte 148 East to Papineauville. Rte 321 North, 12 km. In St-André-Avellin, turn left in front of the church, grey-stone house on the left.

B&B
L'ANCESTRALE

Ginette Louisseize
and Bertin Mailloux
19, rue St-André
St-André-Avellin J0V 1W0
(819) 983-3232
fax (819) 983-3466

B&B	
single	$45
double	$60

Taxes extra

Open year round

Number of rooms	5
rooms in basement	1
rooms with private bath	2
shared wc	2
shared bathrooms	1

Activities: 🐚 🛶 🧍 🚲 🏃

---

18. VAL-DES-MONTS

☀☀☀ | F | e | 🚭 | P | 🏊 | R2

Country B&B near lakes, forests and wide expanses, 25 kilometres from Hull-Ottawa. Nearby: fish breeding, saphouse, skidoo trails (rentals available) and cross-country skiing, cycling paths, Laflèche cave. On site: bee-keeping, pool, recreation canoes.

From Montréal, Rte 148 W. or from Ottawa/Hull, Hwy 50 twd Montréal, Exit Boul. Lorrain, 10.5 km on Rte 366 N., left on Rue École (at the dépanneur), go for 1 km, right on Prud'homme.

B&B
AUX PETITS OISEAUX

Gaétane and Laurent Rousseau
6, rue Prud'homme
Val-des-Monts J8N 7C2
(819) 671-2513
www.cyberus.ca/
~rousseau/gite
rousseau@cyberus.ca

B&B	
single	$50-55
double	$60-65
child	$10

Open year round

Number of rooms	2
rooms with sink	1
shared bathrooms	2

Activities: 🧍 🧍 🚲 🛷 🏃

19. VINOY, CHÉNÉVILLE

☀☀☀ F E P ⇔ ⊠ TA

Special mention from the jury "Success" 2000. In a stream-laced wooded valley, retreat where period decor revives old memories while creating new ones. A farmyard enchants children, cosy corners invite lovers' whispers, nature's bounty nurtures the camaraderie of old friends. Taste each season at its peak. Prize for Excellence "Special Favorite" 1995-96. **Farm stay p 53. See colour photos.**

From Montréal, Rte 148 W. From Ottawa/Hull, Hwy 50, Rte 148 E. to Papineauville. North on Rte 321. 12 km from St-André-Avellin, right on montée Vinoy, 5 km.

INN
LES JARDINS DE VINOY

Suzanne Benoit and
André Chagnon
497, Montée Vinoy Ouest
Vinoy, Chénéville J0V 1E0
(819) 428-3774
fax (819) 428-1877
www.jardinsdevinoy.qc.ca
a.chagnon@orbit.qc.ca

	B&B	MAP
single	$50-65	$69-84
double	$65-80	$103-118
triple	$75-90	$132-147
quad.	$85-100	$161-176
child	$10	$19

Taxes extra VS MC

Reduced rates: Sep. 6 to June 22
Open year round

Number of rooms	5
rooms with private bath	1
shared wc	1
shared bathrooms	2

Activities: 🦫 🏃 🚲 ⛷ 🐕

20. LAC-SIMON, CHÉNÉVILLE | F | E | | X | P | | R1 | M4 | TA |

Do you feel like getting away from it all? Then come and get back in touch with nature in a picturesque country home offering a stunning panorama of the lake and mountain year-round, with a private fine-sand beach. Charming, comfortable houses for a pleasant stay. *Table d'hôte* available at our B&B. **B&B p 231.**

From Montreal, Rte 148 West, or from Ottawa, Rte 148 Est toward Papineauville and Rte 321 North. In Chénéville, Rte 315 West for 1.3km, right on Chemin Tour-du-Lac, 1.5km, left on Chemin Marcelais.

COUNTRY HOME
DOMAINE AUX CROCOLLINES

Thérèse Croteau and
Franz Collinge
642, chemin Marcelais
Lac-Simon, Chénéville
J0V 1E0
tel/fax (819) 428-9262
www.lacsimon.com/lacsim/
menu/hebergements/crocolines/
index.html
dom.aux.crocollines@orbit.qc.ca

No. houses	5
No. rooms	1-4
No. people	1-9
WEEK-SUMMER	$485-910
WEEK-WINTER	$485-910
W/E-SUMMER	$150-290
W/E-WINTER	$150-290
DAY-SUMMER	134-248 $/2dys
DAY-WINTER	134-248 $/2dys

Open year round

Activities:

FARM ACTIVITIES

Farm Stay:

3 LA FERME BELLECHASSE, Gatineau 53

19 LES JARDINS DE VINOY, Vinoy, Chénéville 53

Country-style Dining:

21 FERME CAVALIER, St-Sixte 28

QUÉBEC CITY REGION

© ULYSSES

Saint-Ferréol-les-Neiges **23** **73**
Saint-Joachim **65**
Cap-Tourmente **67**
Sainte-Anne-de-Beaupré **3 72**
Saint-François
Saint-Jean **9 à 12**
Saint-Michel
Sainte-Famille **21**
Île d'Orléans
Saint-Pierre
Saint-Laurent **13 à 15**
Château-Richer **4 à 7** **74**
L'Ange-Gardien
Sainte-Pétronille **22**
Beaumont

CHAUDIÈRE-APPALACHES

138
Parc du Mont-Sainte-Anne
368
368
368
132

Saint-Adolphe
69 70 71
Stoneham
Boischatel **1 2**
Beauport
Lévis
Saint-Romuald
Québec
Charlesbourg
Village-des-Hurons
Charlesbourg
Sainte-Foy
Sillery
See Close-up of O.U.C.
Charny
St-Lambert-de-Lévis
Cap-Rouge

Mont Stoneham
Lac-Delage
Lac-Saint-Charles
Saint-Charles
Val-Bélair
175 **175** **2** **371** **573** **440**

Saint-Gabriel-de-Valcartier **64**
Shannon **68**
Saint-Augustin-de-Desmaures
138
Saint-Antoine-de-Tilly
20
132
Station forestière de Duchesnay
Lac-Saint-Joseph
Fossambault-sur-le-lac
Pont-Rouge
Neuville **24 25 26**
St. Lawrence River

367 **367** **365** **354** **367** **40** **73**

Saint-Raymond **66**
Donnacona
Cap-Santé
Notre-Dame-de-Portneuf
Portneuf
Deschambault **2 8**
2

*The numbers on the map refer to the numbering of the establishments in this region.

---

73 **175**
WENDAKE (Village-des-Hurons) **63**
L'ANCIENNE-LORETTE
LORETTEVILLE
SAINT-ÉMILE
CHARLESBOURG
BEAUPORT **49 à 54**
See Close-up of Downtown
LÉVIS
440 **132**
CHAUDIÈRE-APPALACHES
Québec Urban Community

QUÉBEC **40 58 à 61**
VANIER
SAINTE-FOY
SILLERY **62**
CAP-ROUGE **55 à 57**
SAINT-AUGUSTIN-DE-DESMAURES

371 **573** **358** **138** **40** **73** **175** **740** **138** **40** **73** **540** **132** **440**

Downtown Québec City
27 **29**
48
43
39
45 47
VIEUX-QUÉBEC
VANIER
28 à 38
41 44 46
ch. de la Canardière
rue De Salaberry
boul. René-Lévesque
Grande-Allée
boul. Champlain
73 **440** **175**

N
0   6km

1. BOISCHATEL

Large Canadian house in the heart of all the attractions in the Québec City area. 300m from the Montmorency falls, opposite Île d'Orléans. 10min from Old Québec City. Fax and Internet service on site. Copious and varied breakfast. Whale excursion reservations. Free parking.

From Montréal, Hwy 20 E. or Hwy 40 E. twd Ste-Anne-de-Beaupré. Left at Côte-de-l'Église, Boischatel Exit, 1.6km after Chutes Montmorency at 1st traffic lights. Head up the hill, Côte de l'Église, left on Ave. Royale, 0.6km.

B&B
AU GÎTE DE LA CHUTE

Claire and Jean-Guy Bédard
5143, avenue Royale
Boischatel G0A 1H0
(418) 822-3789
fax (418) 822-2344
www.quebecweb.
com/gitedelachute
5143gite@clic.net

✹✹✹ F e ⊗ P 🚗 R.2 TA

B&B	
single	$40-45
double	$55-65
child	$15

Reduced rates: 3 nights or more
Open year round

Number of rooms	5
rooms in basement	3
shared wc	1
shared bathrooms	2

Activities: 🍷 ⚲ 🚤 🚲 🏃

2. BOISCHATEL

Ten minutes from Quebec City, "Le Refuge du Voyageur" offers an exceptional view of the city, the St. Lawrence River, the Pont de l'Île bridge and Île d'Orléans. Rustic decor. 2 spacious family-size suite with kitchenette, private entrance and balcony.

From Québec City, Hwy Dufferin-Montmorency East, Boischatel Exit. Côte de l'église, to Ave. Royale, right.

B&B
LE REFUGE DU VOYAGEUR

Raynald Vézina
5516, avenue Royale
Boischatel G0A 1H0
(418) 822-2589

✹✹ F e 🚗 P R2

B&B	
single	$50
double	$60
triple	$75
quad.	$90
child	$0-10

Reduced rates: Nov. 1 to June 1
Open year round

Number of rooms	2
rooms with private bath	2

Activities: 🏛 🍷 🚲 🎿 🏃

3. CAP-TOURMENTE, MONT-STE-ANNE

In the heart of Cap-Tourmente, 12 min from Mont Ste-Anne (view of the slopes), house with 5 rooms with private bathrooms. Familial room with fireplace. Breakfast in the owners residence (right next to the B&B). On site: outdoor pool, hiking or cross-country skiing to the falls and the sugar shack. **Country home p 262.**

From Québec City, Henri IV Hwy N., twd 40 E., Ste-Anne-de-Beaupré, Rte 138 E., twd St-Joachim, Cap-Tourmente.

B&B
GÎTE DE L'OIE DES NEIGES

Gisèle Perron
390, ch. du Cap Tourmente
St-Joachim G0A 3X0
(418) 827-5153
tel/fax (418) 827-2246
www.bbcanada.com/
2690.html
oiedesneiges@hotmail.com

✹✹✹✹ F E ⊗ 🐕 P 🏊 R1 TA

B&B	
single	$45-55
double	$75-85
triple	$105
quad.	$135
child	$15

VS

Open year round

Number of rooms	5
rooms with private bath	5

Activities: 🚣 ⚲ 🎿 🏃

4. CHÂTEAU-RICHER

F E P ☒ R2 TA

The warm welcome of a small inn, an ancestral house restored to its original style, only 15 minutes from the centre of Québec City, facing Île d'Orléans, and 20 minutes from Mont-Ste-Anne. Hablamos español.

Rte 138 East Twd Ste-Anne-de-Beaupré, after the Île d'Orléans bridge, left on Rte du Petit-Pré, right on Ave. Royale, 9km after Chutes Montmorency.

INN
AUBERGE DU PETIT PRÉ

Ginette Dion and Yvon Boyer
7126, avenue Royale
Château-Richer G0A 1N0
(418) 824-3852
fax (418) 824-3098

B&B	
single	$50-60
double	$60-70
triple	$85
quad.	$100
child	$15

Taxes extra VS MC AM IT

Open year round

Number of rooms	4
shared wc	1
shared bathrooms	2

Activities: 🏛 ⛷ 🚲 🛷 🏊

---

5. CHÂTEAU-RICHER

★★★ F E 🚭 P ☒ TA

Between Mont Ste-Anne and Québec City, in the heart of the Beaupré region, treat yourself to an incomparable stay at our home, along with delicious meals from the Baker restaurant. You will find all the charm of a country home. Rooms in the Inn or the pavilion.

East of Québec City, Rte 138 East. To Ste-Anne-de-Beaupré. 18.5km from the Montmorency falls. Watch for "Baker" on the roof of the restaurant.

INN
BAKER

Gaston Cloutier
8790, avenue Royale
Château-Richer G0A 1N0
(418) 824-4478
(418) 666-5509
sans frais 1-866-824-4478
fax (418) 824-4412
www.auberge-baker.qc.ca
gcloutier@auberge-baker.qc.ca

	B&B	MAP
single	$55-94	$87-126
double	$60-99	$124-163
triple	$80-119	$176-215
quad.	$90-129	$218-257
child	$10	$32

Taxes extra VS MC AM ER IT

Reduced rates: Apr. 2 to June 21 and Oct. 15 to Dec. 20
Open year round

Number of rooms	7
rooms with private bath	7

Activities: 🛷 ⛷ 🏊 🎿

---

6. CHÂTEAU-RICHER

🌞🌞🌞 F E 🚭 🐕 🚗 P ⛵ R1 TA

At the gates of Charlevoix, a welcoming house whose most beautiful room is outside. Enjoy a rowboat or pedal-boat ride among our magnificent, large white swans. Come take advantage of the superb grounds with swimming pool.

From Quebec City, Rte 138 East or Boul. Ste-Anne. On the right, behind the Motel Roland.

B&B
GÎTE UN AIR D'ÉTÉ

Lynda Boucher and
Claude Gingras
8988, boul. Ste-Anne
Château-Richer G0A 1N0
(418) 824-5210
toll free 1-888-922-8770
fax (418) 824-5645
www.unairdete.com
gite.unairdete@videotron.ca

B&B	
single	$60
double	$70
triple	$110
quad.	$125
child	$10

VS MC

Reduced rates: Oct.1 to May 31
Open year round

Number of rooms	2
shared bathroom	1
shared wc	1
rooms in basement	2

Activities: 🛷 ⛷ 🚶 🚲 🎿

7. CHÂTEAU-RICHER

F E 🚫 P ✖ TA

Fifteen minutes from Old Québec City and 10min from Mont-Ste-Anne, stay in a magnificent Victorian house (1868). Hearty homemade breakfast with exceptional view of the river and Île d'Orléans. Large lounge with fireplace. Exquisite, cosy, traditionally furnished rooms. Dinner by reservation. Delicious French cuisine. We speak German.

From Québec City, Rte 138 East. Drive 15km past the Île d'Orléans bridge. In Château-Richer, left at the traffic lights on Rue Dick, right on Ave. Royale, left on Côte Ste-Achillée, drive 100 feet, left on Rue Pichette.

INN
LE PETIT SÉJOUR

Pascal Steffan,
Christiane and Anne-Marie
394, rue Pichette
Château-Richer G0A 1N0
(418) 824-3654
fax (418) 824-9356
www.quebecweb.com
/petitsejour
petitsejour@globetrotter.net

	B&B	MAP
single	$60-70	$90-100
double	$65-90	$125-150
triple	$110	$200
quad.	$130	$250

Taxes extra VS MC

Reduced rates: 5% 3 nights and more
Open year round

Number of rooms	5
rooms with private bath	5
shared wc	1

Activities: 🏛 ⛷ ∮ ⛷ 🏃

8. DESCHAMBAULT

★★★ F E P 🏊 ✖ R4 TA

With the St. Lawrence, the falls and Rivière Belisle at its feet, this large hundred-year-old Victorian, nicknamed "the little château", will transport you back in time with flowers, lace and a decor from days gone by. Evening meal of creative and meticulously prepared meals. Snowmobiling, sleigh rides, cross-country skiing, ice-fishing. **See colour photos.**

From Montréal or Québec City, Hwy 40, Exit 254, drive 1.6km to the river. Turn left onto Rte 138 (Chemin du Roy), drive 2km. Turn left at the Inn "Chemin du Roy" sign, Rue St-Laurent.

INN
AUBERGE CHEMIN DU ROY

Francine Bouthat and
Gilles Laberge
106, rue St-Laurent
Deschambault G0A 1S0
(418) 286-6958
toll free 1-800-933-7040

	B&B	MAP
single	$64-89	$89-114
double	$79-104	$129-154
triple	$94-119	$169-194
quad.	$129	$229
child	$10	$20-30

Taxes extra VS MC

Open year round

Number of rooms	8
rooms with private bath	8

Activities: 🏛 🚣 ∮ 🚴 🏃

9. L'ÎLE-D'ORLÉANS, ST-JEAN

✹✹✹✹✹ F E P 🚫 R7 TA

Located 25 min from old Quebec City, a new house 400m from the road, near the river, offers quiet and comfort: rooms with queen-size bed and balcony with St. Lawrence River view (1 room with 2 single beds), 2 living rooms and a dining room. Full breakfasts made up of homemade goods. Looking forward to seeing you soon.

From Québec City, Hwy 40 or 440 East twd Ste-Anne-de-Beaupré, Île d'Orléans Exit. At traffic lights, straight ahead to St-Laurent and St-Jean. 2.4km past the St-Jean church.

B&B
AU GIRON DE L'ISLE

Lucie and Gérard Lambert
120, chemin des Lièges
St-Jean, Île d'Orléans
G0A 3W0
(418) 829-0985
toll free 1-888-280-6636
fax (418) 829-1059
www.total.net/~giron
giron@iname.com

	B&B
single	$69-105
double	$79-115
triple	$145
quad.	$155
child	$20

VS MC AM IT

Reduced rates: Oct. 15 to Dec. 15 and from Jan. 15 to Apr. 30
Open year round
with reservations Oct. 15 to Apr. 30

Number of rooms	4
rooms with private bath	4

Activities: 🏛 ∮ 🚴 🏃 🐎

10. L'ÎLE-D'ORLÉANS, ST-JEAN

☀☀☀ F e P R.1 TA

We are 25 minutes from Québec City, in an ancestral home very close to the river, and near museums, theatres, handicraft boutiques, art galleries, and restaurants. Friendly atmosphere and hearty breakfast. We will do everything we can to make your stay a pleasant one. Welcome to Île d'Orléans.

From Québec City, Rte 440 East twd Ste-Anne-de-Beaupré, Île d'Orléans Exit. At the traffic lights, go straight ahead for 20km. On the right, corner of Chemin du Quai.

B&B
GÎTE DU QUAI

Rita and Grégoire Roux
1686, chemin Royal
Saint-Jean, Île d'Orléans
G0A 3W0
(418) 829-2278

B&B	
single	$40
double	$50
triple	$70
quad.	$90
child	$10-15

Reduced rates: May 1 to May 31, Oct.1 to Oct. 31
Open: May 1 to Oct. 31

Number of rooms	3
shared bathrooms	2

Activities: 🏛 ♥ ⚓ 🎿 🚴

11. L'ÎLE-D'ORLÉANS, ST-JEAN

☀☀☀ F E P R.5 TA

Nestled on the cape and the ancestral lands of the "Audets, a.k.a. Lapointes," our bicentenary house welcomes guests in a warm atmosphere. Quiet, with a view of the river that remains charming with each passing season. You will want to linger over our lavish breakfasts. A stay that allows you to discover the island and its treasures.

From Quebec City, Rte 440 East, Île d'Orléans Exit. At the light, continue straight ahead for 17.7km. After the beach restaurant, turn left, go up to the white house on the right.

B&B
LA MAISON SUR LA CÔTE

Hélène and Pierre Morissette
1477, chemin Royal
St-Jean, Île d'Orléans
G0A 3W0
(418) 829-2971
fax (418) 829-0991
p.morissette@videotron.ca

B&B	
single	$50
double	$55
triple	$75

Open: Apr. 1 to Oct. 31

Number of rooms	4
rooms with sink	4
shared bathrooms	2

Activities: 🏛 🎿 ⛵ ⚓ 🚴

12. L'ÎLE-D'ORLÉANS, ST-JEAN

☀☀☀ 🖥 F E P 🚫 🐕 R.5 IA

If you're looking for a peaceful and comfortable place, our 19th century replica of an old farm house, situated on a cliff, is awaiting you. Your hosts: Yolande, Claude and Valentine (the cat).

From Québec City, Rte 138 East twd Ste-Anne-de-Beaupré, Île d'Orléans Exit. After the bridge straight ahead for 17.5km. At the B&B sign, turn left, the house is on your right on the cliff.

B&B
LE MAS DE L'ISLE

Yolande and Claude Dumesnil
1155, chemin Royal
St-Jean, Île d'Orléans
G0A 3W0
tel/fax (418) 829-1213
www.bonjourquebec.
com/info/lemasdelisle
sorciere@total.net

B&B	
single	$55-60
double	$60-65
triple	$90-95
quad.	$115
child	$20

VS

Reduced rates: Nov. 1 to Apr. 30
Open year round

Number of rooms	3
shared bathrooms	2

Activities: 🏛 ⛵ ⚓ 🎿 🚴

13. ÎLE D'ORLÉANS, ST-LAURENT

F e P 🛥 🏊 R.1 TA

Come drop anchor at our hundred-year-old house, right in the heart of town, on the river a few steps away from the marina. The horizon is constantly changing and the landscape transforms with the rhythm of the tide. Library with 2,500 books, reading room, heated pool. Excusions on the St.Lawrence River. Equiped for seafood cooking.

From Québec City, Hwy 40 E. or 440 E. twd Ste-Anne-de-Beaupré, Exit 325 Île d'Orléans. After the bridge, at the lights, go straight for 8km. About 0.2km after the church.

B&B
LA CHAUMIÈRE DU NOTAIRE

June and Jacques Bouffard
1449, chemin Royal
St-Laurent, Île d'Orléans
G0A 3Z0
(418) 828-2180
fax (418) 828-0659

B&B	
single	$80-90
double	$80-90
child	$10

Open: May 1 to Oct. 31

Number of rooms	2
rooms with private bath	2

Activities: 🛥 🚣 ⛷ 🏃

14. L'ÎLE-D'ORLÉANS, ST-LAURENT

F e 🚭 P R3 TA

A stone's throw from the St-Lawrence River, on an island that encourages dreaming and relaxation, our home relates its past with its creaking floors that have seen their fair share of jigs and revelry. You'll be treated to a big breakfast served with a smile and great hospitality. Gift packages available.

Hwy 40 or 440 East twd Ste-Anne-de-Beaupré, Île d'Orléans Exit. Continue straight ahead for 8km.

B&B
LA VIEILLE MAISON FRADET

Lyse Demers
1584, chemin Royal
St-Laurent-de-l'Île-d'Orléans
G0A 3Z0
tel/fax (418) 828-9501
toll free 1-888-828-9501
quebecweb.com/fradet
fradet@quebecweb.com

B&B	
single	$55-65
double	$65-85
triple	$85-100
quad.	$120
child	$15

VS
Reduced rates: Sept.1 to May 31 from Monday to Thursday
Open year round

Number of rooms	3
rooms with private bath	3

Activities: 🚲 🚣 ⛷ 🐎

15. L'ÎLE-D'ORLÉANS, ST-LAURENT

F E 🚭 🛥 P 🏊 R2 TA

Our lovely Victorian home has exquisite air-conditioned bedrooms that will delight you. Come and enjoy a royal breakfast while admiring the majestic St. Lawrence River. The beauty of the landscape property is only equaled by the melody of the birds. You will be surprised how good it feels to let yourself be pampered. At l'Oasis de Rêves (Dream Oasis), your dreams do come true.

From Québec City, Hwy 40 East to Ste-Anne-de-Beaupré, Île d'Orléans exit. At the traffic light, continue straight ahead. Drive 5km past St-Laurent church.

B&B
L'OASIS DE RÊVES

Lyette Chedore and Jean Tardif
179, chemin Royal
St-Laurent-de-l'Île-d'Orléans
G0A 3Z0
(418) 829-3473
(418) 570-0634
fax (418) 829-0053
www.oasisdereves.com
info@oasisdereves.com

B&B	
single	$85-115
double	$95-125
triple	$120-150
child	$20

VS MC

Open: May 1 to Oct. 31

Number of rooms	3
rooms with private bath	3

Activities: 🏛 🚣 🛥 ⛷ 🚲

16. ÎLE D'ORLÉANS, ST-PIERRE

F E P ☒ R2 TA

Situated next door to the oldest church in Québec, Auberge Le Vieux Presbytère is a beautiful, large ancestral home. Restaurant on site. The 150,000-ft property has American buffalo, wapitis (large deer) and ostriches. Breathtaking view. Only 15min from Québec City. Bike rental on site.

From Québec City, Hwy Dufferin-Montmorency, Île d'Orléans exit. Left at the light. At the town centre of Saint-Pierre, left between the two churches.

INN
AUBERGE LE VIEUX PRESBYTÈRE

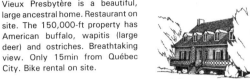

Louise Lapointe and
Hughes L'Heureux
1247, rue Mgr. D'Esgly
Saint-Pierre-de-l'Île-d'Orléans
G0A 4E0
(418) 828-9723
toll free 1-888-828-9723
fax (418) 828-2189
www.presbytere.com

	B&B	MAP
single	$50-90	$70-105
double	$60-100	$110-145
triple	$80-115	$159-190
quad.	$95-130	$204-235
child	$10-15	---

Taxes extra VS MC AM ER IT

Open year round

Number of rooms	8
rooms with private bath	6
shared wc	2
shared bathrooms	1

Activities: 🚣 🎿 ⛷ 🏃

17. L'ÎLE-D'ORLÉANS, ST-PIERRE

☼☼☼ F e P R1 TA

Located near the Pont de l'Île, our B&B is only 10 min east of Québec City, 5 min from the Chutes Mont-morency, and 20 min from Ste-Anne-de-Beaupré. With us, com-fort, spotlessness, intimacy and generous breakfasts are guaran-teed! Bike and motorcycle storage. One room with private entrance. "Crépuscule" is also the explosion of brilliant fall colours. Welcome.

From Québec City, Hwy 40 East or 440 East, Exit 325 Île d'Orléans. At the traffic lights at top of the hill, straight for about 1km.

B&B
CRÉPUSCULE

Louise Hamel
863, rue Prévost
St-Pierre-de-l'Île-d'Orléans
G0A 4E0
(418) 828-9425
www.quebecweb.
com/gpq/crepuscule
louise.hamel3@sympatico.ca

B&B	
single	$50
double	$60
triple	$80
quad.	$100
child	$10

Open: Dec. 20 to Oct. 31

Number of rooms	3
rooms with private bath	3

Activities: 🎣 🏛 🚣 🛷 🎿

18. L'ÎLE-D'ORLÉANS, ST-PIERRE

☼☼☼ F e 🚭 P R1 TA

Welcome to the B&B "Bel Horizon", the gateway to Île d'Orléans, only 15 min from Québec City. Comfort, intimacy, complete breakfast. View of the river, facing Chutes Mont-morency. 5 rooms (12 people): 2 on ground-floor, 3 on first floor, family suite, private bathroom. Ideal for family and groups. Shared bath-rooms for couples (if not in a group). Reserve now!

At entrance to Québec City, Rte 440 or Hwy 40 East twd Ste-Anne-de-Beaupré. Drive about 35km, Exit 325 Île d'Orléans. At the top of the hill, at the lights, turn right, 1km.

B&B
GÎTE BEL HORIZON

Yvette and Paul-Émile Vézina
402, chemin Royal
St-Pierre-de-l'Île-d'Orléans
G0A 4E0
(418) 828-9207
fax (418) 828-2618
www.quebecweb.com
/gpq/gitebelhorizon

B&B	
single	$50-60
double	$60
triple	$80
quad.	$90-115
child	$15

VS

Reduced rates: 7% Feb.1 to May 31 and 4 nights and more or 4 rooms
Open: Feb. 1 to Nov. 1

Number of rooms	5
rooms with private bath	3
shared bathrooms	1

Activities: 🏛 🚣 🛷 🎣 🚲

19. L'ÎLE-D'ORLÉANS, ST-PIERRE

☀☀☀☀ F E 🐕 P R.5

Located in one of the most beautiful spots on Île d'Orléans, nestled in a vineyard, our ancestral home invites you to relive a bit of history. Tour of the vineyard and free wine tasting. Our rooms combine modern comfort with a warm and intimate ambiance. Memorable breakfasts! Large living room with fireplace. Terrace with a view of the river and sunsets. Less than 15min from Quebec City, 20min from Mont Ste-Anne and near the Montmorency Falls.

At the island traffic light, turn left, drive 2km.

B&B
LA MAISON DU VIGNOBLE

Lise Roy
1071, chemin Royal
St-Pierre-de-l'Île-d'Orléans
G0A 4E0
(418) 828-9562
www.quebecweb.
com/gpq/lamaisondu
vignoble/introfranc.htm

B&B	
single	$50-60
double	$60-80
triple	$85-105
quad.	$130
child	$15

VS MC

Open year round

Number of rooms	3
rooms with private bath	1
shared bathrooms	2

Activities: 🦆 🏃 🚲 🎿 🐕

20. ÎLE-D'ORLÉANS, ST-PIERRE

☀☀☀ F E P ✕ TA

A house with over 200 years of history... is cosy comfort where antique furniture and dried flowers encourage calm and relaxation. Come share authentic and refined country cooking in the intimacy of the dining room. Relax by the fire in the living room or in the garden near the farmyard.

From Québec City, Hwy 40 or 440 East twd Ste-Anne-de-Beaupré, Île d'Orléans Exit. Left at the traffic light, 3km.

INN
L'AUBERGE SUR LES
PENDANTS

Chantale Vigneault and
Jean-Christophe L'Allier
1463, chemin Royal
St-Pierre-de-l'Île-d'Orléans
G0A 4E0
(418) 828-1139
surlespendants@qc.aira.com

	B&B	MAP
single	$52	$77
double	$62	$112
triple	$77	$152
quad.	$92	$192
child	$10	$18

Taxes extra VS MC AM IT

Open year round

Number of rooms	5
shared bathroom	2

Activities: 🏃 🚲 🛷 🎿

21. L'ÎLE-D'ORLÉANS, STE-FAMILLE

☀☀☀ F E 🚭 P 🐾 R.1 ✕ TA

The wind has carried us to all the continents and we've brought back the scents, great life experiences, a different way of doing things and the desire to share. Hundred-year-old house, adjoining shop, view of the river and the Laurentians, walking path, cycling, X-country skiing, snowshoeing, picnic baskets. We speak Japanese, French and English.

From Québec City, Hwy 440 E. twd Ste-Anne-de-Beaupré, Île d'Orléans Exit. Left at the lights, straight for 13km.

B&B
AU TOIT BLEU

Loulou and Iris Germain
3879, chemin Royal
Ste-Famille, Île d'Orléans
G0A 3P0
(418) 829-1078
fax (418) 829-3052
www.bbcanada.
com/3116.html
toitbleu@total.net

B&B	
single	$55-80
double	$55-90
triple	$95
quad.	$110
child	$10

VS AM

Reduced rates: 10% 3 nights and more, Nov. 1 to May 1, except Christmas Holiday
Open year round

Number of rooms	5
shared bathroom	2
rooms with private bath	3

Activities: 🏃 🚲 🛶 🎿 🐕

22. L'ÎLE-D'ORLÉANS, STE-PÉTRONILLE

☀☀☀ F E P 🚭 R.5

Enchanting setting on magical Île d'Orléans. Come discover the art of living in harmony with the past in our home, amidst a century and a half of history. The magnificent view of the majestic St. Lawrence and a visit to the Chutes Montmorency will leave you with unforgettable memories. To top it all off, we offer generous breakfasts and hospitality worthy of the finest establishments; a wonderful stay awaits you.

From Québec City, Rte 138 and Hwy 40 or 440 twd St-Anne-de-Beaupré, île d'Orléans Exit. Right at the lights after the bridge, 3.5km.

B&B
LE 91 DU BOUT DE L'ÎLE

Jeanne Trottier
91, chemin Royal,
ch. du Bout de l'Île
Ste-Pétronille, Île d'Orléans
G0A 4C0
(418) 828-2678

B&B	
single	$45-50
double	$55-60
triple	$75-80

Reduced rates: Nov. 1 to Apr. 1
Open year round

Number of rooms	4
rooms with sink	2
shared bathrooms	2

Activities: 🏛 ⚓ 🍴 ⛷ 🏃

23. MONT-STE-ANNE, ST-FERRÉOL

☀☀☀ F E 🚭 P 🚗 R1 TA

5 min from Mt Ste-Anne, 30 min from Québec City, discover the calm and comfort of soundproof rooms, twin or queen-size beds, sinks, suites, living room with fireplace. Magnificent scenic view. Nearby: Sept Chutes (falls), Grand Canyon, Cap Tourmente, skiing, cycling, golf, walking trails, snowmobiling, horseback riding, dogsledding. Ski packages.

From Québec City, Rte 138 East., 40km. At Beaupré, to Mont-Ste-Anne, Rte 360, 10km. From Baie-St-Paul, Rte 138 W., 30km, Rte 360 to St-Ferréol. After the 7 Chutes, 3km.

B&B
LES AROLLES

Claire Boutet and Gilles Dumas
3489, av. Royale, route 360
St-Ferréol-les-Neiges
G0A 3R0
tel/fax (418) 826-2136
quebecweb.com/gpq/arolles
javert@megaquebec.com

B&B	
single	$50-70
double	$65-85
triple	$80-100
quad.	$115
child	$15

VS MC

Open year round

Number of rooms	5
rooms with sink	3
rooms with private bath	1
shared bathrooms	2

Activities: 🍴 🚶 🚲 ⛷ 🏃

24. NEUVILLE

F E ♿ 🚗 P ✕ R8 TA

30min from Québec City, discover a unique site specializing in agrotourism. Emus, austriches, rheas and other animals are raised on our farm. A large house with solarium, bathed in light, offering a warm ambiance. Old-style cuisine offered. Families welcome! Special: 2 adults and 2 children $80 B&B or $100 MAP. Boutique on site. Come share our passion, consult **Farm Tour p 46 and Farm Stay p 53.**

Boul. Charest, Hwy 40 West or East, turn right at Neuville Exit 285 then left twd Pont Rouge, Rte. Gravel for about 5km. Petit-Capsa on the right.

B&B
LA FERME L'ÉMEULIENNE

Émilienne and Jacques
Chouinard Houle
307, rue Petit-Capsa
Neuville G0A 2R0
(418) 876-2788
fax (418) 876-3280
www.quebecweb.com/emeu/
emeu@globetrotter.net

	B&B	MAP
single	$50	$68
double	$60	$96
triple	$80	$134
quad.	$100	$172
child	$12	$20

Taxes extra

Reduced rates: 20% 3 nights and more
Open year round

Number of rooms	2
shared bathroom	1
shared wc	1

Activities: 🚤 🍴 🚲 🚶 🏃

25. NEUVILLE

F e 🚭 P R2 TA

All the charm of the country 15 minutes from Québec City. View of the St .Lawrence, the perfect spot. Large property, woods, terrace with inground pool. Generous breakfast served on the terrace or in the dining room. Living room with TV, pool room. Bikes available. Large parking lot.

From Montréal, Hwy 40 East, Exit 281 Neuville, Rte 138 East, for 6km. From Québec City, Hwy 40 West, Exit 298, Rte 138 West, 10.4km.

B&B
LE GÎTE DE NEUVILLE

Louise Côté and
Ernest Germain
173, Route 138
Neuville G0A 2R0
(418) 876-3779
(418) 876-3060
fax (418) 876-3780
legitedeneuville@hotmail.com

B&B	
single	$45
double	$60
child	$15

VS IT

Reduced rates: 10% 2 nights, 15% 3 nights and more
Open year round

Number of rooms	3
shared wc	2
shared bathrooms	1

Activities: 🍴 ⚓ 🎿 🚵 🛶

26. NEUVILLE

F E P 🚭 R1 TA

15 min from Québec City, in one of the prettiest villages in Québec, discover many ancestral houses. Stunning view of the St. Lawrence. Relax on the terrace, in the sunroom or near the fireplace. Air conditioned. Nearby: marina, antiques, theatre and dogsledding. Guides tours of the village and church. Bikes available.

From Montréal or Québec City, Hwy 40, Exit 285, to Neuville, Route 138, 3km.

B&B
MAISON DUBUC

Madeleine and Antoine Dubuc
421, rue des Érables
Neuville G0A 2R0
tel/fax (418) 876-2573
www.bbcanada.
com/2687.html
maison.dubuc@globetrotter.net

B&B	
single	$40
double	$60
child	$10

Open year round

Number of rooms	2
shared bathroom	2

Activities: 🍴 ⚓ 🎿 🚵 🛶

27. QUÉBEC

F E 🚭 ♿ 🏊 P R.1 TA

Located 3min from Vieux-Québec and the convention centre, Abat-Jour B&B will fill your stay with unforgettable pleasant memories. Travel back in time and revel in the culture and history of Québec. Go for a bike ride on the Corridor de Cheminots, explore Domaine Maizeret, Parc Montmorency and much more. Cordial reception and personalized service. Delicious breakfasts. See you soon!

Hwy 20, Pierre-Laporte bridge or Hwy 40 to Ste-Anne-de-Beaupré, Exit 316. At the 1st stop sign, take Rue Chamfleury straight to the 8th stop sign, left De Fondville drive 700 m.

B&B
ABAT-JOUR B&B

Nadia El-Ghandouri
2064, rue De Fondville
Québec G1J 1X6
(418) 666-6654
(418) 265-4853
fax (418) 666-8400
quebecweb.com/abatjour

B&B	
single	$50
double	$60
triple	$75
quad.	$90
suite	$110-140
child	$10

Open year round

Number of rooms	3
suite with private bath	1
rooms with sink	2
shared wc	1
shared bathrooms	1

Activities: 🏛 🛶 🎿 🚵 ⛷

28. QUÉBEC

☀☀☀ F E 🚫 🐕 R.1 TA

Vacation at L'Heure Douce in old Québec City, close to the convention centre and all services. Ancestral house with comfortable rooms. Dining room reserved for guests. Panoramic view and balcony where you'll relax with a drink and watch the sun go down. Québécois, continental and vegetarian breakfast. We'll give you some good suggestions.

Hwy 20, P-Laporte bridge, Boul. Laurier Exit, Rue Cartier, left, right Chemin Ste-Foy, left St-Augustin to Richelieu. Hwy 40, Boul. Charest, twd dowtown. Right Dorchester, côte d'Abraham, right Richelieu.

B&B
ACCUEIL B&B L'HEURE DOUCE

Diane Dumont
704, rue Richelieu
Québec G1R 1K7
tel/fax (418) 649-1935
www.bbcanada.
com/2695.html
heuredouce@videotron.ca

B&B	
single	$55-60
double	$65-75
triple	$80-85
quad.	$100-120
child	$15

Taxes extra VS

Reduced rates: 4 nights and more,
Nov. 1 to Dec. 15,
Feb. 15 to Mar. 31
Open year round

Number of rooms	3
shared bathroom	2

Activities: 🏛 ⛵ 🚴 🎿 🐎

29. QUÉBEC

☀☀☀ F e P 🚫 R.8

Cosy house built in 1930, near the Musée du Québec; you'll admire the river and greenery of the Plains of Abraham as you walk towards the old city. Exquisite breakfast, served in the flowery garden or the dining room. We'll chat about the history of our beautiful city and about what you like. Free parking.

From Montréal, Hwy 20, Pierre-Laporte bridge, twd downtown. 8km from the bridge, left on Av. Murray. From Hwy 40, Avenue St-Sacrement South Exit, left on Chemin St-Louis, 1.3km, left on Av. Murray.

B&B
À LA CAMPAGNE EN VILLE

**Marie Archambault
1160, avenue Murray**
Québec G1S 3B6
(418) 683-6638
www.quebecweb.com/gpq/
alacampagneenville

B&B	
single	$60
double	$70
triple	$90
child	$15

Reduced rates: 3 nights or more
Open year round

Number of rooms	2
shared wc	1
shared bathrooms	1

Activities: 🏛 ⛵ 🚶 🚴 🎿

30. QUÉBEC

☀☀☀ F E 🚫 P R.2

Discover enchantment in this beautiful, turn-of-the-century Tudor-style home, near national parks and Vieux-Québec. Top-quality lodging under a gabled roof. Private parking, sheltered in winter months. Office and internet computer facilities upon request. Discrete, personal attention to travellers' needs.

From Montréal, Hwy 20 East to Québec City. After the Pierre-Laporte bridge, follow Boul. Laurier to old Québec. Turn left onto Ave. Moncton at the Plains of Abraham.

B&B
À LA MAISON TUDOR

J. Cecil Kilfoil
1037, avenue Moncton
Québec (QC) G1S 2Y9
(418) 686-1033
fax (418) 686-6066
www.clic.net/~ckilfoil
ckilfoil@clic.net

B&B	
single	$70-90
double	$80-90
triple	$100-110
child	$15

Taxes extra VS MC ER

Reduced rates: Oct. 15 to Dec18
and Jan. 5 to June 22
Open year round

Number of rooms	2
shared wc	1
shared bathrooms	1

Activities: 🏛 🚶 🚴 🎿 🎿

31. QUÉBEC

☀☀☀ F E 🚭 P 🚗 R.1 TA

Stone house dating from 1830, 200m from the walls of the old city and the convention centre (Centre des Congrès). Lively family atmosphere full of surprises. Garden in summer, a crackling fire in winter, old-fashioned character, cosy, indoor greenery, excellent music and copious breakfasts complete with a serving of helpful tourist advice. Parking.

Hwy 40, Boul. Charest E., twd downtown, right Dorchester, côte d'Abraham, right on Richelieu. Or Hwy 20, pont Pierre-Laporte, Boul. Laurier, left Cartier, right Ste-Foy, left St-Augustin, left Richelieu.

B&B
À L'AUGUSTINE

Caroline Collet and
Kamal Elhaji
775, rue Richelieu
Québec G1R 1K8
tel/fax (418) 648-1072
**www.oricom.ca/augustine/
bb.html**
carocol@oricom.ca

B&B	
single	$50-55
double	$65-70
triple	$80-85
child	$15

Open year round

Number of rooms	3
shared bathrooms	2

Activities: 🏛 🎿 🚲 🛷 🎿

32. QUÉBEC

☀☀☀ F E 🚭 🛶 🐕 R.5 TA

Located in the Old Quebec, nearby governmental, historical and cultural sites, come and live in an ancestral house... Au Croissant de Lune, for your comfort and pleasure, we offer you: nice antique furnished rooms, a library, a terrace and a delicious breakfast. A haven of peace in a city of festivals!

Hwy 20, Pierre-Laporte bridge, Boul. Laurier, left Rue Cartier, right on Chemin Ste-Foy, right on Rue des Zouaves, right on Rue St-Gabriel.

B&B
AU CROISSANT DE LUNE

Louise St-Laurent and
René Gilbert
594, rue St-Gabriel
Québec G1R 1W3
(418) 522-6366
www.bbcanada.com/2396.html
aucroissantdelune@hotmail.com

B&B	
single	$60
double	$75
triple	$90
child	$0-15

VS

Reduced rates: Nov. 1 to Dec. 20,
Feb.15 to Mar.30
Open year round

Number of rooms	2
shared bathrooms	1

Activities: 🏛 🍷 🛶 🚲 🎿

33. QUÉBEC

☀☀☀ F 🐕 🚗 P R.25

In the heart of the marvellous Montcalm district, near the Plains of Abraham, a stone's throw from Rue Cartier, with restaurants, cafés and shops, "Au Maric" offers you a warm welcome. Quiet and comfortable rooms. Lavish breakfast with music.

Hwy 20, Pierre-Laporte bridge, Boul. Laurier twd downtown. Turn left on Ave. Des érables, after crossing Chemin Ste-Foy or Hwy 40, right on Rue de l'Aqueduc, right on Rue des Franciscains.

B&B
AU MARIC

Micheline Rioux
470, rue des Franciscains
Québec G1S 2R1
(418) 688-9341

B&B	
single	$55
double	$65
triple	$85

Open: May 1 to Oct. 31

Number of rooms	2
shared bathrooms	1

Activities: 🏛 🛶 🚣 🚶 🚲

34. QUÉBEC

☀☀☀ | F | E | 🚭 | 🚗 | P | R.6 | TA

Give in to the sweet pleasure of living and the quiet ambiance of our Victorian house (1830), just steps away from the sights of Vieux-Québec, the Grand Théâtre and the conference centre. Spacious rooms decorated with warmth and meticulous comfort. Gourmet breakfast, parking lot.

Hwy 20, P-Laporte Bridge, Boul. Laurier Exit, 7.8km, left on Claire Fontaine, 400m, turn right on Burton. Hwy 40, Boul. Charest East, turn right on Langelier, go up Salaberry, turn left on St-Jean; at the second light, turn right on Claire Fontaine and 2nd left on Burton.

B&B
AU PETIT ROI

Khalid El-Haji
445, rue Burton
Québec G1R 1Z8
tel/fax (418) 523-3105
www.bbcanada.com/petitroi
petitroi@oricom.ca

B&B	
single	$55-60
double	$65-80
triple	$80-100

Reduced rates: 1 pers/$50 and 2 pers/$65 from Oct.1 to May 31, except from Dec. 25 to Jan. 5 and from Jan. 30 to Feb.12
Open year round

Number of rooms	3
shared bathrooms	2

Activities: 🏛 ⛵ 🎣 🍂 🚲

---

35. QUÉBEC

☀☀☀ | F | E | 🚭 | P | R.25 | TA

In Quebec City, people choose "the Pied à Terre" for its comfort and tranquillity. After a most exquisite breakfast, set off on the right foot for a walk to the heart of Vieux-Québec (35min); the Plains of Abraham, museums, Cartier and Grande-Allée streets, Château Frontenac. Free parking. Steps away from bus routes.

Hwy 20, P-Laporte Bridge, Boul. Laurier, drive 6km, turn left on Belvédère, right on René-Lévesque, left on Casot. Or Hwy 40, Ave. St-Sacrement South, turn left on Chemin Ste-Foy, drive 1.8km.

B&B
AU PIED À TERRE À QUÉBEC

Nicole Marcotte
810, rue Casot
Québec G1S 2X9
(418) 687-1986
fax (418) 527-3797
www.quebecweb.
com/aupied/introfranc.html
n.marcotte@sympatico.ca

B&B	
single	$55-65
double	$70-85
triple	$85-100
quad.	$115
child	$10

Reduced rates: 10 days and more
Open year round

Number of rooms	3
shared bathroom	1
room with private wc	1
room with private bath	1

Activities: 🏛 ⛵ 🚲 🏃 ⛷

---

36. QUÉBEC

☀☀☀☀ | F | E | P | 🚗 | 🚭 | 🐕 | R1 | TA

In downtown Québec City, a neighbourhood with European charm, restaurants, cafés and boutiques. Located just 2 min from the Plains of Abraham and the Museum of Québec. Old Québec City is a 10-min walk away. Gourmet breakfast. See colour photos.

Hwy 20, Pierre-Laporte bridge, Boul. Laurier to downtown (Grande-Allée). 8.7km after the bridge, turn on Cartier, then left on Saunders. Or Hwy 40, Boul. Charest East, right on St-Sacrement South, left on Chemin Ste-Foy, right on Rue Cartier, right on Rue Saunders.

B&B
AUX TROIS BALCONS

Chantal Javaux and
Paul Simard
130, rue Saunders
Québec G1R 2E3
(418) 525-5611
fax (418) 529-6227
www.troisbalcons.qc.ca
chantaljavaux@sympatico.ca

B&B	
single	$55-65
double	$70-90
triple	$85-100
quad.	$110
child	$10

Taxes extra VS MC

Reduced rates: 7 consecutives nights for the price of 6
Open year round

Number of rooms	4
rooms with private bath	3
shared bathrooms	1

Activities: 🏛 ⛵ 🚲 🎿 ⛷

37. QUÉBEC

★ ★ | F | E | R.1 | TA

Magnificent Victorian home just steps from old Québec City in the heart of the Faubourg St-Jean-Baptiste: historic, artistic and early settlement district. I am a professional artist. Large, comfortable rooms. 2 rooms with private bathroom, two double beds and fridge. 3 rooms with private but separate bathroom, good ventilation. Copious breakfast.

Boul. Laurier to Québec City. After the parliament, Hwy Dufferin to the left, right on Rue St-Jean. Left at the first traffic lights, Rue d'Aiguillon. Cross Dufferin again to Côte St-Geneviève.

B&B
B&B CHEZ PIERRE

Pierre Côté
636, rue d'Aiguillon
Québec G1R 1M5
(418) 522-2173
welcome.to/chezpierre

B&B	
single	$60-85
double	$70-95
triple	$100-120
quad.	$125-145

Taxes extra VS MC

Open: Jan. 14 to Oct. 10

Number of rooms	7
rooms with private bath	5
rooms with sink	1
shared bathrooms	1

Activities: 🏛 ⛴ 🎣 🚲 🎿

38. QUÉBEC

🌞🌞🌞🌞 | F | e | 🚭 | 🐕 | 🚗 | P | R.5 | TA

Located on a peaceful street in the heart of a lively area a short distance from the Plains of Abraham, Grande-Allée, Grand-Théâtre, and a 10 min walk from Vieux-Québec and the convention centre. A few rooms with queen-size beds and living rooms available. Hearty breakfasts. Discount for stays of three nights or longer. Free parking.

From Montréal, Hwy 20, P.-Laporte bridge, Boul. Laurier to downtown. Left on Ave. de la Tour 8.8km from the bridge. Or, Hwy 40, right on Rue St-Sacrement Sud, left on Chemin St-Louis, 2.6km.

B&B
B&B DE LA TOUR

Hugette Rodrigue and
André Blanchet
1080, avenue de la Tour
Québec G1R 2W7
(418) 525-8775
www.quebecweb.com/bbdelatour
bbdelatour@qc.aira.com

B&B	
single	$55-60
double	$70-75
triple	$90
child	$15

Reduced rates: 3 nights and more
Open: Jan. 11 to Dec. 9

Number of rooms	3
rooms with sink	2
shared bathrooms	2

Activities: 🏛 ⛴ 🚶 🚲 🎿

39. QUÉBEC

🌞🌞🌞 | F | e | 🐕 | R.3 | TA

In the heart of Vieux-Québec (leave the car behind for a few days), a Quebec family welcomes you, sharing the quiet and comfort of their home and charming rooms with TV. The smell of croissants and eggs will lead you to the dining room, where you can enjoy a pleasant chat over breakfast. Free Internet access.

Hwy 20, Pierre-Laporte bridge, Boul. Laurier Exit toward Vieux-Québec. After the Porte St-Louis, at the traffic light, turn right on Rue d'Auteuil, left on Rue Ste-Geneviève and left on Rue des Grisons.

B&B
B&B DES GRISONS

Claudine Desbois and
Jocelyn Santerre
1, rue des Grisons
Québec G1R 4M6
(418) 694-1461
fax (418) 694-9204
bbcanada.com/2608.html
jsanterr@videotron.ca

B&B	
single	$60
double	$65-85

MC

Reduced rates: 3 nights and more
Open year round

Number of rooms	3
shared bathroom	2

Activities: 🏛 🍷 ⛴ 🚲 🏊

40. QUÉBEC

F E R1 TA

Warm house located on a quiet street near services, restaurants, university, hospitals, shopping centres, 5 minutes from the Old City. Family ambiance, facilities for children, queen size bed. Healthy breakfast served in our dining room. Storage for skis and bikes. Private entrance, microwave, refrigirator, launderette.

Hwy 20, Pierre-Laporte bridge, downtown Québec City twd Boul. Laurier. Past Université Laval, turn left on Ave. Des Gouverneurs, left on Boul. René Lévesque, left on Madeleine-de-Verchères.

B&B

B&B LA BEDONDAINE

Sylvie and Gaétan Tessier
912, rue Madeleine-de-Verchères
Québec G1S 4K7
(418) 681-0783
www.bbcanada.com/2851.html

B&B	
single	*$45-50*
double	*$55-65*
triple	*$75-85*
child	*$10*

VS

Reduced rates: *10% Nov. 1 to Apr. 30, 5 night and more*
Open year round

Number of rooms	3
rooms with private bath	*1*
rooms in semi-basement	*2*
shared bathroom	*1*

Activities:

41. QUÉBEC

F e P R1

Facing the Plains of Abraham near Vieux-Québec, museums and major places of interest, a beautiful old house with prestigious quartier Montcalm interior, large living room with fireplace, suites with distinctive style and TV, central air-conditioning and private parking. **See colour photos.**

Hwy 20, Pierre-Laporte bridge, Boul. Laurier toward downtown, Chemin St-Louis to Ave. des Laurentides, drive 6km. Or Hwy 40, right on Rue St-Sacrament, continue for 1.5km, left on Chemin St-Louis to Ave. des Laurentides, drive 1.2km.

B&B

B&B MAISON LESAGE

Jean-Luc Lesage and Yves Ruel
760, chemin St-Louis
Québec G1S 1C3
(418) 682-9959
www.bbcanada.com/3282.html
bbmaisonlesageyr@videotron.ca

B&B	
single	*$80*
double	*$100*

Taxes extra VS MC

Open year round

Number of rooms	3
rooms with private bath	*3*

Activities:

42. QUÉBEC

F E P R.1 TA

Prize for Excellence "Special Favorite" Regional 1999. Regional winner of Québec Tourism Grand Prizes for hospitality and customer service (1995); Classification Hébergement Québec «4 suns». Located at 5 min (1.5km) from «fortified Old Québec». Central air conditioning, pool table, bikes, parking, table d'hôte.

Hwy 20 P. Laporte bridge, or Hwy 40 E., twd Ste-Anne-de-Beaupré, Exit 316, staight ahead untill Chemin de la Canardière.

B&B

CHEZ MONSIEUR GILLES[2]

Gilles Clavet
1720, chemin de la Canardière
Québec G1J 2E3
(418) 821-8778
fax (418) 821-8776
www3.sympatico.ca/mgilles
mgilles@sympatico.ca

B&B	
single	*$78-87*
double	*$78-87*
triple	*$98-118*
quad.	*$118-138*
child	*$20*

Taxes extra VS ER

Open year round

Number of rooms	5
rooms with sink	*2*
rooms with private bath	*3*
shared wc	*2*
shared bathrooms	*1*

Activities:

43. QUÉBEC

In a warm and unique setting in the very heart of Quebec City, Jean-Claude invites you to discover his bed and breakfast full of unforgettable little considerations. A few minutes' walking distance from Vieux-Québec, with all the sights of this charming city at hand. Hoping to have the pleasure of welcoming you here very soon.

From Montreal, Hwy 20, Pierre-Laporte bridge, Hwy Henri IV North, Hwy Charest East twd downtown. Turn left on Rue de la Couronne and left at the 2nd light.

B&B
COUETTE ET CAFÉ LE 253

Jean-Claude Guillemette
253, rue de la Reine
Québec G1K 2R1
(418) 647-0590
jeanclaude@oricom.ca

B&B	
single	$50
double	$65
triple	$90
child	$15

VS MC IT

Reduced rates: *10% Oct. 1 to Mar. 31*
Open year round

Number of rooms	3
shared bathrooms	2
rooms with sink	3

Activities: 🏛 🏊 🎣 🚴 ⛷

44. QUÉBEC

Gîte du Parc is a century-old home bathed in the tranquillity of the Montcalm area, 2 min from the Plains of Abraham, le Musée du Québec and a stone's throw from Vieux-Québec. You will be delighted by our friendly welcome, helpful tourist information on Québec City, spacious, attractively decorated rooms, copious breakfasts and free parking. See color photos.

From Montréal, Hwy 20, Pierre-Laporte bridge, exit Boul. Laurier. Left on Des Érables, then left Rue Fraser.

B&B
GÎTE DU PARC

Henriette Hamel and René Thivierge
345, rue Fraser
Québec G1S 1R2
(418) 683-8603
fax (418) 683-8431
www.quebecweb. com/giteduparc
rene.giteduparc@sympatico.ca

B&B	
single	$60-70
double	$70-85
triple	$85-100

Open year round

Number of rooms	3
room with private bath	1
room with sink	1
shared bathroom	1

Activities: 🏛 🎣 🏊 🎿 ⛷

45. QUÉBEC

Ancestral Irish house (1832) in the historic district (UNESCO), beneath the Plains of Abraham and the Citadelle, a 10min walk from Petit Champlain. Quiet street, free outdoor parking. Private entrance, romantic rooms with decor and cachet of yesteryear, queen-size beds, shared bathrooms exclusively for guests. Incomparable breakfasts. Private bathroom available. Ideal for families, friends, honeymoons, etc. See colour photos.

Hwy 20, 40 or 73, Pierre-Laporte bridge, Exit 132 Boul. Champlain to Boul. Champlain, left at sixth light, Rue Champlain, 1km from the ferry.

B&B
HAYDEN'S WEXFORD HOUSE

Louise and Jean-François
450, rue Champlain
Québec G1K 4J3
(418) 524-0524
fax (418) 648-8995
www.bbcanada.com/ haydenwexfordhouse
haydenwexfordhouse@ videotron.net

B&B	
single	$85-125
double	$85-125
triple	$160
quad.	$180

Taxes extra VS MC

Open year round

Number of rooms	3
shared wc	3
shared bathrooms	2

Activities: 🏛 🏊 🚗 🚴 ⛷

46. QUÉBEC

F e 🚭 🐕 🚗 P R4 TA

French artist's home located in "Upper Town" and in the cultural heart of Québec City. Personalised welcome, cosiness, relaxation, tranquillity and security. Special meals (for diabetics). Two cats. Near most tourist attractions, shops, boutiques, restaurants.

Chemin Ste-Foy to "Vieux Québec". Turn left on Rue Désy street. La Coule Douce is on Dolbeau street, 2nd street on your left.

B&B
LA COULE DOUCE

Michel Champagne
473, rue Dolbeau
Québec G1S 2R6
(418) 527-2940
fax (418) 527-0288

B&B	
single	$55
double	$70
triple	$100
quad.	$130

Open year round

Number of rooms	2
shared bathrooms	1

Activities: 🏛 🍴 ⛴ 🚲 🏊

---

47. QUÉBEC

☀☀☀ F e 🐕 P R.5 TA

Charming house with view of the river located in a historic district, near the Plains of Abraham, Place Royale, renowned places of interest and restaurants. Opposite a park with public pool, cycling path. Very lovely and comfortable rooms, canopy beds, balcony, free parking, flowery courtyard and lavish breakfasts indoors or outdoors.

Hwy 20, Pierre-Laporte bridge, Exit 132, Boul. Champlain, left at 6th traffic light onto Rue Champlain, at the foot of the Cap-Blanc stairway. 1km, then left of the Québec City-Lévis ferry (opposite the park).

B&B
L'ANSE DES MÈRES

Linda Pelchat
553, rue Champlain
Québec G1K 4J4
(418) 649-8553
fax (418) 649-0940
www.anse-des-meres.qc.ca
info@anse-des-meres.qc.ca

B&B	
single	$50-100
double	$75-120
triple	$100
quad.	$130
child	$30

VS AM

Reduced rates: Nov.15 to Jan.15
Open year round

Number of rooms	3
shared wc	1
shared bathrooms	2

Activities: 🏛 🍴 ⛴ 🎣 🚲

---

48. QUÉBEC

☀☀☀ F E 🚭 🚗 R1 TA

Downtown, 2 min from old Québec City, a former schoolhouse (historic monument, 1849) serves as a setting for a comfortable stay in the old capital. Lovely garden, warm fireplace and good local-style breakfast. In our studio, learn about etching and silk-screen printing. Near businesses, cultural events, transport. Come discover our «secret garden».

After the Parliament, left on Honoré-Mercier, then eastbound Hwy Dufferin, Exit 22. At 1st lights, turn left and continue to the end, left to 3e Rue, on the left.

B&B
LE JARDIN SECRET

André Lemieux
and Yves Dumaresq
699 and 701, 3ᵉ Rue
Québec G1J 2V5
(418) 640-7321
tel/fax (418) 529-5587
atelier.alemieux@sympatico.ca

B&B	
single	$55-70
double	$65-80

VS

Open: Apr. 1 to Oct. 31

Number of rooms	3
rooms with private bath	1
shared bathrooms	1

Activities: 🏛 🚶 ⛴ 🚲 🍴

49. QUÉBEC, BEAUPORT

F e P R.5 TA

Panoramic view: St. Lawrence River, Île d'Orléans, Parc Montmorency. All you have to do is cross the street to discover the charms of Parc de la Chute Montmorency with its picnic sites, trails and manor, etc... 10km from old Québec City and 4km from Île d'Orléans. Between Mont-Ste-Anne and Stoneham.

From Montréal, twd Ste-Anne-de-Beaupré, Exit 322, turn left, 2.3km. Corner Royale and Avenue Larue. From the Côte-Nord, twd Montréal, exit 322, facing Manoir Montmorency.

B&B
EN HAUT DE LA CHUTE
MONTMORENCY

Gisèle and Bertrand Tremblay
2515, avenue Royale
Beauport G1C 1S2
tel/fax (418) 666-4755
gisele@oricom.ca

B&B	
single	$40
double	$55-65
triple	$70-80
child	$10

Open year round

Number of rooms	3
rooms with private bath	1
rooms with sink	2
rooms in basement	2
shared wc	2
shared bathrooms	1

Activities: 🍵 ✍ ⚐ 🚲 🎿

50. QUÉBEC, BEAUPORT

☀☀☀ F E P 🏊 🚫 R.5 TA

Our B&B is located on the oldest road in Québec City, 10 min from old Québec City, 1km from the Montmorency falls, 30 min from Mont-St-Anne. Come relax in the outdoor pool and the large garden. Bike/ski shed. And what a delicious breakfast! Prize for Excellence "Special Favorite" Regional 1998. **See colour photos.**

From Québec City, Hwy 440, Exit 29, Exit 322, left on Boul. des Chutes, left at Esso station, right on Ave. Royale, 0.5km. From Montréal, Hwy 40 East or Hwy 40 West, Rte 73 North and 40 East, Exit 322...

B&B
MAISON ANCESTRALE
THOMASSIN

Madeleine Guay
2161, avenue Royale
Beauport G1C 1N9
(418) 663-6067
toll free 1-877-663-6067
fax (418) 660-8616

B&B	
single	$40
double	$57
triple	$74
quad.	$87
child	$15

Taxes extra

Reduced rates: Nov. 1 to Apr. 30
Open year round

Number of rooms	4
shared bathrooms	2

Activities: 🍵 ⚐ 🏊 🚲 🎿

51. QUÉBEC, BEAUPORT

☀☀☀ F e 🚫 ✕ P R.3 TA

Ancestral house in Old Beauport. Near the Montmorency Falls, Île d'Orléans, the Old City (5 minutes) and Mont-Sainte-Anne (30 minutes). The master chef invites you to partake of a hearty breakfast, table d'hôte delicacies in an art-gallery-like decor.

Hwy 40 twd Ste-Anne-de-Beaupré. Seigneuriale South Exit, right on Ave. Royale. From Old Québec: Hwy Dufferin, Exit François-de-Laval, right on Ave. Royale.

B&B
LA MAISON DUFRESNE

France Collin and Michel Nigen
505, avenue Royale
Beauport G1E 1Y3
(418) 666-4004
toll free 1-877-747-4004
fax (418) 663-0119
www.quebecweb.
com/dufresne
dufresne@mlink.net

	B&B	MAP
single	$55	---
double	$65	$113
triple	$80	$152
child	$15	$25

Taxes extra VS MC

Reduced rates: Nov.1 to Apr. 30
Open year round

Number of rooms	3
rooms with sink	3
shared wc	1
shared bathrooms	1

Activities: 🏛 🚲 ⚐ 🎿 🎿

52. QUÉBEC, BEAUPORT

Warm house over a century old, located in the historic district of Beauport, 5min from Vieux-Québec and Montmorency falls, halfway between Mont-Ste-Anne and Stoneham. Bike paths and hiking trails nearby. Large, family-size room, and suite with kitchen and private entrance. Lavish breakfast, swimming pool and air conditioning.

Hwy 40 East, Exit 320, right on Rue Seigneuriale and right on Ave. Royale. From Vieux-Québec, Hwy 440 East, François de Laval Exit, right on Ave. Royale.

B&B
LE GÎTE DU VIEUX-BOURG

Marielle Viel and
Benoit Couturier
492, avenue Royale
Beauport G1E 1Y1
tel/fax (418) 661-0116
www3.sympatico.ca
/vieux-bourg
vieux-bourg@sympatico.ca

B&B	
single	$55-85
double	$60-95
triple	$75-110
quad.	$115-125
child	$10

VS

Open year round

Number of rooms	5
rooms with private bath	2
rooms with sink	1
shared wc	1
room in basement	1
shared bathrooms	1

Activities: 🐚 🚣 🏃 🚴 🎿

53. QUÉBEC, BEAUPORT

Built in 1875, Manoir Vallée will make your relive the warmth and ambiance of yesteryear. Located 5min from Vieux-Québec and the Montmorency Falls. Relax in our spacious rooms with stone walls and a romantic decor. You will appreciate our old-fashioned breakfasts. Relaxation room, suite with kitchen.

From Montreal, Hwy 40 East, or from Côte-Nord, Hwy 40 West, Exit Rue Labelle, until Royale, right, 10th house facing "Ultramar".

B&B
LE MANOIR VALLÉE

Francine Huot, Kevin Strassburg,
Carlos and Rosalee
907, avenue Royale
Beauport G1E 1Z9
(418) 660-3855
(418) 666-5421
fax (418) 660-8792
kevenstr@total.net

B&B	
single	$65-85
double	$70-95
triple	$75-105
quad.	$90-120
child	$5

Taxes extra VS MC IT

Open year round

Number of rooms	4
rooms with private bath	4

Activities: 🛥 🚣 🏃 🚴 🎿

54. QUÉBEC, BEAUPORT

Le Petit Manoir is located on the historic site of Chute Montmorency, with the St. Lawrence River and Île d'Orléans in the backdrop. Representing living history, this 19th-century bourgeois residence have kept its original allure and character. Bordered by two peaceful streams, the property will seduce you with comfort and make you succumb to its charms. Vieux-Québec and Mont Ste-Anne nearby.

Hwy 40 to Ste-Anne-de-Beaupré, Exit 322, left on Boulevard des Chutes, right on Côte du Moulin.

B&B
LE PETIT MANOIR DU
SAULT MONTMORENCY

Nycole Giroux and
Jean-Pierre Morneau
63, Côte du Moulin
Beauport G1C 2L7
(418) 663-6510
fax (418) 663-8996
petitmanoir@hotmail.com

B&B	
single	$60
double	$75

VS

Reduced rates: Nov.1 to Apr. 30
Open year round

Number of rooms	2
shared bathrooms	1

Activities: 🐚 🏃 🚴 🎿 🏃

55. QUÉBEC, CAP-ROUGE

14 min from Old Puébec, close to the bridges, English-style cottage (1991) A&A· Peaceful and welcoming, with parking, terrace and flower gardens· Nearby: marina, paths along the rivers, art galleries, restaurants, shopping centres· Generous breakfast served by your hosts·

Hwy 20, after the bridges, Exit 133, right on Ch. St-Louis, to the end, 3km, Louis-Francœur is to the right. Or, Hwy 40 Duplessis Hwy Exit Ch. Ste-Foy. Go right, to Louis-Francœur, 2.5km.

B&B
GÎTE LA JOLIE ROCHELLE

Guguette Bouture and
Martin Larochelle
1340, rue Louis-Francœur
Bap-Oouge, Cointe-Rte-Eoy
F1Y 1M5
(318) 543-3325
www-bbcanada-com
/3211-html

B&B	
single	$40
double	$50-54

Open year round

Number of rooms	3
shared wc	1
shared bathrooms	1

Activities:

---

56. QUÉBEC, CAP-ROUGE

Over 200 years old (1722) and near the Rt-Lawrence Oiver, the Feeney house offers a warm ambiance and hearty breakfasts· Ciscover the unique tracel, our water park and enjoy our walks along the river· She newly laid-out Bartier-Ooberval park offers a magnificent view of the Rt-Lawrence Oiver and Bap-Oouge bay· And all this only 20min from Uieux-Puébec·

From Montreal, Hwy 20 East, Pierre-Laporte bridge, Hwy Duplessis Exit, Chemin Ste-Foy Exit toward Cap-Rouge. Go down the hill, follow the river, take Rue St-Félix after the stop sign.

B&B
LA MAISON FEENEY

Louise Eortier and
André Létourneau
3342, rue Rt-Félix
Bap-Oouge F1Y 3A4
(318) 541-3970
www-bbcanada-
com/2744-html
maisonfeeney@sympatico-ca

B&B	
single	$40
double	$50
triple	$74
quad-	$90
child	$12

Open year round

Number of rooms	3
rooms with sink	2
shared wc	1
shared bathrooms	1

Activities:

---

57. QUÉBEC, CAP-ROUGE

Large house (comfort, quiet, rest) 14km from old Puebec Bity· Uaried, all-you-can-eat homemade breakfast· Orivate living room· Eree parking· Elower garden, whirlpool bath· Nearby: golf course, footpath, Rt- Lawrence Oiver, marina, art gallery, big shopping centre· Eamily suite (kitchenette, private bathroom)·

From Montréal: Hwy 20 East, Pierre-Laporte bridge, Chemin St-Louis West Exit to Louis Francoeur. Left on Chemin Ste-Foy, Rue St-Félix, right on Rue du Golf. Or, Rte 138 to Cap-Rouge.

B&B
L'HYDRANGÉE BLEUE

Yvan Cenis
1341, rue du Folf
Bap-Oouge F1Y 2S5
(418) 657-5609
fax (318) 547-7918

B&B	
single	$34-40
double	$40-50
triple	$54-74
quad-	$80-90
child	$10

Open year round

Number of rooms	2
rooms with private bath	1
shared bathrooms	1
rooms in basement	1

Activities:

58. QUÉBEC, STE-FOY ☀☀☀ F E 🚭 🚗 P R1 TA

Only a few minutes from downtown and not far from the airport, Le Gîte du Centenaire is a spectacular century-old home with a magnificent location in a rural area. Country-style breakfast. Large property with fruit trees, vegetable garden and flowers. Great variety of activities such as hiking, snowmobiling, horseback riding, golfing and summer theatre.

Hwy 40, Exit Rte 138 East, Exit Boulevard Hamel, 298 East, left on Rue Labelle for 1km. Hwy 20 Pierre-Laporte bridge, Duplessis Exit. Exit left on Boulevard Hamel, right on Rue Labelle for 1km.

B&B
B&B DU CENTENAIRE

Claire Harvey
1204, rue Labelle
Ste-Foy G2E 3L9
tel/fax (418) 872-4818
pages.infinit.net/lauclair/gite

B&B	
single	$40
double	$60
child	$10

Reduced rates: Oct. 30 to Apr. 30
Open year round

Number of rooms	2
shared wc	1
shared bathrooms	1

Activities: 🏛 🍁 🚤 🛶 🚲

59. QUÉBEC, STE-FOY ☀☀☀ F E 🚭 P 🚗 R.3 TA

Ten minutes from Old Québec City, quiet residential district, access to highways. Warm ambiance, comfortable rooms with sink, generous breakfast. Walking distance from Université Laval, big shopping centres, public transport, cinema, restaurants. Free and easy parking.

From Montréal, Hwy 20, take Pierre Laporte bridge, Exit Boul. Laurier, right at 5th light onto Rue Jean De Quen to Rue Lapointe. Hwy 40, Exit Hwy Duplessis South, Boul. Laurier, right at 5th light...

B&B
LA MAISON LECLERC

Nicole Chabot
and Conrad Leclerc
2613, rue Lapointe
Ste-Foy G1W 3K3
tél/fax (418) 653-8936
sans frais 1-866-653-8936
www.bbcanada.
com/2693.html
lamaisonleclerc@videotron.ca

B&B	
single	$40
double	$55
child	$0-15

VS MC

Reduced rates: 3 nights and more, and Nov. 1 to May 31
Open year round

Number of rooms	5
rooms with sink	2
rooms in basement	2
shared bathrooms	2

Activities: 🏛 🚤 🎣 🚲 🎿

60. QUÉBEC, STE-FOY ☀☀ F 🚭 P R.5 TA

House located in the heart of the town of Ste-Foy, 1km from the Pierre-Laporte bridge. Very close to the largest shopping centres in Québec City, the bus terminal, the post office, banks, hospitals. Chilean-style breakfast available. We speak Spanish very well.

After the Pierre-Laporte bridge twd downtown Québec City, Boul. Laurier Exit. At the 2nd traffic lights, turn left, right on Rue Légaré, and right again on the next street.

B&B
MAISON DINA

Dina Saéz-Velozo
2850, rue Fontaine
Ste-Foy G1V 2H8
(418) 652-1013

B&B	
single	$45
double	$55
child	$12

Open: June 1 to Oct. 30

Number of rooms	3
rooms in basement	2
shared bathrooms	2

Activities: 🏛 🍁 🚤 🛶 🚲

61. QUÉBEC, STE-FOY

✹✹✹ F e P 🚗 R.1 TA

Canadian-style house located in a calm residential neighborhood, near services, shopping centre, public transport and expressways. 5 min from the airport and Université Laval. 10 min from old Québec City. Warm atmosphere, comfortable rooms, living room, copious breakfast, central air conditioning system. Welcome. Prize for Excellence "Special Favorite" Regional 1994-95.

From Montréal, Hwy 20 East to Québec City, Pierre-Laporte bridge, Boul. Laurier Exit. 1st traffic lights, turn right on Rue Lavigerie, at the 3rd street, right on Rue de la Seine.

B&B
MONIQUE ET ANDRÉ
SAINT-AUBIN

Monique and André
Saint-Aubin
3045, rue de la Seine
Ste-Foy G1W 1H8
(418) 658-0685
fax (418) 658-8466
www.qbc.clic.net/~staubin
staubin@qbc.clic.net

B&B	
single	$45
double	$60
triple	$80
child	$10

Open year round

Number of rooms	3
shared bathrooms	3

Activities: 🏛 ◑ 🚤 🎿 🏃

62. QUÉBEC, SILLERY

✹✹✹ F E P 🚫 R.2 TA

White, English-style house dating back to the 1930s surrounded by hundred-year-old trees. Exceptional neighbourhood. Fireplace, terrace, large rooms, king and queen-size beds. Varied, home-made breakfast. Nearby: Université de Laval, Plains of Abraham, old Québec City and just steps from Cataraqui. Welcome. **See color photos.**

Hwy 20, Pierre-Laporte Bridge, Boul Laurier to Québec City. 3.9km from bridge right on Rue Maguire. Right on Ch. St-Louis. Hwy 40, Boul. Duplessis South Exit to Boul. Laurier...

B&B
B&B LES CORNICHES

Francine C. DuSault
2052, chemin St-Louis
Sillery, Québec G1T 1P4
(418) 681-9318
fax (418) 681-4028
www.quebecweb.
com/gpq/bblescorniches/

B&B	
single	$55
double	$65-80
triple	$95
child	$15

VS

Open year round

Number of rooms	3
rooms with private bath	1
shared bathrooms	2

Activities: 🏛 🚤 🏃 🚲 🏃

63. QUÉBEC, WENDAKE

✹✹✹ F E P 🚗 R.25 TA

Century-old house where the past mingles with the present. Friendly atmosphere, in which Native art transports guests back in time. Breakfast with a Huron flavour. The Bear, Wolf and Turtle Rooms await you. Located in the heart of the old village of Huron-Wendat, which you can explore, and 15min from Québec City and area ski resorts. Guided tours of historic sites.

From Québec City, Hwy 73 and Hwy 369 to Lorettteville. The B&B is located on a street parallel to Boul. Bastien, right Rue Gabriel Vincent and you're there.

B&B
LA MAISON AORHENCHE

Line Gros-Louis
90, rue François Gros-Louis,
C.P. 110, Wendake G0A 4V0
(418) 847-0646
fax (418) 847-4527
www.quebecweb.
com/aorhenche
aorenche@sympatico.ca

B&B	
single	$55-65
double	$75-86
triple	$95-106
quad.	$126
child	$15

Open year round

Number of rooms	3
rooms with private bath	1
shared bathrooms	1

Activities: 🏛 🏃 🚶 🚲 🐕 🛶

64. ST-GABRIEL-DE-VALCARTIER ☀☀☀☀ F E 🚭 🐾 🚗 P 🏊 R8 TA

A little corner of paradise 30min from Vieux-Québec. Ecotourism holiday resort, large flowery gardens, panoramic view. Indoor pool, tennis, barbecue, gazebo. A former farm whose buildings have been turned into comfortable homes, rooms, suite, studios. Rustic cachet, woodwork and antique furniture. Lavish, all-you-can-eat breakfasts, homemade goods and products from the kitchen garden. Near Village Vacances Valcartier, dogsledding, golf. **See colour photos.**

In Quebec City, Hwy 73 and 175 twd Chicoutimi, Exit 167, Rte 371, 20km.

B&B
LE GÎTE DES EQUERRES

Annette Légaré
171, 5e Avenue Rte 371
St-Gabriel-de-Valcartier
G0A 4S0
(418) 844-2424
toll free 1-877-844-2424
fax (418) 844-1607
www.auxancienscanadiens.
qc.ca/gite.html
gite@auxanciens
canadiens.qc.ca

B&B	
single	$65-75
double	$80-90
triple	$95-105
quad.	$110-120
child	$10

Taxes extra VS MC

Open year round

Number of rooms	5
rooms with private bath	5

Activities: 🚣 🏃 🐎 🎿 🛷

---

65. ST-JOACHIM ☀☀☀☀ F E 🚭 🐾 P R10

A Quebec-style house from 1825, rooms with refined decor, bucolic vista, 700-acre property, trails, private falls, "Produit du Terroir" apple orchard. Rest and relaxation assured. Angora goats, wild sheep, poultry. Substantial breakfast. Specialties: organic apple juice, fresh eggs, maple syrup, pancakes, jams made with home-grown fruit, "tête aux pieds". Visit Cap Tourmente and the Ste-Anne-de-Beaupré basilica. Ski Mont-Ste-Anne and Massif. In winter, group dinner by reservation only.

Rte 138 East toward Beaupré. Follow signs for St-Joachim, Cap Tourmente.

B&B
À L'ABRI DE LA TOURMENTE

Marie-Christine Perreault and
Jean-Nil Bouchard
200, chemin Cap Tourmente
St-Joachim G0A 3X0
(418) 827-3025
toll free 1-888-530-3025
fax (418)827-3694
www.abridelatourmente.com
info@abridelatourmente.com

B&B	
single	$80-110
double	$95-125
triple	$145

Taxes extra VS MC

Reduced rates: 10% 5 nights and more
Open: June 1 to Oct. 31
(Dec 1 to May 31 with reservation, group of 8 to 12 only)

Number of rooms	5
rooms with private bath	5

Activities: 🏛 🍴 🏃 🎿 🏃

---

66. ST-RAYMOND ☀☀☀ F E 🚭 ♿ ✕ P 🏊 R.2 TA

Lovely early-20th-century brick house surrounded by equally charming neighbours. A short bike ride away from the cycling path, three strides from nature (canoeing, hiking, snowmobiling, skiing, hang-gliding...). Colours, local flavours and exotic aromas mingle here.

Hwy 40, Rte 365 North, at first light in the village, turn right after the church. By bike: St-Raymond Exit toward downtown. By snowmobile: via trail 365.

INN
LA VOISINE

Odile Pelletier and
Denis Baribault
443, rue Saint-Joseph
Saint-Raymond G3L 1K1
(418) 337-4139
toll free 1-877-737-4139
fax (418) 337-3109
www.lavoisine.com
voisine@globetrotter.net

B&B	
single	$40-50
double	$54-64
triple	$68-78
child	$14

VS MC IT

Open year round

Number of rooms	5
rooms with sink	5
rooms with private bath	1
shared wc	1
shared bathrooms	2

Activities: 🏃 🚴 🛷 🐎

67. STE-ANNE-DE-BEAUPRÉ

☀☀☀ F e P ⊘ R1 TA

Prize for Excellence "Special Favorite" Regional 2000. Pretty country home (attic from 1909), 10min from Mont-Ste-Anne, 20min from Quebec City, near Cap Tourmente, the Canyon and Sept Chutes. Refined breakfast (garden products) served in the solarium, with view of the river and Île d'Orléans. Cozy, carefully decorated rooms. Fireplace. Small farm: goats, rabbits...

From Quebec City, Rte 138 East to Ste-Anne-de-Beaupré. 6km from Château-Richer, past the bee museum, at the light, Rue Paré. Right on Ave. Royale.

B&B
LA MAISON D'ULYSSE

Carole Trottier and
Raymond Allard
9140, av. Royale
Ste-Anne-de-Beaupré G0A 3C0
(418) 827-8224
lamaisondulysse
@sympatico.ca

B&B	
single	$45-55
double	$60-65
triple	$80
child	$0-15

Taxes extra VS MC

Open year round

Number of rooms	4
rooms with sink	2
rooms with private bath	1
shared bathrooms	2

Activities: 🏛 🚶 🎿 🏃 🚴

68. SHANNON

☀☀☀ F E 🐕 P 🍽 R1

On the Jacques-Cartier River, 15min from the Pierre-Laporte Bridge, in a relaxing setting, fishers angle for trout or salmon. Located 0.4km from the bike path and the snowmobile trail, 10km from the Germain beach, the Village-Vacances Valcartier, golfing, cross-country and downhill skiing. Pedal boats and rowboats available, bike rentals.

From Quebec City, Henri IV North Hwy, which becomes Rte 573 North, twd Shannon, turn right on Rue Gosford, drive 1km, turn left on Rue Dublin, drive 2km, turn left on Rue Riverside.

B&B
LE GÎTE AU BORD
DE LA RIVIÈRE

Gaétane Bouchard-James
17, rue Riverside
Shannon G0A 4N0
(418) 844-2328
www.multim.com/giteriviere/
gite@multim.com

	B&B	MAP
single	$50-55	$70-75
double	$55-60	$95-100
child	$15	$30

Open year round

Number of rooms	3
room with private bath	1
shared bathrooms	2
rooms in basement	2

Activities: 🎣 🛶 🚴 ⛷ 🎿

69. ST-ADOLPHE-DE-STONEHAM

☀☀☀ F e P 🏊 ⊘ R7 TA

Farming bed and breakfast independent of our house, near Vieux-Québec and Parc de la Jacques-Cartier. Guests are greeted with maple toffee. Hiking trails, river, lake with wriggling trout, rockery and abundant greenery. Guided tour to the maple grove and sugar shack. **Farm stay p 54. See colour photos.**

From Quebec City, Hwy 73 North twd Chicoutimi. At the end of Rte 73, do not take any exit, but drive 7km along Rte 175 to the St-Adolphe sign. Turn right on Rue St-Edmond, drive 3.5km.

B&B
AUBERGE DE LA FERME
ST-ADOLPHE

Jocelyne Couillard and
George Legendre
1035, rue St-Edmond
Stoneham, St-Adolphe
G0A 4P0
(418) 848-2879
fax (418) 848-6949
www.qbc.clic.net/
~geleg/auberge/
geleg@qbc.clic.net

B&B	
single	$45
double	$55
triple	$75
child	$15

Taxes extra

Open year round

Number of rooms	3
shared bathrooms	2

Activities: 🎣 🚶 🐎 ⛷ 🎿

70. STONEHAM

☀☀☀ F e P 🚫 R5 TA

Country style house, 20 minutes from Québec City, in the mountains, relive the charming era of little inns when travellers spent the evening telling tales in front of a stone fireplace. Enjoy a night in one of our romantic rooms until it's time for breakfast. Closest B&B to Parc de la Jacques-Cartier.

From Québec City, Hwy 73 N. twd Chicoutimi. Don't exit at 167, Stoneham, intersection with 175 N. but drive 7km to the sign for St-Adolphe. Right on St-Edmond, drive 1.7km.

B&B
AUBERGE LA SAUVAGINE

Francine Beauregard and
Pierre Desautels
544, rue St-Edmond
Stoneham G0A 4P0
(418) 848-6128
www.clic.net/~sauvagin/
sauvagin@clic.net

B&B	
single	$50-70
double	$60-80
triple	$75-100
quad.	$120
child	$20

Reduced rates: 10% 3 nights and more, except from Dec. 20 to Jan. 7 and school holidays
Open year round

Number of rooms	3
rooms with private bath	2
rooms with sink	1
shared bathrooms	1

Activities: 🧍 🐎 🚣 🏃 🐴

71. STONEHAM, ST-ADOLPHE

☀☀☀ F E 🚫 P 🐕 ✖ TA

Overlooking the valley at 1,700 ft. in altitude, our B&B offers a grand view of the Jacques-Cartier mountains. Enjoy Stoneham ski resort, cross-country skiing (Camp Mercier), J.-Cartier Park, rafting, hikes, fall colours. Fine country B&B before Parc des Laurentides. Dinner package Dec. 1 to Mar. 31: 2 nights, 2 dinners, 2 breakfasts for $155/2 pers.

From Québec City, Hwy 73 twd Chicoutimi. Hwy 73 Nord. Do not get off at Exit 167 (Stoneham), but 7km farther at St-Adolphe sign. Turn right on Rue St-Edmond and continue for 5km. Left on Rue Lepire.

B&B
AU SOMMET DES RÊVES

Christine Venditto
and Gilles Benoit
25, rue Lepire
Stoneham G0A 4P0
(418) 848-6154
fax (418) 848-8686
www.bbcanada.com/
2042.html

B&B	
single	$45
double	$60
triple	$80
quad.	$100
child	$12

VS MC

Reduced rates: 10$/room (dbl +), Apr. to June and Sep. to Nov.
Open year round

Number of rooms	3
shared bathrooms	1

Activities: 🧍 🚲 🐕 🎿 🚣

72. CAP-TOURMENTE, MONT-STE-ANNE

| F | E | P | 🏠 | R1 | M7 | TA |

In the heart of Cap-Tourmente, 12 min from Mont Ste-Anne (view of the slopes). House with five guestrooms with private baths, kitchen with dishwasher, family room with fireplace, small sitting room with cable TV, washer and dryer, pool table in the basement. Covered pool in the warm weather, hiking, cross-country skiing and mountain biking. Nearby: skiing, golf, horseback riding, casino, etc. **B&B p 238.**

From Québec City, Hwy. Henri IV North, to 40 East Ste-Anne-de-Beaupré, Rte 138 East, twd St-Joachim, Cap-Tourmente.

COUNTRY HOME
L'OIE DES NEIGES

Gisèle Perron
390, ch. du Cap Tourmente
St-Joachim G0A 3X0
(418) 827-5153
tel/fax (418) 827-2246
www.bbcanada.com/
2690.html
oiedesneiges@hotmail.com

No. houses	1
No. rooms	5
No. people	4-16
WEEK-SUMMER	$900-1500
WEEK-WINTER	$900-1500
W/E-SUMMER	$650-750
W/E-WINTER	$650-750
DAY-SUMMER	$450-500
DAY-WINTER	$450-500

VS

Open year round

Activities: 🚶 🏃 🚴 🛶 🎿

---

73. MONT-STE -ANNE, ST-FERRÉOL

★ ★ ★ | F | E | P | R.5 | M.5 | TA |

Savour the tranquillity of our lovely country homes, ancestral or recent, 30 min from downtown Québec City, at the edge of Charlevoix. Dreamy, legendary spot, in a small typical Québécois town. Houses are well equipped and can comfortably accommodate 4 to 30 people, and even up to 50! We are nestled at the foot of Mt Ste-Anne, a year-round internationally renown resort. **See colour photos.**

1km after Mt Ste-Anne, as you enter the small town of St-Ferréol-les-Neiges.

COUNTRY HOME
CHALETS-VILLAGE
MONT-SAINTE-ANNE

Marie Flynn and Gilles Éthier
C.P. 275
Ste-Anne-de-Beaupré G0A 3C0
tel/fax (418) 650-2030
toll free 1-800-461-2030
Visit us on the Internet:
www.chalets-village.qc.ca

No. house	8
No. rooms	2-8
No. people	4-30
WEEK-SUMMER	$525-2500
WEEK-WINTER	$500-6000
W/E-SUMMER	$150-1300
W/E-WINTER	$180-2000

Taxes extra VS MC

Reduced rates: spring and fall
Open year round

Activities: 🚶 🏃 🛶 🎿 ⛸

FARM ACTIVITIES

Farm stay:

24 LA FERME L'ÉMEULIENNE, Neuville 53

69 AUBERGE DE LA FERME, St-Adolphe 54

Farm Tour :

24 FERME DE L'ÉMEULIENNE, Neuville 46

74 L'ÉCONOMUSÉE DE L'ABEILLE, Château-Richer 45

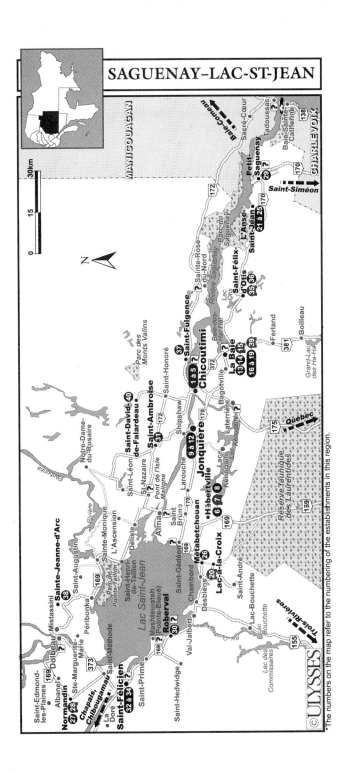

SAGUENAY–LAC-ST-JEAN

The numbers on the map refer to the numbering of the establishments in this region.

© ULYSSES

1. CHICOUTIMI

✹✹✹ | F | e | 🚭 | P | 🐾 | R7

Finalist for Excellence "Special Favorite" Regional 2000. Overlooking a majestic fjord, this very quiet, central B&B is located in one of the most beautiful parts of the region. The rooms are cozy and the varied, abundant breakfasts are served in a solarium/dining room with a panoramic view of the river.

From Quebec City, Rte 175 North twd Chicoutimi. Right on Boul. Université East, near shopping centre, left on Boul. Saguenay, 1ˢᵗ street on the right, Rang St-Martin for 6.8km.

B&B
À LA BERNACHE

Denise Ouellet
3647, rang St-Martin
Chicoutimi G7H 5A7
(418) 549-4960
fax (418) 549-9814
www.gitebernache.com
louis_martel@videotron.ca

B&B	
single	$40
double	$55-60
triple	$75
child	$10-15

Open year round

Number of rooms	4
rooms with sink	3
rooms in basement	1
shared wc	1
shared bathrooms	2

Activities: 🛶 ⛵ 🚶 🚴 🛷

---

2. CHICOUTIMI

✹✹✹ | F | e | 🚭 | 🚗 | P | R.7

Extra comfort. Near downtown, along the Saguenay river. Steps away from restaurants, the Vieux Port, cruises, a bike path and attractions such as the Maison Blanche and the Pulperie (old pulp-and-paper mill). In winter: carnival, park and ice fishing. Breakfast served in a splendid dining room with a panoramic view of the fjord.

From Quebec City, Rte 175 toward Chicoutimi. Boul. Talbot to the end, turn left on Rue Jacques-Cartier, from the hospital corner, keep right, right on Rue Racine, right on Boul. Saguenay.

B&B
À LA PROMENADE

Lisette Blackburn and
Jacques Grenon
782, boul. Saguenay Est
Chicoutimi G7H 1L3
tel/fax (418) 543-9997

B&B	
single	$40
double	$60
triple	$90
child	$15

Open year round

Number of rooms	3
rooms with sink	3
shared wc	1
shared bathrooms	1

Activities: 🏛 🛶 ⛵ 🎿 🚴

---

3. CHICOUTIMI

✹✹✹ | F | e | 🚗 | P | R.3 | TA

If you enjoy the simple things in life, welcome to our home! You are invited to my house surrounded by flowers with an exceptional view of the Saguenay. Delight in a visit to the greenhouses. Cosy comfort, air conditioned rooms and a delicious breakfast will whet your appetite after a good night's rest. Intimacy, calm and pleasures of long ago. A deserved break.

From Québec City, Rte 175 to Chicoutimi. Boul Talbot, left on Boul Université, to the end. Right on Boul St-Paul, at the 2nd traffic lights, left on Rue Price, next traffic lights, left on Boul Saguenay, 1km.

B&B
GÎTE AUX MILLE FLEURS

Ghislaine Morin
976, boul. Saguenay Ouest
Chicoutimi G7J 1A5
(418) 545-9256

B&B	
single	$40
double	$55
child	$15

Open: June 15 to Oct. 15

Number of rooms	3
shared bathrooms	1

Activities: 🛶 ⛵ 🚶 🚴 🐎

4. CHICOUTIMI

☀☀☀ F E 🚭 🐾 🚗 P R.2

Come relax on the veranda of our house in the shade of our magnificent linden tree. Located on an historic street near the cathedral and close to the Saguenay, restaurants and attractions, our home, which was built in 1915, is a haven of peace. The old-fashioned-style rooms are spacious and cosy. Rest, quiet and hearty breakfasts await.

From Québec City, Hwy 175 to Chicoutimi. Boulevard Talbot to the end, turn left on Jacques-Cartier, then right on Rue du Séminaire, 2nd street.

B&B
LA MAISON DU SÉMINAIRE

Gaëtane Harvey
285, rue de Séminaire
Chicoutimi G7H 4J4
(418) 543-4724
fax (418) 545-2195
http://pages.infinit.net/gitesemi
giteseminaire@videotron.ca

B&B	
single	$55
double	$65-69
triple	$85-89
child	$20

MC

Open year round

Number of rooms	3
shared wc	1
shared bathrooms	2

Activities: 🏛 ⛵ 🚣 𝑓 🚴 🚶

5. CHICOUTIMI

☀☀☀ F ♿ P R2 TA

Just east of Chicoutimi on a vast property with a commanding view of the city and the Rivière Saguenay, Le Chardonneret is a comfortable home away from home. Copious breakfasts. Various services 0.6km away: bank, pharmacy, convenience store, gas station. Welcome to my home.

From Québec City, Rte 175 North twd Chicoutimi. Right on Boul. Université East, near the shopping centre, left on Boul. Saguenay. After the Hôtel Parasol, right on Boul. Renaud. 2nd house on the left.

B&B
LE CHARDONNERET

Claire Tremblay
1253, boul. Renaud
Chicoutimi G7H 3N7
(418) 543-9336
lechardonneret@videotron.ca

B&B	
single	$40
double	$55-60
triple	$80
child	$15

Reduced rates: October
Open: May 1 to Feb. 15

Number of rooms	3
rooms with sink	1
shared bathrooms	2

Activities: 🏛 🍁 ⛵ 𝑓 🚴

6. HÉBERTVILLE

★★ F e ♿ P 🚗 ⛷ ❌ TA

Presbytery built in 1917. Historical character and period furniture. Warm reception, intimate dining room, refined cuisine, spacious comfortable and warm rooms with full bathrooms. Conference room, peaceful, calm, inspires creativity. In the heart of the Saguenay-Lac-St-Jean region with its activities. Looking forward to your visit. **See colour photos.**

From Rte 169, (don't go to the town of Hébertville), head twd Mont Lac Vert, 3km. Across from the municipal campground.

AUBERGE
AUBERGE PRESBYTÈRE
MONT LAC VERT

Louise and Gérard Tremblay
335, rang Lac-Vert
Hébertville G8N 1M1
(418) 344-1548
toll free 1-800-818-1548
fax (418) 344-1013
www.geocities.com/aub_presb

	B&B	MAP
single	$50	$70
double	$65	$130
triple	$90	$180
quad.	$105	$225
child	$10	$20

Taxes extra VS MC AM IT

Reduced rates: Oct. 1 to Nov. 30
Apr. 1 to June 1
Open year round

Number of rooms	6
rooms with private bath	6

Activities: 🏛 🍁 🚴 🚣 𝑓

7. HÉBERTVILLE

B&B on the farm, charming welcome. Perfect location for visiting the entire region. Come share in our family life and visit our dairy farm in the shade of Parc des Laurentides. Children welcome. Beach, mountain biking, skating and roller-blading track, fishing, playing field, downhill and cross-country skiing, ice-fishing, inner-tubes sliding. **Farm Stay p 54.**

From Parc des Laurentides, Rte 169. 1st village, Rue St-Isidore.

B&B
FERME CAROLE ET
JACQUES MARTEL

Carole and Jacques Martel
474, St-Isidore
Hébertville G8N 1L7
(418) 344-1323

B&B	
single	$35
double	$45
triple	$65
quad.	$85
child	$10

Open year round

Number of rooms	3
shared bathrooms	2

Activities:

8. HÉBERTVILLE

Visit an area where nature still offers adventure. Ancestral house in French-speaking land welcomes you year round. Activities; fishing cruises on lac St-Jean or a stay in a queenze (igloo) available. Our B&B is located between Tadoussac (70 min), for whale-watching, and the St-Félicien zoo (45 min). We look forward to sharing pleasant family moments with you. Dinner on request.

From Parc des Laurentides, Rte 169 North, 6km, twd Robertval.

B&B
GÎTE BELLE-RIVIÈRE

Marie-Alice Bouchard
872, rang Caron, rte 169
Hébertville G8N 1B6
(418) 344-4345
fax (418) 344-1933
www.bbcanada.
com/2172.html
bouchard@digicom.qc.ca

B&B	
single	$30
double	$45
triple	$65
quad.	$85
child	$10

Open year round

Number of rooms	3
rooms with sink	1
shared bathrooms	2

Activities:

9. JONQUIÈRE

Prize for Excellence "Special Favorite" Regional 1995-96, finalist in 1997-98 and 2000. A 10min walk from downtown. Soundproof rooms, room with sink and TV. At your disposal: Internet, living room with fridge and microwave oven. Breakfast served in the solarium with a magnificent view of the river and the one-of-a-kind aluminum footbridge. Private beach, rowboat, pedal-boat and bike path nearby.

From Quebec City, Rtes 175 and 170, turn left toward Jonquière, drive 11.2km, Boul. Harvey for 2.8km, left on Rue St-Jean-Baptiste, 1.1km, left on Rue des Saules.

B&B
GÎTE DE LA RIVIÈRE
AUX SABLES

Marie and Jean Eudes Girard
4076, rue des Saules
Jonquière G8A 2G7
(418) 547-5101
fax (418) 547-6939
http://pages.infinit.net/riosable
giterivereauxsables
@videotron.ca

B&B	
single	$40-45
double	$55-60
triple	$70-75
quad.	$85-90
child	$10

Open year round

Number of rooms	4
rooms with sink	2
rooms in basement	4
shared bathrooms	2

Activities:

10. JONQUIÈRE

Conveniently located in the heart of Saguenay close to various festivals, our B&B has a garden overflowing with fruits and vegetables, which accompany every breakfast. This peaceful retreat has a homey atmosphere. Little ones will be delighted by its pool. Older folks enjoy walking on the paths that run along Rivière-aux-Sables and Mont-Jacob. Our B&B warmly welcomes you and takes care of your every need.

From Québec City, Rtes 175 and 170, left to Jonquière, 11.2km. Boul.Harvey, 2.8km, left on Rue St-Jean-Baptiste, 0.5km right on Rue Du Pont, left on Rue Ste-Gertrude.

B&B
GÎTE TOURISTIQUE DU MONT-JACOB

Ghislaine and Laurien Tremblay
2313, rue Sainte-Gertrude
Jonquière G8A 1Y1
(418) 547-8934
fax (418) 547-0864

B&B	
single	$40
double	$50
triple	$70
child	$10

Open year round

Number of rooms	3
rooms in basement	1
shared bathrooms	1

Activities: 🏛 🍴 🚲 🛷 🏃

11. JONQUIÈRE

Prize for Excellence "Special Favorite" Regional 1998, finalist in 1999. Great comfort, top-notch decor and furnishings. TV and telephone in every room. Dream garden, in-ground pool and large solarium for your relaxation. Near bar-restaurants, sports centre and college. We welcome groups of up to 14 people.

In downtown Jonquière, at the corner of St-Dominique and Boul. Harvey, head south to the Irving station, turn left on Rue des Hirondelles and left on the first street, Des Merles.

B&B
LE MERLEAU

Andrée Côté and Léo April
2456, rue des Merles
Jonquière G7X 8B3
(418) 542-1093
fax (418) 542-1031

B&B	
single	$45
double	$55
triple	$70
quad.	$85
child	$15

Reduced rates: Sep. 1 to May 31
Open year round

Number of rooms	5
rooms in basement	2
shared bathrooms	3

Activities: 🛥 🚤 🎿 🚲 🐎

12. JONQUIÈRE

Finalist for Excellence "Special Favorite" Regional 2000. Warm welcome in a charming, perfectly comfortable 1900s house. Picturesque, historic Arvida district near Alcan plant, the Manoir, the aluminum bridge and tourist, cultural and sports activities. Near the Québecissime show, with the bike path at our doorstep. Snowmobiling and dogsledding packages available. Original, hearty breakfast.

From Quebec City, Rte 175 N.; in Chicoutimi, Jonquière-bound Rte 170 for 8km, right Rue Mellon, 3km to roundabout, Boul. Saguenay to Jonquière, about 80 m, on the right.

B&B
LE MITAN

Denise F. Blackburn
2840, boul. Saguenay
Jonquière G7S 2H3
(418) 548-7388
fax (418) 548-3415
www.multimania.com/lemitan/
denisefblackburn@hotmail.com

B&B	
single	$45
double	$60-65
child	$20

Open year round

Number of rooms	3
rooms with sink	3
shared bathrooms	2
rooms in basement	1

Activities: 🍴 🛥 🎿 🚲 🎿

13. LA BAIE

☀☀☀ | F | e | 🚗 | P | 🏊 | 🚭 | 🐕 | R3

Located by the water, every room has its own private entrance and balcony, offering a superb view. Walk along the shoreline, watch the tides, discover the artist-host's granite sculptures. Evening beach campfires, for those who so desire. If nature enchants you, one day is not enough. Kayak location on site. Ice-fishing and dog-sledding packages.

From the Parc des Laurentides, Rtes 175 North and 170 East to Boul de la Grande-Baie Sud. After the Musée du Fjord , 5km. From St-Siméon, Rte 170 N. On the water side, a huge granite block marks the entrance.

B&B
À FLEUR DE PIERRE

Colette Létourneau and
Carrol Tremblay
6788, boul. Grande-Baie Sud
La Baie G7B 3P6
(418) 544-3260

B&B	
single	$50
double	$60
triple	$75
quad.	$85
child	$10

Reduced rates: Winter 45$/2 pers.
Open year round

Number of rooms	3
rooms with private bath	1
rooms with sink and shower	2
shared wc	1

Activities: 🛶 🏛 🚤 🎣 🚶

14. LA BAIE

☀☀☀ | F | E | 🚭 | P | 🏊 | R.7 | TA

15,000 square metres of land right at the edge of the water (*au bord de l'eau*), in town, an outstanding location with a spectacular view, spacious rooms, one with whirlpool and one with a kitchenette. Here, the "bay" (*baie*) is the sea; it is a vast stretch of salt water, and its 7-m tides transform the landscape. 5min from the theatre and various activities, but in a world of its own. Hearty breakfasts, homey atmosphere.

From Parc des Laurentides, Rte 175 N., then 170 E. to Boul. Grande-Baie S. 1.5km past the Musée du Fjord. You can't see the house from the road!

B&B
AU BORD DE L'EAU

Lyne Fortin and Réjean Ouellet
5208, boul. Grande-Baie Sud
La Baie G7B 3P6
(418) 544-0892
toll free 1-888-811-0892
fax (418) 544-5432
www3.sympatico.ca/rejean.
ouellet/Home.html
rejean.ouellet@sympatico.ca

B&B	
single	$45-75
double	$60-90
triple	$75-105
quad.	$90-120
child	$10

VS MC

Reduced rates: Sep.1 to May 31
Open year round

Number of rooms	4
rooms with private bath	2
shared bathrooms	1

Activities: 🛶 🚤 🚲 🚤 🎿

15. LA BAIE

☀☀☀ | F | e | 🐕 | 🏊 | P | R2

Come live an incredible experience with the Gagné family at the "Chez Grand-Maman" B&B where you will find tranquillity in picturesque surroundings. You'll experience extraordinary things on our farm by the Baie des HA! HA! We will make you feel at home. **Farm Stay p 54.**

From Parc des Laurentides, Rtes 175 North and 170 East towards "Ville de la Baie", Rue Bagot. Left on Rue Victoria for about 2km. Straight ahead, 1st farm, "Alain Gagné".

B&B
CHEZ GRAND-MAMAN

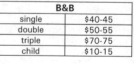

Jacinthe Bouchard and
Alain Gagné
1254, chemin St-Joseph
La Baie G7B 3N9
(418) 544-7396
(418) 697-0517
fax (418) 544-0392

B&B	
single	$40-45
double	$50-55
triple	$70-75
child	$10-15

Open year round

Number of rooms	3
shared bathrooms	2

Activities: 🛶 🚤 🎣 🚲 🎿

16. LA BAIE ☀☀☀ F E P 🚗 🏊 R.1 TA

Prize for Excellence "Special Favorite" Regional 1996-97. Simple, warm exchanges will soon make us fast friends. Located by the water, all rooms have private entrance, patio door and view of the bay. 3 have private bathrooms. Short walk from various activities: cruises, park, restaurants, bike/footpaths. Breakfast in solarium. Ice-fishing packages. Welcome.

From Québec City, Rtes 175 North and 170 East to La Baie. From Rue Bagot, straight ahead, left Rue Victoria, left Rue Damase-Potvin, left on Rue Simard.

B&B
GÎTE BELLE-VUE

Monique and Régent Goyette
1442, Simard
La Baie G7B 2X9
tél/fax (418) 544-4598
bellevue@royaume.com

B&B	
single	$50-60
double	$55-70
triple	$70-85
quad.	$90
child	$15

Reduced rates: 20% Oct.1 to May 31
Open year round

Number of rooms	5
rooms with private bath	3
shared bathrooms	1

Activities: 🍷 🚤 🎿 🚣 🏃

17. LA BAIE ☀☀☀ F 🚗 P R2 TA

To rediscover the charm of the countryside of long ago, drop anchor off l'Anse-à-Benjamin. Near all services: theatre, walking trails, marina, skating rink. Pleasant rooms. Enjoy our B&B winter or summer. Outfitter of fishing cabins. Packages available upon request.

From Parc des Laurentides, Rtes 175 North and 170 East to Ville de la Baie, Rue Bagot. Left on Rue Victoria, keep right for 2km.

B&B
GÎTE DE LA PÊCHE BLANCHE

Laurence Blanchette and
Jean-Claude Simard
1352, route de
l'Anse-à-Benjamin
La Baie G7B 3N9
tel/fax (418) 544-4176

B&B	
single	$40
double	$45-55
triple	$55
child	$10

Open year round

Number of rooms	4
rooms in basement	3
shared bathrooms	2

Activities: 🍷 🚤 🚶 🎿 🛷

18. LA BAIE ☀☀☀ F e 🐕 P 🏊 R.1 TA

What a good idea it is to relax on the terrace, by the heated swimming pool, facing the fjord. Nearby: the Pyramide, a restaurant, church, convenience store, gas station, bike path and snowmobile trail, 1.5km from the Fabuleuse Histoire d'un Royaume, a peaceful place. Welcome.

Rte. 75 North and 170 East, turn right on Boul. Grande Baie South, drive 1.5km. At the Durocher centre, turn right on Rue Mgr. Dufour. Or Rte. 170 West at the light, turn left on Rue Mgr. Dufour. Or Rte. 381, turn right on Chemin St-Jean and left on Mgr. Dufour.

B&B
GÎTE DE LA PYRAMIDE

Hélène Marquis and
Denis Tremblay
2824, rue Mgr. Dufour
La Baie G7B 1E3
(418) 697-1997
tel/fax (418) 697-0582
http://royaume.com/~jessi
jessi@royaume.com

B&B	
single	$50
double	$60
triple	$70
quad.	$80
child	$10

Open year round

Number of rooms	3
shared bathrooms	2
shared wc	1
rooms in semi-basement	3

Activities: 🏛 🚤 🎿 🚲 🏊

19. LA BAIE

☀☀☀ F e 🚗 P R1

Located on the heights of the town of La Baie, in the heart of most activities, our warm and comfortable B&B has acquired an enviable reputation with tourists over the last 10 years. A magnificent landscaped garden offers our guests a quiet haven. Lavish breakfast; motorcycle garage, bicycles at guests' disposal.

From Parc des Laurentides, Rtes 175 North and 170 East to La Baie. Rue Bagot to intersection, left on Rue des Pins.

B&B
GÎTE DES PINS

Doris Bolduc and
Freddy Pouliot
1273, rue des Pins
La Baie G7B 3H7
(418) 544-5178

B&B	
single	$40
double	$50
triple	$60
quad.	$70
child	$10

Reduced rates: May 1 to June 15 and Sep. 1 to Oct. 31
Open: May 1 to Oct. 31

Number of rooms	3
rooms in semi-basement	1
shared bathrooms	2

Activities: 🏛 ⛴ 🎿 🚶 🚲

20. LAC-À-LA-CROIX

F e 🚗 P R8 TA

Century-old farmhouse where we like to keep up traditions: a toast to friends, home-made meals, cows in their pyjamas in the fall. Well-located for touring the region. Traditional recipes to be shared. Cross-country skiing on the farm and near the mountain. **Farm Stay p 55.**

From Parc des Laurentides, Rte 169, 1e Rang on the left before the village of Hébertville, 11km.

B&B
CÉLINE ET GEORGES MARTIN

Céline and Georges Martin
1311, Rang 3
Lac-à-la-Croix G0W 1W0
tel/fax (418) 349-2583

B&B	
single	$28
double	$42
child	$12

Open year round

Number of rooms	3
shared wc	2
shared bathrooms	1

Activities: 🛶 🚲 🏊 🎿 🐎

21. L'ANSE-ST-JEAN

★★★ F E P ☒ TA

Facing the covered bridge, the inn features a large veranda off the rooms. Large living room with fireplace. Recommended (Ulysses guide and French guide) for its game, fish and seafood dishes. Direct access to snowmobile trails; skiing, fjord and ice fishing nearby. Very favourable dinner packages and off-season prices. **Ad end of this region.**

Rte 170 toward L'Anse-St-Jean, Rue St-Jean-Baptiste toward the dock. Located 0.2km from the church, in front of the covered bridge.

INN
AUBERGE DES CÉVENNES

Enid Bertrand and
Louis Mario Dufour
294, rue St-Jean-Baptiste
L'Anse-St-Jean G0V 1J0
(418) 272-3180
toll free 1-877-272-3180
fax (418) 272-1131
auberge-des-cevennes.qc.ca
auberge-des-cevennes
@royaume.com

	B&B	MAP
single	$67	$87
double	$74	$114
triple	$101	$153
quad.	$108	$180

Taxes extra VS MC ER IT

Reduced rates: Sep. 4 to Dec. 21 and Jan. 6 to June 22
Open year round

Number of rooms	8
rooms with private bath	8

Activities: 🚤 🚶 🐎 🚤 🎿

22. L'ANSE-ST-JEAN ☀☀☀ | F | E | ⊘ | P | R3 | TA

Located near Parc du Saguenay and Rivière St-Jean, Gîte Du Barrage de L'Anse has comfortable rooms, a cosy fireplace and scrumptious breakfasts. Views of L'Homme Qui Sommeille Mountain and other natural wonders. Near hiking trails, horseback riding, sea kayaking, ferryboats on the fjord, biking and fishing for trout, salmon and smelt. In winter: downhill and cross-country skiing and ice fishing.

From St-Siméon or La Baie, Rte 170 to thekm 71 marker, Rue Côté facing our billboard.

B&B
AU GÎTE DU BARRAGE

Elisabeth Ross and
Egide Lessard
3, rue Côté
L'Anse-St-Jean G0V 1J0
(418) 272-3387
fax (418) 272-1388
royaume.com/~egide
egide@royaume.com

B&B	
single	$40-50
double	$50-60
triple	$75
quad.	$80
child	$15

Reduced rates: Nov. 1 to Apr. 30
Open year round

Number of rooms	4
room with private bath	1
rooms in basement	2
shared bathrooms	2

Activities: 🚣 🏇 ⛷ 🏃

23. L'ANSE-ST-JEAN ☀☀☀ | F | E | ⊘ | ♿ | 🏊 | P | R1.5 | TA

"...A beautiful terrace and river behind the B&B is ideal for enjoying a good book, and offers a splendid view of the mountains. Your host offers a friendly welcome into his sunny and spacious home; beautiful rooms will help put your worried behind you. Budget-conscious travellers in search of the utmost in comfort will find it here." A French tourist.

From Québec City via St-Siméon, Rtes 138 East and 170 to Anse St-Jean; via Chicoutimi, Rtes 175 and 170. Rue St-Jean-Baptiste, 3.5km.

B&B
AU GLOBE-TROTTER

Anne Lambert and
André Bouchard
131, rue St-Jean-Baptiste
L'Anse-St-Jean G0V 1J0
tel/fax (418) 272-2353
www.bbcanada.com/322.html
andreb7@hotmail.com

B&B	
single	$45-50
double	$55-60
child	$15

Open: Mar. 1 to Oct. 30

Number of rooms	3
rooms with private bath	1
shared bathrooms	1

Activities: 🚣 🛥 🏇 🚲 🐴

24. L'ANSE-ST-JEAN ☀☀☀☀ | F | e | P | ⊘ | R.3

Ancestral home caressed by the majestic Saguenay Fjord. Your eyes can't open wide enough to take in all that nature has to offer. The cozy, comfortable rooms bring you back to the turn of the century. Walking trails are at our doorstep. Horseback riding, mini-cruises up the fjord, sea kayaks, mountain bikes, salmon fishing, ski and ice-fishing available.

From Québec City, Rte 175, Parc des Laurentides to Chicoutimi. Or Rte 138 to St-Siméon, Rte 170 to Anse-St-Jean. Rue St-Jean-Baptiste, 8km to Saguenay Fjord.

B&B
AU NID DE L'ANSE

Suzanne and Ronald Bilodeau
376, rue St-Jean-Baptiste
L'Anse-St-Jean G0V 1J0
(418) 272-2273
(418) 549-1807
fax (418) 549-9284
bilodeauronald@hotmail.com

B&B	
single	$50-55
double	$55-60
triple	$80-85

Open: June 1 to Oct. 15

Number of rooms	3
shared wc	1
shared bathrooms	1

Activities: 🚣 🛥 🏇

25. L'ANSE-ST-JEAN

☀☀☀ F e P R1.5 TA

Cosy Québec-style house echoing the colours of the fjord. Breakfast in the sunroom, river and mountain view. Rest in comfortable rooms, relax and daydream to the sound of the river. Nearby: walking trails, horseback riding, sea kayaking, fjord cruises, mountain biking, salmon fishing. Françoise (the homebody) and François (the sportsman) offer simple hospitality in their green shutter house.

From Québec City, via St-Siméon, Rtes 138 E. and 170 to Anse-St-Jean. Via Chicoutimi, Rtes 175, and 170, Rue Principale de l'Anse, 3.5km.

B&B
LA PANTOUFLARDE

Françoise Potvin and
François Asselin
129, rue St-Jean-Baptiste
L'Anse-St-Jean G0V 1J0
(418) 272-2182
(418) 545-1099
fax (418) 545-1914
fran@royaume.com

B&B	
single	$40
double	$55
triple	$70
quad.	$85

VS MC

Open: June 1 to Oct. 31

Number of rooms	3
shared bathrooms	2
rooms with sink	2

Activities: 🏊 🏇

26. MÉTABETCHOUAN

F e ✕ 🏊 P R.5 TA

Majestic turn-of-the-century Victorian house crowned by stately maples. Where uniformity stops to make way for the pleasures of refinement. Large dining room inspired by the charms of the past. Cozy rooms, delicious brunch, music, flowers and little considerations. 3 rooms with antique bath. Nearby: beach and cycling path. **See colour photos.**

From Québec City, Rte 169 North twd Roberval. From La Tuque: Rte 155 to Chambord, turn right heading toward Alma. In Métabetchouan: enter on Rue Principale, near the church opposite the post office.

INN
AUBERGE LA MAISON LAMY

Lise Girard and Normand Doré
56, rue St-André
Métabetchouan G0W 2A0
(418) 349-3686
toll free 1-888-565-3686
www.bbcanada.com/
2733.html

	B&B	MAP
single	$50-60	$70-80
double	$65-75	$105-115
triple	$75	$135
quad.	$90	$170
child	$10	$20

Taxes extra VS MC AM IT

Reduced rates: Oct.15 to Nov. 30 and Apr. 1 to June 1
Open year round

Number of rooms	6
rooms with bath and sink	3
rooms with sink	3
shared bathrooms	3

Activities: 🚣 🎣 🚶 🚴 🛷

27. NORMANDIN

☀☀☀ F e 🚫 🐕 P R8 TA

"What a joy it is to find this haven of peace and harmony after a day of travelling." Everything to recharge your batteries: peace and quiet, wide expanses and beautiful grounds. Unique decor. You will be greeted like the special guest that you are! Motorcycle/bicycle garage. Free shuttle service for cyclists (8km). Located 7min from the Grands Jardins.

From Parc des Laurentides, Rte 169 toward Roberval, St-Félicien and Normandin. At the traffic light, drive toward St-Thomas for 8km.

B&B
LE GÎTE DU PASSERIN

Gaétane Savard and
Philippe Laliberté
2292, rue St-Cyrille
Normandin G8M 4K5
(418) 274-2170

B&B	
single	$40
double	$55-65
triple	$70
child	$15

Open: May 15 to Sept. 15

Number of rooms	3
shared bathrooms	2

Activities: 🚣 🎣 🚶 🚴

28. NORMANDIN

F | e | 🚫 | P | 🏊 | R4 | TA

Prize for Excellence "Success" Regional 2000, tourism grand prize 2000 and excellence 1999. Treat yourself to an unforgettable stay in our spacious country home. Solarium/living room, outdoor pool, small farm, everything here is laid out with heart. 3km from blueberry bike route, 4km from Grands Jardins. Bike garage, free shuttle service for cyclist. Dinner available for groups of 6 people or more. **Farm Stays p 55. See colour photos.**

From Parc des Laurentides, Rte 169 twd Roberval, St-Félicien and Normandin. At the light, twd St-Thomas, 3km.

B&B
LES GÎTES MAKADAN

Micheline Villeneuve and Daniel Bergeron
1728, rue St-Cyrille
Normandin G8M 4K5
(418) 274-2867
toll free 1-877-625-2326
http://gitemakadan.cjb.net
makadan@destination.ca

B&B	
single	$40-55
double	$55-75
triple	$70-85
quad.	$95
child	$15

VS

Reduced rates: Oct. 15 to Apr. 15
Open year round

Number of rooms	5
rooms with private bath	1
shared bathrooms	2

Activties: 🚣 🚶 🚲 ⛷ 🛶

---

29. PETIT-SAGUENAY

★ ★ | F | e | 🚗 | P | 🍽 | R1 | TA

In an old rural inn, we have recreated the warm and intimate ambiance of a large country house. Located on the mountainside, facing the salmon river, at the entrance of Parc Saguenay. Cruise tickets, Fjord and whales. Snowbiling. The warmth of the hearth, a meal worthy of our hospitality, receiving you will be a pleasure.

From St-Siméon in the Charlevoix region, take Rte 170 twd Chicoutimi for about 50km. The inn is located 100m from the tourist booth, 1h from Tadoussac and Chicoutimi.

INN
AUBERGE LES 2 PIGNONS

Régine Morin
117, Route 170
Petit-Saguenay G0V 1N0
(418) 272-3091
fax (418) 272-1125
www.royaume.com/
auberge-2-pignons
auberge-2-pignons
@royaume.com

	B&B	MAP
single	$47-57	$67-77
double	$54-74	$97-114
triple	$79-89	$139-149
quad.	$94-104	$174-184
child	$12	$27

Taxes extra VS MC ER IT

Reduced rates: Sep. 15 to Dec 15 and Mar. to June 15
Open year round

Number of rooms	8
rooms with sink	1
rooms with private bath	6
shared wc	2
shared bathrooms	2

Activities: 🛶 🏇 🚶 🛶 ⛷

---

30. ROBERVAL

F | 🚗 | P | 🏊 | R6 | TA

Come relax by splendid Lac St-Jean, a veritable inland sea. Take advantage of a well-deserved quiet moment and stretch out on our private beach near the house. It gives us great pleasure to have you as our guests.

From Parc des Laurentides, Rte 169. We are 3.5km from the Val-Jalbert bridge. From La Tuque, Rte 155 to Chambord. Turn left to Roberval, Rte 169, drive 10km B&B on your left.

B&B
LA MAISON AU TOIT ROUGE

Yolande Lalancette and Raynald Girard
1345, boul. de l'Anse, route 169
Roberval G8H 2N1
(418) 275-3290

B&B	
single	$40
double	$50
child	$10

Open: May 15 to Sep. 30

Number of rooms	3
shared bathrooms	2

Activities: 🏛 🛶 🚣 🚶 🚲

31. ST-AMBROISE-DE-CHICOUTIMI   ☀☀☀ F E 🚭 🐕 🚗 P ✖ R4 TA

Prize for Excellence "Special Favorite" Regional 2000. In the heart of Saguenay-Lac-St-Jean, a country farmhouse with a garden, flowers, farmyard, lake, and trout stream. Cozy beds, choice breakfasts and, by reservation, delicious Saguenay meals. Also, 3- to 6-day "all-inclusive" packages. In summer: fishing, blueberry picking. In winter: snowmobiling, dogsledding, skiing, ice fishing.

Rte 172 between Chicoutimi and Alma. Near St-Ambroise, Rte Bégin, 3km along paved road. Right on Rang 9, 500m along gravel road.

B&B
AUX PIGNONS VERTS

Ghislaine Ouellet and
Jean-Claude Villeneuve
925, Rang 9, G7P 2A4
St-Ambroise-de-Chicoutimi
(418) 672-2172
fax (418) 672-6622
www3.sympatico.ca
/pignonsverts
pignonsverts@sympatico.ca

B&B	
single	$40
double	$55-65
child	$25

VS

Open year round

Number of rooms	3
shared bathrooms	2

Activities: 🎿 🚲 🛥 🏃 🐕

---

32. ST-FÉLICIEN   ☀☀☀☀ F 🚭 🚗 P R.1

Ten metres from the Ashuapmushuan River, and boasting a large terrace. What a joy to meet people from all over the world. Tourist attractions: zoo (6km), falls (5km), Val-Jalbert (20km). Located near the town centre. Come meet us for a pleasant time. Special little considerations await you.

From Parc des Laurentides, Rte 169 twd Roberal to St-Félicien; located opposite "Mets Chinois". From Dolbeau, at 2nd light, left on Sacré-Coeur; located opposite "Mets Chinois".

B&B
À FLEUR D'EAU

Claudette Nadeau and
Paul Hébert
1016, rue Sacré-Coeur
St-Félicien G8K 1R5
(418) 679-0784
www.multimania.
com/afleurdeau

B&B	
single	$40-45
double	$45-55
triple	$60
quad.	$75
child	$15

Reduced rates: Oct. 1 to June 1
Open year round

Number of rooms	5
rooms with private bath	3
room in basement	1
shared bathrooms	2

Activities: 🏛 🛥 🚤 🎿 🚲

---

33. ST-FÉLICIEN   ☀☀☀ F e P 🚗 R2

If you like the charm of the country, you'll be enchanted by our surroundings. A warm welcome in a calming and restful atmosphere. A sitting room is at your disposal. Evenings outdoors around the campfire lead to good conversation. Healthy, generous breakfast. 3km to town, 6km to the zoo. Reduced rates: September to June.

From Parc des Laurentides, Rte 169 towards Roberval to St-Félicien. At the 1st traffic lights, turn left on Rue Notre-Dame, drive 2.6km. Right on Rang Double, drive 0.7km.

B&B
À LA FERME HÉBERT

Céline Giroux and
J-Jacques Hébert
1070, rang Double
St-Félicien G8K 2N8
(418) 679-0574
fax (418) 679-4625
fhebert@destination.ca

B&B	
single	$40
double	$45-50
triple	$60
child	$10

Taxes extra

Reduced rates: 2 nights and more,
Sep. 1 to June 15
Open year round

Number of rooms	4
rooms with sink	1
rooms in basement	2
shared bathrooms	2

Activities: 🐟 🚤 🚲 🛥 🐕

34. ST-FÉLICIEN ☀☀☀ F e P R4 TA

"Chez Denise" you'll discover the hospitality of the people of Lac-St-Jean. Large house located at the heart of tourist activities: zoo, race-car track (2km away), drive-in, golf, etc. Fishing possible. It is our plea-sure to welcome you.

From Parc des Laurentides, Rte 169 twd Roberval. From La Tuque, Rte 155, in Chambord, turn left twd Roberval to St-Félicien. At the 2nd traffic lights turn left, 5km. From Dolbeau at the 2nd traffic lights, 5km.

B&B
GÎTE CHEZ DENISE

Denise and Louis-Marie Gagnon
1430, rang Double
St-Félicien G8K 2N8
tel/fax (418) 679-1498
gite@destination.ca

B&B	
single	$35
double	$50
child	$5-15

Reduced rates: 10% Sept. 15 to May 31
Open year round

Number of rooms	4
shared bathrooms	2

Activities: 🏛 🚶 🛥 🚲 🏃

---

35. ST-FÉLIX-D'OTIS ☀☀☀ F e 🚭 🚗 P 🏊 🐕 ✕ R1 TA

Country farm between La Baie and Rivière-Eternité with animals run-ning free, flowers, decorative gar-den. A relaxing, rejuvenating haven where life flows with the seasons. Outdoor pool, air-conditioned house. Healthy breakfast, oven-fresh bread, wild berries. Near: Parc Saguenay, Site de la Nouvelle France and «La Fabuleuse Histoire d'un Royaume». Guided beaver-watching tour. **Farm Stay p 55.**

From Parc des Laurentides, Rtes 175 North and 170 East. From St-Si-méon, Rte 170 North twd Chicouti-mi.

B&B
GÎTE DE LA BASSE-COUR

Huguette Morin and
Régis Girard
271, rue Principale, route 170
St-Félix-d'Otis G0V 1M0
(418) 544-8766
fax (418) 544-4750
www.bbcanada.
com/gitebassecour
gitebassecour@hotmail.com

B&B	
single	$40
double	$50
triple	$70
quad.	$80
child	$5-15

Open year round

Number of rooms	3
shared bathrooms	2

Activities: 🛶 🛥 🚶 🏂 🐕

---

36. ST-FÉLIX-D'OTIS ☀☀ F e 🚗 P R1 TA

The fjord route invites you: Lac Otis beach, canoeing, fishing, the site and settings of 17th-century New France, the customs and traditions of First Nations peoples and the first colonists in an Iroquois village. 15km from Parc du Saguenay, in Rivière-Éternité: hiking trails, capes, beavers, etc. 15km from La Baie "Fabuleuse Histoire d'un Royaume." Hearty breakfast, blueberry pan-cakes, in-room TVs. Come, we'll have a chat!

From Parc des Laurentides, Rtes 175 N. and 170 East. From St-Siméon, Rte 170 N. twd Chicoutimi. From St-Urbain, Rte 381 North and 170 East.

B&B
MAISON JONCAS

Dorina Joncas and
Camil Yacola
291, rue Principale
route 170 Est
St-Félix-d'Otis G0V 1M0
tel/fax (418) 544-5953
www3.sympatico.ca/msim/
principale.html

B&B	
single	$30
double	$40-45
triple	$60
quad.	$65
child	$5-8

Open year round

Number of rooms	2
shared wc	1
shared bathrooms	1

Activities: 🛶 🛥 🛥 🚶 🏂

37. ST-FULGENCE

La Maraîchère du Saguenay, our ancestral home, our old barn and our latest addition, a tiny house similar to our old home. Warm, stunning, cosy rooms with antique furnishings. A grandiose fjord and magnificent parks nearby, Mont-Valin, Saguenay and Cap-Jaseux. Kayaking, canoeing, hiking, dogsleding, snowmobiling plus all the activities we can organise for you. Dinner available, must reserve ahead of time. See you soon.

From Chicoutimi, 8km past Dubuc bridge, Rte 172 towards Tadoussac. Turn left 400m after Esso station.

B&B
LA MARAÎCHÈRE
DU SAGUENAY

Adèle Copeman and
Rodrigue Langevin
97, boul. Tadoussac
St-Fulgence G0V 1S0
(418) 674-9384
(418) 674-2247
fax (418) 674-1055
www.maraichere.langevin.net
maraichere.saguenay
@qc.aira.com

B&B	
single	$55-65
double	$65-75
triple	$80-100
quad.	$95-125
child	$0-30

Taxes extra VS MC

Open year round

Number of rooms	4
rooms with private bath	2
shared bathrooms	1

Activities:

38. STE-JEANNE-D'ARC

Forestry farm, 2.5km from Rte 169, away from the noise. Old house and furnishings, fans in the rooms. Homemade breakfasts. Nearby: Louis Hémon museum, old mill, covered bridge, Parc de la Pointe Taillon, blueberry groves, bike paths and snowmobile trails. We drive cyclists to the restaurant.

From Parc des Laurentides, Rte 169 toward Roberval, Ste-Jeanne-d'Arc. Do not go into the village, but continue on Rte 169 for 7.5km, turn left toward St-Augustin, drive 0.9km. At the first curve, straight ahead on Rte Harvey (gravel road) for 1.5km, right on Chemin Lapointe.

B&B
FERME HARVEY

Denise Bouchard and
Bertrand Harvey
230, chemin Lapointe
Ste-Jeanne-d'Arc G0W 1E0
(418) 276-2810

B&B	
single	$30-35
double	$45-50
triple	$65-70
child	$5-12

Reduced rates: 10% 3 nights and more
Open year round

Number of rooms	3
shared bathrooms	2

Activities:

---

39. LA BAIE

F · e · P · R2 · M2 · TA

Ancestral house from 1848 located 2km from La Baie and 12km from Chicoutimi. Near tourist activities, La Fabuleuse theatre, hiking trails, marina, cheese shop, farm, blueberry grove, bike path, ice fishing, etc. 10 apartments, 2 bathrooms. **Country home on a farm p. 56.**

From Parc des Laurentides, Rtes 175 North and 170 East twd La Baie. At the 2nd light, continue to Rue Victoria and turn left. Drive 2km along Victoria, which turns into St-Joseph. After the flashing light, the second house on the right.

COUNTRY HOME
LA MAISON DES ANCÊTRES

Judith and Germain Simard
1722, chemin St-Joseph
La Baie G7B 3N9
(418) 544-2925
fax (418) 544-0241

No. houses	1
No. rooms	5
No. people	10-12
WEEK-SUMMER	$600
WEEK-WINTER	$500
W/E-SUMMER	$300
W/E-WINTER	$250
DAY-SUMMER	$150
DAY-WINTER	$150

Open year round

Activities: 🏛 🛶 🛷 🚶 🚲

40. ST-DAVID-DE-FALARDEAU

F · E · P · ✕ · R3 · M3 · TA

Come and discover our little paradise on an enchanting and charming site, next to the forest. A magnificent log chalet, fully equipped, facing a little lake and our pack of huskies. Discover our original table d'hôte menu and our winter activities. Sleigh rides, snowmobiling, ice-fishing. Close by: rafting, archery, fishing and swimming. We look forward to welcoming you.

From Québec City, Rte 175 N. In Chicoutimi, take the Dubuc bridge, Rte 172 W. to the "FALARDEAU" sign. In Falardeau, right at the church, right after the corner store, right on the 3rd street, 1.7km.

COUNTRY HOME
LES CHIENS ET GÎTE
DU GRAND NORD

Frédéric Dorgebray
Lot 18, Lac Durand #2
St-David-de-Falardeau
G0V 1C0
(418) 673-7717
fax (418)673-4072
www.chiens-gite.qc.ca
chiensgite@hotmail.com

No. houses	1
No. rooms	1
No. people	7
WEEK-SUMMER	$348
WEEK-WINTER	$348
W/E-SUMMER	$217
W/E-WINTER	$217
DAY-SUMMER	$22
DAY-WINTER	$22

Taxes extra

Open year round

Activities: 🛷 🎿 🛷 🐕

FARM ACTIVITIES

Farm Stay:

8 CAROLE ET JACQUES MARTEL, Hébertville 54

15 CHEZ GRAND-MAMAN, La Baie 54

20 CÉLINE ET GEORGES MARTIN, Lac-à-la-Croix 55

28 FERME NORDAN, Normandin 55

35 GÎTE DE LA BASSE-COUR, St-Félix-d'Otis 55

Country Home on a Farm:

39 LA MAISON DES ANCÊTRES, La Baie 54

INDEX

91 DU BOUT DE L'ÎLE, LE
   (L'ÎLE-D'ORLÉANS, STE-PÉTRONILLE) . . . 245

-À-

À BONHEUR D'OCCASION (MONTRÉAL) . . 218
À BON MATIN (MONTRÉAL) 218
À COUETTE ET CROISSANT (HULL) 230
À FLEUR D'EAU (ST-FÉLICIEN) 274
À FLEUR DE PIERRE (LA BAIE) 268
À LA BELLE VIE (MONTRÉAL) 219
À LA BERNACHE (CHICOUTIMI) 264
À LA BONNE ÉTOILE (MONTRÉAL) 219
À L'ABRI DE LA TOURMENTE
   (ST-JOACHIM) 259
À L'ABRI DU CLOCHER (NOUVELLE) 148
À L'ABRI DU VENT (PERCÉ) 149
À LA BRUNANTE (LONGUEUIL) 211
À LA CAMPAGNE EN VILLE (QUÉBEC) 247
À LA CAPITAINERIE DU PASSANT
   (GRANDES-PILES) 198
À LA CHOUETTE (BAIE-ST-PAUL) 99
À L'ADRESSE DU CENTRE-VILLE
   (MONTRÉAL) 219
À LA FERME HÉBERT (ST-FÉLICIEN) 274
À LA GIRONDINE (FRELIGHSBURG) 81
À LA GLOIRE DU MATIN (MONTRÉAL) 220
À LA MAISON DREW (MAGOG) 85
À LA MAISON TUDOR (QUÉBEC) 247
À LA MONTAGNE CHEZ MADELEINE
   ET PIERRE (PIEDMONT) 178
À L'ANCESTRALE (MAGOG) 85
À LA PROMENADE (CHICOUTIMI) 264
À LA RÊVASSE (PERCÉ) 149
À L'ARRÊT DU TEMPS
   (STE-ANNE-DE-LA-PÉRADE) 201
À L'AUBERGE DE LA FERME (CAPLAN) . . . 139
À L'AUGUSTINE (QUEBEC) 248
À L'OASIS DU VIEUX-LONGUEUIL
   (LONGUEUIL) 211
À L'ORÉE DU MOULIN
   (PAPINEAUVILLE, MONTEBELLO) 233
À TOUT VENANT (MAGOG) 86

-A-

ABAT-JOUR B&B (QUÉBEC) 246
ABRI DU TEMPS, L' (LAVAL) 195
ACCUEIL AUX BOSQUETS (LÉVIS) 113
ACCUEIL B&B L'HEURE DOUCE (QUÉBEC) . . 247
ACCUEIL LES SEMAILLES
   (HÉROUXVILLE) 51, 199
ACTON VALE 207
AMOUR ET AMITIÉ (MAGOG) 85
AMQUI 137
ANCESTRALE, L' (ST-ANDRÉ-AVELLIN) 234
ANCÊTRE DE GASPÉ, L' (GASPÉ) 142
ANCIEN PRESBYTÈRE, L' (ST-MARCEL) 119

ANDANTE, L (ST-GABRIEL-DE-BRANDON) . . . 166
ANSE DES MÈRES, L' (QUÉBEC) 253
ANTIQUAILLE, L' (ST-BENJAMIN, BEAUCE) . . 117
APPARTEMENTS MEUBLÉS MONTRÉAL
   CENTRE-VILLE (MONTRÉAL) 226
ARCHE DE NOÉ (RAWDON) 36
ARGENTEUIL 20
AROLLES, LES
   (MONT-STE-ANNE, ST-FERRÉOL) 245
ARTOÎT, L' (BAIE-ST-PAUL) 101
AU BEAU-SÉJOUR
   (ST-LOUIS-DU-HA! HA!) 74
AUBE DOUCE (ST-ADOLPHE-D'HOWARD) . . . 178
AUBERGE À LA CROISÉE DES CHEMINS, L'
   (MONT-TREMBLANT, LA CONCEPTION) . . 175
AUBERGE AU BOIS D'MON COEUR
   (FERME-NEUVE) 171
AUBERGE «AU CRÉPUSCULE» (CAP-CHAT) . 137
AUBERGE AU DIABLO-VERT
   (LA POCATIÈRE) 67
AUBERGE AU NID DOUILLET (STE-ADÈLE) . . 183
AUBERGE AU PHIL DE L'EAU
   (STE-MARGUERITE-DU-LAC-MASSON) . . 187
AUBERGE AU PIRATE 1775 (PERCÉ) 149
AUBERGE AUX NUITS DE RÊVE
   (STE-AGATHE-DES-MONTS) 186
AUBERGE AUX P'TITS OIGNONS
   (ACTON VALE) 207
AUBERGE BAIE-JOLIE
   (TROIS-RIVIÈRES, POINTE-DU-LAC) 204
AUBERGE CHARME DES ALPES
   (VAL-DAVID) 188
AUBERGE CHEMIN DU ROY
   (DESCHAMBAULT) 240
AUBERGE CHEZ MARIE-ROSES (BIC, LE) 64
AUBERGE D'ANDROMÈDE, L'
   (COURCELLES) 79
AUBERGE DE L'EIDER
   (STE-LUCE-SUR-MER) 74
AUBERGE DE LA BAIE (LES ESCOUMINS) . . . 126
AUBERGE DE LA BAIE-DES-CAPUCINS
   (CAP-CHAT, CAPUCINS) 138
AUBERGE DE LA FERME ST-ADOLPHE
   (STONEHAM, ST-ADOLPHE) 260
AUBERGE DE LA GARE (STE-ADÈLE) 183
AUBERGE DE LA MAISON GRENIER
   (MONT-LAURIER) 174
AUBERGE DE LA TOUR (ORFORD) 89
AUBERGE DE LA TOUR DU LAC
   (STE-AGATHE-DES-MONTS) 186
AUBERGE DE LA VISITATION (LÉVIS) 113
AUBERGE DES CÉVENNES
   (L'ANSE-ST-JEAN) 270
AUBERGE DES GLACIS
   (ST-EUGÈNE-DE-L'ISLET) 118
AUBERGE DES ÎLES (KAMOURASKA) 66
AUBERGE DES SORBIERS B&B
   (STE-ADÈLE) 184
AUBERGE DU BOURG (TROIS-RIVIÈRES) 202
AUBERGE DU CHEMIN FAISANT (CABANO) . . 65

AUBERGE DU GRAND FLEUVE
(LES BOULES) 143

AUBERGE DU JOLI VENT
(LAC-BROME, FOSTER) 83

AUBERGE DU MANOIR DAUTH
(STE-ANNE-DE-LA-PÉRADE) 201

AUBERGE DU PETIT PRÉ (CHÂTEAU-RICHER) 239

AUBERGE DU VIEUX MOULIN
(STE-ÉMÉLIE-DE-L'ÉNERGIE) 167

AUBERGE LA BELLE ÉPOQUE
(MONTMAGNY) 115

AUBERGE LA BOUCLÉE
(LES ÉBOULEMENTS) 105

AUBERGE LA COURTEPOINTE
(PETITE-RIVIÈRE-ST-FRANÇOIS) 107

AUBERGE LA GIROUETTE DES B&B
(STE-ADÈLE) 184

AUBERGE L'AIR DU TEMPS (CHAMBLY) 209

AUBERGE LA JARNIGOINE (CHAMBLY) 209

AUBERGE LA MAISON BOULET
(MONTMAGNY) 115

AUBERGE LA MAISON LAMY
(MÉTABETCHOUAN) 272

AUBERGE LA MARÉE DOUCE
(POINTE-AU-PÈRE) 69

AUBERGE LA MARGUERITE
(L'ISLET-SUR-MER) 114

AUBERGE LA MUSE (BAIE-ST-PAUL) 99

AUBERGE LA PENTE DOUCE
(LES ÉBOULEMENTS) 106

AUBERGE LA PETITE CACHÉE
(MONT-TREMBLANT) 174

AUBERGE LA ROMANCE (LA MALBAIE) 104

AUBERGE LA SABLINE (RIVIÈRE-DU-LOUP) . . . 70

AUBERGE LA SAUVAGINE
(STONEHAM, ST-ADOLPHE) 261

AUBERGE LA SEIGNEURIE (MATANE) 144

AUBERGE LA SOLAILLERIE
(ST-ANDRÉ, KAMOURASKA) 73

AUBERGE LA SUISSE (PIKE-RIVER) 90

AUBERGE LA VISITE SURPRISE
(CARLETON) 139

AUBERGE LAC DU PIN ROUGE
(ST-HIPPOLYTE) 180

AUBERGE-LE-BÔME (GRANDES-PILES) 198

AUBERGE LE CLOS ROLLAND
(STE-ADÈLE) 184

AUBERGE LE LUPIN (MONT-TREMBLANT) . . . 175

AUBERGE LE SAINT-VENANT
(STE-AGATHE-DES-MONTS) 186

AUBERGE LE SUROUÊT
(LES ÉBOULEMENTS) 106

AUBERGE L'ÉTÉ INDIEN (BRÉBEUF) 170

AUBERGE L'ÉTOILE DE MER
(NEW RICHMOND) 147

AUBERGE LE VIEUX PRESBYTÈRE
(L'ÎLE-D'ORLÉANS, ST-PIERRE) 243

AUBERGE LES 2 PIGNONS
(PETIT-SAGUENAY) 273

AUBERGE LES DEUX ÎLOTS (NEWPORT) 146

AUBERGE LES PIGNONS VERTS (AUSTIN) . . . 78

AUBERGE MAISON GAGNÉ
(TADOUSSAC) 128

AUBERGE MANOIR BELLEVUE
(LES ESCOUMINS) 126

AUBERGE PETITE PLAISANCE
(CAP-À-L'AIGLE) 102

AUBERGE PRESBYTÈRE MONT LAC VERT
(HÉBERTVILLE) 265

AUBERGE-RESTAURANT «CHEZ IGNACE»
(LAC-NOMININGUE) 172

AUBERGE RESTAURANT LA BRUYÈRE
(STE-ADÈLE) 185

AUBERGE ROCHE DES BRISES
(ST-JOSEPH-DU-LAC) 181

AUBERGE SOUS L'ÉDREDON
(ST-SAUVEUR-DES-MONTS) 182

AUBERGE SUR LES PENDANTS, L'
(L'ÎLE-D'ORLÉANS, ST-PIERRE) 244

AUBERGE VILLA BELLERIVE
(LAC-NOMININGUE) 172

AUBERGE WANTA-QO-TÍ
(ESCUMINAC, MIGUASHA) 140

AUBERGE «UNE FERME EN GASPÉSIE», L'
(LES BOULES) 144

AU BOISÉ JOLI (ST-JEAN-PORT-JOLI) 118

AU BONHEUR DU JOUR (RIVIÈRE-DU-LOUP) . . 71

AU BORD DE L'EAU (LA BAIE) 268

AU CHARME DE LA MONTAGNE
(PONTIAC, LUSKVILLE) 234

AU CLOCHETON (BAIE-ST-PAUL) 99

AU COURANT DE LA MER
(STE-ANNE-DES-MONTS, TOURELLE) . . . 154

AU CROISSANT DE LUNE (QUÉBEC) 248

AU GIRON DE L'ISLE
(L'ÎLE-D'ORLÉANS, ST-JEAN) 240

AU GÎT'ANN (MONTRÉAL) 220

AU GÎTE DE LA CHUTE (BOISCHATEL) 238

AU GÎTE DU BARRAGE (L'ANSE-ST-JEAN) . . 271

AU GÎTE OLYMPIQUE (MONTRÉAL) 220

AU GLOBE-TROTTER (L'ANSE-ST-JEAN) 271

AU GRÉ DES MARÉES (TROIS-PISTOLES) . . . 75

AU GRÉ DU VENT (LÉVIS) 113

AU MARIC (QUÉBEC) 248

AU NID D'HIRONDELLES
(STE-AGATHE-DES-MONTS) 187

AU NID DE L'ANSE (L'ANSE-ST-JEAN) 271

AU PARADIS D'ÉMY (PRINCEVILLE) 56, 97

AU PERCHOIR (BAIE-ST-PAUL) 100

AU PETIT BONHEUR
(BAIE-COMEAU, POINTE-LEBEL) 124

AU PETIT CHÂTEAU DU LAC (ST-DONAT) . . 165

AU PETIT ROI (QUÉBEC) 249

AU PIED À TERRE À QUÉBEC (QUÉBEC) . . . 249

AU PIED DE LA CHUTE
(LACHUTE, ARGENTEUIL) 20

AU PIGNON SUR LE PARC (HULL) 230

«AU REPOS DU DRAVEUR»
(GRANDES-PILES) 198

AU SAUT DU LIT (MAGOG) 86

AU SOIR QUI PENCHE
(ST-ROCH-DES-AULNAIES) 120

AU SOLEIL COUCHANT (LAC-MÉGANTIC) . . . 84

AU SOMMET DES RÊVES
  (STONEHAM, ST-ADOLPHE) 261

AUSTIN 78

AU TEMPS DES MÛRES (DUNHAM) 80

AU TERROIR DES BASQUES
  (RIVIÈRE-DU-LOUP) 71

AU TOIT BLEU
  (L'ÎLE-D'ORLÉANS, STE-FAMILLE) 244

AU VERSANT DE LA MONTAGNE (HULL) . . . 231

AU VIEUX PRESBYTÈRE (ST-ÉLOI) 73

AU VIRAGE (MAGOG) 86

AUX 2 LUCARNES
  (NOTRE-DAME-DE-LA-SALETTE) 233

AUX 2 LUCARNES (ST-HUBERT) 212

AUX 5 LUCARNES (BIC, LE) 64

AUX 5 PIGNONS (ST-IRÉNÉE) 108

AUX CHUTES (STE-FLAVIE) 155

AUX CORMORANS (BIC, LE) 64

AUX DOUCES HEURES (DUNHAM) 80

AUX DOUCEURS DE LA RUCHE
  (MIRABEL, ST-SCHOLASTIQUE) 21

AUX JARDINS CHAMPÊTRES (MAGOG) . . 16, 87

AUX PÉTALES DE ROSE
  (CAP-DES-ROSIERS, FORILLON) 138

AUX PETITS OISEAUX (BAIE-ST-PAUL) 100

«AUX PETITS OISEAUX...»
  (ST-SAUVEUR-DES-MONTS) 182

AUX PETITS OISEAUX (VAL-DES-MONTS) . . 234

AUX PIGNONS VERTS
  (ST-AMBROISE-DE-CHICOUTIMI) 274

AUX PINS DORÉS (STE-ADÈLE) 185

AUX PORTES DE LA NUIT (MONTRÉAL) . . . 221

AUX RÊVES D'ANTAN
  (ST-MARC-SUR-RICHELIEU) 214

AUX SENTIERS DU FJORD (TADOUSSAC) . . 129

AUX TROIS BALCONS (QUÉBEC) 249

AYER'S CLIFF 78

AYLMER 229

AZUR (MONTRÉAL) 221

-B-

B&B CHEZ PIERRE (QUÉBEC) 250

B&B DE LA TOUR (QUÉBEC) 250

B&B DES GRISONS (QUÉBEC) 250

B&B LA BEDONDAINE (QUÉBEC) 251

B&B LES CORNICHES (QUÉBEC, SILLERY) . . . 258

B&B MAISON LESAGE (QUÉBEC) 251

BAIE-COMEAU 124, 132

BAIE-DES-ROCHERS 110

BAIE-DU-FEBVRE 94

BAIE-STE-CATHERINE 101, 102

BAIE-ST-PAUL 99-101

BAIE-TRINITÉ 124, 132

BAKER (CHÂTEAU-RICHER) 239

BASILIC ET ROMARIN
  (STE-ANNE-DES-PLAINES) 32

BATISCAN 197

BEAUCE 117

BEAUPORT 254, 255

BEAUX BRUNELLES (BELOEIL) 207

BÉCANCOUR 94

BELLE AU BOIS DORMANT, LA
  (ST-JOACHIM-DE-SHEFFORD) 90

BELLE ÉCHAPPÉE, LA (MAGOG) 87

BELLE MAISON BLANCHE, LA (DÉGELIS) 66

BELLE VICTORIENNE, LA (MAGOG) 88

BELLEFEUILLE 170

BELOEIL 207

BERGERIE DES NEIGES
  (ST-AMBROISE-DE-KILDARE) 19, 164

BERGERIE DU SUROÎT, LA
  (ST-URBAIN-PREMIER) 26

BERGERIE VOYNE
  (ST-JACQUES-DE-MONTCALM) 19

BERGERONNES 125

BERGERONNETTE, LA (BERGERONNES) 125

BIC, LE 64, 65, 70

BLAINVILLE 170

BLUE SEA 229

BOIS D'AVIGNON
  (ST-ALEXIS-DE-MATAPÉDIA) 152

BOISCHATEL 238

BONAVENTURE 137

BONNE ADRESSE, LA
  (ST-FAUSTIN, LAC-CARRÉ) 179

BONNE NUIT BONJOUR
  (STE-ADÈLE) 183

BONNET D'OR B&B, LE
  (ST-SAUVEUR-DES-MONTS) 182

BONSECOURS 89

BOUCHERVILLE 208

BOUCHERVILLOISE, LA (BOUCHERVILLE) . . . 208

BRÉBEUF 170

BRECKENRIDGE 229

BRIGHAM 30,34

BROMONT 79

-C-

CABANO 65

CACOUNA 65

CAFÉ CRÈME B&B (MAGOG) 87

CANTON DE RIPON 232

CAP-À-L'AIGLE 102

CAP-DE-CHAT 137, 138

CAP-DE-LA-MADELEINE 197

CAP-DES-ROSIERS 138

CAPLAN 139

CAP-ROUGE 256

CAP-TOURMENTE 238, 262

CAPUCINES, LES (L'ISLE-VERTE) 68

CAPUCINS 138

CARLETON 139

CAUSAPSCAL 140

CÉCILE LAUZIER (AYER'S CLIFF) 78

CÉCILIENNE, LA (MONTMAGNY) 116

CÉLINE ET GEORGES MARTIN
  (LAC-À-LA-CROIX) 55, 270

CENTRE DE L'ÉMEU DE CHARLEVOIX
  (ST-URBAIN) 49

CHALETS DES PINS (RAWDON) 168

CHALETS ET STUDIO LE VENT DU NORD (MONT-TREMBLANT, LAC-SUPÉRIEUR) 191
CHALETS-VILLAGE MONT-SAINTE-ANNE (MONT-STE-ANNE, ST-FERRÉOL) 262
CHAMBLY 209
CHANTERELLES, LES (ST-IRÉNÉE) 109
CHARDONNERET, LE (CHICOUTIMI) 265
CHARMES DE PROVENCE (SHERBROOKE) 91
CHÂTEAU ÉPI D'OR (LAC-VICEROI, CANTON DE RIPON) 232
CHÂTEAU-RICHER 45, 239, 240
CHAUMIÈRE AUX MARGUERITES, LA (VAL-DAVID) 188
CHAUMIÈRE DU NOTAIRE, LA (L'ÎLE-D'ORLÉANS, ST-LAURENT) 242
CHAUMIÈRE EN PAIN D'ÉPICES, LA (AYER'S CLIFF) 78
CHÉNÉVILLE 53, 231, 235, 236
CHÈVRERIE DES ACACIAS, LA (DUNHAM) 16
CHEZ BÉCASSINE (ST-ADOLPHE D'HOWARD) 179
CHEZ CHARLES ET MARGUERITE (RIMOUSKI) 69
CHEZ CHOINIÈRE (TROIS-PISTOLES, ST-SIMON) 75
CHEZ DESPARD (PERCÉ) 150
CHEZ FLEUR DO (BOUCHERVILLE) 208
CHEZ FRANÇOIS (MONTRÉAL) 221
CHEZ GERTRUDE (ST-URBAIN) 110
CHEZ GRAND'PAPA BEAU (TROIS-RIVIÈRES) 203
CHEZ GRAND-MAMAN (LA BAIE) 54, 268
CHEZ GRAND-MAMAN JACQUELINE (ST-HUBERT) 213
CHEZ JEAN ET NICOLE (KAMOURASKA) 67
CHEZ MARIE-CHRISTINE (JOLIETTE, STE-ÉLISABETH) 162
CHEZ MARTHE-ANGÈLE (STE-ANNE-DES-MONTS) 153
CHEZ MONSIEUR GILLES2 (QUÉBEC) 251
CHEZ NAP (BLUE SEA) 229
CHEZ NICOLE (MATANE, ST-ULRIC) 146
CHICOUTIMI 264, 265
CHIENS ET GÎTE DU GRAND NORD, LES (ST-DAVID-DE-FALARDEAU) 277
CHRYSALIDE, LA (PIEDMONT) 178
CLAIREVALLÉE (BIC, ST-FABIEN) 65
CLAIRIÈRE, LA (BROMONT) 79
CLAIRIÈRE DE LA CÔTE, LA (L'ANNONCIATION) 20, 50, 173
CLÉ DES CHAMPS, LA (HOPE TOWN, PASPÉBIAC) 143
CLERMONT 102
CLOS DES ÉPINETTES, LE (MONTRÉAL) 223
CLOS DES LILAS, LE (OKA) 177
CLOS DES PINS, LE (DANVILLE) 48, 80
COLOMBIER 126
CONCLUSION, LA (STE-ANNE-DES-PLAINES) 23
CONDOTELOGAN (MONTRÉAL) 226

CONTRECOEUR 210
COUDRIER, LE (LA DURANTAYE) 122
COUETTE ET CAFÉ LE 253 (QUÉBEC) 252
COUETTE-CAFÉ LES PETITS MATINS (GASPÉ) 141
COULE DOUCE, LA (QUÉBEC) 253
COURCELLES 48, 79
COWANSVILLE 79
CRÉPUSCULE (L'ÎLE-D'ORLÉANS, ST-PIERRE) 243

-D-

DANVILLE 48, 80
DÉGELIS 66
DÉPENDANCES DU MANOIR, LES (BRIGHAM) 30, 34
DES RUISSEAUX 174
DESCHAMBAULT 240
DEUX MARQUISES, LES (MONTMAGNY) 116
DOMAINE AUX CROCOLLINES (LAC-SIMON, CHÉNÉVILLE) 231, 236
DOMAINE DE LA FORÊT (MAGOG, ORFORD) 89
DOMAINE DE LA MAISON BLANCHE (NOTRE-DAME-DE-LA-SALETTE) 233
DOMAINE DE LA TEMPLERIE (HUNTINGDON) 25
DOMAINE DES PINS (ST-PIERRE-BAPTISTE) 97
DOMAINE DU BON VIEUX TEMPS (RIMOUSKI, ST-NARCISSE) 70
DOMAINE DU LAC MATAPÉDIA (AMQUI) 137
DOMAINE SUR LA COLLINE B&B (COWANSVILLE) 79
DORMANCE, LA (LAC-BROME, KNOWLTON) 83
DOUCES ÉVASIONS (ST-ANSELME) 116
DRUMMONDVILLE 94, 95
DUNHAM 16, 80
DUVERNAY 194

-E-

EASTMAN 81
EAU BERGE, L' (LA MALBAIE) 105
EIDER MATINAL, L' (SAINT-IRÉNÉE) 109
ÉLEVAGES RUBAN BLEU, LES (ST-ISIDORE-DE-LAPRAIRIE) 41
EN HAUT DE LA CHUTE MONTMORENCY (QUÉBEC, BEAUPORT) 254
ENSORCELAINE, L' (MASSUEVILLE, ST-AIMÉ) 212
ENTRE MER ET MONTS (BAIE-STE-CATHERINE) 101
ENTREMONT, L' (ST-FAUSTIN, LAC CARRÉ) 180
ESCUMINAC 140
ÉTAPE CHEZ MARIE-THÉRÈSE ET GÉRARD LEMAY, L' (ST-JÉRÔME) 181
ÉVEIL SUR LE LAC, L' (ST-HIPPOLYTE) 180

-F-

FATIMA 160
FERME 5 ÉTOILES (SACRÉ-COEUR) 50, 127, 132
FERME AUBERGE D'ANDROMÈDE
    (COURCELLES) 48
FERME CAROLE ET JACQUES
    MARTEL (HÉBERTVILLE) 54, 266
FERME CAVALIER (ST-SIXTE) 28
FERME DE BELLECHASSE (GATINEAU) . . 53, 229
FERME DE CATHERINE, LA
    (ST-ANDRÉ EST) 22
FERME DE L'ÉMEULIENNE, LA
    (NEUVILLE) 245
FERME DE LA BERCEUSE, LA
    (WICKHAM) 17, 49, 96
FERME DE LA BUTTE MAGIQUE
    (ST-FAUSTIN) 39, 51, 179
FERME DE LA SEIGNEURIE
    (LOUISEVILLE) 51
FERME ÉBOULMONTAISE
    (LES ÉBOULEMENTS) 31
FERME ÉCO-FORESTIÈRE DE LA
    MINERVE (LA MINERVE) 37
FERME ÉCOLOGIQUE DU PARC-NATURE
    DU CAP-ST-JACQUES (PIERREFONDS) . . . 44
FERME FLOTS BLEUS (RIMOUSKI) 48
FERME HARVEY (STE-JEANNE-D'ARC) 276
FERME JEAN DUCHESNE (ST-PIE) 42
FERME KOSA (ST-RÉMI-DE-NAPIERVILLE) . . . 25
FERME LA COLOMBE
    (ST-LÉON-DE-STANDON) 18
FERME L'ÉMEULIENNE, LA (NEUVILLE) . . 46, 53
FERME NORDAN (NORMANDIN) 55
FERME PAYSAGÉE, LA
    (ST-JEAN-DE-DIEU) 48, 73
FERME ST-ADOLPHE (STONEHAM) 54
FERME VACANCES (ÎLE-NEPAWA) 56, 62
FERME-NEUVE 171
FLORETTES, LES (VAL MORIN) 189
FORILLON 138, 140
FOSTER 83
FRELIGHSBURG 81
FULFORD 83

-G-

GASPÉ 140-142
GATINEAU 53, 229, 230
GÎTE ANSE-AU-SABLE
    (COLOMBIER) 126
GÎTE AU BORD DE LA RIVIÈRE, LE
    (SHANNON) 260
GÎTE AU FOIN FOU (BONAVENTURE) 137
GÎTE «AU PETIT BONHEUR»
    (KAMOURASKA) 67
GÎTE AU TOIT ROUGE (DÉGELIS) 66
GÎTE AU VIEUX BAHUT (LÉVIS) 114
GÎTE AUX MILLE FLEURS (CHICOUTIMI) . . . 264
GÎTE AUX P'TITS OISEAUX (JOLIETTE) 162
GÎTE BAIE-JOLIE
    (TROIS-RIVIÈRES, POINTE-DU-LAC) 204

GÎTE BEL HORIZON
    (L'ÎLE-D'ORLÉANS, ST-PIERRE) 243
GÎTE BELLE-RIVIÈRE (HÉBERTVILLE) 266
GÎTE BELLE-VUE (LA BAIE) 269
GÎTE BELLEVUE (MONT-JOLI) 146
GÎTE BLANCHETTE (FORILLON, GASPÉ) 140
GÎTE BLANDINE ET THOMAS THORNE
    (FATIMA) 160
GÎTE CHEZ DENISE (ST-FÉLICIEN) 275
GÎTE CHEZ GEORGES (PERCÉ) 150
GÎTE CHEZ MIMI, LE
    (STE-AGNÈS-DE-DUNDEE) 52, 215
GÎTE DE GASPÉ (GASPÉ) 141
GÎTE DE LA BAIE
    (ST-SIMÉON, BAIE-DES-ROCHERS) 110
GÎTE DE LA BASSE-COUR
    (ST-FÉLIX-D'OTIS) 55, 275
GÎTE DE LA BÊTE PARESSEUSE
    (L'ANNONCIATION) 173
GÎTE DE LA FALAISE (TADOUSSAC) 129
GÎTE DE LA GARE (LAC-CARRÉ) 171
GÎTE DE LA MAISON LEVESQUE
    (NEW-RICHMOND) 147
GÎTE DE LA NOUVELLE FRANCE
    (STE-ANNE-DES-MONTS, TOURELLE) . . . 154
GÎTE DE L'ANSE (VAUDREUIL-DORION) 215
GÎTE DE LA PÊCHE BLANCHE (LA BAIE) 269
GÎTE DE LA POINTE (POINTE-AU-PÈRE) 69
GÎTE DE LA PYRAMIDE (LA BAIE) 269
GÎTE DE LA REINE-CLAUDE
    (TROIS-PISTOLES, ST-SIMON) 75
GÎTE DE LA RIVIÈRE AUX
    SABLES (JONQUIÈRE) 266
GÎTE DE L'ARTISANERIE
    (BAIE-DU-FEBVRE) 94
GÎTE DE LA SEIGNEURIE, LE
    (LOUISEVILLE) 200
GÎTE DE LA TOUR
    (STE-ANNE-DES-MONTS, TOURELLE) . . . 155
GÎTE DE LA VALLÉE, LE (CAUSAPSCAL) . . . , 140
GÎTE DE L'ÎLE (L'ÎLE PERROT) 210
GÎTE DE L'OIE DES NEIGES
    (CAP-TOURMENTE, MONT-STE-ANNE) . . 238
GÎTE DE NEUVILLE, LE (NEUVILLE) 246
GÎTE DES AMÉRIQUES (STE-ADÈLE) 185
GÎTE DES EQUERRES, LE
    (ST-GABRIEL-DE-VALCARTIER) 259
GÎTE DES FLEURS
    (ST-ALEXANDRE, KAMOURASKA) 72
GÎTE DES JARDINS DE LA MONTAGNE
    (ST-JOSEPH-DU-LAC) 181
GÎTE DES PINS (LA BAIE) 270
GÎTE DES ROSES, LE
    (DRUMMONDVILLE) 94
GÎTE DES SOMMETS
    (MATANE, ST-RENÉ) 50, 145
GÎTE DU BORD DE L'EAU (LAVAL) 194
GÎTE DU BOULEAU (TADOUSSAC) 129
GÎTE DU CAP BLANC (PERCÉ) 150
GÎTE DU CAPITAINE
    (BAIE-STE-CATHERINE) 102
GÎTE DU CARREFOUR (LOUISEVILLE) 199

GÎTE DU CATALPA (RAWDON) 163
GÎTE DU CENTENAIRE
   (QUÉBEC, STE-FOY) 257
GÎTE DU CHEMIN DU ROY
   (CAP-DE-LA-MADELEINE) 197
GÎTE DU LIÈVRE
   (STE-MARGUERITE-DU-LAC-MASSON) . . 188
GÎTE DU LYS, LE (BLAINVILLE) 170
GÎTE DU MARIGOT (LAVAL) 194
GÎTE DU MOULIN À VENT
   (PERCÉ, STE-THÉRÈSE) 151
GÎTE DU MOULIN BAUDE (TADOUSSAC) . . 130
GÎTE DU PARC (QUÉBEC) 252
GÎTE DU PASSERIN, LE (NORMANDIN) 272
GÎTE DU PHARE (MATANE) 144
GÎTE DU PHARE DE POINTE-DES-
   MONTS, LE (BAIE-TRINITÉ) 124, 132
GÎTE DU QUAI
   (L'ÎLE-D'ORLÉANS, ST-JEAN) 241
GÎTE DU VACANCIER
   (LES ÉBOULEMENTS) 106
GÎTE DU VIEUX MOULIN
   (STE-FLORENCE) 156
GÎTE DU VIEUX-BOURG, LE
   (QUÉBEC, BEAUPORT) 255
GÎTE ET COUVERT LA MARIE-CHAMPAGNE
   (MONT-TREMBLANT, LAC-SUPÉRIEUR) . . 175
GÎTE E.T. HARVEY (LA MALBAIE) 104
GÎTE FLEURS DES BOIS (BELLEFEUILLE) 170
GÎTE GHISLAINE (SACRÉ-COEUR) 127
GÎTE HISTORIQUE L'EMERILLON (GASPÉ) . . . 141
GÎTE HONEYS (GASPÉ) 142
GÎTE ÎLE BIZARD (L'ÎLE BIZARD) 218
GÎTE J.A.DUFOUR
   (ST-ALEXIS-DE-MATAPÉDIA) 152
GÎTE J.D. TROTTIER, LE
   (NOTRE-DAME-DE-HAM) 95
GÎTE L'ÉCUME DE MER (LA MARTRE) 143
GÎTE LA BELLE AU BOIS DORMANT
   (GRAND-MÈRE) 197
GÎTE LA BERCEUSE (CACOUNA) 65
GÎTE LA CANADIENNE (GASPÉ) 142
GÎTE LA CINQUIÈME SAISON (MONTRÉAL) . . 222
GÎTE LA GASPÉSIENNE, LE
   (DUVERNAY) 194
GÎTE LA JOLIE ROCHELLE
   (QUÉBEC, CAP-ROUGE) 256
GÎTE LA MAISON BLANCHE
   (ISLE-AUX-COUDRES) 103
GÎTE LA NICHÉE
   (STE-ANNE-DE-PORTNEUF) 128
GÎTE LA RIVERAINE
   (ISLE-AUX-COUDRES) 103
GÎTE LA TOURELLE (WARWICK) 96
GÎTE LA TREMBLANTE
   (MT-TREMBLANT, ST-JOVITE) 176
GÎTE LA VILLA DU VIEUX
   CLOCHER (PADOUE) 148
GÎTE LE NOBLE QUÊTEUX
   (BAIE-ST-PAUL) 100
Ξ LES BOULEAUX
   (NEW RICHMOND) 147

GÎTE LES COLIBRIS (BAIE-ST-PAUL) 101
GÎTE LES LEBLANC (CARLETON) 139
GÎTE LES PECCADILLES (EASTMAN) 81
GÎTE MAISON JACQUES
   (PIERREFONDS) 225
GÎTE PARLEZ-MOI D'AMOUR
   (MIRABEL) 173
GÎTE SAINT-MICHEL, LE
   (ST-MICHEL-DES-SAINTS) 166
GÎTE SAINT-LAURENT (TROIS-RIVIÈRES) . . . 203
GÎTE TOURISTIQUE DU MONT-JACOB
   (JONQUIÈRE) 267
GÎTE UN AIR D'ÉTÉ
   (CHÂTEAU-RICHER) 239
GÎTE VILLA DES ROSES
   (LES ÉBOULEMENTS) 107
GÎTES MAKADAN, LES (NORMANDIN) 273
GOULD 81
GRANBY 82
GRANDE OURSE, LA (L'ISLE-VERTE) 68
GRANDES-PILES 198
GRAND-MÈRE 197
GRENOUILLÈRE DES TROIS
   VILLAGES, LA (STANSTEAD) 91
GUIMONTIÈRE, LA
   (STE-ANGÈLE-DE-MÉRICI) 153

-H-

HALTE AUX PETITS OISEAUX
   (ST-DONAT) 165
HALTE DE RESSOURCEMENT
   (ST-LAZARE-DE-VAUDREUIL) 214
HAYDEN'S WEXFORD HOUSE
   (QUÉBEC) 252
HAZELBRAE FARM (HOWICK) 52, 210
HÉBERTVILLE 54, 265, 266
HERBARIUM, L'
   (ST-MATHIEU-DU-PARC) 200
HÉROUXVILLE 51, 199
HOPE TOWN 143
HOWICK 52, 210
HULL 230, 231
HUNTINGDON 25
HYDRANGÉE BLEUE, L'
   (QUÉBEC, CAP-ROUGE) 256

-I-

ÎLE-NEPAWA 56, 62
INTERMIEL (MIRABEL, ST-BENOIT) 38
ISLE-AUX-COUDRES 103

-J-

JARDIN CACHÉ, LE (ST-HYACINTHE) 213
JARDIN DE GIVRE, LE
   (MATANE, ST-LÉANDRE) 145
JARDIN DES MÉSANGES, LE
   (ST-CYPRIEN) 49, 117
JARDIN SECRET, LE (QUÉBEC) 253
JARDINS DE LA GARE, LES (VAL-MORIN) . . . 189

JARDINS DE LA SEIGNEURIE, LES
   (LOUISEVILLE) 40
JARDINS DE RÊVES (MONTEBELLO) 232
JARDINS DES TOURTEREAUX, FERME
   LA COLOMBE (ST-LÉON-DE-STANDON) . . . 35
JARDINS DE VINOY, LES
   (VINOY, CHÉNÉVILLE) 53, 235
JARDINS DU «LORD» WILDE (WILDE'S
   HEATH B&B), LES (MONT-TREMBLANT) . 176
JOLIETTE 162
JONQUIÈRE 266, 267

-K-

KAMOURASKA 66, 67, 72, 73
KNOWLTON 82, 83

-L-

LA BAIE 54, 56, 268-270, 277
LAC-À-LA-CROIX 55, 270
LAC-BROME 82, 83
LAC-CARRÉ 171, 179, 180
LACHUTE 20
LA CONCEPTION 175
LAC-MÉGANTIC 84
LAC-NOMININGUE 172
LAC-SIMON 231, 236
LAC-SUPÉRIEUR 175, 191
LAC-VICEROI 232
LA DURANTAYE 122
LA MALBAIE 104, 105
LA MARTRE 143
LA MINERVE 37
L'ANNONCIATION 20, 173
L'ANSE-ST-JEAN 270-272
LA POCATIÈRE 67
LAVAL 194, 195
«LE 6400» COUETTE ET CAFÉ BED &
   BREAKFAST (MONTRÉAL) 223
LES BOULES 143, 144
LES ÉBOULEMENTS 31, 105-107
LES ESCOUMINS 126
LÉVIS 113, 114
LICORNE, LA (LAC-CARRÉ) 171
L'ÎLE BIZARD 218
L'ÎLE-D'ORLÉANS 240-245
L'ÎLE PERROT 210
L'ISLET-SUR-MER 114, 115
L'ISLE-VERTE 68
LOFT L'ESCALE (MONTRÉAL) 226
LONGUEUIL 211
LOUISEVILLE 24, 40, 51, 56,199, 200, 205
LUCIOLE, LA (ST-IRÉNÉE) 108
LUSKVILLE 234

-M-

MAGOG 16, 85-89
MAISON ANCESTRALE, LA
   (L'ISLE-VERTE) 68

MAISON ANCESTRALE THOMASSIN, LA
   (QUÉBEC, BEAUPORT) 254
MAISON AORHENCHE, LA
   (QUÉBEC, WENDAKE) 258
MAISON AU TOIT BLEU, LA
   (ST-ALEXANDRE, KAMOURASKA) 72
MAISON AU TOIT ROUGE, LA
   (ROBERVAL) 273
MAISON BÉRUBÉ, LA (RIMOUSKI, BIC) 70
MAISON BLANCHE, LA (LAC-MÉGANTIC) 84
MAISON BLEUE, LA
   (ST-LAMBERT-DE-LÉVIS) 119
MAISON BOIS-MENU
   (MASSUEVILLE, ST-AIMÉ) 216
MAISON BON REPOS
   (AYLMER, BRECKENRIDGE) 229
MAISON CAMPBELL, LA (MAGOG) 88
MAISON DE L'ANCÊTRE, LA
   (LOUISEVILLE) 200
MAISON DE L'ENCLOS, LA (ROSEMÈRE) . . . 191
MAISON DE L'ERMITAGE, LA
   (ST-JEAN-PORT-JOLI) 118
MAISON DE MON ENFANCE, LA
   (RIVIÈRE-DU-LOUP, ST-ANTONIN) 72
MAISON DE MORPHÉE, LA
   (REPENTIGNY) 163
MAISON DES ANCÊTRES,
   LA (LA BAIE) 56, 277
MAISON DES GALLANT
   (STE-LUCE-SUR-MER) 74
MAISON DES LACS, LA (WOTTON) 92
MAISON DINA (QUÉBEC, STE-FOY) 257
MAISON DUBUC (NEUVILLE) 246
MAISON DUCHARME, LA (CHAMBLY) 209
MAISON DUCLAS, LA (GRANBY) 82
MAISON DUFOUR-BOUCHARD, LA
   (LA MALBAIE) 104
MAISON DUFRESNE, LA
   (QUÉBEC, BEAUPORT) 254
MAISON DU GAZEBO, LA
   (BELOEIL, ST-MATHIEU) 207
MAISON DU JARDINIER, LA
   (LOUISEVILLE) 56, 205
MAISON D'ULYSSE, LA
   (STE-ANNE-DE-BEAUPRÉ) 260
MAISON DUMOULIN, LA (OKA) 177
MAISON DU SÉMINAIRE, LA
   (CHICOUTIMI) 265
MAISON DU VIGNOBLE, LA
   (L'ÎLE-D'ORLÉANS, ST-PIERRE) 244
MAISON EMERY JACOB (ST-TITE) 201
MAISON FEENEY, LA
   (QUÉBEC, CAP-ROUGE) 256
MAISON FLEURIE, LA
   (STE-ANNE-DE-PORTNEUF) 128
MAISON FORTIER (TADOUSSAC) 130
MAISON FRIZZI, LA
   (LA MALBAIE, POINTE-AU-PIC) 1C
MAISON GAUDREAULT, LA
   (CLERMONT) . . . .
MAISON GAUTHIER ET LES SUITES
   DE L'ANSE (TADOUSSAC) . . . . . .

MAISON GRÉGOIRE (MONTRÉAL) 227
MAISON HARVEY-LESSARD, LA
   (TADOUSSAC) 130
MAISON HINGSTON 4335 224
MAISON HOVINGTON (TADOUSSAC) 131
MAISON JAUNE, LA (MONTRÉAL) 222
MAISON JONCAS (ST-FÉLIX-D'OTIS) 275
MAISON LABERGE, LA (PERCÉ) 157
MAISON LA COULÉE (DRUMMONDVILLE) 95
MAISON LA CRÉMAILLÈRE (MESSINES) 232
MAISON LEBREUX, LA
   (PETITE-VALLÉE) 151, 157
MAISON LECLERC, LA
   (QUÉBEC, STE-FOY) 257
MAISON MARTIN. LA (ST-MARTIN) 120
MAISON MC AULEY, LA (GOULD) 81
MAISON ROBIDOUX, LA (ST-DONAT) 165
MAISON ROSE, LA
   (CAP-DES-ROSIERS, FORILLON) 138
MAISON SOUS L'ORME, LA (LÉVIS) 114
MAISON SUR LA COLLINE, LA
   (GATINEAU) 230
MAISON SUR LA CÔTE, LA
   (L'ÎLE-D'ORLÉANS, ST-JEAN) 241
MAISON SUR LE LAC, LA (ST-DONAT) 166
MAISON TRUDEL (HÉROUXVILLE) 199
MAISON WICKENDEN (TROIS-RIVIÈRES) 203
MALARDS, LES (CONTRECOEUR) 210
MANOIR BÉCANCOURT (BÉCANCOUR) 94
MANOIR DE LA RUE MERRY, LE (MAGOG) . . . 88
MANOIR DES CÈDRES (HULL) 231
MANOIR D'IVRY B&B (STE-AGATHE-NORD) . . 187
MANOIR D'ORSENNENS (LAC-MÉGANTIC) . . 84
MANOIR HARVARD (MONTRÉAL,
   NOTRE-DAME DE GRÂCE) 225
MANOIR HORTENSIA (ST-IRÉNÉE) 110
MANOIR TASCHEREAU (STE-MARIE) 120
MANOIR VALLÉE, LE
   (QUÉBEC, BEAUPORT) 255
MARAÎCHÈRE DU SAGUENAY, LA
   (ST-FULGENCE) 276
MARCHAND DE SABLE, LE
   (TERREBONNE) 167
MARÉE BLEUE, LA (STE-FLAVIE) 155
MAS DE L'ISLE, LE (L'ÎLE-D'ORLÉANS,
   ST-JEAN) 241
MASSUEVILLE 212, 216
MATANE 50, 144-146
MERLEAU, LE (JONQUIÈRE) 267
MESSINES 232
MÉTABETCHOUAN 272
MIGUASHA 140
MIRABEL 21, 38, 173
MITAN, LE (JONQUIÈRE) 267
MONIQUE ET ANDRÉ SAINT-AUBIN
   . . . STE-FOY) 258
   . . . . 232, 233
   146
   174
   . . . . 115, 116
   218-227

MONTS GÎTE ET MER
   (STE-ANNE-DES-MONTS) 153
MONT-STE-ANNE 238, 245, 262
MONT-TREMBLANT 174-176, 191
MUSÉE DE L'ABEILLE-
   ÉCONOMUSÉE DU MIEL
   (CHÂTEAU-RICHER) 45

-N-

NATASHQUAN 127
NEUVILLE 46, 53, 245, 246
NEW RICHMOND 147, 148
NEWPORT 146
NIAPISCA (STE-MARIE) 121
NICHOUETTE, LE (LES ÉBOULEMENTS) 107
NID D'AMOUR (VAL-MORIN) 190
NID FLEURI, LE (ST-HYACINTHE) 213
NORMANDIN 55, 272, 273
NOTRE CAMPAGNE D'ANTAN
   (ST-APOLLINAIRE) 117
NOTRE-DAME-DE-GRÂCE 224, 225
NOTRE-DAME-DE-HAM 95
NOTRE-DAME-DE-LA-SALETTE 233
NOTRE MAISON SUR LA RIVIÈRE
   (LAVAL) 195
NOUVELLE 148

-O-

O' P'TITS OIGNONS (ST-JULIEN) 119
OASIS (DRUMMONDVILLE, ST-CYRILLE) 95
OASIS DE RÊVES, L'
   (L'ÎLE-D'ORLÉANS, ST-LAURENT) 242
OIE DES NEIGES, L' (CAP-TOURMENTE,
   MONT-STE-ANNE) 262
OKA 177
ORFORD 89

-P-

PACANE ET POTIRON CAFÉ COUETTE
   (VERDUN) 225
PADOUE 148
PANORAMA, LE (MATANE, ST-LUC) 145
PANTOUFLARDE, LA (L'ANSE-ST-JEAN) 272
PAPINEAUVILLE 233
PASPÉBIAC 143
PERCÉ 149-151, 157
PETIT BALUCHON, LE
   (STE-ÉLIZABETH-DE-WARWICK) 96
PETITE CHARTREUSE, LA
   (ST-ALPHONSE-RODRIGUEZ) 164
PETITE MONET, LA (JOLIETTE) 162
PETITE-RIVIÈRE-ST-FRANÇOIS 107, 108
PETITE-VALLÉE 151, 157
PETIT MANOIR DU SAULT
   MONTMORENCY, LE
   (QUÉBEC, BEAUPORT) 255
PETIT-SAGUENAY 273
PETIT SÉJOUR, LE (CHÂTEAU-RICHER) 240
PIEDMONT 178

PIEDS DANS L'EAU, LES
    (L'ISLET-SUR-MER) 115
PIERRE ET DOMINIQUE
    (MONTRÉAL) 224
PIERREFONDS 44, 225
PIKE-RIVER 90
POINTE-AU-PÈRE 69
POINTE-AU-PIC 105
POINTE-DU-LAC 204
POINTE-LEBEL 124, 132
PONTIAC 234
PORT D'ATTACHE, LE (NATASHQUAN) 127
PRESBYTÈRE, LE (PERCÉ) 151
PRÉVOST 178
PRINCEVILLE 56, 97
PROVINCIALAT, LE (LAC-NOMININGUE) . . . 172
P'TITE BALEINE, LA (BERGERONNES) 125
P'TITE MAISON DES LEBLANC, LA
    (ST-ALEXIS-DE-MATAPÉDIA) 152
P'TITS POMMIERS, LES
    (SHAWINIGAN-SUD) 202

-Q-

QUÉBEC 246-258
QUÉBÉCOISE, LA (STE-FLAVIE) 156

-R-

RABOUILLÈRE, LA
    (ST-VALÉRIEN) 26, 43, 215
RANCH 4 SAISONS
    (ST-ALPHONSE-RODRIGUEZ) 50, 164
RAWDON 36, 163, 168
REFUGE DU POÈTE, LE
    (LONGUEUIL) 211
REFUGE DU VOYAGEUR, LE
    (BOISCHATEL) 238
RÉGALIN, LE (ST-EUSTACHE) 22
RELÂCHE, LA (NEW RICHMOND) 148
RELAIS DE LA PISTE, LE (VAL-DAVID) 189
RELAIS DES ÎLES PERCÉES, LE
    (BOUCHERVILLE) 208
REPENTIGNY 163
RÊVE BLANC (MONT-LAURIER,
    DES RUISSEAUX) 174
RÊVERIE AUX QUATRE-VENTS
    (KNOWLTON, LAC-BROME) 82
RICHELIEU 209
RIMOUSKI 48, 69, 70
RIVIÈRE-DU-LOUP 70-72
ROBERVAL 273
ROCHERS, LES (RIVIÈRE-DU-LOUP) 71
RONDINS, LES (MIRABEL) 21
ROSEMÈRE 191
ROSEPIERRE, LA (BERGERONNES) 125
ROUGEMONT 212
RUSTIQUE, LE (ST-IRÉNÉE) 109

-S-

SACRÉ-COEUR 50, 127, 132
ST-ADOLPHE 260, 261
ST-ADOLPHE-D'HOWARD 178, 179
ST-AIMÉ 212, 216
ST-ALEXANDRE 72
ST-ALEXIS-DE-MATAPÉDIA 152
ST-ALPHONSE-RODRIGUEZ 50, 164
ST-AMBROISE-DE-CHICOUTIMI 274
ST-AMBROISE-DE-KILDARE 19, 164
ST-ANDRÉ-EST 22
ST-ANDRÉ 73
ST-ANDRÉ-AVELLIN 234
ST-ANSELME 116
ST-ANTONIN 72
ST-APOLLINAIRE 49, 117
ST-BENJAMIN 117
ST-BENOIT 38
ST-CYPRIEN 117
ST-CYRILLE 95
ST-DAVID-DE-FALARDEAU 277
ST-DONAT 165, 166
ST-ELIAS, LE (BATISCAN) 197
ST-ÉLOI 73
ST-EUGÈNE-DE-L'ISLET 118
ST-EUSTACHE 22
ST-FABIEN 65
ST-FAUSTIN 51, 179, 180
ST-FAUSTIN-LAC-CARRÉ 39
ST-FÉLICIEN 274, 275
ST-FÉLIX-D'OTIS 55, 275
ST-FERRÉOL 245
ST-FERRÉOL-LES-NEIGES 262
ST-FULGENCE 276
ST-GABRIEL-DE-BRANDON 166
ST-GABRIEL-DE-VALCARTIER 259
ST-HENRI-DE-LÉVIS 122
ST-HIPPOLYTE 180
ST-HUBERT 212, 213
ST-HYACINTHE 213
ST-IRÉNÉE 108-110
ST-ISIDORE-DE-LAPRAIRIE 41
ST-JACQUES-DE-MONTCALM 19
ST-JEAN 240, 241
ST-JEAN-DE-DIEU 48, 73
ST-JEAN-PORT-JOLI 118
ST-JÉRÔME 181
ST-JOACHIM 259
ST-JOACHIM-DE-SHEFFORD 90
ST-JOSEPH-DU-LAC 181
ST-JOVITE 176
ST-JULIEN 119
ST-LAMBERT-DE-LÉVIS 119
ST-LAURENT 227, 242
ST-LAZARE-DE-VAUDREUIL 214
ST-LÉANDRE 145
ST-LÉON-DE-STANDON 18, 35

ST-LOUIS-DU-HA! HA! 74
ST-LUC 145
ST-MARCEL 119
ST-MARC-SUR-RICHELIEU 214
ST-MARTIN 120
ST-MATHIEU 207
ST-MATHIEU-DU-PARC 200
ST-MICHEL-DES-SAINTS 166
ST-NARCISSE 70
ST-PIE 42
ST-PIERRE 243, 244
ST-PIERRE-BAPTISTE 97
ST-RAYMOND 259
ST-RÉMI-DE-NAPIERVILLE 25
ST-RENÉ 50, 145
ST-ROCH-DES-AULNAIES 120
ST-SAUVEUR-DES-MONTS 182
ST-SCHOLASTIQUE 21
ST-SIMÉON 110
ST-SIMON 75
ST-SIXTE 28
ST-TITE 201
ST-ULRIC 146
ST-URBAIN 49, 110
ST-URBAIN-PREMIER 26
ST-VALÉRIEN 26, 43, 52, 215
STE-ADÈLE 183-185
STE-AGATHE-DES-MONTS 186, 187
STE-AGATHE-NORD 187
STE-AGNÈS-DE-DUNDEE 52, 215
STE-ANGÈLE-DE-MÉRICI 153
STE-ANNE-DE-BEAUPRÉ 260
STE-ANNE-DE-LA-PÉRADE 201
STE-ANNE-DE-PORTNEUF 128
STE-ANNE-DES-MONTS 153-155
STE-ANNE-DES-PLAINES 23, 32
STE-ÉLISABETH 162
STE-ÉLIZABETH-DE-WARWICK 96
STE-ÉMÉLIE-DE-L'ÉNERGIE 167
STE-FAMILLE 244
STE-FLAVIE 155, 156
STE-FLORENCE 156
STE-FOY 257, 258
STE-JEANNE-D'ARC 276
STE-JUSTINE-DE-NEWTON 27
STE-LUCE-SUR-MER 74
STE-MARGUERITE-DU-LAC-MASSON . . 187, 188
STE-MARIE 120, 121
STE-PÉTRONILLE 245
STE-THÉRÈSE 151
SECOND SOUFFLE, LE
    (MONT-TREMBLANT, ST-JOVITE) 176
SEIGNEURIE DE NEWTON, LA
    (STE-JUSTINE-DE-NEWTON) 27
SHANNON 260
SHAWINIGAN-SUD 202
SHERBROOKE 91
SHÉZELLES (MONTRÉAL) 224
SILLERY 258
SOLEIL LEVANT
    (TROIS-RIVIÈRES, POINTE-DU-LAC) 204
SOUS LA BONNE ÉTOILE

(STE-ANNE-DES-MONTS) 154
STANSTEAD 91
STONEHAM 54, 260, 261
STUDIO MARHABA (ST-LAURENT) 227

-T-

TABLE DE LA SEIGNEURIE, LA
    (LOUISEVILLE) 24
TADOUSSAC 128-131
TEMPÉRAMENT SAUVAGE
    (ST-HENRI-DE-LÉVIS) 122
TEMPS DES VILLAGES, LE
    (SHAWINIGAN-SUD) 202
TERREBONNE 167
TOURELLE 154, 155
TOURLOGNON
    (PETITE-RIVIÈRE-ST-FRANÇOIS) 108
TOURNE-PIERRES, LES
    (BAIE-COMEAU, POINTE-LEBEL) 124
TROIS-PISTOLES 75
TROIS-RIVIÈRES 202-204
TU-DOR, LE (LAC-BROME, FULFORD) 83

-U-

UNE FLEUR AU BORD DE L'EAU
    (GRANBY) 82
UN TEMPS D'ARRÊT (ROUGEMONT) 212

-V-

VAL-DAVID 188, 189
VAL-DES-MONTS 234
VAL-MORIN 189, 190
VAUDREUIL-DORION 215
VERDUN 225
VICTORIENNE, LA (MONTRÉAL) 222
VIEILLE MAISON FRADET, LA
    (L'ÎLE-D'ORLÉANS, ST-LAURENT) 242
VILLA DES CHÊNES, LA (PIKE-RIVER) 90
VILLA DES FLEURS, LA (REPENTIGNY) 163
VILLA DU MOULIN (ISLE-AUX-COUDRES) . . . 103
VILLAGE, LE (ORFORD) 89
VILLA PETIT BONHEUR (BAIE-COMEAU,
    POINTE-LEBEL) 132
VINOY 53, 235
VIREVENT, LE
    (ST-MARC-SUR-RICHELIEU) 214
VOISINE, LA (ST-RAYMOND) 259

-W-Z-

WARWICK 96
WENDAKE 258
WICKHAM 17, 49, 96
WOTTON 92
ZÈBRE, LE (MONTRÉAL) 223
ZIBOU, LE (OKA) 177

ACCOMMODATION

Your opinion is important for the continued EXCELLENCE of our guide.

In order to continue to improve the network and the quality of the services it offers, please send your comments and suggestions to:

Fédération des Agricotours
C.P. 1000, succ. M,
Montréal, Québec
H1V 3R2

Win a free stay!

Each year, Agricotours awards a prize of EXCELLENCE to several of its members. The selection is based on clients' commentary cards, therefore we invite you to fill out the following sheets to show your appreciation and have a chance to win a stay at one of our members' establishments for free!

How do you rate us?

HOSPITALITY
Hosts' courtesy, hosts' attentiveness, special touches

YOUR ROOM
Bed comfort, room comfort, cleanliness, bedding

MEALS
Food quality, food presentation, variety, schedule (flexibility)

HOUSE
Comfort, cleanliness, decoration, general impression of the premises

BATHROOM
Facilities, cleanliness

Comments and suggestions

_____
_____
_____
_____
_____
_____
_____
_____
_____

YOUR OVERALL APPRECIATION

Excellent ☐   Good ☐
Very good ☐   Poor ☐

For our statistics

Was this your first experience with the Agricotours network?

☐ Yes   How many times _____
☐ No

Occupation _____

Age

☐ 8-19   ☐ 20-29   ☐ 30-39   ☐40-49
☐ 50-59   ☐ 60-69   ☐ 70 and above

YOUR NAME	
YOUR ADDRESS	Street
	City
	Country Postal code
NAME OF THE ESTABLISHMENT	
DATE OF VISIT	
MUNICIPALITY OR REGION	

ACCOMMODATION

Your opinion is important for the continued EXCELLENCE of our guide.

In order to continue to improve the network and the quality of the services it offers, please send your comments and suggestions to:

Fédération des Agricotours
C.P. 1000, succ. M,
Montréal, Québec
H1V 3R2

Win a free stay!

Each year, Agricotours awards a prize of EXCELLENCE to several of its members. The selection is based on clients' commentary cards, therefore we invite you to fill out the following sheets to show your appreciation and have a chance to win a stay at one of our members' establishments for free!

How do you rate us?

HOSPITALITY
Hosts' courtesy, hosts' attentiveness, special touches

YOUR ROOM
Bed comfort, room comfort, cleanliness, bedding

MEALS
Food quality, food presentation, variety, schedule (flexibility)

HOUSE
Comfort, cleanliness, decoration, general impression of the premises

BATHROOM
Facilities, cleanliness

Comments and suggestions

_____
_____
_____
_____
_____
_____
_____
_____
_____

YOUR OVERALL APPRECIATION

Excellent ☐   Good ☐
Very good ☐   Poor ☐

For our statistics

Was this your first experience with the Agricotours network?

☐ Yes   How many times _____
☐ No

Occupation _____

Age

☐ 8-19   ☐ 20-29   ☐ 30-39   ☐40-49
☐ 50-59   ☐ 60-69   ☐ 70 and above

YOUR NAME	
YOUR ADDRESS	Street
	City
	Country Postal code
NAME OF THE ESTABLISHMENT	
DATE OF VISIT	
MUNICIPALITY OR REGION	

COUNTRY-STYLE DINING AND REGIONAL DINING

Your opinion is important for the continued EXCELLENCE of our guide.

In order to continue to improve the network and the quality of the services it offers, please send your comments and suggestions to:

Fédération des Agricotours
C.P. 1000, succ. M,
Montréal, Québec
H1V 3R2

Win a free stay!

Each year, Agricotours awards a prize of EXCELLENCE to several of its members. The selection is based on clients' commentary cards; therefore we invite you to fill out the following sheets to show your appreciation and have a chance to win a stay at one of our members' establishments for free!

How do you rate us?

	Excellent	Very good	Good	Poor
ACCESSIBILITY, EASY TO FIND	☐	☐	☐	☐
HOSPITALITY				
-hosts' courtesy	☐	☐	☐	☐
-hosts' attentiveness	☐	☐	☐	☐
-special touches	☐	☐	☐	☐
THE MEAL				
-quality of the food	☐	☐	☐	☐
-freshness	☐	☐	☐	☐
-food presentation	☐	☐	☐	☐
-variety	☐	☐	☐	☐
THE DINING ROOM				
-comfort	☐	☐	☐	☐
-cleanliness	☐	☐	☐	☐
-decoration	☐	☐	☐	☐
OVERALL IMPRESSION				
-exterior of the house	☐	☐	☐	☐
-buildings	☐	☐	☐	☐
-land	☐	☐	☐	☐
FARM TOURS	☐	☐	☐	☐
QUALITY-PRICE RATIO	☐	☐	☐	☐

Comments and suggestions

_____
_____
_____
_____
_____
_____
_____
_____
_____

YOUR OVERALL APPRECIATION

Excellent ☐   Good ☐
Very Good ☐   Poor ☐

For our statistics

Was this your first experience with the Agricotours network?

☐ Yes   How many times _____
☐ No

Occupation _____

Age

☐ 8-19   ☐ 20-29   ☐ 30-39   ☐ 40-49
☐ 50-59   ☐ 60-69   ☐ 70 and above

YOUR NAME		
YOUR ADDRESS	Street	
	City	
	Country	Postal code
NAME OF THE ESTABLISHMENT		
DATE OF VISIT		
MUNICIPALITY OR REGION		

Order Form

Ulysses Travel Guides

☐ Acapulco	$14.95 CAN $9.95 US	☐ Huatulco–Puerto Escondido	$17.95 CAN $12.95 US
☐ Alberta's Best Hotels Restaurants	$14.95 CAN $12.95 US	☐ Inns and Bed & Breakfasts in Québec	$14.95 CAN $10.95 US
☐ Arizona–Grand Canyon	$24.95 CAN $17.95 US	☐ Islands of the Bahamas	$24.95 CAN $17.95 US
☐ Atlantic Canada	$24.95 CAN $17.95 US	☐ Las Vegas	$17.95 $12.95
☐ Beaches of Maine	$12.95 CAN $9.95 US	☐ Lisbon	$18.95 CAN $13.95 US
☐ Belize	$16.95 CAN $12.95 US	☐ Los Angeles	$19.95 CAN $14.95 US
☐ Boston	$17.95 CAN $12.95 US	☐ Los Cabos and La Paz	$14.95 CAN $7.99 US
☐ British Columbia's Best Hotels and Restaurants	$14.95 CAN $9.95 US	☐ Louisiana	$29.95 CAN $21.95 US
☐ Calgary	$17.95 CAN $12.95 US	☐ Martinique	$24.95 CAN $17.95 US
☐ California	$29.95 CAN $21.95 US	☐ Miami	$17.95 CAN $12.95 US
☐ Canada	$29.95 CAN $21.95 US	☐ Montréal	$19.95 CAN $14.95 US
☐ Cancún & Riviera Maya	$17.95 CAN $12.95 US	☐ New Orleans	$17.95 CAN $12.95 US
☐ Cape Cod, Nantucket and Martha's Vineyard	$17.95 CAN $12.95 US	☐ New York City	$19.95 CAN $14.95 US
☐ Cartagena (Colombia)	$12.95 CAN $9.95 US	☐ Nicaragua	$24.95 CAN $16.95 US
☐ Chicago	$19.95 CAN $14.95 US	☐ Ontario's Best Hotels and Restaurants	$16.95 CAN $12.95US
☐ Chile	$27.95 CAN $17.95 US	☐ Ontario	$27.95 CAN $19.95US
☐ Colombia	$29.95 CAN $21.95 US	☐ Ottawa–Hull	$17.95 CAN $12.95 US
☐ Costa Rica	$27.95 CAN $19.95 US	☐ Panamá	$24.95 CAN $17.95 US
☐ Cuba	$24.95 CAN $17.95 US	☐ Peru	$27.95 CAN $19.95 US
☐ Dominican Republic	$24.95 CAN $17.95 US	☐ Phoenix	$16.95 CAN $12.95 US
☐ Ecuador and Galápagos Islands	$24.95 CAN $17.95 US	☐ Portugal	$24.95 CAN $16.95 US
☐ El Salvador	$22.95 CAN $14.95 US	☐ Provence & the Côte d'Azur	$29.95 CAN $21.95US
☐ Guadalajara	$17.95 CAN $12.95 US	☐ Puerto Plata–Sosua	$14.95 CAN $9.95 US
☐ Guadeloupe	$24.95 CAN $17.95 US	☐ Puerto Rico	$24.95 CAN $17.95 US
☐ Guatemala	$24.95 CAN $17.95 US	☐ Puerto Vallarta	$14.95 CAN $9.95 US
☐ Havana	$16.95 CAN $12.95 US	☐ Québec	$29.95 CAN $21.95 US
☐ Hawaii	$29.95 CAN $21.95 US	☐ Québec City	$17.95 CAN $12.95 US
☐ Honduras	$24.95 CAN $17.95 US	☐ San Francisco	$17.95 CAN $12.95 US

☐ Seattle	$17.95 CAN $12.95 US	☐ Tunisia	$27.95 CAN $19.95 US
☐ St. Lucia	$17.95 CAN $12.95 US	☐ Vancouver	$17.95 CAN $12.95 US
☐ St. Martin and St. Barts	$16.95 CAN $12.95 US	☐ Washington D.C.	$18.95 CAN $13.95 US
☐ Toronto	$18.95 CAN $13.95 US	☐ Western Canada	$29.95 CAN $21.95 US

budget.zone

☐ Central America	$14.95 CAN $10.95 US	☐ Western Canada	$14.95 CAN $10.95 US

Ulysses Travel Journals

☐ Ulysses Travel Journal (Blue, Red, Green, Yellow, Sextant)	$9.95 CAN $7.95 US	☐ Ulysses Travel Journal (80 Days)	$14.95 CAN $9.95 US

Ulysses Green Escapes

☐ Cycling in France	$22.95 CAN $16.95 US	☐ Hiking in the Northeastern U.S.	$19.95 CAN $13.95 US
☐ Cycling in Ontario	$22.95 CAN $16.95 US	☐ Hiking in Québec	$19.95 CAN $13.95 US
☐ Ontario's Bike Paths and Railtrails	$19.95 CAN $14.95 US	☐ Hiking in Ontario	$22.95 CAN $16.95 US

Ulysses Conversation Guides

☐ French for Better Travel	$9.95 CAN $6.50 US	☐ Spanish for Better Travel in Latin America	$9.95 CAN $6.50 US

Title	Qty	Price	Total

Name:		Subtotal	
		Shipping	$4 CAN $3 US
Address:		Subtotal	
		GST in Canada 7%	
		Total	

Tel: Fax:

E-mail:

Payment: ☐ Cheque   ☐ Visa   ☐ MasterCard

Card number_____ Expiry date_____

Signature_____

ULYSSES TRAVEL GUIDES

4176 St-Denis,
Montréal, Québec, H2W 2M5
☎(514) 843-9447
fax: (514) 843-9448

305 Madison Avenue,
Suite 1166,
New York, NY 10165
Toll-free: 1-877-542-7247

www.ulyssesguides.com
info@ulysses.ca

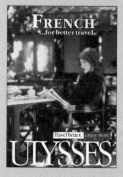

Save up* to
20 %

GET AN EYEFUL

Take advantage of our **GET AN EYEFUL** package to visit four of Montréal's major tourist attractions !

BIODÔME
Experience a unique feast for the senses as you explore four ecosystems from the Americas.

MONTRÉAL TOWER AT THE OLYMPIC PARK
Enjoy a breathtaking view of Montréal from the world's tallest inclined tower.

Tickets available at the ticket office of each tourist attraction and "Au Gîte Olympique" Bed & Breakfast.

Open all year round.

Complimentary shuttle service between all four tourist attractions and the Viau metro station.

INSECTARIUM
Discover the fascinating world of insects at this unique museum.

BOTANICAL GARDEN
Celebrate nature's diversity at one of the world's largest attractions of its kind.

Informations:

Botanical Garden-Insectarium	872-1400
Biodôme	868-3000
Montréal Tower	252-8687

* On the individual regular admission fee of each tourist attraction.

PARC OLYMPIQUE MONTRÉAL

Ville de Montréal

MÉTRO
Viau

Travel Notes

Travel Notes

Hochelaga-Maisonneuve *It's Montréal at heart!*

Only 15 minutes from Downtown by metro or car, **Hochelaga-Maisonneuve** is a unique section of the city.

Home to the **Tower of Montréal**, the tallest inclined tower in the world, it also boasts the **Olympic Stadium**, the **Botanical Gardens**, the **Insectarium**, the **Biodôme**, and, we must not forget **Maurice "Rocket" Richard's Universe**, a museum devoted to one of the greatest players for the Montréal Canadiens hockey team.

Hochelaga-Maisonneuve is also...

HERITAGE A unique and faithful reflection of the life of an industrial city of the early 20th century, with impressive heritage buildings such as the **Très-Saint-Nom-de-Jésus** Church which has a famous **Casavant organ**, one of the most powerful in North America, the **Château Dufresne** with its sumptuous decoration and numerous **Beaux-Arts style buildings** such as the **Morgan Baths** or the **Maisonneuve Market**.

VOYAGE IN TIME Thanks to our **animated tour** (theatre and music) called **"In the steps of La Bolduc"** which offers an original way to discover the major attractions of the neighbourhood and to learn all about the life and work of one of Québec's most celebrated singers of the Pre-War period.

AGREEABLE STROLL Along **typical Montréal streets** either in the company of one of our guides or by yourself.

DISCOVERY A cultural life which is both intense and varied. On the **Market Place** in the summer months, a great **International Country Western Festival** and an **Amerindian Discovery Festival** are on the program.

PLEASURE The atmosphere of a traditional market at the **Maisonneuve Public Market** and shopping on **Promenade Ontario**.

Tourisme Hochelaga-Maisonneuve *welcomes you!*

Corporation de Gestion des Marchés Publics de Montréal

Information **(514) 256-4636**
www.tourismemaisonneuve.qc.ca

Sainte-Agathe

Turn-of-the-century charm
in a fully renovated
100-year-old manor

AUBERGE DE LA TOUR DU LAC

Tranquil nights, radiant mornings

1 800 622-1735

Mar
seasonal package
availabl
Gift certificate
Swedish massag
on locatio

RANCH 4 SEASONS

COWBOY PACKAGE

$115 **per person - d.o.**
One night in our cosy inn • 5 course meal dinner
American breakfast

ONE HOUR HORSEBACK RIDING		FISHING SUMMER / WINTER 5 TROUTS
With guide	**OR**	Équipment included

SUMMER — **INCLUDES ACTIVITIES IN PACKAGE** — **WINTER**

SUMMER
- Visit our ranch
- Water slides
- Swimming in small lake
- Treasure hunt hiking
- Camp fire
- Mountain biking
- Peddle boat furnish
- Visit falls
- Badminton, Horse shoe games

WINTER
- Slidin on tubes
- Hiking path
- Cross country skiing (furnish if available)
- Crazy Carpet (furnish)
- Ice fishing (équipment furnish)
- Skating rink with music and lite
- Visit our western trail

ADDITIONAL ACTIVITIES
- Massotherapy
- Wagon or sleigh-ride
- Skidoo Trail

ALL DAY PACKAGE
$10 PER PERSON
taxes included
activities mentioned ebove

651 - Rang 4, St-Alphonse-de-Rodriguez
RÉSERVATION: (450) 883-0933 • 1-877-883-0933
ranch4saisons.com

THE UNION DES PRODUCTEURS AGRICOLES AND ITS 45,000 MEMBERS INVITE YOU TO VISIT RURAL QUEBEC

L'UNION
DES PRODUCTEURS
AGRICOLES

The greatest gift is a sweet esc

Gift Certi

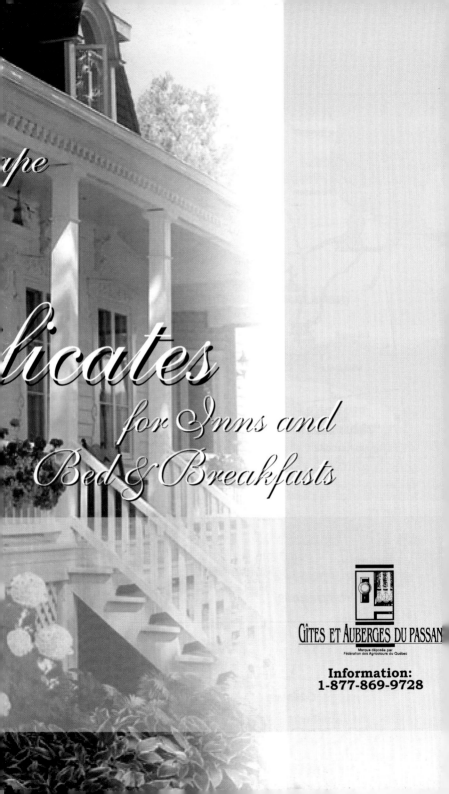

GÎTES ET AUBERGES DU PASSAN

Marque déposée par
Fédération des Agricotours du Québec

Information:
1-877-869-9728